Industrial Organization
and Prices

Industrial Organization
and Prices

JAMES V. KOCH

Department of Economics
Illinois State University

PRENTICE-HALL, INC., Englewood Cliffs, New Jersey

Library of Congress Cataloging in Publication Data

Koch, James V
  Industrial organization and Prices.

  Includes bibliographical references.
  1. Industrial organization (Economic theory)
1. Title.
HD2326.K58   338.6   73-9873
ISBN 0-13-462473-4

HD
2326
.K58

© 1974 by Prentice-Hall, Inc.
Englewood Cliffs, New Jersey

10 9 8 7 6 5 4 3 2

Printed in the United States of America

Prentice-Hall International, Inc., *London*
Prentice-Hall of Australia, Pty. Ltd., *Sydney*
Prentice-Hall of Canada, Ltd., *Toronto*
Prentice-Hall of India Private Limited, *New Delhi*
Prentice-Hall of Japan, Inc., *Tokyo*

To Donna and Beth

Contents

10

Integration, Diversification, and Merger   203

11

Product Differentiation and Advertising   235

12

Oligopoly Behavior and Pricing: Theory   265

13

Oligopolistic Behavior and Pricing: Applied Topics   291

14

A Brief Look at Regulation   337

15

Final Considerations   357

Preface

No book can be all things to all people. This book is not a government and business text in the old tradition, because it emphasizes economic theory rather than court cases and judicial decisions. The book is designed to be a microeconomic theory-oriented approach to the field of industrial organization and is aimed at students who are encountering the field of industrial organization for the first time.

This book attempts to treat the field of industrial organization comprehensively without overwhelming the reader with burdensome and non-essential citations and detail. Its major thrust is the demonstration of how microeconomic theory applies to industrial markets. Empirical evidence is liberally cited wherever possible to shed light on the issues which arise. While courses in intermediate microeconomic theory and beginning statistics are highly desirable forerunners to the use of this text, they are not necessities. The author hopes that this book will be intelligible and useful to the many economic decision-makers whose influence over resource allocation sometimes exceeds their sophistication in formal economic analysis.

The microeconomic view of industrial organization taken in this book is comparatively new. The author's interest and belief in this approach were encouraged in graduate school by Richard Heflebower. The author also owes a debt to Frank Brechling, who by instruction and example imparted to him large doses of economics. Critical and extremely helpful readers of the manuscript during its preparation included James F. Ferguson, Kenneth W. Clarkson, Jeffrey G. Williamson, and Robert L. Sorenson. They cannot, of course, be held responsible for any of the author's shortcomings which may persist in the book.

Industrial Organization
and Prices

1

The Method and Scope
of Industrial Organization

The subject matter of this book is the economics of industrial organization. Industrial organization has in recent years been primarily concerned with the actions of firms as sellers of goods and services in the marketplace. The study of firms as buyers of inputs and the study of the firm's internal organization and behavior are matters of secondary importance to the student of industrial organization and will not be given extensive consideration here.

It is frequently wise to develop definitions of terms or concepts, in order to delimit the nature of the phenomenon being studied. Our definition of industrial organization is the following:

> *Industrial organization is a theoretical and empirical study of how the structure of the organization and conduct of sellers affect economic performance and economic welfare.*

A large proportion of the theoretical apparatus of industrial organization is the static price theory that is taught in courses in microeconomics. Indeed, one of the modern giants in the field of the study of industrial organization, George Stigler, contends that the field of industrial organization does not really exist, that it is nothing more than slightly differentiated microeconomics.[1] This view actually has great merit, because it establishes a solid and rigorous theoretical foundation for our study, while at the same time providing us with a large number of testable hypotheses about the organization structure, conduct, and performance of firms. Further, this view allows us to tailor our study of industrial organization in response to particular sets of problems and circumstances.

Our analysis, then, will typically commence with a theoretical statement that will yield testable hypotheses about the organization structure, conduct, and performance of firms in the market. The theoretical statement will usually be a major implication of price theory and will be followed by the empirical evidence that has been accumulated concerning the hypotheses implied by the theoretical statement. Hence, in Chapter 7, we will note that price theory predicts that firms with market power maintain higher price–cost margins than do other firms. We will then see if existing empirical

[1] George Stigler, *The Organization of Industry* (Homewood, Ill.: Richard D. Irwin, Inc., 1968).

3

evidence affirms or disaffirms the hypothesis. Finally, we will tie the results, theoretical and empirical, to questions of policy.

In a lesser number of instances, the analysis will be inductive in nature. We will observe interesting situations, behaviors, and facts, and will attempt to explain why such phenomena exist. Chapter 13 observes the highly structured market for "big-time" intercollegiate athletics and seeks to explain the existence of such a situation by means of accepted theories of cartelization.

It is convenient to view industrial organization as a set of tools that we will utilize to examine analytically the firm in its selling activities. It is apparent that the primary tool with which we work is static price theory; however, the study of industrial organization could not be carried out successfully without substantial contribution from general equilibrium theory and welfare economics (both of which may be considered to be part and parcel of price theory), mathematics and statistics, and cognate fields such as psychology and sociology. General equilibrium analysis (in which no factors are held constant and in which all feedback effects are analyzed) is necessary if we are to trace the complex interreactions and interrelationships among firms, markets, and sectors of the economy. Welfare economics (the branch of economics in which one attempts to construct noncontroversial statements about what ought to be) must be applied if we are to make judgments about the performance of firms and if we are to formulate intelligent public policy. Both mathematics and statistics must be used repeatedly in order to formulate precise hypotheses and then to perform meaningful tests of those hypotheses. Finally, the study of industrial organization is eclectic by nature and borrows both concepts and methods from fields such as psychology, anthropology, sociology, and history when the need arises.

The systematic tour we shall take of the field of industrial organization presupposes the existence of a market economy in which the basic decisions of *what* shall be produced, *how* it shall be produced, and *for whom* it shall be produced are decided by means of a price system. This does not mean that the study of industrial organization does not exist in command economies dominated by economic planners. The student of industrial organization may study any form of economic organization. Rather, the assumption implies that the theoretical apparatus developed, the institutional constraints imposed, the empirical evidence offered, and the policy prescriptions discussed are representative of a predominantly market economy such as that of the United States and may not be applicable to other forms of economic organization.

The functioning of the price system in the market economy we study may in some cases be free and uninhibited by institutional, governmental, or monopoly interference; in other instances, these interfering influences may prevent the free working of the price mechanism. The field of industrial organization is sufficiently broad to consider both the instances above and many combinations of them.

THE TRADITIONAL MODEL

Since the late 1930's, it has been traditional in the field of industrial organization to conduct most analysis within a specified framework.[2] This framework is based upon broad theoretical assertions, such as, "The organization and structure of the market determine conduct and performance," and suggests general directions of causation in the economics of industrial organization. The traditional framework seeks to explain the performance of the firm in terms of the firm's conduct in the market. The firm's market conduct is in turn presumed to be dependent upon the organization and structure of the market. Market organization and structure are assumed to reflect basic supply-and-demand conditions in the market. Figure 1.1 summarizes this relationship.

We shall have occasion throughout this book to debate the question of whether the basic demand-and-supply conditions and the organization structure of the market necessarily imply certain types of conduct and performance upon the part of firms. If certain market structures (for example, oligopoly) persistently produce certain types of undesirable conduct and performance, then a prima facie case can be made for the mandatory restructuring of all such industries by legal means. Suggestions are made periodically that General Motors Corporation should be broken into its component companies, each company to be an independent competitor;[3] such suggestions are manifestations of the opinion that the organizational-structural characteristics of a market do determine conduct and performance and that conduct and performance can be altered by changing the organization and structure of the market.

It is probable, however, that the direction of causation in the traditional model is two-way in many instances. A facet of market-structure organization such as barriers to entry is assumed to affect market conduct such as pricing. At the same time, pricing tactics may themselves result in entry barriers. Likewise, pricing behavior can influence basic supply-and-demand conditions by reducing the number of substitute goods available. Further,

[2]The earliest evidences of this framework may be found in Edward S. Mason, "Price and Production Policies of Large-Scale Enterprise," *American Economic Review*, 29 (March 1939 Supplement), 61–74; and Mason, "The Current State of the Monopoly Problem in the United States," *Harvard Law Review*, 62 (June 1949), 1265–85. Many modern economists have continued in this tradition, the most well known being Joe S. Bain, *Industrial Organization* (New York: John Wiley & Sons, Inc., 1958), Chap. 1 and throughout.

[3]In the middle of the 1960's, the Antitrust Division of the Department of Justice researched and composed a case designed to strip General Motors Corporation of its Chevrolet Division. The case was never formally filed in any court.

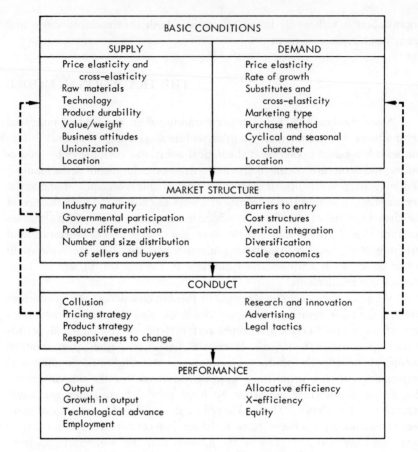

FIGURE 1.1   The Traditional Framework for Industrial Organization Analysis

elements of market structure such as product differentiation clearly have the potential to alter price elasticity of demand. The broken lines in the traditional model of Figure 1.1 indicate possible causation that is the opposite of that usually implied in the traditional model.

THE TYPES OF QUESTIONS WE SHALL SEEK TO ANSWER

We shall utilize, modify, and extend the traditional model in order to provide the evidence necessary for us to formulate intelligent answers to a large number of substantive questions about the behavior of firms in the market. Among the many questions we will consider are these:

Can we measure monopoly power, and welfare losses due to monopoly power? How big are those losses? What are the basic motivations of the modern business firm? Do businesses really maximize profits? What influence does market structure have upon the conduct and performance of business firms? How do entry barriers affect conduct and performance? Do large economies of scale exist with respect to the size of business firms? Is American industry becoming more concentrated, and are large firms pushing out small ones? What are the effects of large firm size on profitability, growth, innovation, and pricing? Are large firms more efficient? Is research and development efficient and profitable? Is the patent system economically justified? Why do firms differentiate their products? Is advertising profitable? Can we explain why so many firms seek to merge? Are mergers, particularly conglomerate mergers, a threat to competition? Do models of oligopoly fully explain and/or predict the conduct and performance that we observe? Do firms really price according to the criterion of marginal cost equal to marginal revenue, or do they price on a cost-plus-markup basis? Are most prices in modern industry competitively determined or are most administered? Can we measure the divergence between price and costs of production? How much collusion exists between business firms, and is it profitable? What is price discrimination, and is it undesirable from a welfare standpoint? How do fair-trade pricing and retail trading stamps affect consumers, and who benefits from their use? When we do discover the existence of monopoly power, what shall we do about it? What public policies can we recommend in order to increase economic efficiency and promote the general welfare?

ANALYTIC DIFFICULTIES

The study of industrial organization is burdened by numerous analytic and conceptual difficulties that reduce the predictive power and the operationality of important hypotheses. Although a great deal of time and effort is spent in the study of industrial organization in analyzing oligopolistic market structures in which only a few interdependent firms exist, there is no definitive theory of oligopoly to guide the analysis. It is perhaps more correct to say that many theories of oligopoly exist, but that no single theory is widely accepted. Hence, the study of this important form of industrial organization often degenerates to a stream of continuous ad hoc formulations with little or no general value.

The fact is that oligopolistic firms or firms with monopoly power are often recognizably and consciously interdependent in their behavior;[4] and this means that models of oligopoly frequently do not yield determinate solutions. Instead of a specific prediction or answer being generated by a model of oligopoly, a range of possible solutions may be specified or a probability distribution attached to possible outcomes. Econometricians—econo-

[4]William Fellner, *Competition Among the Few* (Clifton, N.J.: Augustus M. Kelley, Publishers, 1965).

mists whose analysis relies upon the use of mathematics and statistics—often speak of a "simultaneity" problem when two variables affect each other and the direction of causality cannot be identified. In such a case, a determinate solution may not be obtained without the specification of additional information, sometimes in the form of additional equations that summarize the new information. If the additional information is not forthcoming, then the problem cannot be solved reliably. So it is also in oligopoly. Because firms recognize their interdependence, and act and react almost simultaneously, we often cannot predict the precise outcome of a given situation with any more success than an individual poker player has when he attempts to forecast the results of his actions and his opponents' reactions. A determinate solution does exist, but neither the poker player nor the student of industrial organization ordinarily possesses sufficient information to find that solution. As a result, the theoretical study of industrial organization often involves initially the elimination of outcomes that are very unlikely, and subsequently, the attaching of probabilities to more likely outcomes.[5]

An additional difficulty that tortures the student of industrial organization is his inability to perform laboratory experiments. The study of industrial organization is often carried out on an ex post facto basis, and the student is typically unable to hold important factors constant. Business firms, whether General Motors Corporation or the general store in Hicktown, are seldom amenable to ordering their actions so that the economist can perform the controlled experiments he desires. As we survey the field of industrial organization in this book, we shall see that questions about the reliability of data or the validity of an experiment are frequently keystones of controversy.

A further impediment to the study of industrial organization in an analytic fashion is the reality that many theoretical constructs taken from price theory do not have empirical counterparts that economists can use when seeking to test various hypotheses.[6] Economists may speak of magnitudes such as "marginal cost," but the internal cost-accounting data that businesses typically use are not conducive to the derivation of marginal-cost functions. It is quite obvious that theoretical concepts such as "utility" can at best be only approximated empirically. The result is that data for the purpose of testing hypotheses are often unavailable or in unusable form.

A WORD ABOUT METHODOLOGY

Prior to beginning our formal analysis of the field of industrial organization, we must address ourselves to the question of the methodology of our analysis. Methodology is properly regarded as being a branch of the dis-

---

[5]This has sometimes led to the rejection of *a priori* reasoning in the field of industrial organization and the complete reliance upon empirical tests for information about the true state of the world. This logical positivist view characterizes many articles written in the field of industrial organization.

[6]This has been ably pointed out by Richard Ruggles, "The Value of Value Theory," *American Economic Review*, 44 (May 1954), 140–51.

cipline of logic and does not give us detailed instructions as to how to perform our analysis, or which statistical technique to use. Rather, methodology supplies us with the logical rules that will guide our analysis. Because our analysis will be primarily deductive in nature and will involve ascertaining the worth of alternative theorems, we must have criteria that will separate valuable theorems from those of slight worth. Valuable theorems are those that are (1) valid, (2) operational, (3) broad, and (4) significant.

It is the view of many economists that the decisive test of the worth of a theorem is that theorem's predictive accuracy—that is, validity. This view has especially been associated with Milton Friedman, who also argues that the apparent descriptive accuracy of assumptions underpinning a theorem is not of transcending importance.[7] Whatever position one takes with reference to Friedman's suggestions, it is nevertheless clear that if economics and its child, industrial organization, are to be considered sciences, then economic theorems must have predictive accuracy.

Good theorems and hypotheses are also operational, in terms of both meaningfulness (one can perceive a significant test of the theorem) and feasibility (one can see that a meaningful test can actually be conducted). Unfortunately, some theorems (for example, the theorems of Chapter 4 that impute a utility function to a firm) are operationally meaningful but are often not operationally feasible; they cannot actually be tested, because of known data limitations.

Superior theorems are also broad, in that they apply to a wide range of phenomena. Theoretical breadth, however, is often obtained at the cost of decreased significance. The conflict between the breadth and the validity of a theorem is symptomatic of the frequent conflict between the criteria that determine the worth of a theorem. One must often accept reduced excellence according to one criterion in order to obtain increased excellence according to another.

All economists and students wish to believe that they are concerned with significant, important problems that are deserving of both attention and solution. Needless to say, there is no widespread agreement on precisely which problems are significant, and as a result, general agreement does not exist with respect to the significance of theorems. Students of industrial organization will usually be in general agreement concerning the validity, operationality, and breadth of a certain theorem, but will frequently find no consensus when the significance of the theorem is considered.

Nearly all the theorems utilized in the field of industrial organization are substantive propositions designed to explain and predict. Other theorems are sometimes used simply to describe, file, and limit, by labeling and classifying situations.[8] Still other theorems (for example, the perfectly competitive

[7]Friedman, "The Methodology of Positive Economics," in his *Essays in Positive Economics* (Chicago: University of Chicago Press, 1953).

[8]Fritz Machlup, *The Economics of Sellers' Competition* (Baltimore: Johns Hopkins Press, 1952), is a prime example of theory used to limit and label the world.

market structure) are sometimes used as parables that purport to describe an ideal situation with which other situations may be compared. This yardstick function is extremely important in that it develops norms, goals, and optima with which we may evaluate real-world situations.

SUMMARY

Industrial organization is the study of firms as sellers of output. Industrial organization is highly dependent upon microeconomic theory and is properly viewed as constituting applied microeconomics.

The traditional approach to the study of industrial organization stressed the link between market structure, market conduct, and market performance. The bulk of the analytic work performed in the field still follows this model.

Methodological positions are often considered to be not in the domain of the industrial organization economist. This is clearly not the case, since a great number of the major controversies in the field of industrial organization are methodological in nature. Methodological issues, particularly those that relate to the use of economic theory, are at the center of many current disputes.

PROBLEMS

1. The dichotomy between positive and normative economics, which so many economists insist upon, has been attacked as being false on the grounds that it is impossible to separate values from economic analysis. It is also argued that the very choice of a model to guide economic analysis is in itself a value judgment. Can positive and normative economics actually be separated?

2. Milton Friedman has argued that the descriptive accuracy of the assumptions that underpin a theory is not crucial if the individuals described in the theory "act as if" they behave in the fashion described in the assumptions. Can descriptively inaccurate theorems ever be useful to the economist?

3. Several attempts to test the implications of theories in the field of industrial organization have resulted in coefficients of determination (R^2) of about .10. This means that the explanatory influences in the theory explain about 10 percent of the variation in the dependent variable in the case at hand. Which of the following does this mean? (a) The theory is worthless. (b) The theory is of doubtful use. (c) The theory is a good one. (d) Nothing can really be said.

2

Relevant Theoretical Background

In this chapter we shall review several basic concepts of economic theory and highlight several important predictions about firm conduct and performance that are contained in economic theory. These concepts and predictions will be used many times throughout our study of industrial organization.

The most important theoretical concepts for our purposes are contained in the accepted theories of market structure. Two particular market structures, perfect competition and pure monopoly, are exceptionally instructive, since they delineate polar cases and highlight the welfare economics of market structures. But before we consider market structures, we must define precisely what is meant when we so frequently refer to a "market" or to "competition."

THE CONCEPT OF A MARKET

A market is a collection of firms each of which is supplying products that have some degree of substitutability to the same potential buyers.

The term *market* is not necessarily synonymous with the more commonly used term *industry*, because firms in the same industry may not supply substitutable products and/or may sell their products to quite different sets of customers.[1] Further, some firms that are commonly thought to be in the same industry produce many other products besides the one that caused them to be classified in the industry in question.[2] As a consequence, the economic market for a product may bear little or no relation to the popular notion of the industry producing that product.

The definition of a market that we have presented above suggests additional questions. How much substitutability between products must there be,

[1]The four-digit level of detail in the Standard Industrial Classification System (see Chapter 7) is often regarded as corresponding most closely to the usual conception of an industry. Four-digit SIC Industry 3717, motor vehicles and parts, contains products of low substitutability, such as large semitrailer trucks and small Volkswagen sedans. Further, the subset of customers to whom the truck is sold is substantially different from the subset of customers to whom the sedan is sold.

[2]An example is the Westinghouse Electric Corporation, typically classified as a supplier of electrical goods and equipment. Westinghouse also produces goods as diverse as plywood, television programming, and gas-fired incinerators.

and can this substitutability be measured? Is the geographic structure of suppliers and buyers important? What role does time play in the definition of a market?

These questions arise because a market is not a single-dimensioned concept. A market has at least three significant dimensions: product, geography, and time.[3] From the product standpoint, substitutability is the keystone. If goods are close substitutes for each other, then from the standpoint of the product dimension, they may be said to be in the same market. A measure of substitutability of products is the coefficient of cross-elasticity of demand. Let Θ = cross-elasticity of demand. Then:

$$\Theta = \frac{\% \text{ change in quantity demanded of good number 2}}{\% \text{ change in price of good number 1}}$$

If $\Theta < 0$, the goods in question are complements, whereas if $\Theta > 0$, the goods have some substitutability.[4] Unfortunately, although one can say that the larger the positive value of Θ, the more substitutable are the goods in question, one cannot say that any particular positive value of Θ is necessary in order to state that the two goods are sufficiently substitutable to be classified as being in the same market.

An interesting application of the concept of cross-elasticity of demand has arisen in an antitrust case brought by the U.S. Department of Justice. This case, usually referred to as the *Brown Shoe Case* (1962),[5] developed out of the attempt of the Brown Shoe Company, a supplier of medium-priced shoes, to merge with the Kinney Shoe Company, a supplier of lower-priced shoes. The Department of Justice sued to halt this merger on the grounds that Brown and Kinney were competitors and that their merger would substantially reduce competition. Brown and Kinney replied that they did not compete with each other because they served different markets. Indeed, besides the price differential between the companies' shoes, Brown did sell the greatest proportion of its shoes to men and Kinney did sell most of its shoes to women. Information on cross-elasticity of demand between Brown and Kinney products was subsequently introduced by the Department of Justice. The relevant values of Θ for Brown and Kinney were positive, indicating competitive substitutability within the same market. Whether because of or in spite of the revelation, the Department of Justice won its case and the merger was disallowed.

The geographic dimension of a market is sometimes the most important dimension of that market. Because of high transport costs, or other factors such as convenience or lack of product durability, some markets (for exam-

---

[3] Carl Kaysen and Donald F. Turner, *Antitrust Policy: An Economic and Legal Analysis* (Cambridge, Mass.: Harvard University Press, 1965), pp. 101–2.

[4] This presumes the usual *ceteris paribus* caveat—that is, that all other relevant factors such as income and tastes are held constant.

[5] *United States* v. *Brown Shoe Company*, 370 U.S. 294 (1962).

ple, the milk market) will be primarily local or regional in nature. Other markets, such as national network television, are effectively national markets because of an absence of regional or local cost barriers. Potentially close substitutability of products will be meaningless if geographic considerations do not permit actual competition between suppliers for the same set of customers.

The time dimension of a market also looms large when we remind ourselves that price elasticities of demand and supply increase as time passes. When seeking to determine whether two firms are competitors, we must specify some time period. Given enough time to adjust, nearly any two firms are potential competitors. The relevant time period is neither so short as to include in the market only the existing firms, nor so long as to allow for substantive changes in technology, demand, and tastes that would completely alter the situation.

The product dimension of a market tends to predominate when economists discuss markets. It is useful to bear in mind, therefore, that every market has both geographic and time dimensions as well. The temptation to equate markets with industries must also be avoided whenever possible; however, the fact that the term *industry* is often used when the market is meant presents obvious difficulties. Further, the dictates of empirical research (industry data are widely available, whereas market data are not) will lessen our ability to maintain this distinction.

THE CONCEPT OF COMPETITION: WHAT IT IS AND IS NOT

Few concepts in economics have been as durable and useful as that of competition. McNulty has pointed out that competition is "...a principle so basic to economic reasoning that not even such powerful yet diverse critics of orthodox theory as Marx and Keynes could avoid relying upon it...."[6] Unfortunately, despite the prolific use of the concept of competition in economic theory, it is frequently misunderstood and often misused.

The major historians of the concept of competition, Stigler[7] and McNulty,[8] have pointed out that the concept of competition has evolved from the previous emphasis of Adam Smith[9] on rivalry between firms to the current-day stress upon competition as a situation where there is an absence of effective monopoly power. While Smith was not so naïve as to deny that

---

[6]Paul J. McNulty, "Economic Theory and the Meaning of Competition," *Quarterly Journal of Economics,* 82 (November 1968), 639.

[7]George J. Stigler, "Perfect Competition, Historically Contemplated," *Journal of Political Economy,* 65 (February 1957), 1–17.

[8]McNulty, "Economic Theory," *loc. cit.* See also Paul J. McNulty, "A Note on the History of Perfect Competition," *Journal of Political Economy,* 75 (August 1967), 395–99.

[9]*The Wealth of Nations* (Baltimore: Penguin Books, Inc., 1970).

an absence of barriers to entry and collusion was necessary if meaningful rivalry were to take place, he nevertheless stressed noncollusive rivalry as being the root of competition. In Smith's eyes, the essence of competition was the actions taken by rival firms. Competition could be present even though monopoly power was present. Noncollusive forms of rivalry such as price cutting and product differentiation are therefore competition from the Smithian standpoint.[10]

The prevailing contemporary view of competition is that it exists where there is an absence of monopoly power. That is, there must exist no seller or buyer with price-making power, and further, no single seller or buyer may have a noticeable influence upon market results. Tests of market strength between firms, such as cutthroat pricing contests, therefore become forms of rivalry in the current view. Not price-cutting rivalry, but rather the absence of price-making ability is the keystone of the modern view of competition.

The confusion between rivalry and competition persists today and permeates certain sections of our antitrust law.[11] The distinction between the two concepts is similar to the distinction between conduct and market structure. Rivalry in the modern sense refers to actual conduct; competition refers rather to a structurally determined ability to undertake certain behavior and conduct in the market.

THE STATIC THEORY OF PERFECT COMPETITION

The perfectly competitive model, although predicated upon assumptions that at first blush seem to be unrepresentative of the real world, has nevertheless been used with increasing frequency in economic theory in recent decades. The major reasons for this increasing application and usage are not harmonious in nature. On one hand, the use of the perfectly competitive model reflects the fact that it does yield valid predictions about firm and market behavior in certain circumstances.[12] On the other hand, the perfectly competitive model is frequently used as a parable and is not meant to describe or predict real-world events when so utilized. Rather, the model is employed as a representation of the optimum, a measuring stick against which all other circumstances and market structures may be compared and evaluated. Although our study of industrial organization will not discount the former usage (in fact, the perfectly competitive model used in this sense will be of assistance to us in many circumstances), the latter usage will

---

[10]Stigler, "Perfect Competition," p. 1.

[11]The Robinson-Patman Act, which regulates activities such as price discrimination, is an excellent example of this confusion in operation. See Chapter 13.

[12]The so-called Chicago School of economics has tended to use the assumption of atomistic markets, which closely approximate perfect competition, with great frequency and some success. See Henry L. Miller, Jr., "On the 'Chicago School of Economics,'" *Journal of Political Economy*, 70 (February 1962), 64–69; see also Martin Bronfenbrenner, "A 'Middlebrow' Introduction to Economic Methodology," in Sherman R. Krupp, ed., *The Structure of Economic Science* (Englewood Cliffs, N. J.: Prentice-Hall, Inc., 1966), pp. 5–24.

predominate, because our study of industrial organization will examine so many obviously imperfect competitors and markets.

The assumptions that underpin the perfectly competitive model are the following:

1. A large number of sellers and buyers exist, no single one of which has a noticeable influence upon market price or quantity.

2. Each seller produces a homogeneous product that is undifferentiated and indistinguishable in any way from any rival seller's product.

3. Barriers to entry in the market in the long run are either very minimal or nonexistent.

4. No artificial restraints on supply, demand, or price exist in either the input or the output markets, and resources in general are perfectly mobile.

5. Each seller and buyer has complete and correct information about prices, quantities, costs, and demand in the market in which he participates.[13]

Let us now take the standpoint of a single firm with only one plant in a perfectly competitive market (industry) in the short run.[14] Since the perfect competitor is by assumption a price taker rather than a price maker, the demand function that the firm perceives is a straight line that is parallel to the abscissa. This demand function is simultaneously the average-revenue curve and marginal-revenue curve for the firm. The price that the firm observes is dictated to it by the interaction of supply and demand forces in the entire market where all firms participate.

Assume an initial equilibrium situation such as that of Figure 2.1a. The profit-maximizing firm will equate marginal revenue to marginal cost at point B, and will produce output OQ_1. The selling price of this output is OP_1, and is determined by supply-and-demand forces in the overall market for the product, where every firm participates (Figure 2.1b). The average cost of producing this output is Q_1B per unit, and the "pure" profit (*economic rent* is the technically correct term)[15] per unit is BA. Since the average-cost curve already includes as a cost a "normal" profit,[16] magnitude BA is profits per unit that may be regarded as being in excess of the amount

[13]This assumption of "perfect information" is the feature that effectively differentiates perfect competition from pure competition.

[14]The short run is a time period of indefinite length when the firm possesses certain resources that are fixed in supply. The short run is sufficiently long to permit the firm to employ differing amounts of variable inputs, but not so long that the firm can react and adjust all its decision variables in response to fundamental changes in such things as demand, tastes, and technology. During the short run, for example, the firm might hire extra workers, but is unable to build new productive capacity. The primary distinction between the short run and the long run is that in the long run, the price elasticity of supply of inputs increases substantially.

[15]An economic rent is the difference between the amount paid a factor of production and that factor's opportunity cost. Pure profit is an economic rent because it represents profit in excess of the profits necessary to keep that factor input engaged in production.

[16]Profit, the return to the entrepreneurial factor of production, is a cost that must be included in the average-cost curve. The amount of profit included in the average-cost curve is a "normal" profit: the profit per unit that is just sufficient to retain the entrepreneurial resource at this firm in this market. It is in fact the opportunity cost of the entrepreneurial input. Total profits, then, consist of normal profits plus pure profits, although there is no guarantee that the firm will necessarily earn either type of profit. By way of contrast, "accounting" profits represents a concept of profit where the opportunity cost of the entrepreneurial factor of production is ignored; it is a situation where neither normal nor pure profits are included in the average-cost curve.

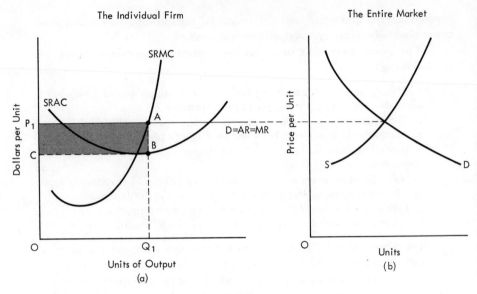

The Individual Firm   The Entire Market

FIGURE 2.1

necessary to retain the firm's resources in this line of activity. Total pure profits earned by the firm are equal to the area of rectangle CP_1AB.

Pure profits per unit (economic rents) are the motivating force of competitive capitalism, according to the static theory of the firm, since they ordinarily attract entry into the market by new firms.[17] *Ceteris paribus*, higher than usual rates of profit will attract new firms into the market. In the short run, however, the entry of new firms cannot occur because of the existence of fixed factor inputs.

As time passes, firms throughout the economy observe pure profits being earned in this market and enter it by opening new plants. Existing firms in this market may also seek to increase the pure profits they are earning and will sometimes choose to expand their existing productive capacity. Figure 2.2b illustrates the shift in the market-supply curve (from S_1 to S_2) that gradually occurs as new firms enter and existing firms expand. Each individual firm in the market observes the lower market price per unit, OP_2, in Figure 2.2a.

As long as pure profits remain, and no entry barriers exist, there is incentive for new firms to enter the market and for existing firms to expand productive capacity. Since price OP_2 still allows for pure profits, entry and expansion will continue to occur until the price each individual firm sees is OP_3. This will be brought about by a shift in the market-supply curve from

---

[17]Conversely, the existence or expectation of negative pure profits will stimulate firms to leave the market in question. In terms of Figure 2.1a, the product price per unit, OP_1, would be less than the average cost of production per unit, OC, in such an instance.

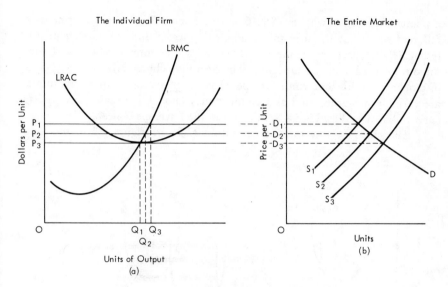

FIGURE 2.2

S_2 to S_3. Price OP_3 includes no pure profits, and entry and expansion will therefore cease.

Despite the absence of pure profits, the long-run individual-firm equilibrium described in Figure 2.2a at point D (price $= OP_3$; output $= OQ_3$) is profit-maximizing in nature, because the firm has equated marginal revenue with marginal cost. A closer look reveals that marginal revenue equals average revenue equals long-run marginal cost equals long-run average cost at this individual-firm equilibrium; that is, $MR = AR = LRMC = LRAC$. The relationship between price and marginal cost is particularly important. $P = MC$ is an optimal result and a frequently used welfare criterion. Price is a rough measure of the value and utility that consumers attach to a unit of a good, while marginal cost per unit is a rough measure of the opportunity cost to society of the resources being used in the production of that unit of the good. When $P > MC$, society would like more units of this good to be produced, whereas when $P < MC$, less units of the good are desired. $P = MC$, then, indicates that we are producing the "correct" output of the good in question in a societal cost–benefit sense. We shall shortly see that the pure-monopoly market structure generates the prediction that $P > MC$, and hence that the monopoly firm will depart from optimality and engage in output restriction.

One final welfare result can be derived from the long-run equilibrium of the firm in perfect competition. The long-run average-cost curve for the firm as drawn in Figure 2.2a is a simplification. The actual $LRAC$ curve is an envelope of $SRAC$ curves such that each point on the $LRAC$ curve represents a point of tangency with an *SRAC* curve. Each *SRAC* curve represents a different scale that the firm might adopt;[18] since an infinite number of different *SRAC* curves exist, the *LRAC* curve is therefore a smooth and continuous locus of points of tangency. The firm may choose any of these points of tangency in this long-run envelope, because in the long run, all its inputs are variable in nature, and as a result it may choose any scale (any *SRAC* curve) that it wishes. Figure 2.3 illustrates the envelope concept.

The cheapest way to produce output OQ_1 in Figure 2.3 in the long

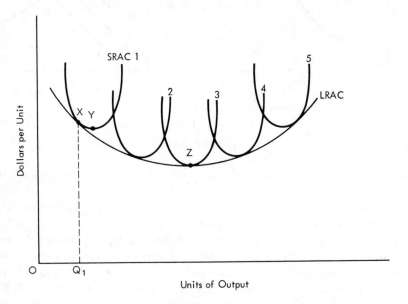

FIGURE 2.3

run is to choose the scale indicated by $SRAC_1$. It is true that scales 2 and 3 offer lower average costs per unit; however, if we wish to produce only OQ_1 units of output, scale 1 is cost minimizing. Points X and Y on $SRAC_1$ represent different rates of utilization of scale 1. The "best" rate of utilization from society's viewpoint is that given by point Y, because point Y represents the lowest average costs of production available with scale 1. Nevertheless, note that when we wish to produce output OQ_1 with scale 1, it is cost minimizing to "underutilize" scale 1 (point X) rather than to realize the lowest possible average costs per unit of production with scale 1.

---

[18]Scale is determined by the quantities of fixed resource available and sets the upper limit on the rate of output per unit of time that the firm may attain. Leftwich has cleverly illustrated this by using the example of a meat grinder. The meat grinder is a fixed resource; meat that is pushed through the grinder is a variable resource. The size of the meat grinder obviously limits the amount of meat that can be ground during any time period. The upper limit to the rate of output per unit of time—scale—is therefore determined in this example by the fixed resource, the meat grinder. Richard H. Leftwich, *The Price System and Resource Allocation,* 4th ed. (Hinsdale, Ill.: The Dryden Press, Inc., 1970), p. 148.

Underutilization of scale means that the firm chooses to operate at a point on a given *SRAC* curve that is to the left of the lowest point on that *SRAC* curve.

The perfectly competitive firm of Figure 2.2a was seen to choose a scale similar to scale 3 in Figure 2.3. That is, the perfectly competitive firm in the long-run equilibrium will choose to produce the output that offers lowest average costs per unit. Further, the perfectly competitive firm will, in the long run, operate this scale at the optimum rate, as represented by point *Z* in Figure 2.3. In the long run, the perfectly competitive firm neither underutilizes nor overutilizes the plant it operates.

We noted in Figure 2.2a that in the long run, competition will force price into equality with average costs of production. Hence, from a welfare standpoint, the most desirable scale for the firm to adopt is the one that offers lowest possible average costs per unit, because this will enable it to offer lower prices to consumers. It is also clear that underutilization of a given scale of plant (that is to say, the continued existence of unused productive capacity) is undesirable from a welfare standpoint. We would like firms to adopt scales of operation, and rates of utilization, similar to point *D* in Figure 2.2a and point *Z* in Figure 2.3. It is hardly surprising, therefore, that such a result is termed perfect competition. We shall soon observe that the introduction of monopoly into the model will destroy this welfare-maximizing result.

Does perfect competition actually exist? The answer to this question is a qualified no. Industries such as wheat farming and cotton textiles may approach perfect competition in nearly all respects, except that buyers of the products may have some monopsony power.[19] Most agricultural markets approximate perfect competition, and many factor markets as well. However, even if perfect competition exists nowhere and is a worthless fairy tale (as some contend), it will still function usefully in the fashion of an illustrative parable outlining optimal circumstances and performance.[20]

THE STATIC THEORY OF PURE MONOPOLY

A pure monopolist is one who is the only seller in a given market. When a firm is the only seller in a given market, that firm clearly has power over product price and quantity in that market. In general, we can state that monopoly power exists when a firm or individual has the ability to influence product price or quantity in the market. According to this definition, most sellers in the American economy have some monopoly power.

[19]See Lloyd Reynolds, "Competition in the Textile Industry," in Walter Adams and Leland Traywick, eds., *Readings in Economics* (New York: The Macmillan Company, 1948).

[20]A frequent modern exponent of the sterility and uselessness of the perfectly competitive model is John Kenneth Galbraith, whose most recent work, *The New Industrial State* (Boston: Houghton Mifflin Company, 1967), restates this thesis.

Monopoly power is the ability to influence price or quantity in the market.

When we speak of pure monopoly, however, we are referring to a situation where only one seller exists in a given market. No ready substitutes for the monopolist's product exist, and the threat of potential entry by new firms is quite low. With respect to substitutability, this is equivalent to saying that the coefficient of cross-elasticity of demand between the monopolist's product price and any other product's quantity demanded is either positive and very small, or negative. Further, the slight chance of entry by new firms may be translated into a coefficient of cross-elasticity of supply between the monopolist's product price and any other possible competing product's quantity supplied which hovers around zero.

The assumptions that are basic to our model of pure monopoly are the following:

1. A single seller exists in the market for this product.
2. The single seller produces a differentiated product for which there are no ready substitutes.
3. Substantial barriers to entry exist.

The third assumption above is critical to the maintenance of monopoly power in the long run. Barriers to entry must exist if the monopolist is to remain the sole producer of a good in the long run while at the same time earning the pure profits that induce entry. The most common alleged barriers to entry are due to (1) demand conditions, (2) control over input supplies, (3) legal-institutional factors, (4) scale economies, (5) large capital requirements, and (6) technology. The reader is referred to Chapters 5 and 6, where the issue of barriers to entry is discussed in some detail.

The profit-maximizing monopolist will in the short run equate marginal revenue with marginal cost. Because the monopolist is a price maker rather than a price taker, his demand curve will be downward sloping, and at any given quantity sold, marginal revenue will be less than price, because the monopolist must successively lower his price in order to sell additional units of output. Figure 2.4 illustrates the situation in which a profit-maximizing firm decides to produce OQ_1 units of output and charge price OP_1.

Pure profits per unit for the monopolist in Figure 2.4 are BA per unit, and total pure profits earned by the monopolist are equal to the area of rectangle CP_1AB. Pure profits ordinarily attract the entry of new firms. Since this firm is a monopolist, and entry barriers exist that prevent the entry of new firms into the market, the price–quantity solution indicated in Figure 2.4 will also be the long-run solution unless demand or cost conditions change.

Figure 2.5 illustrates the monopolist's choice of scale and rate of utilization of scale in the long run. The monopolist chooses a less-than-optimal scale $(SRAC_1)$ and operates that scale at a less-than-optimal rate (point A

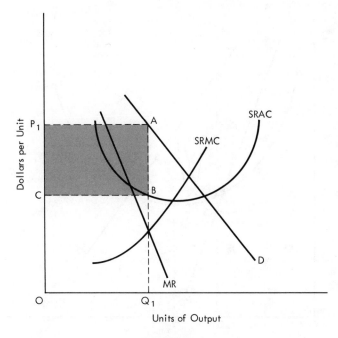

FIGURE 2.4

rather than point B). The result is output restriction, since the perfectly competitive firm's output would have been OQ_2 rather than OQ_1.

The gap between price and marginal cost (vertical distance CD in Figure 2.5) is also of interest. $P > MC$ for the monopolist in Figure 2.5, indicating that the monopolist is violating our welfare criterion by restricting output.

Actual examples of pure monopoly in the American economy are rare. We frequently observe firms in areas such as the public utilities (for example, a municipal gas company) that are the only sellers in their respective markets. Public policy and legal restraints often prevent the existence of more than one firm. Yet even these firms with monopoly power are not pure monopolists, because highly substitutable goods such as electricity exist. Wilcox, in his famous monograph, *Competition and Monopoly in American Industry,* listed aluminum, shoe machinery, telephone communications, Pullman railroad cars, nickel, magnesium, and molybdenum as markets that approach pure monopoly.[21] More than three decades have passed since Wilcox's monograph was written, and a large number of these markets no longer approach pure monopoly. Nevertheless, however rare the examples of pure monopoly may be, the static theory of pure monopoly is the polar case with reference to perfect competition and will serve both as a yardstick for pur-

[21]Clair Wilcox, *Competition and Monopoly in American Industry,* Temporary National Economic Committee Monograph Number 21 (Washington, D.C.: U.S. Government Printing Office, 1940).

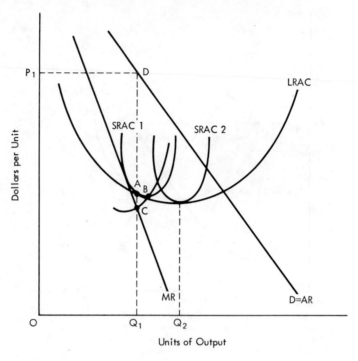

FIGURE 2.5

poses of evaluation of new situations and as a generator of testable predictions about the conduct and performance of firms with monopoly power.

SUMMARY

We may now summarize our theoretical predictions by contrasting the conduct and performance of the firm that is a monopolist with that of a perfectly competitive firm. By way of contrast with the perfectly competitive firm, the monopolist will (*ceteris paribus*) (1) charge a higher product price; (2) produce fewer units of output; (3) choose to operate a less-than-optimal scale of plant; (4) operate that less-than-optimal scale of plant at a less-than-optimal rate, resulting in excess capacity; (5) be the beneficiary of barriers to entry that he himself may create; and (6) charge an output price greater than marginal costs of production.

PROBLEMS

1. The cross-elasticity of demand between two products is +1.00. Are the two products in the same market? How great must cross-elasticity of demand and substitutability be in order for two products to be considered in the same market?

2. Distinguish between the terms *competition, potential competition,* and *rivalry.* Which of these three concepts is measured by the coefficient of cross-elasticity of supply?

3. The major distinction between perfect competition and pure competition is that perfect competition assumes "perfect knowledge." The use of the perfectly competitive market structure instead of the purely competitive market structure has been attacked on the grounds that information and knowledge are economic goods that are bought and sold in the market. Hence, the assumption of perfect competition incorrectly implies that information and knowledge are free goods. Do you agree?

4. Why do pure profits (economic rents) arise? What does the existence of pure profits in the long run imply?

5. Assume a monopolist who faces a linear, downward-sloping demand curve that is both price elastic and inelastic, depending upon the price. Would this monopolist ever knowingly set his price on the inelastic portion of his demand curve?

6. Barriers to entry are the key to the maintenance of monopoly power in the long run. Are most barriers to entry created by the monopolist himself, or are they given to the monopolist by government and other agencies?

3

Alternative Theories of the

Motivation of the Firm

It has long been customary for the price theorist to assume that the basic motivating influence behind the firm's behavior is the desire of the firm's owner-managers to maximize profits. The profit-maximizing assumption permeates economic theory to such an extent that upon occasion it has been wrongfully assumed that the rational operation of the firm requires profit maximization. It is crucially important to realize, however, that a firm may behave rationally (that is, it may consistently strive toward some set of goals) without engaging in profit maximization, since that firm's complex of aims and goals may not include profit maximization.

Despite the vested interest that economists and analysts of industrial organization might have in maintaining the profit-maximization assumption that underpins so much of economic theory, both intellectual honesty and everyday empirical observation of the economy draw one to an examination of alternative theories of the motivation of the firm. Theories based upon the profit-maximization assumption and theories that assume other types of motivation do not produce identical predictions about firm behavior and performance. The nature and importance of these different theoretical predictions, as well as any existing empirical evidence concerning these theories, are therefore of considerable interest in the study of industrial structure and performance.

Numerous theories of the motivation of the firm have been proposed as alternatives to profit maximization. These alternative formulations can be usefully examined by dividing them into five general classes of theories, based upon (1) sales maximization, (2) growth maximization, (3) emphasis upon managerial behavior, (4) "Realism in Process,"[1] and (5) the theory of games.

Basic to any of these alternative theories is the belief that rational firm behavior does not necessarily require profit maximization. Scitovsky has skillfully demonstrated that profit maximization is an assumption rather than a fundamental prediction of basic economic theory, and that profit maximization and utility (satisfaction) maximization behavior will only rarely be

[1] "Realism in Process" is a term suggested by O.E. Williamson in his *Economics of Discretionary Behavior: Managerial Objectives in a Theory of the Firm* (Chicago: Markham Publishing Co., 1967), p. 11.

equivalent for the entrepreneur guiding the firm's actions.[2] Let p^* be the sum of normal and pure profits that can be earned by the entrepreneur who must choose between leisure (L) and income-generating work (W) in any given time period. The entrepreneur's leisure–work preferences are contained in the indifference map for p^* and W, L found in Figure 3.1.

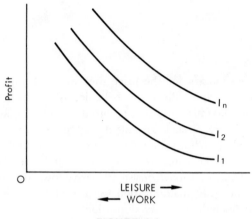

FIGURE 3.1

The various leisure–profit alternatives open to the entrepreneur are represented by the locus found in Figure 3.2. OY hours of work exist in the time period in question. The profit-maximizing combination of leisure and work is given by point M, and is seen to be OX hours of leisure and YX hours of work.

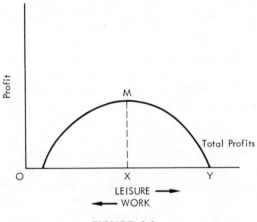

FIGURE 3.2

[2]Tibor Scitovsky, "A Note on Profit Maximization and Its Implications," *Review of Economic Studies*, 11 (1943–44), 57–60.

Figure 3.3 shows that the utility-maximizing combination of leisure and work is given by point M', and consists of OZ hours of leisure and YZ hours of work. Only if the indifference map of the entrepreneur for profits and leisure or work had a very unorthodox shape (for example, indifference curves parallel to the horizontal axis) would points M and M' be identical.

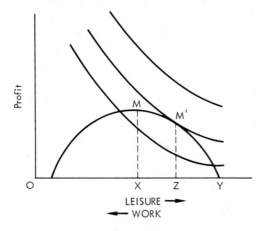

FIGURE 3.3

Scitovsky showed that this unusual type of indifference map would presuppose that the ten-millionth dollar the entrepreneur earns is just as valuable to him as is the first dollar he earns. This sort of Puritan psychology implies that the amount of income an entrepreneur has earned has no relation to his desire for leisure or for work. Such thinking and behavior is probably not widespread. As a result, profit maximization is properly considered to be an assumption that must be justified by empirical evidence and predictive ability; it is not an invariant and absolute prediction of economic theory.

SALES MAXIMIZATION

Sales maximization has attained the status of being the best-known alternative theory of the motivation of the firm. This popularity derives from the fact that the sales-maximization hypothesis is easily understood, and also that casual empirical observations seem to offer considerable support for the hypothesis. Nevertheless, several careful attempts to test the sales-maximization hypothesis have failed to produce any evidence that the hypothesis is empirically valid.

Few proponents of sales maximization contend that it obtains in a "pure" form where firms maximize sales revenues without reference to any behavioral constraint such as profits or security. The classic exposition of the sales-maximization hypothesis by Baumol assumes that firms maximize sales revenues subject to a minimum-profit constraint.[3] Consider Figure 3.4, where P_0 is the minimum level of profits acceptable to the firm in a single-period situation. The firm's total sales revenues, total costs, and total profits are represented by functions labeled TR, TC, and TP, respectively. X_p represents the output that a profit-maximizing firm would produce, and X_s is the output that a "pure" sales-maximizing firm would produce. X_c is the output the sales-maximizing firm will produce when constrained by minimum-profit constraint P_0. The difference between maximum possible level of profits and minimum-profit constraint is termed "sacrificeable profits" by Baumol, since

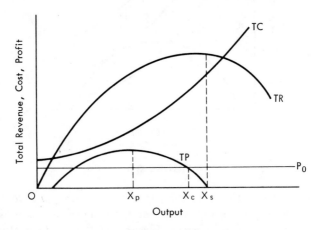

FIGURE 3.4

these profits will be voluntarily given up in order to increase sales revenues (for example, by opening or maintaining an unprofitable sales outlet). Marginal considerations guide the dispensation of these sacrificeable profits: Each dollar of such profits will be used where it generates the greatest additional amount of sales revenue.[4]

Baumol has argued in support of the sales-maximization hypothesis by means of intuitively appealing examples and impressionistic evidence. He notes a host of reasons why firms tend to be preoccupied with sales revenues:

> 1. A small change in sales usually brings with it great changes in selling and technology that are not typically brought about by an equivalent change in profits.
> 2. Consumers may shun the firm's product if they feel that it is declining in popularity.
> 3. Financial institutions and the money market may be unresponsive to a firm with constant or falling sales.

[3]William J. Baumol, *Business Behavior, Value and Growth*, revised edition (New York: Harcourt Brace Jovanovich, Inc., 1967).

[4]Consider a firm producing two products. The equilibrium condition with respect to the use of any given amount of sacrificeable profits is MR_1/Profit Given Up by Producing Output 1 = MR_2/Profit Given Up by Producing Output 2.

4. Firms with constant or falling sales may have difficulty finding or maintaining retail distributors.

5. Constant or falling sales may cause morale problems internal to the firm.

6. Declining sales may mean reduced market power, and consequently increased vulnerability to the actions of competitor firms.

7. Separation of ownership and management in the modern corporation may mean that management is more concerned with sales than with profits.

8. Executive salaries have been found to be more highly correlated with the scale of operations of the firm than with its profitability.[5]

9. In response to the question, "How's business?" an executive will typically reply in terms of what his firm's sales levels are.

10. Firms only reluctantly abandon market areas or products, even when they are unprofitable.

11. Firms that boast that they maintain a national system of sales outlets may be forced to maintain unprofitable outlets in order to fulfill that boast.

The proponents of sales maximization do not contend that it is a universally true explanation of firm behavior, nor do they maintain that sales maximization is always inconsistent with profit maximization.[6] The empirical evidence on the issue is almost unanimous in casting doubt upon the validity of profit-constrained sales maximization by firms.[7] It is true that few tests have actually been conducted, because of the difficulty of devising a meaningful test of one or more of the implications of the hypothesis for firm behavior.

The most careful test of the sales-maximization hypothesis has been performed by Hall.[8] The specific hypothesis under investigation by Hall asserted that changes in the firm's profits above the minimum required level should affect the firm's sales. That is, increased amounts of sacrificeable profits should lead (in subsequent time periods) to increased sales. Hall used the mean profit rate in the firm's industry and the mean profit rate for his entire sample of firms (*Fortune's 500* for the years 1960–62) as a proxy for the minimum acceptable level of profit. He found that ". . . our findings lend no support to the sales revenue maximization thesis."[9]

It is apparent that if the firm's minimum acceptable profit level is less than the profit-maximizing level, then the firm possesses sacrificeable profits that can be used to augment sales revenues. The general lack of evidence of this type of behavior does not mean that it never occurs. Casual observation indicates that firms do sacrifice profits upon occasion in order to stimulate sales or growth. The tenor of the evidence does suggest, however, that these

---

[5]J.W. McGuire, J.S.Y. Chiu, and A.O. Elbing, "Executive Incomes, Sales and Profits," *American Economic Review*, 52 (September 1962), 753–61.

[6]See, for example, William J. Baumol, "Sales Maximization vs. Profit Maximization: Are They Consistent?: Comment," *Western Economic Journal*, 6 (June 1968), 242.

[7]The single notable exception is Robert J. Saunders, "The Sales Maximization Hypothesis and the Behavior of Commercial Banks," *Mississippi Valley Review of Business and Economics*, 5 (Fall 1970), 21–32.

[8]Marshall Hall, "Sales Revenue Maximization: An Empirical Investigation," *Journal of Industrial Economics*, 15 (April 1967), 143–56.

[9]*Ibid.*, p. 154.

instances are isolated in nature—perhaps confined only to certain industries —and that in the long run, such behavior is often profit-maximizing in nature.

GROWTH MAXIMIZATION

A plausible objective of a firm is to maximize the rate of growth of a certain aspect of its activities—for example, its sales revenues, its profits, its assets, or some other variable that describes its activities. The conventional static theory of the firm does not adequately deal with this prospect. In the conventional theory, the firm selects an equilibrium level of output that will maximize its profits. In the absence of any new disturbance, there is no reason for the firm to change its level of output, and hence no reason for the firm to grow.

In reality, of course, firms are vitally interested in growth for many of the same reasons that firms might be interested in maximizing sales. In order to finance growth, the firm must generate considerable profits internally or borrow in the outside capital markets. Despite the opportunity cost attached to the use of internally generated funds, the servicing and payment of outside debt will, *ceteris paribus,* be a drain upon the firm's future growth capacity. Hence, the decision to maximize growth will ordinarily constrain the firm to behave in a manner not dissimilar to that of profit maximization.

It is hardly surprising, then, that the major theoretical contributions that postulate growth maximization on the part of the firm also assign considerable importance to the generation of profits by the firm. A well-known firm-growth model by Baumol is predicated on the assumption that growth is desired primarily as a means to greater profitability.[10] The firm seeks to determine the optimal short-run rate of growth that will make a maximal contribution to long-run profitability. Figure 3.5 relates total revenue, total cost, and total profit (the vertical distance between total revenue and total cost) to the rate of growth of the firm. Total revenue is assumed to be a rising function of the rate of growth, whereas total cost rises even more rapidly than total revenue at higher rates of growth, because of imperfect capital markets, disproportionately high construction and expansion costs associated with accelerated growth, diminishing returns to the fixed management factor, and the increased risk that may accompany high growth rates.

The firm described in Figure 3.5 finds it unprofitable in the short run to expand either too slowly or too rapidly. An intermediate rate of growth, 10 percent, is the most profitable rate for the firm. The long-run solution cannot be illustrated by means of Figure 3.5; however, the most profitable rate of growth is once again an intermediate rate. In the long run, the firm

---

[10]Baumol, *Business Behavior, Value and Growth,* Chap. 10.

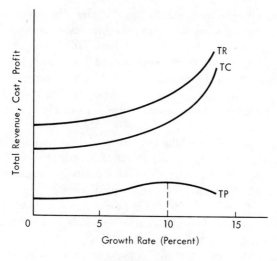

FIGURE 3.5

must consider the present discounted value of each alternative profit stream associated with every possible growth rate.

The preceding example did not actually involve growth maximization; rather, it entailed profit maximization by means of growth. The Baumol apparatus may be adjusted, however, to deal with the case where the firm wishes to maximize its own growth, subject to a minimum-profit constraint. Figure 3.6 is identical to Figure 3.5 except that a total-profit constraint has been added. The firm may now choose between growth rates of 8 percent

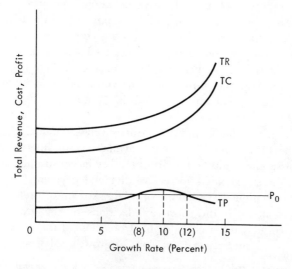

FIGURE 3.6

and 12 percent, since either growth rate satisfies the minimum-profit constraint. The latter rate involves both higher revenues and higher costs. *Ceteris paribus,* the growth-maximizing firm will choose the 12 percent growth rate, since it apparently believes that it derives advantage from growth per se. It should be noted, nevertheless, that rapid growth may be accompanied by greater risk and may also bring with it instability inside the firm. In such a case, the lower growth rate is probably the more attractive choice.

An instructive variant of the growth-maximization hypothesis has been offered by Marris.[11] The firm in the world of Marris maximizes growth subject to minimum constraints relating to the security of the management in its position. The need of executives for managerial security against job dismissal and take-over raids owing to their own failure severely constrains the available range of actions. Managerial security demands that leverage (the firm's ratio of debt to assets) be sufficiently high to support and stimulate growth, but not so high as to imply a type of imprudent, debt-ridden behavior on the part of the manager, which might cause him to be dismissed from his job. Further, the manager must endeavor to keep the firm's liquidity ratio (the ratio of the firm's liquid assets to its total assets) low enough so that the firm's earning power will be increased, but not so low as to endanger the firm's ability to meet its expected current obligations. Finally, the prudent manager will wish to keep the firm's retention ratio (the ratio of the firm's undistributed profits to its total profits) as high as possible in order to have funds available to finance the firm's growth, but not so high as to anger the stockholders who desire large dividend payments.

The Marris firm grows by diversifying into new products and techniques. The proportion of successful diversification attempts can be increased by increasing budgets for research and development and for advertising, and by charging moderate prices. Such actions are costly, however, and the increased growth such actions generate must be balanced in the manager's mind against the reduced security implied by using funds to generate growth rather than, for example, using the same funds as dividend payments to stockholders. The optimal rate of growth is the highest rate of growth that satisfies all the constraints.

In both the Baumol and the Marris growth models, the long-run growth of the firm depends upon the availability of internally generated profits. Likewise, the ability of the firm to satisfy its constraints (for example, the desire of the stockholders to receive dividend payments) is also dependent upon the continued availability of a large stream of profits. It becomes apparent that although the short-run decisions of the growth- or sales-maximizing firm may differ considerably from those of the profit-maximizing firm, the long-run interests and decisions of growth, sales, and profit maxi-

[11] Robin Marris, "A Model of the 'Managerial' Enterprise," *Quarterly Journal of Economics,* 77 (May 1963), 185–209.

mizers alike are virtually identical. Policies that maximize the long-run growth of a variable such as sales or assets will necessarily approximate profit-maximizing policies.

The empirical validity of growth maximization as an explanation of firm behavior has yet to be determined. If firms maximize growth subject to some set of constraints, then these constraints must be clearly identified. The problem is that no means is available for specifying precisely how much profitability or security is regarded as being necessary by each firm. Hence, while growth maximization is at present an operationally meaningful proposition, that proposition cannot be tested and therefore is not operationally feasible.

MANAGERIAL THEORIES

A substantial body of literature concerning the motivation of the firm focuses attention on the behavior of the managers who operate the firm. The foundation stone of the contributions in this area is the concept of "separation of ownership and management." The individuals who operate and manage the modern corporation are typically not the primary owners or stockholders of that corporation. Larner has shown that only 30 out of the 200 largest nonfinancial corporations in the United States could still be classified as being "owner-controlled" by the mid-1960's.[12] This separation of ownership and management is alleged to have important implications for the behavior of managerial personnel and for the performance of the firm.

Berle and Means were the first to suggest that the separation of ownership and management results in economically important phenomena.[13] The owners-stockholders, argued Berle and Means, are primarily interested in high dividend payments and therefore typically favor profit-maximizing actions by the firm. Managers, however, are subject to different forces, and have their own set of motives, needs, and desires. Managers may be more interested in the size of their offices, the number of employees who report to them, the absolute size of the firm, and, in general, the perquisites that accompany their job. These interests will usually not be consistent with profit maximization.

Two additional implications of the separation of ownership and management are relevant to the theory of the firm. Berle and Means allege a loss of corporate democracy because of the separation of identity; that is, not only will managers and owners have diverging interests, but also, the owners will have little recourse or power to change the policies of the modern

---

[12]Robert J. Larner, "Ownership and Control in the 200 Largest Nonfinancial Corporations, 1929 and 1963," *American Economic Review*, 56 (September 1966), 777–87.

[13]A.A. Berle and G.C. Means, *The Modern Corporation and Private Property* (New York: Commerce Clearing House, 1932).

corporation should they so desire. Further, the vastness of the modern corporation, which requires professional management by individuals other than the ownership, will also mean that the corporation will be able to generate its needed capital internally through retained profits. It will not be necessary for the corporation to use the external capital markets where its activities will be evaluated with a critical eye by banker and investor alike. The result is that the managers will be able to pursue their own interests without fear of discipline from the external capital markets that presumably seek after and reward profit-maximizing behavior.

A more recent proponent of the importance of the separation of ownership and management in the modern corporation is Galbraith. In a series of three books, he has presented the original Berle–Means theme with provocative variations.[14] Traditional models of economic theory, Galbraith charges, have little to say about the modern American economy, which is dominated by giant corporations with monopoly and monopsony power. These corporations are run by a "technostructure" of managers who represent the power elite of society, despite the fact that they are not the owners of the corporations. The management of the gigantic firm makes decisions about product price, product quantity, and consumer tastes without fear of market reaction or of stockholders. The monopoly power of the firms and implicit cartelization of the market enable them to virtually ignore consumer sovereignty; the separation of ownership and management makes the technostructure of management substantially immune to stockholder pressures.

Both the Berle–Means explanation and the Galbraithian variant of it depend crucially upon the effective existence of the separation between ownership and management. Although the existence of such a separation is hardly to be doubted, the importance of that separation is open to question. If separation of ownership and management results in the profit-maximizing interests of stockholders being ignored, then we might expect to find evidence that profit rates are lower in manager-controlled firms than in owner-controlled firms. This contention has not been established. Kamerschen, in a study of the largest nonfinancial corporations during the time period 1959–64, found not only that the extent of the management control does not affect profit rates in a noticeable fashion, but also that a change in control from owner-controlled to manager-controlled status for a given firm was associated with increased profit rates.[15] This latter finding contradicts the Berle–Means–Galbraith prediction. It is true that two other studies have given support to the Berle–Means–Galbraith hypothesis; however, both studies suffer from deficiencies in the sample being used to test the hypothesis.

The first study, by Shelton, of identical branch restaurants in a national

---

[14]J.K. Galbraith, *American Capitalism: The Concept of Countervailing Power* (Boston: Houghton Mifflin Company, 1952); *The Affluent Society* (Boston: Houghton Mifflin Company, 1958); and *The New Industrial State* (Boston: Houghton Mifflin Company, 1967).

[15]David R. Kamerschen, "The Influence of Ownership and Control on Profit Rates," *American Economic Review*, 58 (June 1968), 432–47.

chain, reported that those managed by their owners were more profitable than those run by nonowning managers.[16] The sample consisted of only 22 branch restaurants. The second study, by Monsen, Chiu, and Cooley, found profit rates to be much higher in owner-controlled firms than in manager-controlled firms, but there is reason to believe that the sample (72 firms taken from *Fortune's* largest 500 firms in 1963) is unrepresentative.[17]

Additional evidence, which is destructive to the Berle–Means–Galbraith position, has been produced by Lewellen.[18] He points out that the separation between ownership and management is not as absolute as might be implied by the Berle–Means–Galbraith hypothesis. The pure-separation thesis states that managers will not be interested in the profit-maximizing behavior that stockholders desire. Lewellen, in a study of the 50 largest manufacturing firms for the period 1940–63, found that a great deal of executive compensation takes the form of stock options or grants and profit sharing. On the grounds that profit maximization is statistically equivalent to maximizing the share price of the firm's stock, Lewellen argues that nearly every action the manager takes will affect the share price of the firm's stock and therefore the manager's own welfare. As a result, the separation of financial interests between management and ownership implied by some researchers does not exist if a broader definition of compensation is employed.[19]

A more useful version of the theories of the firm that are based upon managerial behavior is the managerial discretion model of Williamson.[20] The Williamson model is analytically rigorous and yields testable results; it has considerable appeal as a description of the real-world behavior of managers and firms. In contrast to the Berle–Means–Galbraith explanation of managerial behavior, noteworthy empirical evidence exists to support the validity of the assumptions underpinning the Williamson model and its *a priori* prediction.

Williamson takes heed of the separation of ownership and management in the modern corporation and concludes that managers can pursue their own self-interest once they have achieved the goals of keeping profits at an acceptable level, paying sufficient dividends to the stockholders, and causing the firm to grow.

Williamson argues that a manager's utility and self-interest depend

[16]John P. Shelton, "Allocative Efficiency vs. 'X-Efficiency': Comment," *American Economic Review*, 57 (December 1967), 1252–58.

[17]R.J. Monsen, J.S. Chiu, and D.E. Cooley, "The Effect of Separation of Ownership and Control on the Performance of the Large Firm," *Quarterly Journal of Economics*, 82 (August 1968), 435–51.

[18]Wilbur G. Lewellen, *Executive Compensation in Large Industrial Corporations* (New York: National Bureau of Economic Research, 1968). See also Wilbur G. Lewellen and Blaine Huntsman, "Managerial Pay and Corporate Performance," *American Economic Review*, 60 (September 1970), 710–20.

[19]In a previously cited piece of evidence in support of the sales-maximization hypothesis, McGuire, Chiu, and Elbing found that executive salaries are more highly correlated with the scale of operations of the firm than with the profitability of the firm. Hence, an important separation of financial interests exists in the firm between management and ownership. Lewellen's findings, based upon a wider definition of executive compensation, contradict this conclusion. See McGuire, Chiu, and Elbing, "Executive Incomes," pp. 753–61.

[20]Williamson, *The Economics of Discretionary Behavior*.

upon (1) his salary and other forms of compensation; (2) the number and quality of personnel who report to him; (3) the type and amount of non-income perquisites that are beyond the amount needed for the firm's operations; and (4) the amount of discretionary spending and investment he directs. The crucial distinction is that many other things beside wages and salaries influence the manager. In particular, managers frequently crave nonessential management perquisites (for example, a chauffeured limousine) and tend to extract such things from the firm when the firm is prosperous. In the tradition of the behaviorists, these nonessential items are referred to as "management slack."

Our brief tour of the various alternative theories of the motivation of the firm has revealed several models that approximate Williamson's. The noteworthy aspect of the Williamson model, however, is that a managerial utility function is maximized and testable predictions result with respect to how managers will adjust output, staff expenditures, and profits when faced by a change in demand, a change in tax rates, or a lump-sum tax. In general, firms guided by a Williamson utility-maximizing manager will spend more on staff expenditures and maintain more organizational slack than will a profit-maximizing firm.

The empirical evidence offered by Williamson is mildly supportive of the managerial-discretion hypothesis, but suffers from several deficiencies.[21] He attempted to explain the compensation of the top executive of firms in 26 industries by means of arguments such as staff expenditures, industry concentration ratios, industry entry barriers, and the freedom of the management to make independent decisions. Williamson found the magnitude of staff expenditures to be a highly significant explanatory variable of executive compensation in the years 1953, 1957, and 1961, and concluded that profit-maximizing activities were not carried out by the firms in the sample.

Such evidence is, of course, hardly definitive, and Williamson admits this.[22] The measure of executive compensation employed is deficient in that it fails to give sufficient attention to compensation other than wages and salaries. Hence, like the McGuire-Chiu-Elbing study, the Williamson study may be seriously underestimating the profit-maximizing interests of managers in the modern corporation.

REALISM-IN-PROCESS THEORIES

Several students of the theory of the firm have voiced the opinion that a reorientation of the theory is needed that would construct it in more descriptively realistic terms. That is, the theory should describe the way busi-

---

[21]O.E. Williamson, "Managerial Discretion and Business Behavior," *American Economic Review*, 53 (September 1963), 1032–57.
    [22]*Ibid.*

nessmen actually act and do it in terms of the types of real-world concepts and data that businessmen actually deal with in their day-to-day activities. In this spirit, Boulding and Cooper have separately asserted that this "new" theory of the firm should be based on balance-sheet considerations, because this would make the theoretical apparatus immediately useful to business-men.[23] Additionally, both Boulding and Cooper imply that such theories would be more valid predictors of actual firm behavior, although they do not provide any evidence of this.

More thorough formulations of realism-in-process theories of the firm have been offered by Cyert and March, who emphasize the behaviorist ap-proach, and Simon, Cohen, and Cyert, who offer a "satisficing" solution. Before considering these alternatives, it would be wise to place in perspec-tive the controversy over the need for descriptive realism in the theory of the firm. Whereas students of firm behavior associated with the realism-in-process approach contend that the theory must be descriptively realistic in assumptions and rules of application, many other economists (notably Fried-man) have insisted that this is not necessary. Friedman, in his essay on the positive economic philosophy, insists that the decisive test of a theorem is its ability to predict accurately the class phenomena it purports to explain.[24] Descriptive realism of a theory's underlying assumptions is not necessary if the firm "acts as if" it behaves in the manner the assumptions indicate.

An illustrative example of the "act as if" usage is the Williamson model, which presumes utility-maximizing behavior on the part of the firm's managers. Williamson does not contend that managers know precisely what their staff expenditures are, what the exact value of their managerial prero-gatives are, or even what utility is. Rather, it is sufficient for Williamson's purposes that managers "act as if" they had this knowledge, because this will result in a theory of firm behavior that can be used to explain or predict this behavior.

Detractors of the positive economic methodology maintain that such theories are not useful because they may be the result of finding spurious correlations between two variables when no actual causality exists. Further, such theories are often based upon descriptively naïve or unrealistic assump-tions about behavior (for example, utility maximization), which make them unusable to the businessman-practitioner in the field.

The discussion concerning the need for descriptive realism in the theory of the firm is not settled. The majority of the existing theories of the firm and received economic theory in general are in the tradition of positive economic philosophy. Despite this, alternative formulations of the theory of the firm, such as the behaviorist approach, have been quite successful in

---

[23]Kenneth Boulding, "Implications for General Economics of More Realistic Theories of the Firm," *American Economic Review*, 42 (May 1952), 30–44; and W.W. Cooper, "Theory of the Firm—Some Suggestions for Revision," *American Economic Review*, 39 (December 1949), 1204–22.

[24]Milton Friedman, "The Methodology of Positive Economics," in his *Essays in Positive Economics* (Chicago: University of Chicago Press, 1953).

predicting company decisions. It is therefore appropriate to consider these approaches in greater detail.

Cyert and March have developed a behavioral theory of the firm that is predicated on the assumption that firms do not usually behave in an "optimal" fashion—that is, maximize profits or sales or minimize costs.[25] Cyert and March examine in detail the decision-making process inside the firm, whereas the conventional theory of the firm attacks broad questions such as resource allocation between markets, but not inside markets. The conventional theory has typically assumed that resources are used efficiently inside the firm, but Cyert and March make no such assumption, and in fact, expect to find otherwise.

Behavioral theories of the firm are directed at answering a different set of questions from those of profit-maximizing theories. The behaviorist approach is in a sense an explanatory complement to profit-maximizing theories, because behaviorism emphasizes factors such as resource allocation, information flows, decision making, and property rights inside the firm, which are either assumed to be optimal or ignored in profit-maximizing formulations. Such an emphasis does not remove behaviorism from the sphere of interest of industrial organization; however, the study of industrial organization has traditionally emphasized the role of the firm as a seller of outputs rather than the firm's activities as a purchaser or organizer of productive inputs.

Cyert and March conceive of the firm as being a group of coalitions that compete and cooperate in order to arrive at decisions. The goals of the firm are often quite normative ("We must be the largest firm in the industry") and are often vague, contradictory, and ill-conceived. Ordinarily, the minimum amount of resources that must be allocated to the various coalitions inside the firm in order to keep the firm operating is less than the actual amount of resources available. This difference between these minimum necessary resource payments and the resources available is conceptually similar to the concept of "pure profits" and is termed "organizational slack."[26] Nearly everyone in the firm receives an organizational-slack payment (for example, in the form of an unnecessary secretary for an executive) at some time. Clearly, the opportunities for expanding organizational slack are greater when the firm is prosperous and economic conditions are good.

Behavioral models are based upon the actual decisions made by the firm, and the predictions made by the behavioral models of the firm's behavior are often quite accurate. Yet the status of behaviorism as a theory of the firm is somewhat questionable. It is not sufficient for behaviorism to observe the past behavior of firms, simulate the situation with the help of a computer, and then predict a certain pattern of action for the firm. Such an

[25]Richard M. Cyert and James G. March, *A Behavioral Theory of the Firm* (Englewood Cliffs, N.J.: Prentice-Hall, Inc., 1963).

[26]Organizational slack is closely related to the concept of X-Inefficiency inside the firm, which will be discussed in the next chapter.

approach is obviously empirical in nature, but is not a theory. Theories should be capable of explaining *why* an action has occurred, and should be generally applicable to a large number of situations. Behavioral theories, on the other hand, predict that a firm will behave in a certain fashion because past experience and knowledge of what firms do indicates that a certain course of action is probable. Such predictions are often ad hoc in nature and applicable only to a given situation. Behaviorism, then, does not appear to be a general theory of the firm, but rather a valuable empirical study of firm and managerial behavior that can serve as the basis for the construction of a generalized theory of the firm.

An intriguing variant of the general class of realism-in-process theories is the "satisficing" theory originally proposed by Simon.[27] The satisficing firm does not attempt to maximize or minimize any particular function, but rather to meet reasonable goals in the various areas that interest the firm (for example, sales and profits). The standards of achievement that the firm adopts are often minimum standards, designed to guarantee the firm's existence, and seldom to achieve any single goal such as the maximization of profits.

The firm that satisfices a set of goals closely resembles the firm of behaviorist models, in that organizational slack is assumed to exist and that the firm is a coalition of coalitions. Since the firm does not have a well-defined objective function that dictates its behavior, its actions cannot be predicted except by a detailed examination of its decision process. The exact properties of satisficing models (which are based upon reasonable assumptions about the firm and its behavior) are often not discovered unless a computer simulation of the model is undertaken. This is done by specifying initial values for the parameters in the equations representing the reasonable assumptions about the firm's behavior, and then observing the values that key variables such as profits and organizational slack assume as successive time periods pass. Such a computer simulation based on satisficing behavior by a firm has been performed by Cohen and Cyert.[28] They simulated a non-maximizing monopoly model of a firm for 10,000 periods in an attempt to predict firm behavior.

The predictive success of a satisficing computer simulation is limited primarily by how realistically the decision process of the firm is represented. Nevertheless, however accurate the representation made of the firm's behavior, the satisficing computer simulations are (like the behaviorist models) appropriately viewed as being empirical bases for future inductive theorizing. A satisficing model is not at present a generalized theory of firm behavior applicable to many different situations in the same sense as profit-, sales-, or growth-maximizing models are.

[27]Henry A. Simon, *Models of Man* (New York: John Wiley & Sons, Inc., 1957).

[28]Kalman J. Cohen and Richard M. Cyert, *Theory of the Firm: Resource Allocation in a Market Economy* (Englewood Cliffs, N.J.: Prentice-Hall, Inc., 1965).

GAME-THEORETICAL MODELS

In the decade of the 1940's, Von Neumann and Morgenstern published a book that opened new vistas for the study of conflict behavior.[29] The book was hailed by economists as a breakthrough in the study of market structures such as duopoly and oligopoly. Von Neumann and Morgenstern dealt with various types of rational behavior and illustrated that market structures that previously were thought to produce indeterminate solutions could under reasonable sets of assumptions produce determinate solutions.

The Von Neumann and Morgenstern theoretical framework is designed to apply to any conflict situation, economic or otherwise. They specifically dealt with the firm's problem of selecting an optimal market strategy, given that the optimal strategy depends upon what actions the firm believes its competitors might take. Uncertainty as to competitors' precise actions and reactions is assumed to exist.

The key aspect of the theory of games from the standpoint of our current discussion is the fact that a wide range of alternative motivations can be assumed to hold true for a firm. The theory of games is not based exclusively upon profit- or sales-maximizing behavior. Consider the following simple game representing the behavior of two duopolists, illustrated in Figure 3.7. Each duopolist has four strategies that he may pursue. The dollar amounts in the payoff matrix represent profits to oligopolist A. It will be assumed that only a total of $40 of profit can be earned by the duopolists; thus, if duopolist A lowers his prices and earns $30 of profits, duopolist B automatically earns $10 of profits if he chooses the strategy of raising his prices.

Duopolist A conceivably distrusts duopolist B and may fear that duopolist B will discover what duopolist A is doing and adjust accordingly. Hence, if A chooses to increase his advertising expenditures, the most profitable behavior for B would be to lower his prices. Profoundly distrusting B, A might therefore attempt to reach the best possible solution, given that B is assumed to be doing what is worst for A. Regardless of what action he pursues, A perceives, it will be most profitable for B to lower prices. As a result, A chooses also to lower his prices, for in so doing he maximizes the minimum gain that he can receive. This strategy, referred to as a "maxmin" strategy, involves maximizing the various row minima, and is a somewhat conservative strategy. B's strategy may be described as "minmax" (since B chooses to minimize the various column maxima) and is also a somewhat conservative strategy, because it eliminates the possibility of large gains and losses.

Because a $20 profit is the best he can do if B lowers his prices, A is

[29]John Von Neumann and Oskar Morgenstern, *Theory of Games and Economic Behavior*, 3rd ed. (New York: John Wiley & Sons, Inc., 1953).

B's Possible Strategies

		Raise Prices	Prices Unchanged	Lower Prices	Increase Advertising
A's Possible Strategies	Raise Prices	$ 21	$ 12	$ 8	$ 19
	Prices Unchanged	$ 30	$ 26	$ 14	$ 17
	Lower Prices	$ 36	$ 28	$ 20	$ 22
	Increase Advertising	$ 28	$ 29	$ 16	$ 18

FIGURE 3.7

satisfied with his own decision to lower prices. Likewise, B optimizes by lowering his prices if A does the same. The result is a type of equilibrium known as a "saddle point." Saddle points are characterized by the congruence of the opponents' strategies. Neither A nor B will alter his decision, given the actions of the other. Saddle points do not always exist in every conflict situation; however, the introduction of "mixed" strategies, which realistically permit each duopolist to attach probabilities to each of the courses of action open to him, ensures the existence of a saddle point.

The theory of games is not limited in application to the duopoly case. A potentially unlimited number of firms may be included in a single game. Coalitions may be formed among the firms, and cartelization is permissible. The range of permissible behavior for a firm is not limited to such staple behavioral criteria as minmax or maxmin. Shubik, a pioneer in the study of the theory of games, has pointed out that some thirty or forty different solution concepts have been applied in the theory.[30] Each solution concept is based upon a given type of rational behavior that implies a particular motivation behind the actions of the firm.

It is apparent that the potential applicability of the theory of games to

[30]Martin Shubik, "A Curmudgeon's Guide to Microeconomics," *Journal of Economic Literature,* 8 (June 1970), 425.

the theory of the firm is quite great. Nevertheless, the actual usefulness of the theory of games has never approached the promise that the theory seems to hold. Although the theory of games has proved to be a fertile ground for innovative thoughts about the theory of the firm, it has not produced any widely accepted models that are empirically valid. The theory is appealing, in that it permits us to assume many alternative motivations for the actions of a firm's managers. Yet the frequent indeterminateness of solutions one encounters, the strong assumptions that are frequently required in order to obtain results, and the general lack of other than impressionistic evidence in support of particular game-theoretical formulations have seriously limited the worth of the theory of games to the economist.

EVALUATION

The critics of the profit-maximization assumption are legion. Our discussion has highlighted the major alternatives to profit maximization that have been proposed. We must now ask, Is profit maximization a useful assumption? The critics of profit maximization argue that (1) it is not rational for entrepreneurs to maximize profits (the Scitovsky argument) ; (2) managers live in a world of uncertainty and lack the knowledge of demand, costs, and future events necessary to maximize profits;[31] (3) in general, managers pursue many goals besides profit maximization in the complex modern firm (Baumol, Marris, Williamson, Cyert and March, Simon, et al.) ; (4) the separation of ownership and management in the modern corporation causes the firm's managers to have only a muted desire to maximize profits (Berle and Means, Galbraith, et al.) ; and (5) risk-averting, security-conscious managers will seldom choose a policy designed to maximize profits, because such policies are associated with the increased risk and instability that they abhor.

Against this mass of criticism, defenders of the profit-maximization assumption have replied with three major arguments. First, they point out that there is only scanty empirical evidence in support of any of the alternatives to profit maximization that have been proposed. In point of fact, decisive empirical evidence in support of any theory of the motivation of the firm, including profit maximization, does not exist.

[31]Profit maximization has many dimensions, and one of the most important of these is time. The firm must decide when to realize profits. Maximizing current-period profits is seldom the same as maximizing the present discounted value of a stream of profits over time. If a firm discounts future profits at a very high rate, then the firm's managers will choose to wring the highest possible profits out of the market in the current period, perhaps by a policy that emphasizes high product prices in price-inelastic markets. Such a policy will inspire entry by competitor firms and will reduce profits in future time periods. Alternatively, a longer time horizon and lower discount rate will lead to a policy of lower prices. This strategy will not maximize current-period profits, but will maintain the size of the future profit stream and discourage entry. Which strategy the firm chooses will depend upon management's knowledge of the shape of the stream of expected future profits as well as upon the firm's rate of discount.

A second argument made in defense of the profit-maximization assumption was first made by Machlup[32] and has since been generalized by Friedman.[33] Machlup ingeniously used the example of an automobile that is attempting to pass another automobile on a two-lane highway. The driver must consider as relevant variables the position, speed, and acceleration of his own car, the car he is attempting to pass, and any oncoming cars in other lanes. Further, he must consider road conditions, lighting, and weather conditions. The automobile driver (like the firm attempting to maximize profits) must consider a host of factors and arrive at an optimal decision. A rigorous solution to his problem would involve an exercise in higher mathematics. The typical driver, however, solves this problem intuitively and then applies his result. So also, Machlup contends, it is with profit maximization. Perfect knowledge and the absence of uncertainty on the part of the firm's managers need not exist. The entrepreneur can nevertheless seek after profit maximization as his intuition suggests. Machlup suggests that both the automobile driver and the firm that attempts to maximize profits are ordinarily successful in pursuing their aims.

Friedman has extended the argument one step further, by stating that whether or not entrepreneurs say that they maximize profits (or have the ability to work with higher mathematics), if they act as if they do, then the profit-maximization motivation is an empirically valid description of firm behavior. Both Friedman and Machlup therefore reject arguments stating that the firm's managers have insufficient information available to maximize profits. Further, Friedman doubts the significance of statements by the managers of firms in which they imply that they do not pursue profit-maximizing goals. Friedman feels that the managers act as if they maximize profits, and statements to the contrary are best disregarded.

The keystone of support for the assumption of profit maximization is the "natural selection" proposition.[34] Simply stated, the natural-selection argument maintains that firms that do not approximate the maximization of profits will be unable to meet the rigors of competition and will be driven out of the market. Further, the example of these disappearing firms will not be lost on the surviving firms, which will be encouraged to pursue profit-maximizing activities in order to avoid a similar fate. Hence, only profit-maximizing firms will survive in the long run.

The natural-selection argument depends upon the existence of vigorous competition. The absence of competition in a market will ordinarily imply a diminishing of the natural-selection process. Monopolists need not fear the

[32]Fritz Machlup, "Marginal Analysis and Empirical Research," *American Economic Review,* 36 (September 1946), 519–54.

[33]Friedman, "The Methodology of Positive Economics."

[34]Armen A. Alchian, "Uncertainty, Evolution and Economic Theory," *Journal of Political Economy,* 58 (June 1950), 211–21. See also Armen A. Alchian and Ruben Kessel, "Competition, Monopoly, and the Pursuit of Pecuniary Gain," in *Aspects of Labor Economics* (Princeton, N.J.: National Bureau of Economic Research, 1962).

actions of profit-maximizing competitors and therefore might be expected to engage in practices at variance with profit maximization—for example, the wasteful maintenance of management slack.[35] It is not surprising that proponents of alternative theories of the motivation of the firm, such as Baumol, Williamson, Cyert and March, and Simon, argue that their non-profit-maximizing models most accurately describe oligopolistic markets, in which competitive forces are of minimal importance.

On the grounds that profit maximization is undoubtedly a major goal of the firm, and also because it is a useful point of departure for our studies, we shall proceed to assume profit maximization as the basic motivating force of the firm. Empirical evidence does not discourage this viewpoint. With the recognition that profit maximization is not universally true, we will proceed with our analysis of industrial organization and performance.

PROBLEMS

1.   Several empirical studies have revealed that as much as 80 percent of the capital raised by large firms is raised internally by the firms themselves. That is, the firms do not go to the outside capital markets. If this information is true, what implications does it have for any alleged conflicts between growth-maximization and profit-maximization theories of the motivation of the firm?

2.   Some observers of industrial organization claim that the fact that firms contribute to the United Fund, give Christmas parties, maintain pretty lawns and flower beds, and grant severance pay is evidence that firms do not maximize profits. Is this true, or is it evidence that firms maximize long-run instead of short-run profits?

3.   "The requirement of the theory of games in terms of information is impossibly great. In order to be able to implement game-theoretical models, one must have in one's possession unrealistically large amounts of data, most of which a single firm is not party to and never will be." Comment.

4.   Is it possible for organizational slack to exist in a competitive market? Can a firm choose to take portions of its profits in the form of organizational slack?

5.   Assume that the rate of growth of the firm is greater than the firm's rate of discount in a Baumol type of growth-maximization model. What problems does this cause?

6.   Maxmin and minmax are conservative, risk-averting strategies in the theory of games. The idea of minimaxing "regret" has also been proposed. "Regret" is the difference between the actual outcome and the best possible outcome that the firm could have received. Minimaxing regret is a Monday-morning-quarterback sort of criterion. Is it a reasonable criterion?

---

[35]In a related vein, Hicks has stated that "the best of all monopoly profits is a quiet life." Presumably Hicks had in mind the monopolist who is not forced to maximize profits and who therefore tolerates inefficiency and slack in his enterprise because he finds it utility maximizing to do so. J.R. Hicks, "Annual Survey of Economic Theory: The Theory of Monopoly," *Econometrica*, 2 (January 1935), 8.

4

The Identification and
Measurement of
Monopoly Power

We have said that monopoly power is the ability to influence perceptibly the price or quantity in the market. Many firms have monopoly power, and it seems clear that some firms have more than others. In this chapter we seek to identify monopoly power in a theoretical sense and then to measure it in a quantitative sense. Unfortunately, monopoly power has many sources and many outlets, and no single measure of it or single index number can fully capture the many nuances of its real or potential exercise in the market. The pessimistic Mason has commented, "It is not possible, nor will it ever be possible, by calculating market shares, dividing price minus marginal cost by price, or other hocus pocus, to present an unambiguous measure of the degree of monopoly. Market power has many dimensions."[1]

A host of other difficulties present themselves when one attempts to measure monopoly power. The economist who wishes to do so must decide first whether he seeks to measure the *actual* exercise of monopoly power or the *potential* for such exercise. We shall see that economists have been schizoid with respect to this issue; they have not firmly decided what it is they wish to measure. It must also be emphasized that nearly every index of monopoly power that has been proposed is based upon the static theories of competition and monopoly. This not only limits the indexes to the logical constructs and terminology contained in those theories, but also prevents the indexes from being truly dynamic and recording the time path of changes in monopoly power. Finally, the majority of the proposed indexes of monopoly power are nonoperational in nature and therefore cannot actually be utilized.[2]

[1] Edward S. Mason, "Market Power and Business Conduct: Some Comments," *American Economic Review*, 46 (May 1956), 480.

[2] This point and others are summarized in John P. Miller, "Measures of Monopoly Power and Concentration: Their Economic Significance," in *Business Concentration and Price Policy*, ed. George J. Stigler (Princeton, N.J.: Princeton University Press, 1955), pp. 119–39.

INDEXES OF MONOPOLY POWER

The Lerner Index

Although concentration ratios are a more frequently used index when empirical studies are being performed, the Lerner Index is easily the best-known index of monopoly power.[3] The Lerner Index is defined as:

$$I = \frac{\text{Price} - \text{Marginal Cost}}{\text{Price}}$$

We have seen in Chapter 2 that when perfect competition exists, $P = MC$; therefore, the Lerner Index assumes a value of zero. When $P > MC$, indicating the existence of monopoly power, the Lerner Index becomes positive and varies between zero and 1. The closer it is to the value of 1, the more monopoly power the firm is said to possess. It should be noted, however, that the Lerner Index can also assume negative values. If the firm mistakenly produces too much output, $P < MC$, and the Lerner Index will assume negative values.

It can easily be demonstrated that the Lerner Index is equal to the reciprocal of the coefficient of price elasticity of demand when the firm is maximizing profits and is in equilibrium. We begin this demonstration by writing a fundamental equation that relates marginal revenue, price, and price elasticity of demand:

(1) $MR = P\left[1 + \dfrac{1}{\eta}\right]$ where η = the coefficient of price elasticity of demand

If the firm in question is maximizing profits and is in equilibrium, then

(2) $MC = P\left[1 + \dfrac{1}{\eta}\right]$

(3) $MC = P + \dfrac{P}{\eta}$

(4) $MC - P = \dfrac{P}{\eta}$

(5) $P - MC = -\dfrac{P}{\eta}$

(6) $\dfrac{P - MC}{P} = -\dfrac{1}{\eta}$

If we use the absolute value (positive value) of the coefficient of price

[3]Abba P. Lerner, "The Concept of Monopoly and the Measurement of Monopoly Power," *Review of Economic Studies*, 1 (June 1934), 157–75.

elasticity of demand, we may write

$$(7) \quad \frac{P - MC}{P} = \frac{1}{|\eta|}$$

The statement that the Lerner Index is the reciprocal of the absolute value of the coefficient of price elasticity of demand is equivalent to saying that the Lerner Index measures the degree of monopoly in terms of the deviation of the slope of the demand curve away from a value of zero.[4]

The Lerner Index is a measure of actual conduct and does not measure the potential for monopoly behavior on the part of a firm. As such, it may hide relevant information from us. Further, the Lerner Index is based upon static price theory and is incapable of telling whether or not a current divergence between price and marginal cost is a justifiable result of past behavior or is perhaps a societal cost, which is defensible in light of the future societal benefits that might accrue.[5] In any case, the Theory of the Second Best, a keystone of modern welfare economics, has considerable relevance in this area.[6] The Theory of the Second Best seeks to answer questions such as, Is it welfare maximizing to eliminate some monopoly power while being unaware of, or ignoring, other monopoly power that exists? Assume that a given firm is adjudged to possess considerable monopoly power on the basis of a computed Lerner Index. Would society be better off if that monopoly power were eliminated but other monopoly power remained? The Theory of the Second Best cautions us that we cannot show logically that welfare is increased (or even that welfare will not decline) when we selectively eliminate monopoly power.

The Lerner Index concept has been applied with mixed success in empirical studies. Kalecki has attempted to determine the degree of monopoly for the entire American economy.[7] Dunlop has used the Lerner Index in an attempt to ascertain the effects of the business cycle upon monopoly power.[8] Maddox has sought to explain patterns of sexual discrimination in hiring by using a Lerner Index.[9] A related sort of empirical

[4]This follows from the relationship between price and marginal revenue that is implied in the Lerner Index. For a profit-maximizing firm in equilibrium, $I = (P - MR)/P$. The index will be larger when the gap between P and MR is greatest. The gap between P and MR will be greatest when the slope of the demand curve becomes increasingly negative in an absolute sense.

[5]An example might be a technological advance that is engendered by the funds accumulated by exercise of monopoly power.

[6]See Kelvin Lancaster and R.G. Lipsey, "The General Theory of the Second Best," *Review of Economic Studies*, 24 (December 1956), 11–32; also M. McManus, "Comments on the General Theory of Second Best," *Review of Economic Studies*, 26 (June 1959), 209–24; E.J. Mishan, "Second Thoughts on Second Best," *Oxford Economic Papers*, N.S., 14 (October 1962), 205–17. Numerous other articles have since appeared that have amended and extended this basic work.

[7]M. Kalecki, "The Determinants of the Distribution of National Income," *Econometrica*, 6 (April 1938), 97–112.

[8]John T. Dunlop, "Price Flexibility and the Degree of Monopoly," *Quarterly Journal of Economics*, 53 (August 1939), 522–33.

[9]Lola P. Maddox, "The Impact of Market Structure on Sexual Discrimination in Selected Manufacturing Industries" (Master's thesis, Illinois State University, 1972).

study (that of the so-called deadweight loss due to monopoly, which we will review later in this chapter) has caused problems, however. Two firms might have identical Lerner Indexes while causing quite different deadweight losses. This issue will be considered shortly.

The Concentration Ratio

The most commonly used measure of monopoly is the concentration ratio. Of the many different measures of concentration that are available, the four-firm concentration ratio is the most popular. The four-firm concentration ratio reports the proportionate share of the market held by the four largest firms in that market, where the size of the firms and of the market may be measured by variables such as value of shipments, value added, or employment. Similar concentration ratios are computed for the largest eight, twenty, and fifty firms.[10] The higher the concentration ratio, the greater the monopoly power that is said to exist in the industry.[11]

Economic theory, particularly the accepted theories of duopoly and oligopoly, predicts that highly concentrated markets that are characterized by the existence of a few large firms will be guilty of most of the abuses and departures from efficiency associated with pure monopoly.[12] Empirical evidence to be presented in Chapter 7 also suggests that the performance of firms in highly concentrated markets is often demonstrably inferior to the performance of firms in less concentrated markets. Thus, the assertion that market concentration is related to monopoly power is not without theoretical and empirical basis.

The use of market concentration ratios as a measure of individual-firm monopoly power is nevertheless subject to a large number of criticisms. The most obvious of these is that a concentration ratio such as the four-firm concentration ratio gives us information about a slice of the entire market, but tells us little about the individual firms in that market. The size, conduct, and performance of the individual firm are largely disguised by the concentration ratio.

Concentration ratios are not a reliable guide to the number of points of initiative in a market or to the number of alternatives available to consumers.[13] Some have contended that they are; and if this contention were true, a concentration ratio would be a rough guide to potential competition

[10]See Chapter 7 for a lengthy discussion of the measurement and effects of concentration.

[11]An example of this type of usage is Lester G. Telser, "Advertising and Competition," *Journal of Political Economy,* 72 (December 1964), 537–62. See also, among many others, R.W. Kilpatrick, "Stigler on the Relationship Between Industry Profit Rates and Market Concentration," *Journal of Political Economy,* 76 (May–June 1968), 479–88.

[12]Saving has also shown that it is possible under certain conditions to construct a theoretical connection between concentration ratios and monopoly power, where monopoly power is measured by means of a Lerner Index or the Rothschild Index. Thomas R. Saving, "Concentration Ratios and the Degree of Monopoly Power," *International Economic Review,* 11 (February 1970), 139–46.

[13]Miller, "Measures of Monopoly Power," p. 130.

and monopoly. The four-firm concentration ratio, however, is based upon only four firms and is not a summary measure of concentration taking into account all the firms in the market. A four-firm concentration ratio of 80 simply means that the four largest firms in the market have 80 percent of the market, and that at least one firm has 20 percent of that market. It does not tell us how many firms are in the market. Hence, the number of points of initiative and/or alternatives open to consumers cannot be accurately determined by means of the four-firm concentration ratio.

Concentration ratios differ from other measures of monopoly power in many ways. One of the most important of these is that concentration ratios seek to measure the *potential* for monopoly power evident in an *entire market,* whereas other measures (for example, the Lerner Index) seek to measure the *actual* monopoly power exercised by a *single firm* in a market.

Monopoly power has many possible sources, of which high market concentration is only one. Despite the frequency of their use as indicators of monopoly power and/or market imperfections (the reader is again referred to Chapter 7), concentration ratios are not the ideal measure of either, and should be used with caution.

Slope of Demand Curves (Rothschild)

K.W. Rothschild has suggested that the degree of monopoly power exercised by a firm might be approximated by a ratio that is the slope of the product-demand curve faced by the firm, divided by the slope of the demand curve for the same product in the entire market.[14] The Rothschild Index, which is based upon the work of Chamberlin and Copeland in the area of monopolistic competition, may vary between the values of zero (for a perfect competitor) and 1 (for a pure monopolist).[15]

Figure 4.1 illustrates the derivation of the Rothschild Index. Let dd be the demand curve that the firm feels it faces when it charges any given price on that demand curve but all other firms in the same market keep their prices constant at P_1. DD is the demand curve the firm feels it faces if all other firms in the market charge prices identical to the price charged by this firm. Demand curve dd is more price-elastic than demand curve DD at most relevant prices because demand curve dd assumes that other firms will not react to price changes by the firm in question. Hence, the firm will sell many fewer units if it raises its price and no other firm follows, and it will sell many additional units if it lowers its price and no other firm follows suit.

In pure monopoly, only one firm exists, and demand curves dd and

[14]K.W. Rothschild, "The Degree of Monopoly," *Economica*, 9 (February 1942), 24–40.

[15]E.H. Chamberlin, *The Theory of Monopolistic Competition* (Cambridge, Mass.: Harvard University Press, 1933); and M.A. Copeland, "The Theory of Monopolistic Competition," *Journal of Political Economy*, 42 (August 1934), 531–36.

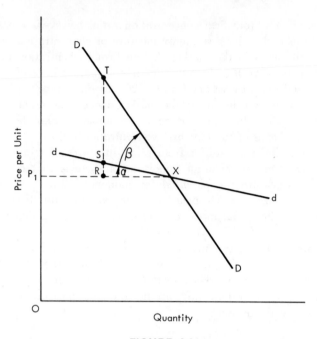

FIGURE 4.1

DD are identical. Since the slopes of the two demand curves are identical, the value of the Rothschild Index is 1. In perfect competition, the demand curve that faces the firm is horizontal, and therefore the Rothschild Index will be zero. In the case of an imperfect competitor, the greater the absolute value of the slope of the dd demand curve, the greater is said to be the monopoly power of the firm. In Figure 4.1, the slope of the dd demand curve is the tangent of angle α, and is equal to the ratio RS/RX. The slope of the DD demand curve is the tangent of angle β, and is equal to the ratio RT/RX. The Rothschild Index can be seen to be

$$I = \frac{RS/RX}{RT/RX} = \frac{RS}{RT} = .15$$

The deficiencies of the Rothschild Index are of two types: (1) economic and (2) pragmatic. The economic criticisms are simple and obvious. The Rothschild Index assumes very specific price expectations on the part of the individual firm; the dd and DD demand curves reflect these expectations. The worth of the index depends largely upon the accuracy of these assumptions. Also, the index is based totally upon demand considerations and ignores the effects of supply and cost upon the exercise of monopoly power.

Whatever the economic shortcomings of the Rothschild Index, the pragmatic problems associated with it are more critical. Even if sellers' price expectations are as Rothschild postulated, and even if supply and cost considerations are not important sources of monopoly power, the Rothschild Index is of little use except as a theoretical artifact unless one can actually estimate the slopes of the *dd* and *DD* demand curves from market data. E.J. Working showed years ago that it is often impossible to estimate a demand curve unless certain strict conditions are fulfilled.[16] In the case at hand, one of these conditions is that the firm whose monopoly power we seek to measure must have engaged in considerable price variation during the time period in question; the same must be true for the entire market. Further, one must be able to distinguish true changes in demand, because of factors such as changing income or tastes, from mere changes in the quantity demanded. Econometricians today label these difficulties the "identification problem," which remains one of the most vexing of all econometric problems. Consequently, no empirical study of monopoly power has ever relied upon the Rothschild Index.

Profit Rates

Bain has proposed that profit rates be used to measure monopoly power.[17] He argues that when a particular firm persistently earns excess profits for a long period of time, this is prima facie evidence of the existence of monopoly power. We may restate this proposition in the terminology of Chapter 2. If pure profits are persistently earned by a firm, there is a great probability that this firm possesses monopoly power. The greater the pure profits, and the longer the duration of time that these pure profits are earned, the greater is said to be the monopoly power.

Bain chose to define the rate of profit as, "that rate which, when used in discounting the future rents of the enterprise, equates their capital value to the cost of those assets which would be held by the firm if it produced its present output in competitive equilibrium."[18] This rate of profit is compared to the normal rate of profit (the rate of interest acts as a proxy for the normal rate of profit) in order to determine if pure profits exist.

The Bain Index is operational in nature, although when one constructs a profit rate, one must often depend upon unsatisfactory and unreliable data. Few firms have identical accounting practices, and therefore the construction of a given firm's profit rate is necessarily an ad hoc process. In particular, when computing a rate of profit as a percent return on invested capital, one must confront the well-known problem of evaluating the

[16]E.J. Working, "What Do Statistical 'Demand Curves' Show?" *Quarterly Journal of Economics*, 41 (February 1927), 212–35.

[17]Joe S. Bain, "The Profit Rate as a Measure of Monopoly Power," *Quarterly Journal of Economics*, 55 (February 1941), 271–93.

[18]*Ibid.*, pp. 276–77.

firm's assets either in terms of their original cost to the firm or in terms of a guesstimate of their current value or replacement cost to the firm. Deceptively high rates of profit may appear if the firm's assets are undervalued or simply because the firm is quite efficient. Likewise, deceptively low rates of profit might indicate overvaluation of assets,[19] or possible inefficiency, or the fact that the firm has expended considerable resources on activities such as advertising that are designed to erect barriers to entry. It is not clear, then, that persistently high rates of profit must necessarily indicate the existence of monopoly power.[20]

An interesting comparison is possible between the Bain Index and the Lerner Index. When the Bain Index proclaims that monopoly power has been exercised, the Lerner Index will be in agreement. The converse, however, is not true. When the Lerner Index indicates that monopoly power exists, the Bain Index may or may not be in agreement. Figure 4.2 demonstrates this. In Figure 4.2a, $P_1 > AC > MC$ at profit-maximizing output

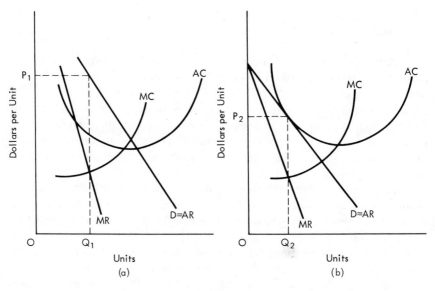

FIGURE 4.2

Q_1, and both Bain and Lerner would agree that monopoly power exists. Bain is in agreement because $P > AC$, and Lerner is in agreement because $P > MC$. In Figure 4.2b, $P_2 = AC > MC$ at profit-maximizing output Q_2, and no pure profits exist. Because no pure profits exist, and $P = AC$, the Bain Index does not identify monopoly power in this circumstance. Notwithstand-

[19]Fritz Machlup has demonstrated this in his book, *The Political Economy of Monopoly* (Baltimore: Johns Hopkins Press, 1952), p. 493.

[20]K.W. Rothschild, "A Further Note on the Degree of Monopoly," *Economica*, 10 (February 1943), 69–71.

ing, the Lerner Index will be positive (indicating monopoly power) because $P > MC$. Note that if we assume constant returns to scale (constant costs), then $AC = MC$, and the conflict disappears.

The Papandreou Index

Papandreou has suggested that monopoly power be measured in terms of what he has called coefficients of penetration and insulation.[21] Papandreou argued that one must determine the firm's ability to penetrate other markets by means of lowering its price (the coefficient of penetration measures this ability) and the firm's ability to ward off the price attacks of its rivals (the coefficient of insulation is relevant here). In both cases, the absolute amount of penetration or insulation is measured in terms of sales.

Papandreou's two coefficients, which are designed to represent both demand and supply factors, may be approximated by estimating cross-elasticities of supply and demand.[22] The difficulty with adopting a measure such as the coefficient of cross-elasticity of demand as a measure of monopoly power is that one might logically expect a coefficient equal to zero for both the case of pure monopoly and its antithesis, perfect competition. It is true that the pure monopolist's product has no ready substitutes and therefore that the product has a cross-elasticity of demand equal to zero with respect to any other product. This follows from the fact that when any other firm alters its product price, this will have no effect on the sales of the pure monopolist because of the lack of substitutable products. It may also be predicted, however, that the coefficient of cross-elasticity of demand for a perfect competitor's product will also be zero. Since no single perfect competitor is able to influence overall market quantity, when one perfect competitor changes his price, it will not elicit any measurable reaction in the sales of any other perfect competitor.

The issue of classifying competitors and entire market structures on the basis of cross-elasticities has been discussed in great detail since the latter 1930's.[23] These discussions have not resolved the fundamental conceptual problem outlined above. Additionally, the same identification problem that plagues the estimation of any supply–demand relationship is also present when attempts are made to compute cross-elasticities or coefficients of penetration and insulation. Such numbers can be readily computed; the relevance and accuracy of these numbers is not clear.

[21]A.G. Papandreou, "Market Structure and Monopoly Power," *American Economic Review,* 39 (September 1949), 883–97.

[22]The cross-elasticity of supply is relevant because of the frequent Papandreou emphasis upon the ability or capacity of a firm to supply prospective customers in response to price variations of its own and those of other firms.

[23]The literature in this area is mountainous. The reader who has any significant time constraint is referred to Mancur Olson and David McFarland, "The Restoration of Pure Monopoly and the Concept of the Industry," *Quarterly Journal of Economics,* 76 (November 1962), 613–31.

EMPIRICAL STUDIES OF THE EFFECTS OF
MONOPOLY POWER

We will now alter our emphasis and examine empirical studies that purport to measure the actual loss in welfare that occurs because of the exercise of monopoly power. These studies are of two types: (1) those studies that attempt to ascertain the amount of losses in consumer surplus because of the misallocation of resources between monopolist and competitor firms; and (2) those studies that attempt to measure welfare losses due to "X-Inefficiency."[24]

Losses in Consumer Surplus

It is necessary to define in a nonrigorous fashion the term "consumer surplus" before we can proceed further.

Consumer surplus is the difference between what the consumer would have been willing to pay for each unit of a good or service purchased and what the consumer actually had to pay for those same units.[25]

Figure 4.3 illustrates the concept of consumer surplus. Assume that a given consumer purchased three units of a certain commodity at the equilibrium price, P_E per unit. According to his demand schedule, the consumer would have been willing to pay a maximum price of P_1 for the first unit; however, he paid only P_E for that unit when he purchased three units at price P_E. The area of rectangle $P_E P_1 OP$ corresponds to the excess satisfaction (consumer surplus) the consumer received when he did not have to pay price P_1 for the first unit. In like fashion, the area of rectangle $P_E P_2 QR$ represents consumer surplus received from the second unit because the consumer paid price P_E rather than price P_2, the maximum he would have been willing to pay per unit for two units. It should be noted that part of rectangle $P_E P_2 QR$ was counted previously when we derived consumer surplus for the first unit purchased. The area that was counted previously was the area of rectangle $P_E P_2 SP$. Total consumer surplus derived from the purchase of two units is therefore the noncheckered area of triangle $P_E NM$.

---

[24]The term "X-Inefficiency" was coined by Harvey Leibenstein in "Allocative Efficiency vs. X-Efficiency," *American Economic Review*, 56 (June 1966), 392–415.

[25]A more rigorous definition of consumer surplus ties the concept to the area of the triangle under the demand curve by means of an integral. Let the demand curve be represented by $P = f(Q)$. If the consumer purchases Q_x units at price P_x, his total expenditure on the commodity in question is $P_x Q_x$. The area under the demand curve above price P_x from the origin to Q_x represents the sum of money that the consumer would have been willing to pay for Q_x units but did not have to, because he purchased those units at price P_x. The difference between what the consumer would have been willing to pay for each unit of the good and what the consumer actually pays may be written as $\int_0^{Q_x} f(Q)\, dQ - P_x Q_x$ and is consumer surplus.

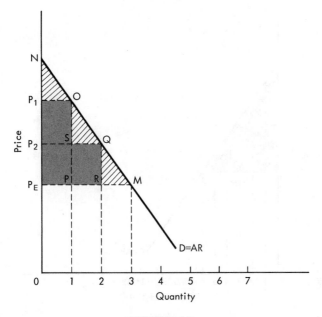

FIGURE 4.3

The purchase of the third unit brought with it no additional consumer surplus, since the consumer paid price P_E per unit for three units, and this is the maximum that he was willing to pay for three units according to his demand schedule.

Assume now that at the equilibrium price, P_E, the consumer could buy six units of the good in question instead of three. If this is true, the result is six checkered triangles that are not included in consumer surplus (see Figure 4.4) instead of the three observed in Figure 4.3. Consumer surplus, which is represented by the noncheckered areas of triangles $P_E NM$ and $P_E AB$, can be seen to be larger in Figure 4.4 than in Figure 4.3. At the limit, when the units of the commodity are very small (or where the commodity in question is perfectly divisible, like gasoline), total consumer surplus will closely approximate the area of triangle $P_E NM$ in Figure 4.3, or in terms of Figure 4.4, the area of triangle $P_E AB$. While several alternative methods of computing consumer surplus exist, we will adopt the method outlined above, which results in consumer surplus being the area of the triangle formed by the product price, the ordinate, and the demand curve.

The relevant question at this point is whether or not the allocation of resources in the entire economy between monopolists and competitors causes consumer surplus to be reduced. Harberger, in a landmark study, investigated this question empirically.[26] Following Harberger, assume that price

[26]Arnold C. Harberger, "Monopoly and Resource Allocation," *American Economic Review,* 44 (May 1954), 77–87.

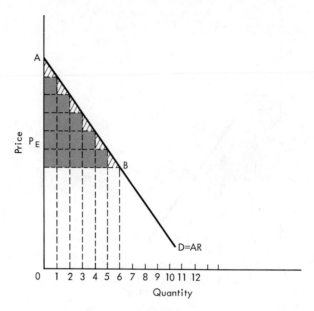

FIGURE 4.4

P_c in Figure 4.5 is the price a perfectly competitive firm would charge ($P =$ MC), whereas P_m is the price a monopolist would charge. Q_c and Q_m are the analagous outputs for each firm. Profit-maximizing behavior and constant costs (such that $MC = AC$) are assumed throughout.

In Figure 4.5, consumer surplus under conditions of perfect competition is the area of triangle P_cAC; under conditions of monopoly, consumer surplus is the area of triangle P_mAB. Because of the existence of monopoly, consumer surplus declines by an amount equal to the area of trapezoid P_cP_mBCD. With regard to this reduction in consumer surplus, the amount equal to the area of rectangle P_cP_mBD is taken by the monopolist. The area of triangle DBC, however, is also lost to the consumer, but is not gained by the monopolist, and hence is termed "deadweight loss" due to monopoly. The area of triangle DBC is the welfare loss to society owing to the misallocation of resources caused by monopoly. It is this deadweight loss in consumer surplus that Harberger and others after him have attempted to measure.

Three considerations are particularly crucial to the computation of the deadweight loss due to monopoly. First, what items should be included as costs? Second, is it appropriate to assume constant costs? Third, what value should one assume for price elasticity of demand? Let us consider these issues in order. Kamerschen and Tullock have contended that certain types of costs are in fact "quasi-monopoly" profits, and should not be counted in

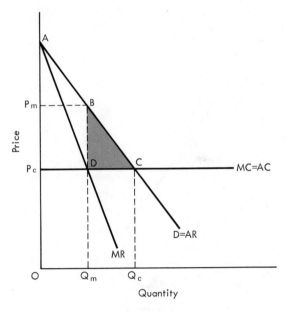

FIGURE 4.5

the same fashion as other costs.[27] In this light, advertising and selling costs may be alleged to be entirely manipulative, entirely directed at the creation of monopoly power, and not in any way directed at increasing information in the market.[28] If one adopts this viewpoint, such costs should not be included in the average-marginal-cost curve, and as a result, the deadweight loss due to monopoly will be larger.

The wisdom of assuming constant unit costs is open to question. While continuing to bear in mind Figure 4.5, consider Figure 4.6, where the same demand conditions exist but the firm in question is subject to increasing average costs. Note that in Figure 4.6, a substantial portion of the deadweight loss due to monopoly is eliminated (the shaded area). If one assumes the typical U-shaped long-run average-cost curve for the firm, and, further, that the firm is already near the bottom of that curve, then when output is expanded in that industry (that is, when resources are transferred to that industry in order to eliminate the output retardation associated with monopoly), such output will be high-cost output at the margin, and the

[27]David Kamerschen, "An Estimation of the 'Welfare Losses' from Monopoly in the American Economy" (Doctoral dissertation, Michigan State University, 1964); and Gordon Tullock, "The Welfare Costs of Tariffs, Monopolies and Theft," *Western Economic Journal*, 5 (June 1967), 224–32. See also David R. Kamerschen, "An Estimation of the 'Welfare Losses' in the American Economy," *Western Economic Journal*, 4 (Summer 1966), 221–36.

[28]One might also include costs devoted to activities that result in patents, trademarks, franchises, goodwill, royalties, and all types of product development. See Dean A. Worcester, Jr., "Innovations in the Calculation of Welfare Loss to Monopoly," *Western Economic Journal*, 7 (September 1969), 234–43.

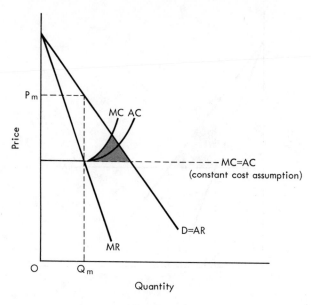

FIGURE 4.6

monopolist will succeed in taking part of the overall reduction in consumer surplus.

We have seen that the deadweight loss due to monopoly may be represented by the area of a particular triangle. The area of a triangle is equal to one-half its base times its height. In the case at hand, the triangle's base is the amount of resources that must be transferred in order to drive the price down to the competitive level, and the height of the triangle is the divergence of the monopoly price from the competitive level. Harberger has approximated the divergence of price from the competitive level by the percent divergence of any given industry's profit rate from the average industry profit rate. Those industries with a higher-than-average profit rate were said to have too few resources; industries with lower-than-average profit rates were said to have too many resources. Consequently, a transfer of resources between industries would be necessary in order to drive profit rates to equality. The amount of this transfer of resources, however, depends upon the value of price elasticity of demand. Harberger assumed unit price elasticity of demand. This meant (for example) that a 10 percent increase in resources in a given industry would be necessary to reduce that industry's price (profit rate) by 10 percent. If Harberger had assumed a coefficient of price elasticity of demand of -2.00, then twice as great a transfer of resources (a 20 percent increase, in terms of our previous example) would have been necessary to eliminate monopoly pricing. The more price-elastic demand is, the greater the transfer of resources that will be necessary to eliminate monopoly pricing and profits, the greater will be the base of the triangle containing the deadweight loss due to monopoly, and the larger will be that deadweight loss.

Using data for the time period 1924–28, Harberger arrived at a total welfare loss of $59 million for all manufacturing industries; this was less than 1 percent of national income during this time period. Translated into 1955 prices (the date of Harberger's article), this loss was less than $1.50 for every individual in the United States. The obvious implication of these results was that "our economy emphatically does not seem to be monopoly capitalism in big red letters. We can neglect monopoly elements and still gain a very good understanding of how our resources are allocated."[29] A subsequent study by Schwartzman, for the United States for the 1950's, lent credence to this finding.[30]

Since the advent of the Harberger and Schwartzman studies, the primary innovations in the area of loss of consumer surplus have been the result of work by Kamerschen. His most notable contribution consisted of relaxing the assumption of unit price elasticity of demand and instead using a distinctive estimate of price elasticity of demand for each industry.[31] Further, Kamerschen considered various types of selling costs, such as advertising, to be quasi-monopoly profits and did not include them in his cost curves. Following Stigler's suggestion,[32] Kamerschen based the average profit rate upon all types of business establishments, not just those in the area of manufacturing. Since the overall average rate of profit is lower than the average rate of profit in manufacturing (which Harberger used), the deviations of monopoly price from competitive price were estimated to be larger. Depending upon the particular set of assumptions chosen, Kamerschen found the deadweight loss due to monopoly in the economy to range from 3.9 to 8.0 percent of national income.[33]

If the deadweight loss due to monopoly is only 1 percent of national income (as Harberger and Schwartzman contend), then the monopoly problem is hardly one about which we need to worry.[34] If, on the other hand, the deadweight loss is 3.9 to 8.0 percent of national income (as Kamerschen states), then the wastages of monopoly are substantial, and considerable benefit might accrue to society if it pursued an antitrust policy directed at reducing the amount of monopoly in the economy.

One disturbing facet of the deadweight-loss studies is that the results of such studies can be inconsistent with the judgments provided by other measures of monopoly power. For example, two firms might have precisely

[29]Harberger, "Monopoly and Resource Allocation," p. 87.

[30]David Schwartzman, "The Burden of Monopoly," *Journal of Political Economy,* 68 (December 1960), 627–30.

[31]Kamerschen, "An Estimation of the 'Welfare Losses'," *loc. cit.*

[32]George J. Stigler, *Capital and Rates of Return in Manufacturing Industries* (Princeton, N.J.: Princeton University Press, 1963).

[33]Kamerschen, "An Estimation of the 'Welfare Losses'," p. 115.

[34]See, for example, David Schwartzman, "The Economics of Antitrust Policy," *The Antitrust Bulletin,* 6 (May–June 1961), 235–44.

the same Lerner Index of monopoly power even though the deadweight loss due to monopoly associated with each firm is quite different. Figure 4.7 demonstrates this possibility. Firms A and B face demand curves D_A and D_B, respectively. Both firms charge price P_1 for their output and have marginal costs equal to MC_1 per unit. Hence, the value of the Lerner Index is the same for both firms, namely, $(P_1 - MC_1)/P_1$. Note, however, that the deadweight loss caused by firm A (shown by the triangle labeled A) is much smaller than the deadweight loss caused by firm B (the triangle labeled B). The Lerner Index, then, and the concept of a deadweight loss due to monopoly are not always consistent with respect to their evaluations of monopoly power and performance.

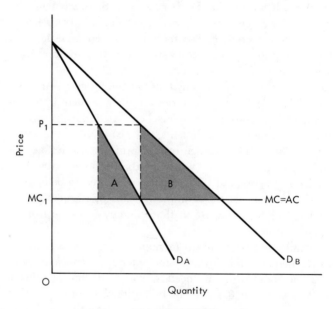

FIGURE 4.7

Nonallocative (X-Inefficiency) Losses Due to Monopoly

Microeconomics has traditionally been concerned with allocative efficiency—the resource allocation between monopolist and competitor firms in the economy. The studies of Harberger, et al., are of this vein. Largely ignored has been the question of resource allocation that is internal to the firm. Economists have tended to assume that the allocation and use of resources inside the firm are optimal and that the firm's managers and employees perform their duties with efficiency and dispatch.

Such internal efficiency, of course, need not be the case. Given firms may have inefficient internal resource allocations and inefficient managers and employees. The existence of such internal inefficiency has intuitive appeal; few among us can claim that he or she has not encountered some doltish employee in some business who "ought to be fired." Firms that maintain inefficient resource allocations are in a suboptimal equilibrium such that the firm could (via differing internal allocations or management techniques) actually increase output without any increase in inputs. This is equivalent to saying that a given level of output could be produced at lower cost.

Leibenstein has stated that such inefficient, suboptimal equilibria are evidence of what he has labeled "X-Inefficiency."[35] X-Inefficiency can alter any production function or production relation.[36] Factors such as incompetent or unpopular management, lack of employee motivation, and the incorrect organization of inputs are the meat and bones of X-Inefficiency. Leibenstein has listed numerous examples, largely taken from the area of economic development, of the existence of X-Inefficiency. He has cited the example of two identical petroleum refineries in Egypt, one of which was efficient by output standards, the other of which was inefficient by the same standards. The introduction of a new manager at the inefficient refinery brought an immediate improvement in output there and a spectacular improvement in output after some time had passed. As we saw in Chapter 3, there are several theories seeking to explain the general motivation and operation of the firm that rely heavily upon the existence of X-Inefficiency or a counterpart concept, organizational slack.

Although X-Inefficiency can affect either monopolist or competitor firms, there is reason to believe that it may affect monopolists to a greater degree.[37] This is because a monopolist is not disciplined by competition. In industries that are very competitive in nature, there should be few firms where X-Inefficiency is in evidence, because the rigors of competition will drive internally inefficient firms out of existence.

To the extent that X-Inefficiency exists because monopolists are not subject to competitive pressures, the effects of such inefficiency should be included in any measurement of the welfare loss due to monopoly. When the possibility of X-Inefficiency is recognized, the total welfare loss due to monopoly becomes the sum of two different types of measurable losses—the conventional allocative deadweight loss *and* an allocative loss due to X-Inefficiency—plus a nonallocative loss due entirely to X-Inefficiency.[38]

Figure 4.8 will assist in making apparent the distinction among the

[35]Leibenstein, "Allocative Efficiency," *loc. cit.*

[36]James Ferguson has pointed out to the author that the question of X-Inefficiency internal to the firm is actually a question of how the firm chooses to structure or exercise its own property rights. Ferguson also contends that the optimum structure of property rights is not connected to market structure.

[37]Note that any firm might choose to take portions of its profits as "X-Inefficiency" via thick carpets, limousines, or extra sleep at the expense of work.

[38]The reader is referred to William S. Comanor and Harvey Leibenstein, "Allocative Efficiency, X-Efficiency, and the Measurement of Welfare Losses," *Economica*, 36 (August 1969), 304–9.

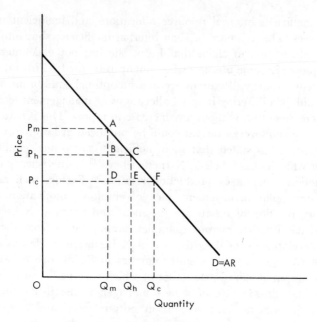

FIGURE 4.8

various components of welfare loss. Assume that $P_m Q_m$ is the price–output combination chosen by a firm that is a monopolist. Following Harberger, a transfer of resources of amount $Q_m Q_h$ to the monopolist would drive the price down to P_h. Price P_h is a competitive price similar to the one in Harberger's work and may be the result of some degree of X-Inefficiency. The conventional deadweight loss due to monopoly is the area of triangle *BAC*.

As Comanor and Leibenstein have insisted, the introduction of competition may have a cost effect in addition to the price effect noted above.[39] Competition may also eliminate X-Inefficiency, in the sense of reducing production costs and thereby reducing even further the amount of allocative welfare loss. This cost effect on the allocative welfare loss may be represented by trapezoid *DBCF*. The ability to produce at lower unit costs will lower price and stimulate output. The total allocative loss due to monopoly, then, is the area of triangle DAF.

The area of rectangle $P_c P_h BD$ is the welfare loss of a nonallocative nature due to X-Inefficiency. This loss occurs because higher costs were used to produce a restricted output, and it is totally nonallocative in character, since it refers to the loss that occurs because a given level of output (Q_m) was produced at higher costs than those competitive forces would have dictated for that same level of output.

[39]*Ibid.*

When X-Inefficiency is considered, the welfare loss due to monopoly increases. The allocative loss becomes larger, and a nonallocative loss is newly identified and must be considered. The Comanor–Leibenstein suggestions have not yet been subjected to empirical testing. Two important reasons why no testing has occurred are the inability of researchers to define precisely the amount of X-Inefficiency present in any given situation and the relatively short period of time that has passed since the appearance of the hypothesis.

SUMMARY

Adam Smith long ago commented that "monopolists, by keeping the market constantly understocked, by never fully supplying the effectual demand, sell their commodities much above the natural price, and raise their emoluments, whether they consist in wages or profit, greatly above the natural rate."[40] In this chapter, we have examined various alternative measures of the ability of firms to behave in the fashion of Smith's monopolists. No single measure of monopoly power that was explored was found to be wholly satisfactory, because no single index is capable of including the many diverse factors that create monopoly power. Further, economists have not yet decided whether they should measure potential monopoly power, the actual exercise of monopoly power, or both. Finally, many of the indexes that have been considered are found to be sadly lacking in terms of the criterion of operational feasibility that was discussed in Chapter 1.

In the latter part of the chapter, we turned to studies of the welfare loss due to monopoly. Empirical researchers do not agree concerning the magnitude of the allocative loss in consumer surplus due to monopoly. The recent suggestion that the internal organization and management of the firm are also adversely affected by monopoly power has not yet been given the testing that so important a hypothesis deserves.

It would, of course, be comforting to have a definitive measure of firm monopoly power. Reliable empirical evidence with respect to the precise effects of monopoly power on welfare would also make life much easier for economist and policy maker alike. Unfortunately, as the tenor of this chapter has indicated, neither of these millenia has yet arrived.

PROBLEMS

1. Which should a measure of monopoly power reflect, actual conduct or potential conduct? Is it possible to devise a measure that would reflect both actual and potential conduct in the market?

[40]Adam Smith, *The Wealth of Nations* (Baltimore: Penguin Books, Inc., 1970), p. 164.

2.   Given two markets, A and B. In market A, only two firms exist, and each of these firms has one half of market sales. In market B, the largest firm has 50 percent of the market, and the rest of the market is split among some 100 other firms. Which market is the more competitive, which the more monopolistic? Why?

3.   A Chicago-based producer of creamery butter recently replied to a charge that it was a monopoly by stating that the national four-firm concentration ratio was only 11. Hence, said the spokesman for the creamery, it could hardly be accused of being a monopoly. Do you agree?

4.   An econometric study reveals that the price elasticity of demand for one firm is -4.00 and the price elasticity of demand for another firm is $-.50$. Which firm is the monopolist?

5.   Studies of the deadweight loss due to monopoly utilize a datum that is the percentage by which monopoly prices are alleged to be greater than competitive prices. Demonstrate that such a percentage approximates the Lerner Index.

5

The Elements of
Market Structure
and the Traditional Model

We have already observed that the traditional model of analysis in the field of industrial organization centers upon the structure–conduct–performance relationship. In this chapter we shall explore the concept of market structure in greater detail.

Our study of market structure will begin with a discussion of what market structure is and how it fits into the traditional model proposed by Mason; however, it will become apparent in the course of our discussion that the direction of causation implied in the traditional model is not the only legitimate way to analyze contemporary industrial organization and behavior. The causal and empirical validity of the structure–conduct–performance link is frequently in doubt and will be subjected to scrutiny in subsequent chapters. Further, we shall see that a distinction can be made between the basic supply-and-demand conditions in a market and the elements of market structure in that market. Our overview of the issues surrounding market structure will conclude with a consideration of the crucial role that barriers to the entry of new firms assume in the structure–conduct–performance trichotomy.

THE CONCEPT OF MARKET STRUCTURE AND THE TRADITIONAL MODEL

The definition of market structure that we will adopt is the following:

Market structure is the strategic elements of the environment of a firm that influence, and are influenced by, the conduct and performance of the firm in the market in which it operates.

The traditional analytical model of industrial organization was proposed by Edward S. Mason in the 1930's.[1] The model emphasized the causal link between market structure, conduct, and performance. The firm's environmental market structure was presumed to affect the firm's conduct

---

[1] Mason, "Price and Production Policies of Large-Scale Enterprise," *American Economic Review,* 29 (March 1939 Supplement), 61–74.

and activities in the market. The firm's conduct in the market could in turn be evaluated in terms of welfare-performance norms. Figure 5.1 summarizes this analytical model.

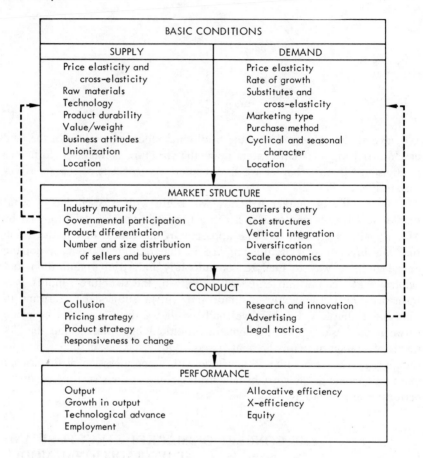

FIGURE 5.1   The Traditional Framework for Industrial Organization Analysis

The structure–conduct–performance model of analysis of industrial organization soon became the dominant methodology in the field.[2] The adherents of this approach, who were on occasion jestingly referred to as "Masons" in recognition of Professor Mason's role, felt that this analytic

[2]An example of the domination of this approach in the contemporary study of industrial organization is the statement by Caves that "market structure is important because the structure determines the behavior of firms in the industry and that behavior in turn determines the quality of the industry's performance." Richard Caves, *American Industry: Structure, Conduct, Performance,* 2nd ed. (Englewood Cliffs, N.J.: Prentice-Hall, Inc., 1967), p. 17.

approach to the study of industrial organization gave the field the structure that it had previously lacked and that this would rescue the field from its previous dependence upon normative institutional analyses. Meaningful hypotheses could now be formulated and tested that related conduct and performance to market structure.

The adoption of the structure–conduct–performance analytical model was not unanimous. Critics of the approach, such as E.G. Nourse, contended that there is no necessary relationship between market structure and performance.[3] Rather, firm conduct and performance, said Nourse, are a function primarily of the individual idiosyncrasies of the firm's managers. This viewpoint still has some currency. Kaysen and Turner have warned that "we can neither predict market performance from market structure, nor can we tell from structure alone how competitive the processes of the market are."[4]

The disagreement between these two approaches stems at least partially from the fact that the structure–conduct–performance triad cannot and should not be considered to be a rigidly deterministic relationship.[5] Whereas price theory and empirical evidence support the contention that there is some sort of causal relationship in which structure determines performance, the same tools may be utilized to demonstrate possible causation in the reverse direction. Conduct and performance do alter market structure. Tactics such as predatory pricing and frequent product style changes may drive competing firms out of the market and alter market structure. The direction of causation is therefore often two-way. As a result, the study of industrial organization frequently proceeds initially by observing desirable types of conduct and performance and then by asking what types of market structures will most often generate such "good" conduct and performance.

A further difficulty with the traditional model is related to the antitrust laws that regulate competition. These laws, which clearly constitute a relevant institutional feature in industrial markets, are typically not concerned with market structure. Rather, statutes such as Sections 2-(a) and 2-(b) of the Robinson-Patman Act are aimed at eliminating certain types of conduct —namely, price discrimination. The particular market structures that tend to generate such conduct are ignored, as is the ultimate desirability of price discrimination in imperfectly competitive markets. The effect is to reduce

---

[3]E.G. Nourse and H.B. Drury, *Industrial Price Policies and Economic Progress* (Washington, D.C.: The Brookings Institution, 1938); see also E.G. Nourse, *Price Making in a Democracy* (Washington, D.C.: The Brookings Institution, 1941).

[4]Carl Kaysen and Donald F. Turner, *Antitrust Policy: An Economic and Legal Analysis* (Cambridge, Mass.: Harvard University Press, 1965), pp. 60–61.

[5]A detailed discussion of this problem may be found in James W. McKie, "Market Structure and Function: Performance versus Behavior," in J.W. Markham and G.G. Papanek, eds., *Industrial Organization and Economic Development: Essays in Honor of E.S. Mason* (Boston: Houghton Mifflin Company, 1970), pp. 3–25.

seriously the applicability of the traditional model to the analysis of these situations. Questions of market structure and its implications for conduct and performance are largely irrelevant in this framework.[6]

Bain, who is perhaps the foremost contemporary exponent of the traditional model, has stated that the four salient aspects of market structure are these: (1) the degree of seller concentration; (2) the degree of buyer concentration; (3) the degree of product differentiation; and (4) the conditions of entry.[7] There is little disagreement among economists concerning this, but there is no consensus on the issue of which market characteristics should be considered to be elements of market structure and which should be classified as basic supply-and-demand conditions of the market. Basic conditions are those fundamental supply-and-demand conditions (for example, location) that determine the market structure that is actually observed. Location influences seller and buyer concentration as well as entry conditions. Other facets of markets—for example, price elasticity of demand—are sometimes considered to be basic conditions and at other times elements of market structure.[8] The distinction is not crucial. The most general definitions of market structure are inclusive of basic conditions and the commonly recognized elements of market structure. Except for possible increased clarity of nomenclature, there seems to be little to be gained from arguments about what features of industrial markets are to be termed basic conditions and which should be labeled elements of market structure. We shall seldom make a distinction between the two concepts in succeeding chapters.

The ultimate virtue of the traditional structure–conduct–performance approach is crucially dependent upon the empirical evidence that can be marshalled in its support. The basic tenet of the pure structure–conduct–performance analytical apparatus is actually rather naïve, in that it assumes in Cournot-like fashion that structural market characteristics determine market behavior and that existing competitors do not respond adaptively to each other in a given situation.[9] Such a descriptively inaccurate assumption is useful only if it results in empirically valid predictions about the behavior of firms. A large portion of this book is devoted to the consideration of the

[6]An exception to the general neglect by antitrust law of structural considerations is Section Seven of the Clayton Act, as amended. Section Seven deals with firm mergers and prohibits the development of market structures via the merger route that might lessen competition or tend to create a monopoly. Although this language is hardly precise, the structure–performance link in Section Seven is apparent.

[7]Joe S. Bain, Industrial Organization (New York: John Wiley & Sons, Inc., 1958) is the classic modern statement of the Mason-inspired traditional model.

[8]Scherer considers price elasticity of demand to be a basic demand condition. F.M. Scherer, Industrial Market Structure and Economic Performance (Skokie, Ill.: Rand McNally & Co., 1970). Caves, in American Industry, considers price elasticity of demand to be an element of market structure.

[9]A valuable discussion of this point may be found in Almarin Phillips, "Structure, Conduct, and Performance—and Performance, Conduct, and Structure?" in Markham and Papanek, Industrial Organization and Economic Development, pp. 26–37. The original Cournot models may be found in Augustin Cournot, Researches into the Mathematical Principles of the Theory of Wealth, translation (New York: The Macmillan Company, 1927).

existing empirical evidence concerning the structure–conduct–performance link.

Bain has pointed out that our ability to produce evidence that speaks to the validity of the traditional model is contingent upon a reasonable degree of stability in the basic features of market structure.[10] If market structure is constantly changing, it may be very difficult to trace any causal relationship between structure, conduct, and performance. The traditional model, as enunciated by Mason, is a long-run relationship. In the long run, structure is assumed to determine conduct and performance. If, however, market structure is itself changing in the long run, then our current analytical techniques may not be sufficiently sophisticated to ferret out the true relationship. Two of Bain's four salient aspects of market structure are somewhat unstable in nature. Barriers to entry change over time, and the degree of product differentiation is often quite volatile, particularly in consumer-goods industries. Consequently, the needed *ceteris paribus* assumption with respect to the elements of market structure cannot be fulfilled in the long run.

The possible variability of market structure has led many researchers to emphasize (1) cross-sectional studies, which take a snapshot view of firms at a given point in time (and which, therefore, "freeze" market structure at that given point in time); and (2) univariate studies, which relate only one element of market structure, such as seller concentration, to market conduct and behavior.[11] Cross-sectional observations of firms at a given point in time are potentially deficient in that they may catch firms in a disequilibrium position as these firms react to recent changes in their environment. The firms may not have fully adjusted to such shocks. Time-series studies of market structure, on the other hand, describe the behavior of firm and market as they move toward an equilibrium position as time passes. Such observations are more likely to reveal whether market structure does affect conduct and performance.

Univariate studies—for example, those relating seller concentration to average market price–cost margins—yield interesting results; however, these results are frequently irrelevant, because the determination of performance indicators such as price–cost margins is a function of many factors, and seller concentration is only one of these factors. Consequently, although univariate explanatory studies often generate strong relationships between a given indicator of market structure, such as seller concentration, and a measure of performance in the marketplace, such as price–cost margins, this relationship may deteriorate and even disappear when other relevant deter-

---

[10] Joe S. Bain, "The Comparative Stability of Market Structure," in Markham and Papanek, *Industrial Organization and Economic Development,* pp. 38–46.

[11] The subtle pressures of data availability may be primarily responsible for these research characteristics, however. A great deal of the data published by agencies such as the Bureau of the Census are cross-sectional in nature and are centered around the concept of seller concentration in the market.

minants of price–cost margins (for example, the degree of product differentiation and the rate of technical change) are considered simultaneously in the analysis.[12]

THE CRUCIAL ROLE OF BARRIERS TO ENTRY

As Figure 5.1 indicates, a host of different indicators of industry market structure exist. Many of these indicators are not uniquely independent of each other and may in fact measure the same things. For example, the degree of product differentiation and price elasticity of demand are often highly correlated with each other and may in certain cases represent the same phenomenon. In markets where the degree of product differentiation is very high (perhaps owing to high advertising expenditures), the absolute value of the coefficient of price elasticity of demand may be low, because of factors such as increased buyer loyalty to given products.

In an attempt to bring order to this chaos, Bain identified the four salient aspects of market structure enumerated earlier in this chapter. Of these four elements, the static theories of competition and monopoly emphasize the singular importance and role of barriers to the entry of new firms. Monopoly power cannot exist in the long run except where it is supported and protected by barriers to entry. Hence, the key to understanding and evaluating industrial markets is to be found in the conditions of entry into those markets by new firms. This view is reflected in Bain's well-known book, *Barriers to New Competition*.[13]

In the long run, then, existing firms will be able to persistently earn pure profits only if the entry of new firms is somehow barricaded. The imagination of entrepreneurs, monopolist or otherwise, is seemingly infinite. A host of potential barriers to entry exist, among the most prominent of which are those alleged to result from (1) demand conditions, including product differentiation and price elasticity; (2) control over input supplies; (3) legal and institutional factors; (4) scale economies; (5) large capital requirements; and (6) technological factors.

There is no agreement about what actually constitutes a barrier to entry. One school of thought, typified by Bain, contends that a barrier to entry is simply any advantage held by existing firms over those firms that might potentially produce in a given market. It has been suggested that a proxy for this advantage is the dollar amount by which established firms can persistently raise their prices above the competitive level without attracting entry into the market.[14] With respect to the work of Bain in this

---

[12]James V. Koch, "Industry Market Structure and Industry Price–Cost Margins" (Unpublished manuscript).

[13]Joe S. Bain, *Barriers to New Competition* (Cambridge, Mass.: Harvard University Press, 1965).

[14]*Ibid.*, pp. 3–5.

area, however, another caveat is needed. His definition of entry itself is notable, in that he refers only to the production of new output in a market when he speaks of entry having occurred. Such expansion could emanate from an already-existing firm or from a new firm. Thus, it is not necessary in Bain's eyes for a new firm to actually enter the market in order for entry to have occurred.

The competing view of what constitutes a barrier to entry is most often identified with Stigler.[15] Stigler argues that a barrier to entry is ". . .a cost of producing at some rate of output (or at any rate) which must be borne by a firm which seeks to enter an industry, but which is not borne by firms already in the industry."[16] The act of entry itself consists only of the entry of new firms not previously in the market; hence, the expansion of output by already-existing firms is not entry in the Stiglerian framework.[17]

The substance of these two divergent viewpoints may best be contrasted by means of an example. Scale economies are sometimes considered to be a barrier to entry of new firms on the grounds that firms seeking to enter a market may be forced to enter it at low levels of output. If the typical average-cost-per-unit-of-output curve of a firm in this market is U-shaped, then low levels of output may dictate high average costs per unit of production for the entrant. Therein lies the alleged disadvantage for the entrant relative to existing firms, which are assumed to be realizing the lowest possible average unit costs of production. The Stiglerian view of such a cost situation is that it does not constitute a barrier to the entry of new firms because existing firms face exactly the same cost conditions. Any circumstance in the market that either affects all firms in the same fashion (for example, capital requirements) or is equally available to all firms (for example, scale economies) is not a barrier to the entry of new firms in Stigler's eyes because all firms, new or old, must confront these identical particulars in the market. Hence, no "advantage" exists.

By way of contrast, Bain disregards the question of whether the particular feature of the market in question is encountered by all firms, new or old; instead, he asks in pragmatic fashion, Does this factor deter the entry of new firms into the market? If it does, then Bain regards it as a barrier to entry, which can be approximated in size by the excess of market price over the price that would have been obtained under competitive circumstances. Bain and Stigler agree when they label such factors as location, advertising, product differentiation, legal–institutional factors, and scarce resources as having the potential to act as barriers to entry. However, while Bain would also place in this category scale economies, large capital requirements, and

---

[15]George Stigler, *The Organization of Industry* (Homewood, Ill.: Richard D. Irwin, Inc., 1968), pp. 67–70.

[16]*The Organization of Industry*, p. 67.

[17]The disagreement between Bain and Stigler over what constitutes a barrier to entry is complicated by their further disagreement over what entry itself actually is. Our analysis of barriers to entry is predicated upon the Stiglerian version of what constitutes entry.

inadequate demand, Stigler considers such factors to be determinants of firm size rather than barriers to entry.

From a technical standpoint, the Stiglerian perception of what constitutes a barrier to the entry of new firms is superior. A barrier to entry is some obstruction that applies to some firms but not to others; if a given circumstance applies equally to *all* individuals or firms, then it cannot be termed a barrier to entry. Therefore, from the standpoint of logic, the position of Stigler is preferable.

Pragmatically, however, the Bain viewpoint has great appeal. Elements of market structure such as large capital requirements, scale economies, and inadequate demand apparently do effectively retard the entry of some new firms into certain markets, even though these features apply to all firms and even though they may actually be the result of efficient economic behavior by other decision units. An example in point is the steel industry. Few prospective entrepreneurs possess the credit standing and the productive know-how concerning steel to warrant the extension of a loan for the large amount of capital necessary for a new firm to begin steel production at lowest possible unit costs. Hence, many prospective new competitors are excluded from the steel market even though their exclusion is primarily a reflection of efficient economic discrimination.

Since our underlying aim is to understand the operation of industrial markets, we must examine market situations where large capital requirements reduce the flow of entrants. In so doing, we will find constant temptation to bow to popular usage and label such factors as economies of scale as barriers to entry. However, it should be borne in mind that a circumstance that applies uniformly to all competitors does not qualify as a barrier to entry.

EMPIRICAL EVIDENCE ON BARRIERS TO ENTRY

Succeeding chapters will explore in greater detail individual elements of market structure that may act as barriers to entry. In this section we will examine the empirical evidence that is available on various types of such barriers.

The seminal empirical study in the area of barriers to entry was performed by Bain.[18] Bain isolated a nonrandom sample of twenty manufacturing industries and used survey-obtained information and his own expertise in order to classify the barriers to entry in each of these industries as being "very high," "substantial," or "moderate to low." The twenty industries, which were primarily oligopolies, were generally large in size and contributed almost 20 percent of total value added in the 452 manufacturing in-

---

[18]Bain, *Barriers to New Competition.*

dustries that existed in the year 1947.[19] Table 5.1 summarizes Bain's results for the individual barriers to entry that he examined. It is apparent that the product-differentiation barrier to entry assumes great importance in the twenty industries. Table 5.2 records Bain's evaluations of aggregate, overall entry barriers in the same industries. Note that several of Bain's "barriers to entry" are not barriers according to our definition.

Any student of industrial organization has the right, if not the ability, to classify entry barriers in a given subsample of industries. The merit of such an activity depends upon whether or not there are observable behavioral differences among the groups of industries so classified. Bain argued that when "very high" entry barriers exist, established firms may be able to elevate their prices by 10 percent or more above minimal average costs per unit without attracting the entry of new firms into that industry; with "sub-

TABLE 5.1

Summary of Relative Heights of Specific Entry Barriers in 20 Industries (Higher Numbers Denote Higher Entry Barriers)

Industry	Scale-Economy Barrier	Product-Differentiation Barrier	Absolute-Cost Barrier	Capital-Requirement Barrier
Automobiles	III	III	I	III
Canned Goods	I	I to II	I	I
Cement	II	I	I	II
Cigarettes	I	III	I	III
Copper	n.a.	I	III	n.a.
Farm Machinery	II	I to III	I	n.a.
Flour	I	I to II	I	φ
Fountain Pens	n.a.	I to III	I	I
Gypsum Products[b]	n.a.	I	III	I
Liquor	I	III	I	II
Meat Packing	I	I	I	φ or I
Metal Containers[b]	n.a.	II	I	I
Petroleum Refining	II	II	I	III
Rayon	II	I	I	II
Shoes	II	I to II	I	φ
Soap	II	II	I	II
Steel	II	I	III	III
Tires and Tubes	I	II	I	II
Tractors	III	III	I	III
Typewriters	III	III	I	n.a.

[a]Alternative ratings refer generally to different product lines within an industry.
[b]Product-differentiation ratings refer to the period subsequent to 1950. A rating of III is probably indicated for earlier periods.
Source: *Reprinted by permission of the publishers from Joe S. Bain,* Barriers to New Competition (*Cambridge, Mass.: Harvard University Press), Copyright, 1956, by the President and Fellows of Harvard College.*

[19]*Ibid.,* p. 44.

TABLE 5.2

Ranking of 20 Manufacturing Industries According to the Estimated Height of the Aggregate Barrier to Entry

A. Industries with very high entry barriers:

Automobiles
Cigarettes
Fountain pens ("quality" grade)
Liquor
Tractors
Typewriters

B. Industries with substantial entry barriers:

Copper
Farm machines (large, complex)
Petroleum refining
Shoes (high-priced men's and specialties)
Soap
Steel

C. Industries with moderate to low entry barriers:

Canned fruits and vegetables
Cement
Farm machinery (small, simple)
Flour[a]
Fountain pens (low-priced)
Gypsum products[b]
Meat packing[a]
Metal containers[b]
Rayon
Shoes (women's and low-priced men's)
Tires and tubes

[a]The barriers to entry for meat packing generally, and for major segments of the flour and canned-goods industries, lie at the "low" extreme.
[b]Refers to period subsequent to 1950. Classification under group B is indicated for earlier periods.
Source: *Reprinted by permission of the publishers from Joe S. Bain,* Barriers to New Competition *(Cambridge, Mass.: Harvard University Press), Copyright, 1956, by the President and Fellows of Harvard College.*

stantial" barriers the corresponding percentage was estimated to be 7 percent; with "moderate to low" barriers to entry, an estimated 1 to 4 percent.[20] The proof of the pudding, however, is empirical evidence of such behavior. If entry is forestalled in certain industries, and existing firms in those industries are able to raise their prices above minimal average costs per unit, then the average profit rates of firms in such industries should be persistently higher than the average profit rates of firms in industries with low entry barriers. Table 5.3 summarizes Bain's results for the time periods 1936–1940 and 1947–1951, and the analogous results of H. Michael Mann for 30 industries during the time period 1950–1960. It is apparent in Table 5.3 that mean industry profit rates are higher in industries that have high

[20]*Ibid.*, p. 170.

TABLE 5.3

The Relationship Between Barriers to Entry, Mean Profit Rates, and Concentration in Selected Time Periods

Time Period	8-Firm Industry Concentration Ratio*	Profit Rates, Number of Industries, and Height of Industry Barriers					
		"Very High" N		"Substantial" N		"Moderate to Low" N	
1936 to 1940 (Bain)	Greater than 70	5	19.0	5	10.2	2	10.5
	Less than 70	0	—	3	7.0	5	5.3
1947 to 1951 (Bain)	Greater than 70	5	19.0	5	14.0	2	15.4
	Less than 70	0	—	3	12.5	5	10.1
1950 to 1960 (Mann)	Greater than 70	8	16.4	8	11.1	5	11.9
	Less than 70	0	—	1	12.2	8	8.6

*The percent share of the industry's total value added that was obtained by the largest 8 firms.

Sources: Reprinted by permission of the publishers from Joe S. Bain, Barriers to New Competition (Cambridge, Mass.: Harvard University Press). Copyright, 1956, by the President and Fellows of Harvard College; and H. Michael Mann, "Seller Concentration, Barriers to Entry, and Rates to Return in Thirty Industries," Review of Economics and Statistics, 48 (August 1966), 296–307.

entry barriers and high seller concentration. However, entry barriers and seller concentration have independent influences upon profit rates. Reading across a particular row in Table 5.3 from left to right (thus holding seller concentration constant in a given time period), one can see that given any level of concentration, mean industry profit rates are nearly always higher when industry barriers to entry are higher. A host of caveats are associated with profit-rate studies, however, and these reservations are the center of an extended discussion in Chapter 8.

Evidence is also available that points to possible output restriction by firms in industries having high barriers to the entry of new firms.[21] Further, collateral evidence at the industry level indicates that industries character- ized by high barriers to entry are typically industries with slower growth rates.[22] Both firm and industry growth rates are of course determined by a complex of factors, including the growth of the entire economy and the growth of related industries.[23] Nevertheless, the slender reeds of evidence cited above indicate retardation of growth both at the firm and the industry level when entry barriers are present.

The evidence relating entry barriers to measures of conduct and per- formance is not limited to profit rates. Several examples will be cited here. The thrust of recent research in the economics of invention, innovation, and technological change emphasizes that some barriers to entry and some monopoly power are necessary in an industry for technological advance to be rapid. At the same time, extremely high barriers to entry and high degrees of monopoly power seem to retard technological change. There appears to be an optimal height for entry barriers and an optimal amount of monopoly power with respect to their effects upon invention, innovation, and technological change.[24] The complex economics of technological change is considered in detail in Chapter 9.

The static theories of monopoly and competition predict that the price–cost margins of firms will be higher when entry barriers exist. There have been several attempts to test this hypothesis. The pioneering work in this area has been performed by Collins and Preston.[25] They used the aver-

[21]Roger Sherman, "Entry Barriers and the Growth of Firms," *Southern Economic Journal*, 38 (October 1971), 238–47.

[22]James V. Koch, "Market Structure and Industry Growth Rates," *Rivista Internazionale di Scienze Economiche e Commerciali*, 17 (December 1970), 1145–63.

[23]It is not clear that the traditional model of monopoly, which predicts output restriction by mono- polistic firms, also implies output restriction by all firms in an industry. For example, it may be quite rational for a profit-maximizing monopolist to accept a declining share of a growing industry's sales. The frequently cited decline of dominant firms such as U.S. Steel Corporation could reflect nothing more than this type of strategy in operation.

[24]See, for example, William S. Comanor, "Market Structure, Product Differentiation, and Industrial Research," *Quarterly Journal of Economics*, 81 (November 1967), 639–57.

[25]Norman R. Collins and Lee E. Preston, "Concentration and Price–Cost Margins in Food Manu- facturing Industries," *Journal of Industrial Economics*, 14 (July 1966), 226–42; see also Collins and Preston, *Concentration and Price–Cost Margins in Manufacturing Industries* (Berkeley, Calif.: University of California Press, 1970); also Collins and Preston, "Price–Cost Margins and Industry Structure," *Review of Economics and Statistics*, 51 (August 1969), 271–86.

age industry capital-to-output ratio as a proxy for a possible capital-requirements "barrier." Their results, which were based upon a cross-sectional sample of 417 manufacturing industries for the year 1963, supported the theoretical prediction that average industry price–cost margins will be higher when a capital-requirements "barrier" exists.

SUMMARY

The traditional approach to the study of industrial organization is associated with Professor Mason of Harvard, who noted the links between structure, conduct, and performance. Although the direction of causation most often runs from structure to conduct and performance, the reverse is also sometimes true. The direction of causation is often joint and structure, conduct, and performance affect each other.

Market structure is the environment in which firms live. Even though it is impossible to rank given elements of market structure ordinally in terms of their importance, it is clear that barriers to entry play a crucially important role. Following Stigler, a barrier to entry is any advantage that existing firms enjoy that is not equally available to possible entrant firms. According to this definition, economies of scale and capital requirements are not barriers to the entry of new firms.

In general, the existence of barriers to entry and/or substantial economies of scale and capital requirements have been found to be positively associated with high profit rates and high price–cost margins. The quality of the empirical studies upon which these conclusions are based, however, leaves something to be desired in many cases.

PROBLEMS

1. A perennial problem facing the Antitrust Division of the Justice Department is whether to focus upon market structure or market conduct, or both. What are the advantages associated with a policy that makes judgments on the basis of market structure? On market conduct? What are the disadvantages?

2. Many structuralists contend that the predictions of economic theory are sufficiently precise, and the empirical evidence supporting these theories is sufficiently strong, that the mere appearance of certain types of market structures should be cause for antitrust actions on the part of the Antitrust Division of the Justice Department. Does economic theory generate such clear-cut predictions?

3. Several studies have revealed that firm-level capital requirements are associated with higher-than-usual price–cost margins, higher-than-usual profit rates, and lower-than-usual rates of market growth. Is this evidence that (contrary to the view of Stigler) capital requirements are apparently a barrier to the entry of new firms?

6

Scale Economies

and Capital Requirements

It is customary for economists, when studying the productive processes of a firm, to speak of two major laws of production. The first, the law of diminishing returns, is a short-run law that hypothesizes that output will grow at a decreasing rate (and eventually begin to fall) when successive units of a variable-factor input are added to other inputs that remain fixed in number and quantity.[1] The second law treats the case in which all inputs in the productive process are variable in nature. This law deals with returns to scale and describes the relationship between inputs and output in the long run, when the individual firm has complete flexibility in determining the character of its productive process. The subject of returns to scale is the primary focus of this chapter. As we shall see, several important policy questions can be answered only when we have definitive information about the existence or nonexistence of returns to scale.

THE MEANING OF SCALE ECONOMIES

At any moment in time, each firm in a given market finds itself producing a certain rate of output within the limitations of its current "scale."

Scale is the rate of output per unit of time of the firm when all the firm's inputs are variable.

The term *economies of scale*, or its mirror image, *returns to scale*, refers to the relationship of average costs per unit of production to the scale of the firm. Economies of scale are reflected in the shape of the long-run average cost of the plant or firm, and they are said to exist when the long-run average-cost curve has a negative slope; diseconomies of scale are identifiable when the long-run average-cost curve has a positive slope.[2] Figure 6.1 illus-

[1]The law of diminishing returns is often called the law of variable proportions, because it is predicated upon changes in the ratio of variable to fixed inputs. As this ratio is altered, output is assumed to vary in a predictable fashion.

[2]The economies and diseconomies of scale we refer to are those that arise internally, within the firm. Such internal economies determine the shape of a given firm's long-run average-cost curve. External economies and diseconomies also exist, but are represented by a shift in a given firm's long-run average-cost curve, rather than by a movement along an already-existing one.

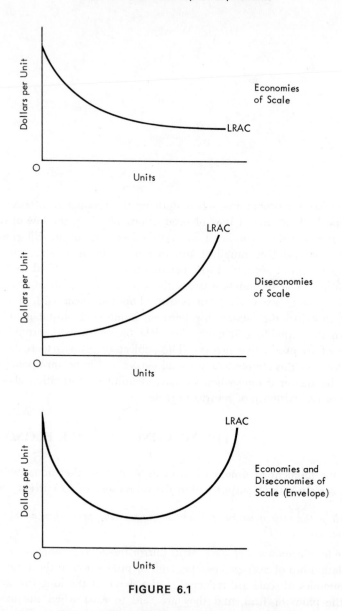

FIGURE 6.1

trates each case. The emphasis here upon the long-run time period is crucial, since the concept of economies of scale is dependent upon the economic
decision unit's ability to vary all its inputs as it desires. By way of contrast,
a short-run average-cost curve assumes that the economic decision unit in
question possesses some inputs that are fixed in nature (for example, the
size of a firm's plant may be invariant in the short run). The essence of

economies of scale is the behavior of average unit costs of production when all inputs are potentially variable and output is increased.

It is necessary to distinguish between plant-level and firm-level economies of scale. A firm that operates a single plant in a single location may realize economies or diseconomies of scale at that plant for a variety of reasons. Also, there may be certain economies and diseconomies of scale that are peculiar to multiplant firms. Adelman's classic study of the Great Atlantic and Pacific Tea Company was partially motivated by a desire to ascertain if A&P's size and geographic decentralization around the United States allowed it to realize scale economies in production, distribution, and input purchases.[3] (Adelman's verdict was positive—certain multiplant economies of scale did exist, but only during particular time periods.)

The long-run average-cost curve, which is the graphic representation of whatever economies or diseconomies of scale may exist, is actually an envelope of short-run average-cost curves (see Figure 2.3, page 20), each of which represents an alternative short-run choice of scale by the firm. Such an envelope, however, ordinarily assumes that the firm operates each and every scale at its most efficient rate of output and that factors such as X-Inefficiency are absent. This may not be true in many industrial markets. A firm's actual output is often less or greater than its optimal output. Hence, when the firm expands and its scale increases, the expansion may be uneven in nature and not perfectly synchronized with production needs. A given scale may be underutilized initially, and overutilized later as production expands. The result is average unit costs exceeding those associated with the optimal utilization of scale that is implied in the smooth long-run average-cost curves of Figures 2.3 and 6.1. As successive additions to the firm's plant are built and scale is increased, the end result of such a piece-by-piece expansion may be a plant that is considerably less efficient at any given rate of production than a plant built *de novo* to the required scale. An example in point is the steel industry. Virtually none of the plants operated by the largest steel producers were originally built to the current optimal scale; instead, they were expanded in a spasmodic, irregular fashion. The consequence has been that an entirely new plant, built to the same scale, would usually offer lower average unit costs at most, if not all, rates of production. Figure 6.2 illustrates this phenomenon.

The long-run average-cost curves that are estimated empirically represent the actual situation of a firm, and not, except in unusual cases, what the firm would have done had it possessed accurate foresight. The implication is that *de novo* plants, built to the appropriate scale and utilizing newly available technology, may often offer lower average unit costs of production than do the existing plants producing for a given market. The superiority of

[3]M.A. Adelman, *A&P: A Study in Price–Cost Behavior and Public Policy* (Cambridge, Mass.: Harvard University Press, 1959).

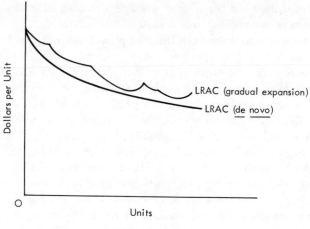

FIGURE 6.2

the basic oxygen steel-refining process to the older, basic open-hearth process is an instructive example.[4]

A RATIONALE FOR ECONOMIES OF SCALE

Why might economies and diseconomies of scale arise? What factors in the firm's environment and operations cause the firm's long-run average-cost curve to be other than horizontal? Two general classes of factors are usually cited in response to these questions. Economies of scale are said to arise because of "real" factors (for example, specialization and division of labor, indivisibilities, human administration, uncertainty) and because of "pecuniary" factors (for example, input price concessions, ability to raise capital at low cost, reduced variability of performance that attracts investors). We shall consider real and pecuniary economies of scale in some detail.

Real Economies of Scale

Real economies of scale represent increased efficiency of operation on the part of the firm. The typical expositions of real economies of scale concentrate upon two major classes of phenomena that are capable of generating other than long-run constant returns to scale (constant long-run average unit costs). These two categories are *indivisibilities* and *human administration*. Adam Smith, who emphasized the specialization and division of labor as a source of increased productivity, convincingly used the example of a pin

---

[4]An interesting and provocative (although slightly polemical) examination of the technological innovations in the steel industry has been provided by Walter Adams and Joel Dirlam, "Big Steel, Invention, and Innovation," *Quarterly Journal of Economics,* 80 (May 1966), 167–89.

factory to point out that the specialization and division of labor would help avoid input indivisibilities, and also might avert the failures of human administration that conceivably arise when a worker is assigned a greater number of tasks than he can reasonably master.[5] Smith did not use the dichotomy between indivisibilities and human administration, but he was nevertheless aware that the potential for the specialization and division of labor is much greater in a large firm than in a smaller one.

Modern assembly-line methods of production in a large firm are a visible demonstration of how the specialization and division of labor creates real economies of scale. An assembly-line-produced Caterpillar tractor, for example, is reliant upon specialization and division of labor to such an extent that a single worker may be responsible for only tightening a nut on a bolt on each tractor that passes him on the line. Assembly-line methods are frequently not feasible in a small firm, because the small firm's total production is not sufficient to support the minute specialization and division of labor required of each worker.[6] Hence, the ability to engage in the division and specialization of labor is a potential cause of real economies of scale in industrial firms.

The major types of indivisibilities that exist are the result of (1) technological machine characteristics, (2) marketing, (3) financial factors, (4) research and development, and (5) integration and diversification. With regard to the first type, it is clear that certain machines used in production have an optimal rate of utilization. For example, in the pottery industry, tile presses that shape and stamp out ceramic tile cannot be operated efficiently above a certain rate of output per unit of time, because they quickly become overheated when operated rapidly, and an overheated tile press frequently produces poor-quality tile that has nicks and scratches in it and must be discarded. Consequently, there exists an optimal rate of utilization of the tile presses.

Another type of technological indivisibility associated with machines is related to their repair and upkeep. The plant or firm must hold in its inventory certain spare parts that can be used to replace worn-out parts in existing machines. As the plant or firm increases its output, and uses an increasing number of a given type of machine, the number of spare parts that must be held in inventory against the possibility of a machine breakdown grows more slowly than the output of the plant or firm. This potential scale-economies-inducing force is a standard result of inventory-theoretic models.[7]

[5] Adam Smith, *The Wealth of Nations* (Baltimore: Penguin Books, Inc., 1970), especially Chaps. 1–3.

[6] In some cases, assembly-line methods are feasible in a small firm; however, because the firm's output is so small, each worker on the assembly line must perform many different tasks rather than one particular task. In such cases, an assembly line does not result in significant specialization and division of labor.

[7] See, for example, James L. Riggs, *Economic Decision Models for Engineers and Managers* (New York: McGraw-Hill Book Company, 1968), pp. 68–76.

Still another type of indivisibility associated with machines has to do with the relationship between the size and surface area of a machine and the machine's capacity and output. The cost of constructing a machine is usually related to its size and surface area. Its capacity and output, on the other hand, are often more closely related to its internal volume.[8] As the surface area of the machine is expanded, the volume of that machine (particularly if it is cylindrical in shape) expands more than proportionately. This means that the output of the machine can potentially expand faster than the cost of expanding the machine. Further, labor costs and the costs of inputs used in operating the machine will in general expand less rapidly than the capacity and output of the machine. This unique geometric relationship between inputs and outputs has been termed the ".6 rule" and is examined in greater detail in a later section of this chapter.

Indivisibilities of marketing can also cause economies and diseconomies of scale. A salesman for a firm may be able to handle and sell an extra item in an already-large product line with little or no additional effort or expense. The incremental cost to Avon Products, Inc., of adding an extra item to their already-substantial product line, which is sold door to door by its ubiquitous representatives, is undoubtedly less than proportionate to the increase in the size of the product line. On the other hand, it is apparent that marketing indivisibilities do not always result in the economies of scale cited above. If a firm's salesmen or distributors are forced to carry and market additional items, the increased product line that results may sometimes be obtained at considerable cost. The salesmen and the distributors may incur high inventory and service costs in order to market the new items; further, their lack of expertise about the new items may not only reduce the sales of those items, but also may detract from the sales of the older items in the line. The apparent reluctance of large automobile producers to allow their retail distributors to market an unlimited number of different makes of automobiles may reflect the feeling that the distributors cannot do so efficiently.[9]

Real economies of scale may accrue to a firm because of financial indivisibilities. Although the empirical evidence concerning the economic effect of advertising expenditures is often conflicting (see Chapter 11), there is mixed empirical support for the contention that economies of scale do exist for firms with respect to their advertising expenditures.[10] This might

---

[8]See, for example, John Haldi and David Whitcomb, "Economies of Scale in Industrial Plants," *Journal of Political Economy*, 75 (August 1967), 373–85. See also F.T. Moore, "Economies of Scale: Some Statistical Evidence," *Quarterly Journal of Economics*, 73 (May 1959), 232–45.

[9]Other possible reasons for such behavior include a simple desire to foreclose a portion of a given market, and the recognition of the benefits of specialization in a complex market.

[10]Those who have argued strongly for the existence of scale economies in advertising include John M. Blair, in *Hearings on Economic Concentration,* Part Five, Subcommittee on Antitrust and Monopoly, Senate Judiciary Committee, 9th Cong., 2d sess. (Washington, D.C.: U.S. Government Printing Office, 1966), pp. 1888–1910; John M. Blair, "Conglomerate Mergers—Theory and Congressional Intent," in J. Fred Weston and Sam Peltzman, eds., *Public Policy Toward Mergers* (Pacific Palisades, Calif.; Goodyear

occur because a certain minimal level of advertising expenditures and advertising messages is required in order for the advertising to make any impression upon the typical consumer. Further, since advertising expenditures are appropriately viewed as an investment that will yield returns in the future, the firm that has already established consumer recognition of its product may be able to maintain that recognition with a lower level of advertising intensity than the level that was necessary to achieve the original product recognition by consumers.[11]

Another possible financial indivisibility relates to the cost of investigating a loan prospect or the cost of investigating a new investment opportunity. It is doubtful that the cost of investigating the worth of a $500 loan or investment is substantially different from the cost of investigating a $1,000 loan or investment. If the cost of investigating loans and investment opportunities increases at a slower rate than the rate of increase in the size of the loans or investments, then scale economies exist that will benefit larger firms.

It has frequently been alleged that there are indivisibilities in research and development that discriminate against the small firm.[12] This contention will be examined in greater detail in Chapter 9; however, we may note here that existing evidence shows that small firms (with less than 1,000 employees) often do not even maintain research and development establishments.[13] There is little convincing evidence pointing to serious diseconomies of scale in research and development for firms that are large enough to maintain such an establishment; nevertheless, the potential for scale economies in research and development is present.

Real economies and diseconomies of scale may also be prompted by horizontal, vertical, and conglomerate mergers. The argument in favor of this position relies partially upon the elimination of indivisibilities in areas such as advertising and research via the merger route. Further, it is contended that uncertainty and earnings variability might be reduced, input supplies secured, markets for output made certain, and transport and distribution costs reduced by securing plant locations in alternative geographic

---

Publishing Co., Inc., 1969), pp. 179–96; William S. Comanor and Thomas A. Wilson, "Advertising and the Advantages of Size," *American Economic Review*, 59 (May 1969), 87–98; and Peter Asch and Matityahu Marcus, "Returns to Scale on Advertising," *The Antitrust Bulletin*, 15 (Spring 1970), 33–41. A summary of the entire evidence and the opposite viewpoint may be found in Julian L. Simon, *Issues in the Economics of Advertising* (Urbana, Ill.: University of Illinois Press, 1970).

[11]The contrary view—that competitive struggles between firms can result in continually higher levels of advertising expenditures—has been voiced by James V. Koch, "Plateaus of Selling and Product Variation Costs," *Economic and Business Bulletin*, 22 (Winter 1970), 31–36. See also Henry G. Grabowski and Dennis C. Mueller, "Imitative Advertising in the Cigarette Industry," *The Antitrust Bulletin*, 16 (Summer 1971), 257–92.

[12]One example of this argument, among many, is John Kenneth Galbraith, *The New Industrial State* (Boston: Houghton Mifflin Company, 1967), pp. 4ff.

[13]National Science Foundation, *Research and Development in Industry, 1967* (Washington, D.C.: U.S. Government Printing Office, 1969), especially pp. 26–41.

sections of the market. The economics of integration and diversification are studied in detail in Chapter 10.

It should be noted parenthetically that any consideration of real economies of scale assumes a given state of technology. Many indivisibilities are functions of the state of technical know-how. Suppose, however, that the state of technical know-how is itself a function of the total volume of output produced by the firm. That is, assume that the firm is capable of "learning by doing" and becomes more efficient as its total volume of output increases.[14] Economies of scale are represented by the shape of the long-run average-cost curve at any and all rates of output per unit of time. Learning by doing, however, relates the shape of the long-run average-cost curve to the cumulative level of output produced by the firm over many time periods. This cumulative volume of output is one of the factors that is held invariant by the *ceteris paribus* assumption that surrounds every cost curve.[15] When the cumulative volume of production does change substantially and the change does affect the cost of producing that output, this is reflected by a shift in the entire long-run average-cost curve, rather than by a movement along the curve. This shift follows from the fact that we are conceptually in a different time period in terms of production when the cumulative volume of production is altered.

Learning by doing was initially observed by Wright in the 1930's.[16] Wright noticed that the number of man-hours required to produce an airframe decreased substantially as the number of airframes produced increased.[17] It has also been suggested that a portion of the success of IBM in the computer market has been due to the learning-by-doing phenomenon.[18] Customers purchase IBM computer systems because they feel that IBM's well-developed software packages, which accompany the basic computer, will enable them to learn how to use the entire system more quickly than will computer packages marketed by IBM's rivals.

It is further apparent that the cumulative output of the firm or industry may affect the managers and employees of a given firm. Their skills may be honed by the acquisition of experience. Such advances are represented by a shift in the long-run average-cost curve. But this example assumes that economies of scale are obtained as the firm and industry expand;

---

[14]The seminal theoretical article in the area of learning by doing has been contributed by Kenneth Arrow, "The Economic Implications of Learning By Doing," *Review of Economic Studies,* 29 (June 1962), 155–73.

[15]Following Buchanan, the *ceteris paribus* assumption in this case is not that the cumulative volume of output does not change during any given time period; rather, it is that it does not change sufficiently during any given time period to make any difference in a learning-by-doing context. See James M. Buchanan, "*Ceteris Paribus:* Some Notes on Methodology," *Southern Economic Journal,* 24 (January 1958) 259–70.

[16]T.P. Wright, "Factors Affecting the Cost of Airplanes," *Journal of Aeronautical Science,* 3 (1936), 122–28.

[17]This phenomenon has also been discussed in Harold Asher, *Cost Quantity Relationships in the Airframe Industry,* (Santa Monica, Calif.: The Rand Corporation, 1956), R–291.

[18]Ferdinand K. Levy, "An Adaptive Production Function," *American Economic Review,* 55 (May 1965), 386–96.

and quite the opposite may actually occur. As the firm expands, the fixed factor of management may be spread over a larger and larger firm.[19] If each manager must assume additional duties, characterized by increasing complexity and responsibility, he may have to neglect other duties and responsibilities. The end result may be that managerial talents are spread so thin over the growing firm that the overall quality of management declines and diseconomies of scale occur. Such diseconomies are not always averted by hiring additional new management. Newly hired management personnel need to be trained and acclimated to their jobs, and this process requires time and resources. Also, some firms, particularly owner-managed "family" firms, refuse to hire new management personnel.

The popular concepts of "red tape" and bureaucracy are often functions of failures of human administration. In very large firms, top management may be effectively isolated from the actual operations and problems of the firm, because of the numerous layers of intermediate supervisory and managerial personnel between the top management and line operations. Heavily structured and often cumbersome lines of communication develop in large organizations. Censure, delay, and opposition frequently greet anyone (even the owner of the firm) who attempts to leapfrog or violate such established lines of communication and authority. President Kennedy is said to have despaired at his inability to sidestep the conventional bureaucracy in government agencies in order to get immediate action on a pressing problem. There have been many attempts to streamline and/or reform the decision-making process in firms. General Motors Corporation's decentralization of operations and decision making is a prime example of such an attempt. Chapter 10 will devote considerable attention to this and similar issues.

It has been alleged by Robinson that large firms suffer from an inability to correct their own mistakes.[20] That is, once a given action is taken, that action or its result becomes institutionalized and is seldom altered. Top-level management in large firms may seek to correct such mistakes, but may be unable to do so with any speed. The unprofitable experience of the Ford Motor Company with its unpopular Edsel automobile speaks strongly in support of the point that large organizations are often unresponsive to management desires.

The advent of large firms has also brought with it the potential for a loss of identity on the part of employees.[21] Employees in a large organization

---

[19]A detailed discussion of returns to scale to management may be found in Edith T. Penrose, *The Theory of the Growth of the Firm* (Oxford, England: Blackwell's, Inc., 1959). A more recent consideration of these issues, rigorous in nature, is O.E. Williamson, "Hierarchical Control and Optimum Firm Size," *Journal of Political Economy*, 75 (April 1967), 123–38.

[20]E.A.G. Robinson, *The Structure of Competitive Industry* (Chicago: University of Chicago Press, 1958), p. 41.

[21]An excellent sociological summary of the causes and effects of loss of identity and alienation by workers is Michael Aiken and Jerald Hage, "Organization Alienation: A Comparative Analysis," in *The Sociology of Organizations*, eds. Oscar Grusky and George A. Miller (New York: The Free Press, 1970), pp. 517–26. For empirical evidence of the effects of alienation upon worker productivity, see Richard Armstrong, "Labor 1970: Angry, Aggressive, Acquisitive," *Fortune*, 80 (October 1969), 94–97.

such as General Motors, which employed 695,000 people in the year 1970, or even International Harvester Company, which employed "only" 101,000 in 1970, may feel that they are anonymous—that their contributions are neither recognized nor appreciated by the gigantic organizations for which they toil.[22] As a consequence, their productivity may vary inversely with the size of the firm. Economists have generally paid little attention to problems such as this, on the grounds that such problems have a distinctly sociological and psychological flavor. But we can see that the possible loss of identity on the part of employees is capable of causing diseconomies of scale in the large firm.

The effects of uncertainty upon the performance of management, and therefore upon economies of scale, have also been examined by Robinson, who contended that uncertainty about any feature of a market will tend to limit the size of the firms in that market.[23] This hypothesis has been given affirmation by Schwartzman, who scrutinized the behavior of department stores in the United States during the mid-1950's.[24] Schwartzman found that the presence of uncertainty induced diseconomies of scale with respect to firm size, presumably because the large firm's management was unable to deal effectively with the many conflicting and competing signals, problems, and unknowns that vary as an increasing function of firm size.

Pecuniary Economies of Scale

The real economies of scale discussed in the preceding section resulted from increased efficiency of operation on the part of the firm. Real economies of scale represent a net gain to society, because they allow a given level of output to be produced with a smaller amount of inputs. Pecuniary economies of scale, however, do not depend upon efficiency of operation such as specialization and division of labor. Pecuniary economies of scale are often the result of one firm's utilizing monopoly or monopsony power to squeeze another firm. Because the effect of such behavior is simply to redistribute profits from one firm to another (without any increased ability on the part of society to produce a given output), pecuniary economies of scale are not regarded as constituting an improvement in society-wide efficiency. The firm that reaps pecuniary economies of scale is behaving in a privately efficient maximizing fashion. From a welfare standpoint, nevertheless, one firm's gain can be the other's loss where pecuniary economies are concerned. Hence, the realization of pecuniary economies of scale is a mixed blessing from the viewpoint of the entire economy.

Pecuniary economies and diseconomies of scale usually result from input price concessions that are forced upon one economic decision unit by

---

[22]Personnel figures from "The Fortune Directory," *Fortune*, 83 (May 1971), 173.

[23]Robinson, *The Structure of Competitive Industry*, Chap. 6.

[24]David Schwartzman, "Uncertainty and the Size of the Firm," *Economica*, 30 (August 1963), 287–96.

another. Within this broad rubric, however, several interesting variations are observable. The most common case involves the large firm's whipsawing its input suppliers in order to force them to offer it input prices that are lower than those that would be justified by the costs of producing for and serving the large firm. Such behavior, which may be supported by thinly veiled threats that the firm will change input suppliers, redistributes profits from the input suppliers to the large firm.

Another variation on the basic theme revolves around the possibility that large firms may be better able than small firms to hire quality labor inputs. Further, they may be able to hire labor inputs of a given quality at a lower price. It has been pointed out that the presumably talented graduates of prestigious business schools do not generally work for small firms and seldom if ever are found in a "Ma and Pa" grocery-store type of situation.[25] But although this advantage of bigness may result in pecuniary economies of scale, the very existence of the large firm is often an open invitation to labor unions to unionize its employees. Unionization, as epitomized in the Galbraithian concept of "countervailing power,"[26] can conceivably penalize the large firm for its size and result in a welfare transfer of profits from the large firm to the labor union and its membership. Levinson has argued that the weight of unionization falls most heavily on the large firms and has cited the automobile industry as an example.[27]

The size of the firm has also been found to be negatively correlated with the firm's average cost of raising needed capital. Certain of these observed reductions in the cost of capital with respect to firm size may be interpreted as real economies of scale, on the ground that the reduced cost of capital actually reflects superior economic efficiency, reduced risk, and lower transactions costs. It is probable, however, that a portion of the observed negative relationship may be due to price concessions extracted by the large firms.

The relationship between firm size and various aspects of performance is given considerable attention in Chapter 7, and we do not wish to duplicate such coverage here. Therefore, it will suffice at this point to mention briefly several important pieces of research that have a bearing upon the issue of pecuniary scale economies. The transactions costs a firm incurs in floating a loan or a bond issue have been found to be negatively related to firm size.[28] Also, several studies have found that firm profit rates are less

---

[25]Sheldon Zalaznick, "The M.B.A.: The Man, the Myth, and the Method," *Fortune*, 77 (May 1968), 168–71ff.

[26]John Kenneth Galbraith, *American Capitalism: The Concept of Countervailing Power* (Boston: Houghton Mifflin Company, 1952).

[27]Harold M. Levinson, "Pattern Bargaining: A Case Study of the Automobile Workers," *Quarterly Journal of Economics*, 74 (May 1960), 296–317. See also Levinson's more comprehensive *Determining Forces in Collective Wage Bargaining* (New York: John Wiley & Sons, Inc., 1966).

[28]Stephen H. Archer and Leroy G. Faerber, "Firm Size and the Cost of Externally Secured Equity Capital," *Journal of Finance*, 21 (March 1966), 69–83; also, F.R. Edwards, "The Banking Competition Controversy," *National Banking Review*, 3 (September 1965), 1–34.

variable in large firms than in smaller ones.[29] The implications of this cost and profit variability are twofold: (1) The cost of raising capital does not rise proportionately with the size of the firm; and (2) investors will tend to favor those firms whose earnings are not uncertain.

The distinction between real and pecuniary economies of scale is not always clear. We have already seen that the fact that large firms pay lower prices for inputs is not necessarily evidence of pecuniary economies; rather, it may be an indication of real economies of scale associated with the large size of the firm. The same may be said for financial indivisibilities associated with advertising expenditures. The alleged economies of scale in advertising expenditures may be due to the market penetration indivisibilities cited earlier, or may be obtained by the exercise of monopsony power and be pecuniary in nature. It is particularly difficult to differentiate between real and pecuniary economies of scale when joint costs are involved. Joint costs are costs of production that cannot easily be allocated to one particular output. The classic example of a joint cost, from Alfred Marshall, consists of the cost of feeding sheep from which both mutton and wool are obtained.[30] What proportion of the cost of the feed is assignable to the mutton, and what proportion to the wool? The inability to assign costs to a particular output makes it difficult to determine if price concessions are being exacted for a given product, or even whether overall economies of scale are in fact being realized with respect to that product.

MEASURING ECONOMIES OF SCALE

We now turn from our examination of possible causes of economies and diseconomies of scale to the empirical measurement of such economies and diseconomies. A serious defect of some of the studies that have been performed is that they have not always been undertaken by disinterested individuals. Many studies have been conducted by researchers who started out with very strong notions about the existence or nonexistence of economies of scale. It is not surprising, then, that few if any studies have uncovered evidence that contradicted the prior views of the researchers conducting them.

Two polar schools of thought exist with respect to the existence of economies of scale. For want of better names, we shall label these polar

[29]H.O. Stekler, *Profitability and Size of Firm* (Berkeley, Calif.: Institute of Business and Economic Research, University of California, 1963); H.O. Stekler, "The Variability of Profitability with Size of Firms, 1947–1958," *Journal of the American Statistical Association,* 59 (December 1964), 1183–93; Charles E. Ferguson, *A Macroeconomic Theory of Workable Competition* (Durham, N.C.: Duke University Press, 1964), pp. 172–74; Marshall Hall and Leonard Weiss, "Firm Size and Profitability," *Review of Economics and Statistics,* 49 (August 1967), 319–31.

[30]Alfred Marshall, *Principles of Economics,* 8th ed. (London: Macmillan and Company, Ltd., 1961), pp. 321–23.

viewpoints the American School and the British School.[31] These names do not, of course, imply that all American or British economists subscribe to these views, or even that a majority of each group does so. Most economists reside in neither intellectual camp. Rather, these names indicate the location of the strongest initial modern-day proponents of each of these opposing views.

The American School developed in the early University of Chicago tradition typified by Henry Simons and Frank Knight.[32] The American School argued that full exploitation of available scale economies at both the plant and firm levels would nevertheless result in small firms. Indeed, small firms were thought to be the most efficient, because of the general absence of real and pecuniary economies of scale. As a result, the proponents of the American School argued, although many segments of American industry are dominated by large firms, this need not be the case. This viewpoint has always attained great favor because of the traditionally strong anti-monopoly bias of many Americans.[33] Modern Chicagoites, while not unanimous in their acceptance of the argument, nevertheless continue to regard available scale economies as being negligible beyond very small scales.[34]

By way of contrast, the British School asserted that one should ordinarily expect economies of scale to be associated quite substantially with firm size, and that economies of scale would particularly accrue to large multiplant firms.[35] Consequently, the existence of large firms and heavily concentrated industries was thought to be simply an indication of the inevitable economic facts of life. Public policies designed to promote bigness and mergers were, therefore, deemed to be appropriate.

The basic task involved in estimating economies and diseconomies of scale is to determine the shape of the long-run average-cost curve. This is not easily achieved, however. Johnston, in his important volume, *Statistical Cost Analysis,* listed four circumstances that must hold in order to ensure accurate estimation of the long-run average-cost curve: (1) The individual observations of cost and output must not span so long a time period that they actually represent averages that might disguise the real cost–output relationship present; (2) the cost and output observations must be properly paired, so that a given period's costs are associated with the same period's

[31] These labels were suggested by Joe S. Bain, *Barriers to New Competition* (Cambridge, Mass.: Harvard University Press, 1965), pp. 59–61.

[32] Henry C. Simons, *A Positive Program for Laissez-Faire* (Chicago: University of Chicago Press, 1934); also, Henry C. Simons, *Economic Policy for a Free Society* (Chicago: University of Chicago Press, 1948). Frank H. Knight, *Risk, Uncertainty and Profit* (New York: Harper Torchbooks, 1965).

[33] Neale reports the existence of "The National Anti-Monopoly Cheap Freight League" during the latter part of the nineteenth century. A.D. Neale, *The Antitrust Laws of the United States of America* (Cambridge, England: Cambridge University Press, 1962), p. 23.

[34] See, for example, George J. Stigler, "The Economies of Scale," *Journal of Law and Economics,* 1 (October 1958), 54–71.

[35] Perhaps the most articulate proponent of this view has been Robinson, *The Structure of Competitive Industry.* See also P. Sargant Florence, *The Logic of British and American Industry* (London: Routledge & Kegan Paul, Ltd., 1953).

output; (3) a wide range of different levels of output must be represented in the cost–output observations, so that the effects of these differing levels of output upon unit costs can be observed; and (4) the observations must not be contaminated by other factors (for example, a change in technology) that are irrelevant to the cost–output relationship.[36] Such conditions are seldom if ever obtainable in a dynamic world; hence, the typical scale-economies study contains imperfections. The crucial question is whether or not those imperfections are of such a nature that they invalidate the empirical findings of the study in question.

Four major types of scale-economies studies have been performed. The alternative methodologies represented in these four types of studies have been based upon (1) profit rates, (2) the survivor test, (3) straightforward statistical estimation, and (4) engineering studies. We will consider each of these approaches in turn and will exercise care in separating plant-level economies-of-scale studies from those that are multiplant (firm level) in character.

Profit Rates

The profit-rate studies are actually not economies-of-scale studies, because the latter, strictly considered, should relate unit costs to output levels. Profit-rate studies, which relate firm size to firm profit rates, do not do so. Nevertheless, the profit-rate studies may contain implications about economies of scale. If scale economies are realized by large firms, then the large firms will be able to produce their outputs more cheaply and more efficiently than can smaller firms, and as a result will earn higher rates of profit if entry is impeded. Unfortunately, while economies of scale may affect profit rates, it does not necessarily follow that high profit rates are an indication of economies of scale. High profit rates, as our discussion in Chapter 4 indicated, may be the result of monopoly power or a host of other factors. Therefore, higher-than-normal profit rates are neither necessary nor sufficient evidence that scale economies exist.

The existing empirical evidence of the relationship between firm size and firm profit rates is extensive;[37] it may be summarized by the statement that there appears to be a positive (although sometimes mild) relationship between the two, particularly in recent time periods.[38] Within the extensive limitations cited above, this evidence, which is dealt with extensively in

---

[36]J. Johnston, *Statistical Cost Analysis* (New York: McGraw-Hill Book Company, 1960), pp. 26–27.

[37]Early examples are Ralph C. Epstein, "Profits and Size of Firm in the Automobile Industry, 1919–1927," *American Economic Review*, 21 (December 1931), 636–47; and Ralph C. Epstein, *Industrial Profits in the United States* (New York: National Bureau of Economic Research, 1934). More recent efforts include S.S. Alexander, "The Effect of Size of Manufacturing Corporation on the Distribution of the Rate of Return," *Review of Economics and Statistics*, 31 (August 1949), 229–35; Stekler, *Profitability and Size of Firm*; Stekler, "The Variability of Profitability"; and Hall and Weiss, "Firm Size and Profitability."

[38]Hall and Weiss, "Firm Size and Profitability."

Chapter 7, can be interpreted to mean that economies of scale do exist at the firm level.

Survivor Test

The survivor test is a comparatively recent development popularized by Stigler,[39] although Stigler has hastened to point out that Mill suggested such a technique during the nineteenth century.[40] The basis of the survivor technique is the belief that competition in any given market will in the long run drive out inefficient plants and firms. Accordingly, the "survivors" of such competition, who have passed the competitive market test, are deemed to be privately efficient in their operations.

The actual empirical estimation of economies of scale by means of the survivor test commences by a classification of all the firms in a given market by size. Then, if the share of the total market output emanating from a given-size class increases, that size of firm is considered to be privately efficient. Conversely, a declining share on the part of a given-size class of firm is interpreted to mean that such a size of firm is relatively inefficient. The efficient firm is the one that passes the market test by meeting all the diverse problems that confront a modern firm, whether these problems be domestic competition, import competition, changes in technology, government regulation, labor relations, or whatever.

The survivor test considers firms found in size classes where the share of output is declining to be either too large or too small. The optimal size of firm can therefore be ascertained by finding those size classes of firms whose share of output is rising. The survivor technique has been applied to most manufacturing industries by Stigler, Saving, and Weiss, and has typically produced results implying that many different firm sizes are consistent with the attainment of lowest-possible unit costs, and that large firm sizes are not needed in order to realize available economies of scale.[41]

The concept of minimum optimal scale also has relevance to the survivor technique.

Minimum optimal scale is the smallest output per unit of time at which the plant or firm can realize the lowest-obtainable unit costs of production.

The results generated by the survivor technique strongly suggest that the minimum optimal scale for either plant or firm is generally a very small proportion of the total market concerned. The overall impact of the sur-

[39]Stigler, "The Economies of Scale."

[40]John Stuart Mill, *Principles of Political Economy* (New York: Longmans, Green, and Company, 1929), p. 134.

[41]Stigler, "The Economies of Scale"; T.R. Saving, "Estimation of Optimum Size of Plant by the Survivor Technique," *Quarterly Journal of Economics,* 75 (November 1961), 569–607; and Leonard W. Weiss, "The Survival Technique and the Extent of Suboptimal Capacity," *Journal of Political Economy,* 72 (June 1964), 246–61. See also a corrective note by Weiss, "The Extent of Suboptimal Capacity: A Correction," *Journal of Political Economy,* 73 (June 1965), 300–301.

vivor technique is to question seriously the existence and importance of economies of scale at both the plant level and the firm level.

The survivor technique has been subjected to telling criticisms by Weiss and Shepherd.[42] The technique is based upon the hypothesis that competition will drive out inefficient firms; but the precise character of that competition is not specified. Conceivably, the competition referred to could involve the foreclosure of markets for outputs, monopolization of input markets, predatory pricing, and the like. Survival, then, might be an indicator of private efficiency but not of social efficiency. Further, it is possible that the technique may be distorted by a price-umbrella effect. Efficient firms may set their prices at such a high level that inefficient firms can also survive and prosper.[43] The efficient firms may choose to price in this fashion because of price elasticity of demand and also because they may wish to deter entry into the market by new firms. Where the umbrella of the efficient firms also allows the inefficient firms to survive, the survivor technique will not be capable of discerning which size of firm is actually efficient. Also, it is clear that the survivor technique cannot be applied to a given market unless a large number of firms exist in the market, and the time period being considered is sufficiently long that the firms involved have full opportunity to adjust their operations in response to their environment.[44] Finally, the estimates produced by the survivor test have sometimes been conflicting, and have on occasion resulted in the confusing statement that three or four quite different firm sizes are all optimal in nature.[45]

The strength of the survivor technique lies in its easy applicability and the manner in which it sidesteps problems that have reduced the effectiveness of other approaches. The survivor test can be implemented with readily available census data, and the researcher need not worry about problems such as whether or not he has computed the relevant rate of profit. Nevertheless, the weaknesses of the technique that were discussed above should make us wary of the estimates that the survivor test produces.

Statistical Studies

Statistical studies utilize historical cost–output data in order to make inferences about economies of scale. The most famous of these studies is that performed by Bain for twenty manufacturing industries.[46] Bain utilized ques-

[42]Weiss, "The Survival Technique"; and William G. Shepherd, "What Does the Survivor Technique Show About Economies of Scale?" *Southern Economic Journal,* 34 (July 1967), 113–22.

[43]The post–World War II oil industry in the United States is an example of a market where the largest firms have maintained a price umbrella over the entire market such that smaller, inefficient firms can survive with shares of the market less than minimum optimal scale.

[44]An industry with a small number of firms (for example, the automobile industry) cannot effectively be analyzed via the survivor test because the small size of the sample seriously reduces the reliability of the estimates. It should be pointed out that many of the major markets in the American economy are oligopolistic in nature, and therefore are difficult if not impossible to examine via the survivor test.

[45]Shepherd, "What Does the Survivor Technique Show?"

[46]Bain, *Barriers to New Competition,* Chap. 3.

tionnaires to assemble the data necessary for his scale-economies estimates. His results—which are becoming dated because they pertain to the late 1940's and the early 1950's—imply that both plant-level and firm-level economies of scale are not substantial in most manufacturing industries. These results are summarized in Table 6.1.

Although Bain's sample included such major oligopolies as automobiles, cigarettes, copper, and tires and tubes, in only six of the twenty markets did his estimates reveal that the minimum optimal scale of a *plant* would exceed 4 to 5 percent of the market's total productive capacity. Further, the average size of the largest *firms* in the twenty markets surveyed was more than three times as large as the mimimum optimal *plant* scale in fifteen of the twenty markets. The immediate conclusion was that many plants and firms are larger than they need to be in order to realize the available economies of scale. Therefore, public policies designed to reduce market concentration and firm size would not result in the realization of diseconomies of scale.

The weaknesses of the Bain work are characteristic of most statistical studies, but should not be permitted to obscure the fact that it is regarded as an important advance in the field.[47] The data Bain used to construct his scale-economies estimates were based upon questionnaire responses. Such tools are sometimes notoriously unreliable. In the case at hand, it is unlikely that the manager or personnel in a given plant or firm would class that plant or firm as being of an inefficient size.[48] Hence, the tendency is to exaggerate the range of optimal sizes. Further, the cost–output data obtained by Bain is representative of all types of firms—inefficient and efficient. Such data, therefore, may not represent the minimum-possible unit cost of producing a given output. As a result, the cost curves and scale-economies estimates that are generated may approximate the non-optimal cost curve found in Figure 6.2. The cost figures used by Bain are subject to the same deficiencies that plague most statistical studies; they are supplied by the plants and firms and represent whatever arbitrariness might exist in the plants' and firms' definitions and allocations of costs. In the long run, positive rents earned by a given plant or firm often become expected in nature and are capitalized permanently into the cost structure; likewise, persistent negative rents may not be recognized and often are ignored.[49]

[47]The Bain study is considered by some observers to be an example of an engineering study. [F.M. Scherer, *Industrial Market Structure and Economic Performance* (Skokie, Ill.: Rand McNally & Co., 1970), pp. 83–85.] This does not seem to be an appropriate classification, because the Bain study differs from other statistical studies only in that the necessary cost–output data were collected by means of questionnaires. Engineering studies, on the other hand, do not directly collect cost–output data; rather, they typically infer cost–output relationships from physical and technical rules, such as the so-called .6 rule that is discussed in the next section.

[48]This point has been made by William G. Shepherd, *Market Power and Economic Welfare* (New York: Random House, Inc., 1970), p. 168. Shepherd, in turn, has attributed the idea to his private conversations with Donald Dewey.

[49]A thorough critique of the strengths and weaknesses of accounting data for use in scale-economies studies may be found in Caleb A. Smith, "Survey of the Empirical Evidence on Economies of Scale," in *Business Concentration and Price Policy*, ed. George J. Stigler (Princeton, N.J.: Princeton University Press, 1955), pp. 213–30. See also the perceptive comment by Milton Friedman, *op. cit.*, pp. 230–38.

TABLE 6.1

Plant-Level and Firm-Level Economies of Scale in 20 Manufacturing Industries

Industry	Average Market Share of Top 4 Firms, 1947[a]	Mean Estimate of Percent of National Industry in One MOS Plant	Ratio of Actual Av. Firm Size to Estimated Plant MOS	Estimated Maximum Extent of Multiplant Economies (As Percent of Total Unit Cost)	Number of Optimal Plants that Would Be Contained in the Av. of the Largest 4 Actual Firms in Industry
Copper	23.1[b]	10.0	2.3	None	2.3
Cigarettes	22.6	5.5	4.1	Slight	4.1
Automobiles	22.5[c]	7.5	3.0	No Estimate	3.0
Gypsum Products	21.2	2.5	8.5	Small	8.5
Typewriters	19.9	20.0	1.0	None	1.0
Soap	19.8	5.0	4.0	.5 to 1	4.0
Rayon	19.6	5.0	3.9	No Estimate	3.9
Metal Containers	19.5	1.2	16.7	No Estimate	16.7
Tires and Tubes	19.2	2.0	9.3	No Estimate	9.3
Distilled Liquor	18.7	1.5	12.5	No Estimate	12.5
Tractors	16.8	12.5	1.3	No Estimate	1.3
Fountain Pens	14.4	7.5	1.9	None	1.9
Steel	11.2[d]	1.8	6.4	2 to 5	6.4
Meat Packing (Diversified)	10.3[e]	2.3	4.6	None	4.6[e]
Petroleum Refining	9.3	1.8	5.3	None	5.3
Farm Machinery	9.0	1.3	7.2	No Estimate	7.2
Cement	7.4	.9	8.2	Small, or 2 to 3	8.2
Flour	7.3	.3	24.3	No Estimate	24.3
Shoes	7.0	.3	21.8	Small, or 2 to 4	21.8
Canned Fruits	6.6	.4	17.6	None	17.6

[a]Percentages of 1947 value of shipments per Census of Manufactures, unless otherwise indicated.
[b]Percentage of copper-refining capacity in United States, 1947.
[c]Percentage (approximate) of total passenger-car registration, 1951.
[d]Percentage of value added per Census of Manufactures, 1947.
[e]Percentage of value added per Census of Manufactures, 1947; firm percentage refers to wholesale fresh-meat packing and diversified firms.

Reprinted by permission of the publishers from Joe S. Bain, Barriers to New Competition. Cambridge. Mass.: Harvard University Press, copyright, 1956, by the President and Fellows of Harvard College.

The number of statistical studies that have been performed in an attempt to estimate economies and diseconomies of scale is quite large. Johnston has summarized the most prominent of these studies for the pre-1960 period.[50] Since that time, the output of statistical studies of economies of scale in American industry has declined.

Engineering Studies

Engineering studies of economies of scale, although often performed by noneconomists, can nevertheless be quite valuable to the economist. Engineering studies are frequently based upon important technological relationships about which most economists are partly or totally ignorant. The relationship between the volume of a cylindrical machine and the maximum output of that machine, a typical basis for engineering studies of economies of scale, is not the centerpiece of many economic theories.

The physical relationship between volume and output, alluded to above, is the basis for an oft-cited relationship known as the ".6 rule." The .6 rule states that the increase in cost associated with an increase in machine capacity will be equal to the increase in machine capacity raised to the .6 power. That is,

$$C_2 = C_1(X_2/X_1)^{.6}$$

where C_2 = cost of running an expanded machine
C_1 = cost of running the existing machine
X_2 = capacity of expanded machine
X_1 = capacity of the existing machine

The .6 rule is dependent upon the relationship between the surface of a machine and the volume of that machine. The surface of the machine represents the machine's cost, whereas the volume represents its output capacity. As the surface of the machine expands, its volume expands, but more than proportionately. Hence, output increases at a faster rate than costs, and economies of scale can be realized.

The .6 rule, which appears to have some empirical validity, was called to economists' attention by Moore.[51] Moore surveyed several productive processes (for example, aluminum) and concluded that some scale economies did exist in several of these processes and that these economies could be represented as having occurred because of the phenomena enclosed in the .6 rule. The .6 rule does not, however, have universal applicability. It applies only to single pieces of equipment, not to batches of equipment. Further, it applies only to the expansion of existing equipment, and not to the purchase of new equipment. Finally, the rule is representative of reality

[50] Johnston, *Statistical Cost Analysis.*
[51] Moore, "Economies of Scale," pp. 232–48.

only in those industries with productive processes that are susceptible to the cost–surface–volume–capacity type of analysis.

Haldi and Whitcomb have applied a variant of the .6 rule to a total of 687 separate pieces of industrial equipment used in a variety of different industrial markets.[52] Over 94 percent of the pieces were found to be subject to increasing returns to scale as their capacity was expanded. The Haldi–Whitcomb data also suggested that scale economies based upon the surface–volume phenomenon were available up to and including the very largest equipment sizes.[53]

Any survey of engineering studies of economies of scale would be incomplete without mention of the classic study of oil pipelines performed by Cookenboo.[54] Cookenboo analyzed oil pipelines, which have a "throughput" of oil rather than the conventional concept of output. The throughput of oil was made a function of the diameter of the oil pipe and the horsepower applied to pushing the oil through the pipe. Cookenboo used his knowledge of physical laws instead of historical data in order to analyze the relationship between throughput and diameter–horsepower. He found increasing returns at the margin to pipe diameter (horsepower held constant), because a larger pipe reduced the friction of the oil flowing through it. Diminishing returns were found for horsepower (pipe diameter held constant). When both pipe diameter and horsepower were increased in the same proportion, throughput increased more than proportionately.[55] The beauty of the Cookenboo study lies in its clear exemplification of an engineering study of economies of scale and in the fact that the productivity curves and isoquants generated by the analysis neatly approximated those one finds in economics textbooks.

ECONOMIES OF SCALE AND ANTITRUST POLICY

Let us assume that significant economies of scale do exist and that two firms attempt to realize these economies by merging rather than by growing internally.[56] The merger is simultaneously desirable, in that unit cost savings

[52]Haldi and Whitcomb, "Economies of Scale in Industrial Plants." Haldi and Whitcomb estimated an equation of the form $C = aX^b$, where C = cost, a = constant, X = output capacity, and b = scale coefficient.

[53]It is notable that many noneconomists who study the problem of scale economies generally conclude that scale economies are large at both the plant and the firm levels. See, for example, S.C. Schumann and S.B. Alper, "Economics of Scale: Some Statistical Evidence: Comment," *Quarterly Journal of Economics*, 74 (August 1960), 493–97.

[54]Leslie Cookenboo, Jr., *Crude Oil Pipelines and Competition in the Oil Industry* (Cambridge, Mass.: Harvard University Press, 1955).

[55]This finding should emphasize the point that a given production function may realize diminishing returns to given inputs and increasing returns to scale.

[56]The probability of economies of scale being realized as the result of the merger of two existing firms should not be overemphasized. The long-run average-cost curve of the firm assumes that *de novo* firms of alternative sizes are built. If such a cost curve is downward-sloping, then the merger of two small firms with high unit costs will result in a merged firm with unit costs above the long-run average-cost curve of the firm. Only if some factor such as complementarity of resources exists will the merger result in the realization of economies of scale.

are realized, and possibly undesirable, in that the merged firm may use its increased size and market power to increase its market price over the competitive level. If both these effects accrue because of a merger, then the ultimate worth of that merger from the viewpoint of society depends upon the comparative size of each of the aforementioned effects.

Williamson has suggested an ingenious apparatus as a means of explicating the precise tradeoffs involved in the type of merger described above.[57] The apparatus relies upon the static theory of the firm, with which we are already familiar. Assume that firms wishing to merge are realizing constant long-run average-cost curves such that $LRAC = LRMC$. Let MC_1 in Figure 6.3 represent the premerger marginal-cost curve of each of the firms involved. MC_2, therefore, is their joint marginal-cost curve after the firms have merged. The premerger price–quantity combination is P_1, Q_1 (assuming the existence of competition, and $P = MC$); the postmerger price–quantity combination is P_2, Q_2. P_2 is greater than P_1 because of our assumption of increased market power on the part of the newly merged firm. The loss in consumer's surplus owing to the merger may be approximated by the area of the triangle labeled A_1 in Figure 6.3. The gain in efficiency owing to the merger may be approximated by the area of rectangle A_2.

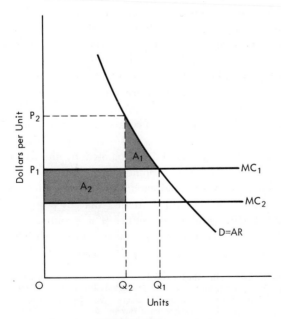

FIGURE 6.3

[57]O.E. Williamson, "Economies as an Antitrust Defense: The Welfare Tradeoffs," *American Economic Review*, 58 (March 1968), 18–36.

Rectangle A_2 represents a gain to society, because fewer resources are now needed in order to produce any given output.[58]

The desirability of the merger can be ascertained by subtracting the area of triangle A_1 from the area of rectangle A_2. The merger, according to Williamson, is desirable if area A_2 minus area A_1 is greater than zero. Unfortunately, a host of complications can be and probably need to be introduced into this naïve model in order to increase its applicability. Among these are the recognition that many gains and losses owing to merger do not occur immediately and therefore must be discounted over time. Also, in some markets, the firms seeking to merge may already possess positive amounts of monopoly power. In such a case, the loss in consumer's surplus because of the merger will be smaller.[59] Further, the effects of different price elasticities of demand and the variability of costs can also alter the results substantially. The effects of the merger on other firms' behavior, upon technological innovation, and upon political power must be considered. Finally, Williamson himself has noted that it is not obvious that any substantial cost or price variations result from the usual merger.[60]

Williamson, within the context of his simple model, concluded that (given "reasonable" values for price elasticity of demand, and so on) only a small reduction in costs of production owing to a merger was necessary to offset relatively large increases in price because of any simultaneous increase in market power. This conclusion has been attacked with great vigor by subsequent contributors to this discussion.[61]

It is clear that one cannot evaluate the welfare effects of mergers without having a great deal of market information about prices, quantities, costs, and elasticities. The problem is essentially similar to the one confronting researchers who attempt to measure the so-called deadweight loss due to monopoly, except that additional information is required in this case. Consequently, there has been no immediate attempt to apply the Willliamson model, despite the wave of mergers that has characterized the late 1960's and early 1970's. The fundamental issue posed by the Williamson model, however, is real and substantial. Should the growth to large firm sizes by means of either merger or internal expansion be encouraged, particularly in view of the possible concomitant increased market power and seller concentration? What gains and losses result? The philosophic clash between what were referred to earlier as the American and British schools of thought on the subject of economies of scale permeates this dispute. The existing

[58]It is possible, however, that the increased market power of the newly merged firm may be used by the firm to make management-slack payments. The net result is simply an increase in X-Inefficiency.

[59]This point has been made by Michael E. DePrano and Jeffrey B. Nugent, "Economies as an Antitrust Defense: Comment," *American Economic Review*, 59 (December 1969), 947–53. See also Raymond Jackson, "The Consideration of Economies in Merger Cases," *Journal of Business*, 43 (October 1970), 439–47.

[60]Williamson, "Economies as an Antitrust Defense," p. 33.

[61]DePrano and Nugent, "Economies as an Antitrust Defense: Comment"; and Jackson, "The Consideration of Economies."

empirical evidence does not provide an answer sufficiently clear to settle the imbroglio. It is interesting, however, that the judicial attitude has typically been to disallow any merger that might conceivably result in increased market power.[62] This attitude, which is examined in Chapter 10, represents a particular but perhaps extreme viewpoint and evaluation of the gains and losses owing to merger when economies of scale are thought to exist.

CAPITAL REQUIREMENTS

The existence of economies of scale does not necessarily imply the existence of high capital requirements. Nevertheless, capital requirements are often high when substantial economies of scale exist either at the plant or the firm levels. The *capital requirements* of a plant (firm) refers to the dollar amount of capital that must be possessed by that plant (firm) in order for it to produce at the minimum optimal scale in the market concerned. This definition is not unambiguous. One may value existing capital in many different ways. For example, a given machine may be valued either at its current replacement cost or in terms of its original purchase price. The two valuations need not correspond. As a result, the comparability of plant or firm asset and capital sizes is indeed often an inexact science.

A frequently alleged reason that a capital-requirements barrier to entry exists is "imperfections in the capital market."[63] Properly understood, an imperfect capital market means that a *fully qualified* borrower cannot obtain (or must pay higher prices for) the capital he wants. Capital markets are not called imperfect because they discriminate against *unqualified* borrowers, who presumably bring with them increased risk of default or failure. Such capital markets are in fact functioning efficiently. Hence, what is often thought to be a capital-requirements barrier is actually efficient market discrimination against inefficient, risky entrepreneurs. It is true that in certain markets, substantial amounts of capital are needed in order for a plant or firm to operate at its minimum optimal scale. The fact that any and every entrepreneur cannot easily procure such amounts of capital does not mean that a capital-requirements barrier exists. It is therefore inaccurate to equate the exclusion of certain entrepreneurs from a given market for reasons of insufficiency of capital with the existence of a capital-requirements barrier.

Although the argument above is logically impeccable, it is nevertheless a fact that only a very small number of entrepreneurs possess or are capable of obtaining the use of the $19 billion worth of capital that Standard Oil of New Jersey utilized in the year 1970.[64] The higher the capital requirement,

---

[62]*United States* v. *Brown Shoe Company*, 370 U.S. 294 (1962), p. 374. See also *Federal Trade Commission* v. *Proctor and Gamble Company*, 87 S. Ct. 1224 (1967), pp. 1230–31.

[63]George J. Stigler, "Imperfections in the Capital Market," in *The Organization of Industry* (Homewood, Ill.: Richard D. Irwin, Inc., 1968), pp. 113–22.

[64]*Fortune*, 83 (May 1971), 172.

the fewer the number of truly qualified entrepreneurs who possess or can obtain the needed amount of capital. In this sense, one can make limited use of the concept of a capital-requirements barrier.

The variability of capital requirements in American industry can be seen in Table 6.2, which records the gross book value of assets per establishment (plant) in selected manufacturing industries.[65] The gross book value of assets per employee is a reflection of the industry's capital-to-labor ratio. As Table 6.2 indicates, this varies from a low of $1,620 per employee in the men's and boys' shirts and nightwear industry to a high of $121,100 per employee in the petroleum refining industry. Table 6.3 reports similar information for selected firms in *Fortune* magazine's list of the 500 largest industrial corporations in 1970. It is apparent that the firms with the largest volume of sales also tend to have large asset/employee ratios. Indeed, the lowest asset/employee ratio among the 500 firms is still larger than several of the average industry asset/employee ratios found in Table 6.2. The size of the firm is positively and significantly correlated with its asset/employee ratio.[66] Therefore, to the extent that only a few qualified entrepreneurs exist who are capable of acquiring the large amounts of capital needed in certain productive processes, there may exist capital requirements that discourage the entry of new firms, even though such requirements are not a barrier to entry in the technical sense.

The asset/employee ratio is not a straightforward measure of capital requirements, however. Some industries—for example, the fur-goods industry —are very labor-intensive and may have a capital-to-output ratio that is less than 1.00. Others, such as the coal-tar industry, may have a capital-to-output ratio that is greater than 100, because of the capital-intensive modes of production utilized.[67] Hence, the asset/employee ratio will not always accurately portray the actual capital needs of a plant, because it is easily biased by the labor or capital intensity of the productive process.

Table 6.2 also reports the average gross book value of depreciable assets per establishment (plant) in a wide range of manufacturing industries. The capital requirements of plants of minimum optimal scale are generally less than those of an average-sized firm in the industry concerned. Nevertheless, the data recorded in Table 6.2 that relate to assets per establishment (plant) give a clearer indication of the actual absolute capital requirements in a given market than does the assets-per-employee statistic. Absolute capital requirements are often quite large (for example, $33 million in the cigarette industry) and can conceivably retard the entry of new firms. At the same

[65]The reader should bear in mind the difficulties involved in evaluating the dollar worth of assets. The reader is also warned that the resemblance between assets and capital can sometimes be superficial.

[66]The simple correlation coefficient between firm size and the asset/employee ratio for the sample of firms in Table 6.3 is .89. This coefficient is statistically significant at the .01 level.

[67]Norman R. Collins and Lee E. Preston, *Concentration and Price–Cost Margins in Manufacturing Industries* (Berkeley, Calif.: University of California Press, 1970), Tables A-4 and A-9.

TABLE 6.2

Use of Capital in Selected Manufacturing Industries

SIC Code	Industry	Gross Book Value of Depreciable Assets per Employee, 1968	Gross Book Value of Depreciable Assets per Establishment, 1967
2011	Meatpacking Plants	$ 8,500	$ 526,000
2037	Frozen Fruits & Vegetables	9,810	1,113,000
2061	Raw Cane Sugar	50,400	4,253,000
2082	Malt Liquors	32,720	10,259,000
2111	Cigarettes	14,380	33,250,000
2271	Woven Carpets & Rugs	10,700	1,754,000
2321	Men's & Boys' Shirts & Nightwear	1,620	230,000
2411	Logging Camps & Logging Contractors	10,320	46,100
2511	Wood Household Furniture	4,600	240,000
2647	Sanitary Paper Products	14,500	2,896,000
2731	Book Publishing	6,170	326,000
2791	Typesetting	5,670	99,000
2812	Alkalies & Chlorine	74,560	27,114,000
2813	Industrial Gases	107,440	1,907,000
2821	Plastics Materials & Resins	37,430	4,197,000
2841	Soaps & Other Detergents	22,930	1,030,000
2871	Fertilizers	55,690	4,183,000
2895	Carbon Black	96,500	5,676,000
2911	Petroleum Refining	121,100	29,652,000
3011	Tires & Inner Tubes	20,450	11,462,000
3111	Leather Tanning & Finishing	15,180	395,000
3211	Flat Glass	32,910	11,313,000
3255	Clay Refractories	16,310	1,462,000
3271	Concrete Block & Brick	15,810	208,000
3312	Blast Furnaces & Steel Mills	42,340	68,857,000
3323	Steel Foundries	10,350	2,378,000
3332	Primary Lead	37,000	3,469,000
3352	Aluminum Rolling & Drawing	30,040	9,234,000
3444	Sheet Metalwork	6,910	158,000
3511	Steam Engines & Turbines	14,000	19,703,000
3566	Power Transmission Equipment	9,840	1,055,000
3572	Typewriters	9,950	7,960,000
3612	Transformers	9,940	2,458,000
3641	Electric Lamps	9,680	2,830,000
3651	Radio & TV Receiving Sets	5,040	1,585,000
3711–12	Motor Vehicles	12,120	23,442,000
3721	Aircraft	5,520	17,432,000
3861	Photographic Equipment & Supplies	16,070	2,713,000
3941	Games & Toys	4,950	434,000

Source: *U.S. Department of Commerce, Bureau of the Census, Annual Survey of Manufactures, 1968, Book Value of Fixed Assets, Rental Payments for Buildings and Equipment, and Labor Costs, M68 (AS)-7 (Washington, D.C.: U.S. Department of Commerce, 1971); also, U.S. Department of Commerce, Bureau of the Census, Census of Manufactures: Summary and Subject Statistics (Washington, D.C.: U.S. Department of Commerce, 1971), pp. 28–42.*

TABLE 6.3

Assets per Employee of Selected Firms from *Fortune's 500*, 1970

Name of Firm	Rank of Assets per Employee Among the Largest 500 Firms, 1970	Assets per Employee, 1970	Sales Rank Among Largest 500 Firms, 1970
Coastal States Gas Producing	1	$323,378	320
Amerada Hess	2	212,160	111
Texas Gulf Sulphur	3	205,270	424
Commonwealth Oil Refining	4	203,861	418
Marathon Oil	5	170,965	118
Union Oil of Calif.	6	152,815	57
Standard Oil of Calif.	7	147,804	14
Getty Oil	8	147,599	95
Gulf Oil	9	141,473	11
Atlantic Richfield	10	140,327	30
.	.	.	.
.	.	.	.
.	.	.	.
National Service Industries	496	8,234	322
VF	497	8,142	416
Rath Packing	498	8,135	355
Interstate Brands	499	7,349	384
American Bakeries	500	6.591	323

Source: *"The Fortune Directory of the 500 Largest Industrial Corporations,"* Fortune, *83 (May 1971),* 191.

time, it should be emphasized that firms can and do enter given markets at rates of output per unit of time that are less than the output associated with the minimum optimal scale in that market. If the cost disadvantage that accompanies entry at a suboptimal scale is not great, then many firms may not need to acquire large amounts of capital in order to enter an industry.[68]

There have been several attempts made to determine the effects of capital requirements upon the performance of firms and markets. The static theory of the firm predicts that, *ceteris paribus,* prices will be higher, output lower, and profit rates higher in markets characterized by high entry barriers. Large capital requirements are a possible cause of high entry barriers. Bain, whose work on entry barriers has been cited previously, used questionnaire data to estimate the height of what he considered to be any capital-requirements barrier that might have existed in twenty manufacturing markets.[69] Table 6.4 summarizes his result. Bain considered the capital-requirements barrier to be "high" in the automobile, cigarette, petroleum

[68]This issue will be given detailed consideration in Chapter 12.
[69]Bain, *Barriers to New Competition.*

refining, steel, and tractor markets.[70] It is probable that the capital requirements of a plant of minimum optimal scale, as he reported them, are high estimates. Survivor-technique estimation of capital requirements reveals that the range of optimal scales and the amount of capital needed for production are frequently only a fraction of the capital requirement estimated by Bain. He incorporated his estimate of capital requirements into an overall measure of barriers to the entry of new firms. This overall measure was found by Bain and by Mann to be positively related to firm profit rates even after the influence of seller concentration was eliminated.[71] (See Table 5.3, page 83.)

Hall and Weiss, in a study designed primarily to determine the effects of firm size on firm profit rates, hesitantly concluded that firm profit rates (variously measured) rise almost 20 percent in markets where the minimum optimal scale of a plant was large enough to require at least $500 million worth of capital for efficient production.[72] Two recent studies performed by researchers in a multivariate context have revealed a strong and positive relationship between the capital requirements of a plant of minimum optimal scale and industry profit rates.[73] Collins and Preston, Koch and Fenili, and Koch found average market price–cost margins to be strongly and positively associated with the capital intensity of the markets.[74] This relationship survived even when the influence of other relevant factors, such as seller concentration, the geographic dispersion of the market, the rate of technical change, and the degree of product differentiation, were considered. Evidence previously cited in Chapter 5 points to output restriction, both at the plant and the market levels, in markets where barriers to entry are substantial. One of these studies, that performed by Koch, used two separate measures of the capital requirements for a plant of minimum optimal scale.[75] For either measure, the market growth rate was found to be negatively related to the plant-level capital requirements, even after other relevant indicators of market structure were taken into account.

[70]Ibid., pp. 158–59.

[71]Ibid., pp. 192–200; and H. Michael Mann, "Seller Concentration, Barriers to Entry, and Rates to Return in Thirty Industries," Review of Economics and Statistics, 48 (August 1966), 296–307.

[72]Hall and Weiss, "Firm Size and Profitability."

[73]Roger Sherman and Robert Tollison, "Advertising and Profitability," Review of Economics and Statistics, 53 (November 1971), 397–407; and Louis Esposito and Frances Ferguson Esposito, "Foreign Competition and Domestic Industry Profitability," Review of Economics and Statistics, 53 (November 1971), 343–53.

[74]Norman R. Collins and Lee E. Preston, "Concentration and Price–Cost Margins in Food Manufacturing Industries," Journal of Industrial Economics, 14 (July 1966), 226–42; Collins and Preston, "Price–Cost Margins and Industry Structure," Review of Economics and Statistics, 51 (August 1969), 271–86; James V. Koch and Robert N. Fenili, "The Influence of Industry Market Structure upon Industry Price–Cost Margins," Rivista Internazionale di Scienze Economiche e Commerciali, 18 (November 1971), 1037–45; and Koch, "Industry Market Structure and Industry Price–Cost Margins" (Unpublished manuscript).

[75]James V. Koch, "Market Structure and Industry Growth Rates," Rivista Internazionale di Scienze Economiche e Commerciali, 17 (December 1970), 1145–63. The two measures of plant-level capital requirements for a plant of minimum optimal scale differed only in the amount of scale economies that each measure attributed to a representative plant.

TABLE 6.4

Classification of Industries According to Capital Requirements for a Single Optimal Plant, and Related Information

(1) Industry	(2) Capital Requirement for One Plant of Minimum Optimal Scale (Millions of Dollars)	(3) Percentage of Largest Submarket Supplied by One Optimal Plant	(4) Estimated Shape of Plant Scale Curve at Suboptimal Scales	(5) Existence of Production Economies of Multiplant Firms	(6) Incidence of Economies of Large-Scale Scales Promotion
I. Industries with very large capital requirements per plant (generally above $100 million):					
Steel	265 to 665	2 1/2 to 6 1/4	Moderately sloped	Yes	Negligible
Automobiles	250 to 500[a]	10 to 20	Moderately sloped	No estimate	Promotional economies up to size of optimal plant
Petroleum Refining	225 to 250[b]	4 1/3	Relatively flat	No	Promotional economies up to size of optimal plant
Tractors	125	10 to 15	Relatively flat	No estimate	Promotional economies up to size of optimal plant
Cigarettes	125 to 150	5 to 6	Relatively flat	Yes	Promotional economies of multiplant firms possible
II. Industries with large capital requirements per plant (generally $10 to $50 million):					
Rayon	50 to 75[c]	4 to 6	Relatively steep	No estimate	Negligible
Liquor	90 to 135[d]	1 1/4 to 1 3/4	Relatively flat	No estimate	Promotional economies of multiplant firms possible
Cement	30 to 42	4 to 5	Relatively steep	Yes	Negligible
Tires and Tubes	15 to 30	1 3/8 to 2 3/4	Moderately sloped	No estimate	Promotional economies of multiplant firms possible
Soap	13 to 20[e]	4 to 6	Moderately sloped		Promotional economies of multiplant firms possible
Meat Packing (Diversified)	10 to 20	8 to 10	Relatively flat	No	Negligible

(1)	(2)	(3)	(4)	(5)	(6)
III. *Industries with moderate capital requirements per plant (generally $2.5 to $10 million):*					
Fountain Pens	6	10 to 15	No estimate	No	Promotional economies up to size of optimal plant, for "quality" pens
Metal Containers	5 to 20	2 to 12	No estimate	No estimate	Promotional economies of multiplant firms possible
Gypsum Products	4 to 6	8 to 12	No estimate	Yes	Negligible
Canned Fruits and Vegetables	2 1/2 to 3	2 1/2 to 5	Moderately sloped	No	Negligible for standard items; multiplant economies for specialties
IV. *Industries with small capital requirements per plant (generally under $2 million):*					
Flour	7/10 to 3 1/2	1/3 to 1 1/2	No estimate	No estimate	Negligible for promotional economies for commercial and private-label sales; multiplant economies for miller's-brand sales
Shoes	1/2 to 2	3/5 to 1 1/5	Moderately sloped	Yes	Negligible for most lines; multiplant economies for high-priced men's or specialties
Meat Packing (Fresh)	under 1	1/10 to 1	Relatively flat	No	Negligible
V. *Nonclassified industries (capital requirements not estimated):*					
Typewriters	No estimate	10 to 30	Relatively steep	No	Promotional economies up to size of optimal plant
Farm Machinery	No estimate	4 to 6	Moderately sloped	No estimate	Promotional economies of multiplant firms probable
Copper	No estimate	10	No estimate	No	Negligible

[a]Supposes integration of bodies and engines, but not of maximum range of components.
[b]Includes crude-oil transport facilities (average requirement).
[c]Acetate rayon.
[d]Viscose rayon.
[e]Excludes working capital.

Reprinted by permission of the publishers from Joe S. Bain, Barriers to New Competition. Cambridge, Mass.: Harvard University Press, Copyright, 1956, by the President and Fellows of Harvard College.

SUMMARY

The scale of a firm or plant was defined as the firm's rate of output per unit of time when all inputs are variable. The subject of economies of scale has always excited economists and others to such an extent that competing *a priori* positions have been staked out concerning the subject, and then staunchly defended almost without reference to empirical evidence.

Many reasons can be adduced as to why economies and diseconomies of scale should appear in the operation of plants and firms. The empirical verification of the existence or nonexistence of economies of scale is sparse and often of doubtful value; however, except for engineering studies, the evidence points in general to the existence of a wide range of optimal scales in most markets. That is, both very small plants and firms and their very large competitors are often found to be realizing all scale economies available.

If substantial economies of scale exist, then the growth of firms via the merger route is sometimes defensible on the ground that it spurs the development of efficiency. However, the realization of economies of scale through firm merger is probably uncommon. Williamson has proposed a simple although debatable model for use in evaluating the welfare tradeoff between any increased efficiencies that might result from a merger and the possible increased market power that might also result.

The concept of a capital-requirements barrier is often mistakenly confused with so-called imperfections in the capital markets. Even though discrimination by an efficient capital market against unqualified borrowers is not properly regarded as evidence of a capital-requirements barrier in our context, the inability to borrow a sufficient amount of capital may retard the entry of some firms. The limited empirical evidence available points to less-desirable performance in markets characterized by large capital requirements.

PROBLEMS

1. Under what, if any, circumstances can a market be competitive in nature if the long-run average-cost curve of every firm in that market is continuously declining?

2. The survivor technique has been criticized for many reasons. One criticism is that it measures private efficiency, not social efficiency. When there exists a divergence between private and social efficiency, will firms ever choose the socially efficient route? Should public policy be one of (a) encouraging privately efficient actions and then compensating afterwards for externalities that arise; or (b) demanding and encouraging only socially efficient actions?

3. Schwartzman has contended that the presence of uncertainty effects a limitation upon the number of firms in the market. How can we measure uncertainty? Is variability of the firm's profit rate an appropriate measure?

4.   Assume that each of two firms is producing 100 units of output at an average cost per unit of $1.00 in a given time period. Under what circumstances is it possible for these two firms to merge and form a firm producing 200 units at an average unit cost of $.75?

5.   Certain of the proponents of the ".6 rule" concerning economies of scale have contended that nearly all economic phenomena (and particularly those involving the firm) can be explained by analogy to the laws of physical science. Ultimately, this contention amounts to the notion that there exist certain universal laws of physical behavior and that these laws apply to the firm just as they apply to other things. Do you agree?

6.   The law of diminishing returns is usually viewed as a short-run law, whereas the concept of returns to scale is usually viewed as a long-run phenomenon. Nevertheless, we often speak of diminishing returns to the fixed factor of management as a cause of diseconomies of scale. Is this use of diminishing returns improper?

7

The Economics of Firm Size

The subject of firm size is intimately related to factors such as economies of scale. In part, the size of an existing firm is determined by the availability and exploitation of such economies. However, as we shall see, large firm size is not synonymous with the existence and exploitation of economies of scale. Further, the effects of firm size upon the conduct and performance of firms in the market are not the same as the effects of economies of scale upon conduct and performance. Therefore, we must in this chapter attempt to untangle the relationship between firm size and elements of market structure such as economies of scale. Our analysis will begin with a statistical look at the actual size distribution of firms in a large number of industrial markets. Then, having looked at "what is," we will attempt to nail down the determinants of firm size. Finally, in the tradition of the classical model of industrial organization, we will evaluate existing empirical evidence that reports the influence of a particular aspect of market structure (firm size) upon the conduct and performance of firms.

The Size Distribution of Firms

We live in an economy that supports a wide range of different firm sizes, only some of which are efficient. The largest firms are typically multiplant, multiproduct firms with billions of dollars in assets. Table 7.1 reports the fifteen largest industrial corporations in terms of assets in the year 1970. The value of the assets of a single firm, Standard Oil of New Jersey, is greater than the gross national product of all but eighteen nations in the world.[1]

Big business is indeed big, as Table 7.1 confirms. Such bigness does not pervade the entire economy, however. Tables 7.2 and 7.3 record respectively the number and the percent of corporations that possessed given amounts of assets in various sectors of the economy during 1968. Over 89 percent of all corporations engaged in manufacturing owned less than $1 million in assets in 1968, and fully 93.7 percent of all corporations in all sectors of the

[1]*World Economic Survey, 1969–70* (New York: United Nations, 1971), pp. 177–79.

TABLE 7.1

The Fifteen Largest Industrial Corporations (by Assets), 1970

Rank	Company	Assets*
1	Standard Oil (N.J.)	$19,241,784,000
2	General Motors	14,174,360,000
3	Texaco	9,923,786,000
4	Ford Motor	9,904,100,000
5	Gulf Oil	8,672,298,000
6	International Business Machines	8,539,047,000
7	Mobil Oil	7,921,049,000
8	General Telephone and Electronics	7,739,272,000
9	International Telephone and Telegraph	6,697,011,000
10	Standard Oil of Calif.	6,593,551,000
11	U.S. Steel	6,311,038,000
12	General Electric	6,309,945,000
13	Standard Oil (Ind.)	5,397,471,000
14	Chrysler	4,815,772,000
15	Shell Oil	4,609,763,000

*Year-end assets, less depreciation and depletion.
Source: *"The Fortune Directory of the 500 Largest Industrial Corporations,"* Fortune, *83 (May 1971), 172·*

economy owned less than $1 million in assets. Most of the firms in the majority of the sectors of the economy are miniscule in size when compared to giants such as Standard Oil of New Jersey or International Business Machines. The "bigness" of business refers not to the number of big firms but to the gargantuan size of the largest firms. This generalization is supported by Table 7.4, which discloses that 42 percent of the value added in manufacturing in the year 1966 was accounted for by the 200 largest manufacturing firms.[2] The remaining 185,000+ manufacturing firms accounted for the residual 58 percent of value added in manufacturing. It is apparent, then, that the activities and work of the manufacturing "heartland" of the economy are performed predominantly by large firms that possess hundreds of millions of dollars in assets.[3]

The reader must be reminded parenthetically at this point not to equate firm size with efficiency of conduct and performance. True, many large firms are demonstrably efficient in conduct and performance. Nevertheless, the empirical evidence to be introduced shortly, and that already presented in Chapter 6, does not provide strong encouragement for the view that bigness and efficiency always walk hand in hand.

Data on the assets of firms undoubtedly give an accurate general portrayal

[2]Stripped to its bare essentials, *value added* is the dollar value of output minus the dollar value of the inputs used to produce the output. Gross national product, therefore, may be viewed as the grand total of the value added of productive activities.

[3]The original use of the term "heartland" was by John Kenneth Galbraith, in *The New Industrial State* (Boston: Houghton Mifflin Company, 1967).

TABLE 7.2

The Size Distribution of U.S. Corporations in the Year 1968

Sector of Economy	Number of Corporations	Number of Corporations in Asset Size Classes (millions of dollars)								
		0–.05	.05–.1	.1–.25	.25–.5	.5–1.0	1.0–5.0	5.0–50.0	50.0–250	Over 250
Agriculture, Forestry, Fisheries	31,248	11,434	5,180	7,587	3,876	1,845	1,223	100	2	1
Mining	12,713	4,761	1,893	2,253	1,577	989	889	289	52	10
Construction	124,989	57,722	20,994	22,229	12,081	6,748	4,593	599	21	2
Manufacturing	191,915	57,259	28,769	41,705	25,332	16,340	17,395	4,180	673	262
Transportation, Communications, Utilities	65,554	29,931	10,314	12,348	5,639	3,383	2,800	806	180	153
Wholesale and Retail Trade	476,252	181,591	87,982	109,857	51,051	27,086	16,557	1,938	154	36
Finance, Insurance, Real Estate	407,199	149,103	66,524	83,589	43,027	24,335	24,174	13,914	1,969	564
Services	227,904	138,667	32,203	31,670	13,552	6,644	4,424	673	58	13
Other	6,051	5,305	326	345	32	29	13	1	0	0
Total	1,543,825	635,773	254,185	311,583	156,167	87,399	72,068	22,500	3,109	1,041

Source: U.S. Treasury Department, Internal Revenue Service, Statistics of Income, 1968, Corporation Income Tax Returns (Washington, D.C.: U.S. Government Printing Office, 1971).

TABLE 7.3

The Size Distribution of U.S. Corporations in the Year 1968

Sector of Economy	Number of Corporations	Percent of Corporations in Asset Size Classes (millions of dollars)								
		0–.05	.05–.1	.1–.25	.25–.5	.5–1.0	1.0–5.0	5.0–50.0	50.0–250	Over 250
Agriculture, Forestry, Fisheries	31,248	36.6%	16.6%	24.3%	12.4%	5.9%	3.9%	.3%	—	—
Mining	12,713	37.4	14.9	17.7	12.4	7.7	7.0	2.3	.04	—
Construction	124,989	46.2	16.8	17.8	9.7	5.4	3.7	.1	—	—
Manufacturing	191,915	29.8	15.0	21.7	13.2	8.5	9.1	2.2	.04	.01
Transportation, Communications, Utilities	65,554	45.7	15.7	18.8	8.6	5.2	4.3	1.2	.03	.02
Wholesale and Retail Trade	476,252	38.1	18.5	23.1	10.7	5.7	3.5	.04	—	—
Finance, Insurance, Real Estate	407,199	36.6	16.3	20.5	10.6	6.0	5.9	3.4	.05	.01
Services	227,904	60.8	14.1	13.9	5.9	2.9	1.9	.03	—	—
Other	6,051	87.7	5.4	5.7	.05	.05	.02	—	—	—
Total	1,543,825	41.2%	16.5%	20.2%	10.1%	5.7%	4.7%	1.5%	.02%	.01%
Cumulative		41.2%	57.7%	77.9%	88.0%	93.7%	98.4%	99.9%	99.9%	99.9%

Source: *U.S. Treasury Department, Internal Revenue Service, Statistics of Income, 1968, Corporation Income Tax Returns (Washington, D.C.: U.S. Government Printing Office, 1971).*

TABLE 7.4

Share of Total Value Added by Manufacture Accounted for by Largest Manufacturing Companies in 1966 and Previous Years

Company Rank group in Given Year	Percent Value Added by Manufacture*					
	1966	1963	1962	1958	1954	1947
Largest 50 firms	25	25	24	23	23	17
Largest 100 firms	33	33	32	30	30	23
Largest 150 firms	38	37	36	35	34	27
Largest 200 firms	42	41	40	38	37	30

*Value added is the value of shipments for products manufactured, plus receipts for services rendered, minus the costs of materials, supplies, containers, fuels, purchased electricity, and contract work.

Source: *U.S. Department of Commerce, Bureau of the Census, Annual Survey of Manufactures, 1966 (Washington, D.C.: U.S. Government Printing Office, 1969), p. 445.*

of firm sizes.[4] Asset data are, however, subject to great variability, depending upon the method used to value assets. It has previously been pointed out that a firm can in good conscience choose to value its assets either in terms of the original cost to the firm of those assets, or in terms of their current replacement cost. Differing methods of depreciation can also scramble asset data. The consequence is that measurements in terms of the value of assets can indicate general firm size but should not be regarded as constituting precise statistics.

The major alternatives to the use of assets as the coin of the realm in measuring firm size are fourfold: (1) value-added, (2) value of shipments, (3) sales, and (4) employment. The value-added, value-of-shipments, and sales measurements are susceptible to price inflation and deflation, and the employment measure can be seriously compromised by technological change, which alters capital-to-labor ratios used in production. The unfortunate conclusion is that none of these four alternatives is particularly well suited as a unit of measurement of firm size. The asset measure, while not optimal, may be the best choice of those available.

The ideal measure of firm size would rely upon a physical unit of output rather than the possibly biased units of measurement proposed above. Internally consistent indexes of physical output are, however, not easily obtained, if for no other reason than the fact that most types of output (for example, automobiles or television sets) change drastically as time passes. Sands, in a pioneering effort, constructed physical indexes of output for 46 manufacturing industries for the time period 1904-47.[5] He found that mean plant size expanded at an average rate of 15 percent every five years, or

[4]See M.A. Adelman, "The Measurement of Industrial Concentration," *Review of Economics and Statistics*, 33 (November 1951), 272-74.

[5]Saul S. Sands, "Changes in Scale of Production in United States Manufacturing Industry, 1904-1947," *Review of Economics and Statistics*, 43 (November 1961), 365-68.

about 3 percent each year. In only one of the 46 industries did mean plant size contract during the time period considered.

Markets may grow either by the expansion of already existing firms or by the entry of new firms. If existing firms expand at the average annual rate of 3 percent (Sands's finding), then there will be no room for new entrants into these established markets unless the markets are expanding at an annual rate that exceeds 3 percent. The real rate of growth of the American economy during the period 1904–47 was probably greater than 3 percent per year.[6] Hence, even though Sands found absolute firm sizes to be rising, it is apparently true that firm size relative to the size of the market concerned declined in many markets during this time period. Of course, this finding need not imply that relative firm size necessarily declined in any single one of Sands's 46 markets.

THE DETERMINANTS OF FIRM SIZE

The determinants of the size of firms may be divided into those factors that are of a supply nature and those that are of a demand nature.[7] The supply factors condition the firm's ability to grow in size and indicate the efficiency of that growth. The demand factors reflect the desires and needs of society for the increased output that could be obtained by increased firm size. Both supply and demand factors must be considered in every individual circumstance, for it is evident that neither factor taken by itself exclusively determines firm size. It is clear that the ability of a firm to grow efficiently to a large size will not imply large firm size if there exists little or no demand for the firm's output. Likewise, large market demand need not dictate large firm sizes, because existing cost conditions and the state of technology can conceivably rule out as inefficient any except the smallest firm sizes.

The supply factors that help influence firm size may be summarized by the firm's long-run average-cost curve—that is, by available economies of scale. The determinants of economies and diseconomies of scale have already been examined in detail in Chapter 6. It will suffice at this point to mention the following factors that shape the firm's long-run average-cost curve and hence affect firm size: (1) division and specialization of use of inputs, including management; (2) the state of technology; (3) indivisibilities; (4) capital requirements; (5) the degree and effects of product differentiation; (6) market and firm maturity; (7) pecuniary advantages; and (8) risk and uncertainty. A change in any one of these factors will change the shape of the long-run average-cost curve and therefore influence firm size. For exam-

[6]See the *Economic Report of the President, 1971* (Washington, D.C.: U.S. Government Printing Office, 1971), p. 198.

[7]The reader is referred to George Stigler, "Barriers to Entry, Economies of Scale, and Firm Size," in *The Organization of Industry* (Homewood, Ill.: Richard D. Irwin, Inc., 1968).

ple, an innovation that can be utilized by even the smallest firm will not, *ceteris paribus,* encourage the growth of large firms. The introduction of the basic oxygen steel-refining process is an example of an innovation that strengthened the position of small firms becaues of its inexpensive cost of installation and operation relative to the existing open-hearth process, and because of its ready adaptability to the small-scale productive processes of the small firms.[8]

The demand factors that influence firm size are actually the various characteristics of the demand facing individual firms in a given market. The most important characteristics of demand with reference to firm size are its (1) absolute size, (2) degree of product homogeneity or differentiation, (3) geographic configuration, (4) time pattern, (5) price elasticity, (6) dependence upon supply-and-demand conditions in other markets, (7) variability, and (8) predictability.

Additional consideration of the demand factors that determine firm size is merited, because the discussion of economies of scale in Chapter 6 emphasized supply factors rather than demand factors. The absolute size of demand is an important determinant of firm size. One of the causes of a "natural monopoly" is market demand that is sufficient to support only one firm. (Another major cause is a circumstance in which economies of scale are so great that they cannot be fully realized by a single firm.) The insufficient-demand scenario can totally cancel any trend to large firms that might result because of the existence of substantial economies of scale. The natural-monopoly circumstance is alleged to explain the existence of only one large firm in utilities and in transportation, and, on the local level, the reason that only one gasoline station can profitably exist in a given location or area.

It is altogether obvious that one can talk about the size of demand only by clearly delimiting the market in which that demand is measured. This requires an assumption concerning how much product differentiation may exist inside a given market, what geographic area is to be considered, and what time period is relevant. The various dimensions of markets have been considered in Chapter 2, and that discussion will not be repeated here.

Price elasticity of demand, while possibly reflecting the degree of product differentiation, will also affect the response of market output to changing conditions on the supply side of the market. Assume that in a given competitive market, an innovation is introduced that reduces average unit costs of production by 5 percent. Given competition, such a cost reduction should also result in a price reduction of about 5 percent. A necessary condition for average firm size in a market to increase when no firms are leaving the market is that market output expands. Market output will expand more when price elasticity of demand is greater. For example, when the coefficient of

---

[8]The low cost of installation could be viewed as a reduction in any capital-requirements barrier that existed.

price elasticity of demand is unity, market output will expand by 5 percent, whereas it will expand by 10 percent when the coefficient of price elasticity of demand is -2.00. Hence, the potential for an increase in the average firm size in a market is greater when demand is more price-elastic.

It may nevertheless be true that a high degree of product differentiation (which may reduce price elasticity of demand) in a given market may result in large firm sizes. If, as Bain has contended, product differentiation is the major barrier to the entry of new firms in many manufacturing industries,[9] then new firms may be excluded and existing firms may grow large in size when the product-differentiation barrier is very high in a given market. The possibility that various firms may engage in varying degrees of product differentiation may also influence firm sizes. Within a major market —for example, book publishing—many submarkets exist. One company may choose to specialize in the publishing of economics textbooks, while another may publish novels that titillate the public and bend or stretch conventional moral standards. The point of importance is that the market for economics textbooks is probably much smaller in size than the market for books containing prurient material. Product differentiation, whether or not undertaken in a conscious fashion, does delimit the market facing a firm and can constrain or stimulate the growth of a firm.

In some markets, demand is profoundly influenced by the supply-and-demand conditions existing in other markets. Consider the relationship between metal cans and glass bottles: These are ordinarily thought to be produced in two different markets; nevertheless, they are often sold in the same market. Metal cans and glass bottles compete as receptacles for products such as pharmaceutical preparations and beer. Any circumstance that affects supply or demand conditions in the glass-bottle market will undoubtedly have an impact upon the demand for metal cans. An example in point is the advent of the throwaway "no deposit, no return" glass bottle. This innovation curtailed the use of metal cans in the beer market and thereby influenced firm sizes in the metal-can market.

The demand function facing a firm usually shifts as time passes. Certain of these shifts are predictable in nature and are due to seasonal, temporal, or other factors. Producers of rock salt are well aware that the approach of winter will greatly affect the demand for their product by towns and cities that use it on their streets to reduce hazardous driving conditions. E.A.G. Robinson has contended that large firms possess "economies of massed reserves" that enable them to adjust to large fluctuations in demand more rapidly than can small firms.[10] This argument, however, rests upon the crucial assumption that the fluctuations in demand cannot be foreseen. If

---

[9]Joe S. Bain, *Barriers to New Competition* (Cambridge, Mass.: Harvard University Press, 1965), p. 142.

[10]E.A.G. Robinson, *The Structure of Competitive Industry* (Chicago: University of Chicago Press, 1958), pp. 26–27.

they can be foreseen, than all firms, large or small, can prepare for such fluctuations, and size of firm need not be a liability. Since no firm, large or small, has perfect foresight, the question devolves to one of which can forecast most accurately, large firm or small firm; and further, which type of firm handles most efficiently the inevitable deviations from expected conditions. We have previously cited the evidence of Schwartzman, who found that large department stores did not handle uncertainty as well as did smaller department stores.[11] Schwartzman, well aware of the limitations of his study, concluded that uncertain conditions would tend to place large firms at a disadvantage.

Some actions and events in the marketplace seem to be the result of random factors. An interesting statistical experiment with considerable bearing upon the distribution of firm sizes has been performed by Scherer.[12] Scherer hypothesized a market consisting of fifty firms of equal size; then he assumed a mean firm growth rate of 6 percent per year in the industry, and a 16 percent standard deviation of firm growth rates in a given year. Despite the fact that the expected growth rate of each firm in any given year was 6 percent, the size distribution of firms became progressively more unequal as time passed. By the fortieth year after the conceptual experiment was begun, the four largest firms, instead of having 8 percent of the market, had an average of 27 percent of the market. Although the assumption that all firms in a given market start at the same point and have the same probability of growing a given percent per year may not be correct, the result of the Scherer experiment clearly contains powerful implications for firm size distributions. The random vagaries of market demand, even when potentially applicable to all firms in the market in equal doses, will tend to produce an unequal size distribution of firms in the market.

THE EFFECTS OF FIRM SIZE UPON FIRM CONDUCT AND PERFORMANCE

In this chapter we have examined the actual size distribution of firms and have attempted to explain the basic determinants of firm size. Now we must address ourselves to the possible effects of firm size upon the conduct and performance of firms in the markets in which they operate. We will consider in turn the relationship between firm size and firm (1) profit rates, (2) growth rates, (3) capital-market activities, and (4) technological change.

[11] David Schwartzman, "Uncertainty and the Size of the Firm," *Economica*, 30 (August 1963), 287–96.

[12] F.M. Scherer, *Industrial Market Structure and Economic Performance* (Skokie, Ill.: Rand McNally & Co., 1970), pp. 125–27.

Firm Size and Firm Profit Rates

Economic theory predicts that competition will drive profit rates on invested capital to equality, other factors such as risk held constant. The existence of market power and barriers to entry could prevent such competitive adjustments from occurring, however. Steindl and Baumol have argued that the market power conferred by large firm size, and the capital-requirements barrier that may result from large firm size, will increase firm profit rates.[13] According to Steindl and Baumol, large firms are capable of undertaking any investment open to smaller firms and can in addition take advantage of some opportunities for investment that would be impossible for the smaller firm to contemplate because of lack of capital.

The view that a positive relationship exists between firm size and firm profit rates has always had many detractors. Marshall asserted that very large firms would earn lower profit rates,[14] and Robinson and Kaldor contended that large firms would experience lower profit rates because of diminishing returns to the fixed factor of management.[15] More recently, Haines has denied the existence of any positive relationship between firm size and firm profit rates.[16]

The empirical evidence concerning the relationship between firm size and firm profit rates is most notable for the variety of different conclusions it supports. Early evidence from the 1920's and 1930's, provided by Summers and Epstein, indicated an inverse correlation between firm size and firm profit rates,[17] whereas Crum found the opposite.[18] Several postdepression studies found medium-sized firms earning the highest profit rates, while small and large firms earned distinctly lower rates.[19] Recent studies by Stekler and by

---

[13]Joseph Steindl, *Small and Big Business: Economic Problems of the Size of Firms* (Oxford, England: Oxford University Press, 1945), p. 33; and William Baumol, *Business Behavior, Value and Growth* (New York: Harcourt Brace Jovanovich, 1967), p. 37.

[14]Alfred Marshall, *Principles of Economics*, 8th ed. (London: Macmillan and Company, Ltd., 1961), p. 239.

[15]Robinson, *The Structure of Competitive Industry*, pp. 39–40; and Nicholas Kaldor, "The Equilibrium of the Firm," *Economic Journal*, 44 (March 1934), 60–76.

[16]Walter W. Haines, "The Profitability of Large-Size Firms," *Rivista Internazionale di Scienze Economiche e Commerciali*, 17 (April 1970), 321–51.

[17]Harrison B. Summers, "A Comparison of the Rates of Large-Scale and Small-Scale Industries," *Quarterly Journal of Economics*, 46 (May 1932), 465–79; Ralph C. Epstein, "Profits and Size of Firm in the Automobile Industry, 1919–1927," *American Economic Review*, 21 (December 1931), 636–47; and Epstein, *Industrial Profits in the United States* (New York: National Bureau of Economic Research, 1934).

[18]William L. Crum, *Corporate Size and Earning Power* (Cambridge, Mass.: Harvard University Press, 1939).

[19]S.S. Alexander, "The Effect of Size of Manufacturing Corporation on the Distribution of the Rate of Return," *Review of Economics and Statistics*, 31 (August 1949), 229–35; Joseph L. McConnell, "Corporate Earnings By Size of Firm," *Survey of Current Business*, 25 (May 1945), 6–12; Joseph L. McConnell, "1942 Corporate Profits by Size of Firm," *Survey of Current Business*, 26 (January 1946), 10–16; Richards C. Osborn, *Effects of Corporate Size on Efficiency and Profitability* (Urbana, Ill.: University of Illinois Press, 1950); Richards C. Osborn, "Efficiency and Profitability in Relation to Size," *Harvard Business Review*, 29 (March 1951), 82–94; Temporary National Economic Committee, *Relative Efficiency of Large, Medium-Sized, and Small Businesses* (Washington, D.C.: U.S. Government Printing Office, 1941).

Hall and Weiss have found a strong correlation between firm size and firm profitability,[20] but this evidence too has been disputed by the work of Haines.[21]

The conflicting nature of the evidence can be seen by examining in greater detail the two most recent studies: those of Hall–Weiss and Haines. Both used as their basic sample the activities of firms listed in the annual *Fortune* directory of the 500 largest industrial firms.[22] Hall and Weiss analyzed 341 of the firms for the period 1956–62: Haines examined the entire sample of 500 firms in each year during the period 1956–67. Both Hall–Weiss and Haines thereby avoided one of the major pitfalls associated with previous studies—namely, overaggregation of the data. Most previous studies had examined the activities of aggregative size classes of firms rather than individual firms. Such aggregation presumably can obscure important individual peculiarities of the firms and of the industries in which they operate.

Hall and Weiss assumed that firm profit rates are determined by many factors, only one of which is firm size. Hence, their basic analysis made the individual firm's profit rate a function not only of firm size, but also of market concentration, market growth, and economy-wide growth and fluctuations. Depending upon the regression specification utilized (and after considering the influence upon firm profit rates of factors other than firm size), Hall and Weiss discovered either a strong positive association between firm size and firm profit rates (as illustrated in Figure 7.1) or a U-shaped relationship between the same variables (Figure 7.2).

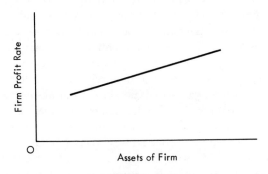

FIGURE 7.1

[20]H.O. Stekler, *Profitability and Size of Firm* (Berkeley, Calif.: Institute of Business and Economic Research, University of California, 1963); Stekler, "The Variability of Profitability with Size of Firms, 1947–1958." *Journal of the American Statistical Association*, 59 (December 1964), 1183–93; and Marshall Hall and Leonard Weiss, "Firm Size and Profitability," *Review of Economics and Statistics*, 49 (August 1967), 319–31.

[21]Haines, "The Profitability of Large-Size Firms."

[22]"The Fortune Directory of the 500 Largest Industrial Corporations," *Fortune* (issued annually in May).

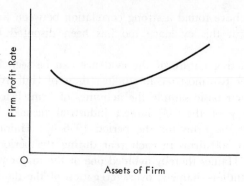

FIGURE 7.2

Haines, on the other hand, relied primarily upon simple correlations between firm size and firm profit rates for his evidence. He found that "the firms that appear most frequently among the 10, 50, or 100 most profitable are small or medium-sized rather than large. For the whole list, the rank correlation coefficient between profitability and invested capital is effectively zero."[23] Haines, therefore, rejected the contention of Steindl, Baumol, and Hall–Weiss that firm profitability is positively related to firm size.

The Hall–Weiss effort is easily the more sophisticated and carefully done of the two. The statistical techniques utilized and the introduction of explanatory influences upon firm profit rates other than firm size lend considerable credence to the study. The Haines study, while interesting, is not controlled for the undoubtedly important influences of market structure, market growth, and economy-wide fluctuations upon firm profit rates. Because the Haines study utilizes the entire sample of the 500 largest industrial firms in each year, its results could be dependent upon other, extraneous factors, such as diversification or barriers to entry, rather than firm size. The Hall–Weiss study eliminated such firms from the analysis.

The evidence, then, points to a positive relationship between firm size and firm profitability, although this relationship is not always strong and is hardly universal in occurrence. Despite the lack of agreement about the relationship between the *mean* profit rate and firm size, there is widespread agreement that the *variability* of profit rates is inversely related to firm size.[24] The greater variability in the profit rates of small firms reflects the fact that that some small firms are marginal in nature and are ultimately driven out of the industry, while others entering an industry experience a very rapid growth rate. Further, large firms are often found in mature, stabilized markets, where the opportunities for radical change and innovation are usually less than in other markets.

---

[23]Haines, "The Profitability of Large-Size Firms," pp. 319–31.

[24]Stekler, *Profitability and Size of Firm;* Stekler, "The Variability of Profitability"; Charles E. Ferguson, *A Macroeconomic Theory of Workable Competition* (Durham, N.C.: Duke University Press, 1964), pp. 172–74; and Hall and Weiss, "Firm Size and Profitability."

Firm Size and Firm Growth Rates

It is widely believed that there is no relationship between the size of the firm and the mean growth rate of the firm.[25] The statistical underpinning of most studies that have led to this conjecture is known as Gibrat's law, also referred to as the law of proportionate effect.[26] Gibrat's law states that the probability of a given firm's growing x percent is independent of the size of that firm. That is, the probability of a large firm's growing at a mean rate of 10 percent per year is no different from the probability of a small firm's growing at the same rate during the time period. Gibrat's law also implies that the variance of the growth rates of various size classes of firms should be equal, although this implication is not crucial to the prediction relating firm sizes and mean firm growth rates.

It has been demonstrated that Gibrat's law usually holds when the distribution of firm sizes is sharply skewed to the right.[27] Such a distribution,

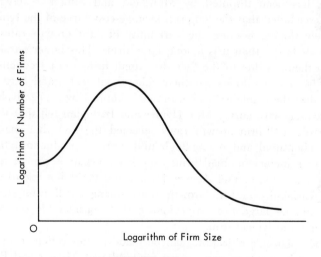

FIGURE 7.3

[25]See especially Herbert Simon and C.P. Bonini, "The Size Distribution of Business Firms," *American Economic Review*, 48 (September 1958), 607–17; Stephen Hymer and Peter Pashigian, "Firm Size and Rate of Growth," *Journal of Political Economy*, 70 (December 1962), 556–69. Irwin H. Silberman, "On Lognormality as a Summary Measure of Concentration," *American Economic Review*, 62 (September 1967), 807–31, finds that log normal distribution is only approximately accurate as a descriptive tool. A negative view is that of Edwin Mansfield, "Entry, Gibrat's Law, Innovation, and the Growth of Firms," *American Economic Review*, 52 (December 1962), 1031–34. The reader is warned that a considerable portion of the empirical evidence concerning Gibrat's law, both favorable and unfavorable, relates to the economy of the United Kingdom and has not been reported here.

[26]Gibrat's law was originally brought to the attention of English-speaking economists by Michal Kalecki, "On the Gibrat Distribution," *Econometrica*, 13 (April 1945), 161–70; the law has been ably dissected and explained by P.E. Hart, "The Size and Growth of Firms," *Economica*, 29 (February 1962), 29–39.

[27]A wide range of different distributions is actually consistent with the predictions of Gibrat's law. Likewise, a large number of different random growth processes will result in skewed distributions similar to that of Figure 7.3. See Herbert Simon, "On a Class of Skew Distribution Functions," *Biometrika*, 52 (December 1955), 425–40; see also Richard E. Quandt, "On the Size Distribution of Firms," *American Economic Review*, 56 (June 1966), 416–32.

illustrated in Figure 7.3, is often termed "log normal" in nature, because it closely approximates a normal distribution when firm size and frequency of occurrence of firm size are stated in terms of logarithms. Figure 7.4 represents a plot of the actual size distribution of corporate firms in 1968, as it was reported in Table 7.2. Because the fit of this distribution roughly approximates Figure 7.3, Gibrat's law, at least as it applies to mean firm growth rates, is ordinarily thought to be empirically valid.

The evidence concerning firm size and firm growth rates in the American economy has been provided by Hymer and Pashigian and by Mansfield.[28] This evidence indicates that there is no systematic difference in the mean growth rates of different-sized firms, and that the variability of firm growth rates decreases as firm size increases.[29] The former finding is consistent with Gibrat's law, whereas the latter is not.[30]

Hymer and Pashigian have argued that their findings imply that the long-run average-cost curve of a typical firm declines continuously.[31] (This conclusion has been disputed by Mansfield and Simon.)[32] Hymer and Pashigian concluded that the long-run average-cost curve of the typical firm is negatively sloped, because the variability of firm growth rates among small firms is larger than it is among large firms. This larger variance, according to them, is due to the fact that small firms must frequently grow very rapidly in order to escape their suboptimal scales and because they wish to realize the available scale economies implied by a negatively sloped long-run average-cost curve. Also, Hymer and Pashigian felt that the larger variability of small-firm growth rates reflected the fact that many small firms are suboptimal and realize high unit costs of production; therefore, many of these inefficient small firms experience negative growth rates and are driven out of the market. Hence, Hymer and Pashigian regard evidence of higher variability of firm growth rates among small firms and lower variability among large firms as evidence that considerable economies of scale exist for the typical firm.

Several plausible objections can be made to this retionale in support of a declining long-run average-cost curve. Although Hymer and Pashigian argue that the variability of the growth rates of small firms will be larger than that of large firms because the small firms will expand faster in order

---

[28]Hymer and Pashigian, "Firm Size and Rate of Growth"; and Mansfield, "Entry, Gibrat's Law."

[29]Evidence from Great Britain is also strongly supportive of the "no difference in mean growth rate, but difference in variability of growth rates" conclusion that has been reported for the United States. See, for example, P.E. Hart and S.J. Prais, "The Analysis of Business Concentration," *Journal of the Royal Statistical Society*, 119 (Part I, 1956), 150–91.

[30]Important discussions of the implications of Gibrat's law for firm growth rates may be found (in addition to other sources already cited) in Simon and Bonini, "The Size Distribution of Business Firms." A discussion of the Hymer–Pashigian and Mansfield research mentioned in the text may be found in Herbert A. Simon, "Comment: Firm Size and Rate of Growth," *Journal of Political Economy*, 72 (February 1964), 81–82; and Stephen Hymer and Peter Pashigian, "Reply," *Journal of Political Economy*, 72 (February 1964), 83–84.

[31]Hymer and Pashigian, "Firm Size and Rate of Growth," pp. 556–59.

[32]Mansfield, "Entry, Gibrat's Law"; and Simon, "Comment."

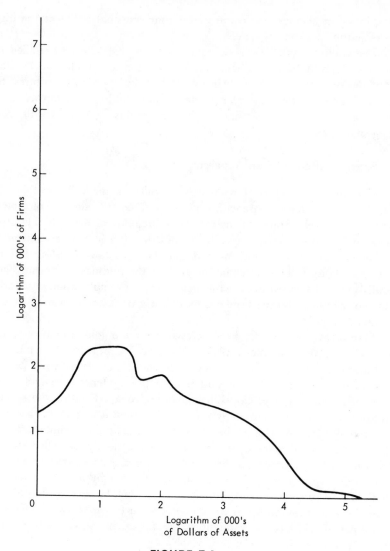

FIGURE 7.4

to realize available economies of scale, it is not obvious why small firms should necessarily expand faster than large ones if the long-run average cost curve is negatively sloped for both firm sizes. Small firms might well grow faster than large firms if the long-run average-cost curve declines at a decreasing rate. This would mean that each incremental amount of output generated by expansion would elicit proportionately less economies of scale. Note, nevertheless, that this implies that the long-run average-cost curve will eventually bottom out and that constant unit costs will eventually be realized. Hymer and Pashigian, however, argue in favor of a continuously falling long-run average-cost curve rather than one that is flat at the high rates of output per unit of time.

The ability of small firms to expand rapidly may also be curtailed by their lack of profitability to finance such expansion, or by efficient capital-market discrimination against their relatively risky expansion ventures. So it is not clear that one may infer a continuously falling long-run average-cost curve from the acknowledged higher variability of firm growth rates among small firms.

Sidelight: Resolving an Apparent Conflict

The weight of empirical evidence surveyed thus far indicates that (1) mean firm profit rates increase with firm size and that (2) the rate of growth of firms is positively related to the rate of profitability of firms. If these two statements are true, then it logically follows that larger firms should grow at faster rates than smaller firms and that Gibrat's law therefore has no empirical validity.[33] This latter implication of the findings above has been skillfully examined by Marcus, who then offered an explanation as to why we do not actually observe firm size and firm growth to be related in any meaningful way.[34]

Marcus asserts that the firm's growth rate is a joint function of the firm's rate of profit and the firm's market share. A large market share, in the Marcusian view, will inhibit firm growth because the large firm's actions greatly affect market conditions and market price. Hence, the large firm may be reluctant to pursue destabilizing rapid growth. Further, the spectre of antitrust action may loom large in the firm's vision if its market share expands rapidly. Hence, Marcus has hypothesized that the stimulant effects of higher firm profit rates upon firm growth are neatly cancelled by the depressant effects of growth in firm market shares. The smattering of empirical evidence offered by Marcus for nine three-digit industries for the period 1961–64 supports this hypothesis. This finding, however, seems almost too simple, and more empirical work is needed in the area. Nevertheless, if the findings of Marcus are valid, then the apparent conflict between the profitability and growth evidence is resolved.

Firm Size and the Firm's Capital-Market Activities

It has already been observed, in Chapter 6, that pecuniary economies of scale exist when the firm is able to obtain price concessions in its purchase

---

[33] A crude illustrative example is helpful in making this point clear. Let π = the firm's profit rate; S = firm size; and G = the firm's growth rate. Then, statement (1) above in the text implies that $\pi = f(S)$; let us arbitrarily assume that the relationship is such that $\pi = 2S$. Statement (2) in the text implies that $G = f(\pi)$; let us arbitrarily assume that $G = 4\pi$. What then is the relationship between G and S? $G = 8S$; that is, the firm's growth rate is a positive function of firm size, contrary to Gibrat's law, which has nevertheless been found to be empirically valid. Herein lies the apparent contradiction.

[34] Matityahu Marcus, "A Note on the Determinants of the Growth of Firms and Gibrat's Law," *Canadian Journal of Economics*, 2 (November 1969), 580–89.

of inputs because of its large scale. A major input market is the market for capital. Some firms generate their needed funds for capital expenditures by retaining all or portions of the profits they have earned in their operations, but many firms must raise capital by means of (1) obtaining loans, (2) issuing stock, and (3) issuing bonds. Although the method used by a firm to raise capital depends upon many factors, including the term structure of interest rates, the most common method of raising capital is the stock issue, followed by bond floatation and loans, in that order.[35]

The costs of raising capital have often been found to be inversely related to the size of the firm, primarily because the probability of loan repayment varies between small and large firms. Two studies, which are now somewhat dated, revealed that interest rates charged firms on loans varied inversely with the size of the firm receiving the loan.[36] Edwards, who has examined this and related issues, has confirmed this finding.[37] The transactions costs associated with the making of loans or the floatation of a stock or bond issue also tend to vary inversely with firm size. This is because the transactions costs of the loan or floatation are usually fixed in amount; therefore, the larger the loan, the lower the transactions costs per dollar borrowed. Given the assumption that large firms borrow greater amounts of capital than do small firms, it follows that the large firms will pay less per dollar of borrowed capital than will small firms. Empirical work performed by Archer and Faerber concerning the transaction costs of firm borrowing in the early 1960's supports this hypothesis.[38]

Firm Size and Technological Change

The process of technological change and the research and development activities that stand behind it are of such importance to the study of industrial organization that we will devote an entire chapter (Chapter 9) to that and related topics. Our current approach is to anticipate this coverage by quickly surveying the relationship between research and development activities and firm size. As Table 7.5 reveals, over 80 percent of all dollars spent on research and development by private firms in 1967 were spent by firms with more than 1,000 employees.

Despite the fact that most research and development activities are performed by large firms, there is little evidence that programs of a given scale are carried out more efficiently in large firms than in small firms, or

[35]William E. Dunkham, *Money, Credit and Banking* (New York: Random House, Inc., 1970), Chap. 11.

[36]Federal Reserve Board, *Studies of Bank Loan Rates in 1955 and 1957* (Washington, D.C.: U.S. Government Printing Office, 1959); U.S., Congress, Senate, Subcommittee on Monopoly of the Senate Select Committee on Small Business, *The Cost and Availability of Credit and Capital to Small Business,* 82d Cong., 2d sess., Subcommittee Print No. 8 (Washington, D.C.: U.S. Government Printing Office, 1952).

[37]F.R. Edwards, "The Banking Competition Controversy," *National Banking Review,* 3 (September 1965), 1–34.

[38]Stephen H. Archer and Leroy G. Faerber, "Firm Size and the Cost of Externally Secured Equity Capital," *Journal of Finance,* 21 (March 1966), 69–83.

TABLE 7.5

Funds Expended for Research and Development Activities, by Size of Company, 1956–57

Size of Company (Employees)	Yearly Research and Development Expenditures (millions of dollars)											
	1956	1957	1958	1959	1960	1961	1962	1963	1964	1965	1966	1967
Less than 1,000	369	542	532	546	581	612	633	619	632	659	621	688
1,000 to 4,999	550	632	642	740	892	949	990	1,022	1,035	956	1,043	1,111
5,000 to 9,999 }	5,686	6,557	7,215	8,332	9,036	9,347	9,840	10,989	11,846	12,569	793	869
10,000 or More }											13,092	13,752

Source: *National Science Foundation, Research and Development in Industry, 1967 (Washington, D.C.: U.S. Government Printing Office, 1969), p. 27.*

that substantial economies of scale exist with respect to their performance.[39] Indeed, above the very smallest, a wide range of firm sizes all appear to be conducive to efficient research and development activities.

The sources and effects of technological change, and the diffusion of technological change, are complex issues that require more thorough treatment. This will be provided in Chapter 9.

SUMMARY AND CONCLUSIONS

The typical firm in a manufacturing industry in the American economy is small and possesses less than $100,000 in assets. The share of total output produced by such small firms is declining, however, and the share generated by large firms with billions of dollars of assets has been steadily climbing in recent years.

The major determinants of firm size are supply factors such as economies of scale and demand conditions. Neither factor solely determines firm size.

Despite frequent opinions to the contrary, little evidence exists clearly linking efficient economic performance to market structures dominated by large firms. Large firm size does appear to increase firm profitability and to reduce the variability of firm profits and growth, and may actually induce diseconomies of scale in certain types of research and development activities.

Both the extent of small-firm efficiency and the degree of large-firm domination of the American economy have often been exaggerated. Many alternative firm sizes are capable of producing efficient behavior in most markets. At the same time, large firm size frequently brings with it market power that can be utilized to the advantage of the large firm. Nevertheless, despite the growth in size of large firms and their considerable diversification, the end of the smalll firm does not seem near in most industrial markets.

PROBLEMS

1. The firm's scale is defined as its rate of output per unit of time when all the firm's inputs are variable. How does the concept of firm scale differ from the concept of firm size?

2. The analysis in this chapter has suggested that one may conceptually think of firm size as being determined by supply-and-demand factors. An increase in costs influences the supply side of a market and has predictable *a priori* effects upon a supply curve. Do we have sufficient knowledge to be able to state the effect of a change in costs (or any other variable) upon expected firm size?

[39]The economics of technological change is considered in detail in Chapter 9. For a useful summary, however, see Edwin Mansfield, *Microeconomics: Theory and Applications* (New York: W. W. Norton & Company, Inc., 1971), Chap. 16.

3. The share of output produced by the 100 and 200 largest firms in the economy has tended to increase in recent years. Is this evidence that these firms are more efficient than smaller firms?

4. Much of the recent growth of some firms has been accomplished by the merger route. Critics of this type of growth have charged that growth by merger "bypasses the market test." That is, such firms do not have to prove their efficiency by growth internally; rather, they simply purchase larger size. Does growth by merger bypass the market test, and if so, should the growth of large firms via merger be prohibited?

8

Concentration: Definition, Measurement, Effects

Concentration is the best-known and most often used indicator of market structure. Concentration indicators, particularly the overworked four-firm concentration ratio, have been cited and examined so often that an uninformed observer might well conclude that no other aspects of market structure exist. Although the initial publication of concentration ratios by the Bureau of the Census did not signal the beginning of the millenium in the field of industrial organization, concentration indexes and concentration ratios have been and continue to be useful tools in the hands of knowledgeable analysts. In this chapter, therefore, we will examine concentration as an aspect of market structure. We will survey the various indexes of concentration available, their strengths and weaknesses, and the effects of concentration upon economic conduct and performance.

CONCENTRATION INDEXES

Let us begin appropriately with a definition of concentration.

Concentration is the number and size distribution of sellers and buyers in the marketplace.[1]

The major controversies surrounding the construction of concentration indexes have been these: (1) the choice of the unit of measurement to be used; (2) the decision whether to include in the index all or only some portion of the firms in a given market; and (3) the meaning and appropriateness of including a measure of the dispersion of firm sizes in the index.

The appropriate unit of measurement for a concentration index is not immediately obvious. In Chapter 7, we indicated that each of the commonly used measuring units of firm size (assets, sales, value of shipments, value added, and employment) was potentially deficient in some respect. These same liabilities extend to the construction and use of concentration indexes.

[1] The number and size distribution of buyers in the marketplace is clearly a datum of some consequence to the student of industrial organization. However, such information is not readily available and therefore has tended to be ignored despite its obvious importance.

With regard to the issue of which firms to include in a given concentration index, there exist partial indexes and summary indexes. Partial indexes typically report the percent of market value of shipments (or some other unit of measurement) held by a portion of the firms in that market (for example, the 4, 8, 20, or 50 largest firms in that market). Summary indexes, on the other hand, take into account all the firms in the market.

The discussion over dispersion stems from a difference of opinion about the consequences of an uneven size distribution of firms in a given market. Does an uneven size distribution of firms profoundly affect the economic conduct and performance of firms, or is the important fact simply that an uneven size distribution often brings with it a fewness of the number of firms? Hart and Prais have argued that concentration is synonymous with the unevenness and dispersion of firm sizes,[2] whereas Adelman has contended that dispersion per se has no real economic consequences.[3] Rather, Adelman has argued, it is the fewness of firms in the market that is of import, and that is what concentration indexes should attempt to capture. Conventional price-theory models of oligopoly, duopoly, and monopoly give support to the view of Adelman in that they emphasize the fewness of firms. Nevertheless, recent commentators such as Shepherd and Worcester have attributed great importance to the disparity of firm sizes in a given market and have attempted to demonstrate that asymmetry among those sizes (which is not precluded by the existence of a large number of firms) is a crucially important determinant of the conduct and performance of firms in the market.[4]

The preceding discussion may be summarized by the statements that no single concentration index can capture all the nuances of the number and size distribution of firms in a given market. Fault can always be found with the unit of measurement employed. Partial concentration indexes ignore all but a portion of the firms in the market, and summary indexes typically overemphasize the importance of small, marginal firms. Further, both the dispersion of firm sizes and the fewness of firms in a given market affect the conduct and performance of firms in that market. However, no existing concentration index successfully incorporates both these influences. The perfect concentration index, like the perfect statistical index number, has yet to be constructed. We shall see that each concentration index highlights particular aspects of the number and size distribution of firms. Hence, the

---

[2] P.E. Hart and S.J. Prais, "The Analysis of Business Concentration," *Journal of the Royal Statistical Society*, 119 (Part I, 1956), 150–91.

[3] M.A. Adelman, "The Measurement of Industrial Concentration," *Review of Economics and Statistics*, 33 (November 1951), 272–74.

[4] William G. Shepherd, *Market Power and Economic Welfare* (New York: Random House, Inc., 1970), pp. 63–65 and throughout; and Dean A. Worcester, Jr., *Monopoly, Big Business and Welfare in the Postwar United States* (Seattle, Wash.: University of Washington Press, 1967).

choice of concentration index must be guided by the measurement needs and peculiarities of the situation at hand.[5]

Partial Indexes

Partial indexes of concentration are by far the most commonly used, and the concentration ratio is the most frequently used and discussed partial index. The distinguishing characteristic of a partial index is the fact that such an index is based upon only a portion of the total number of firms in a given market. Concentration ratios, which indicate the percent of the total size of a given market that is accounted for by the few largest firms, have been used innumerable times in studies of industrial organization as a proxy for things as diverse as monopoly power, an indicator of the probable degree of collusion, and a measure of an industry's receptivity to technological change. In the computation of a concentration ratio, market size may be measured in terms of any of the units discussed eariler, but is most often measured in terms of value of shipments. The Bureau of the Census, which frequently publishes concentration ratios for manufacturing markets, computes separate concentration ratios for the four, eight, twenty, and fifty largest firms in each market. For example, in 1967, the four-firm concentration ratio for the meatpacking-plants market was 26; this means that the four largest firms accounted for 26 percent of the total value of shipments in that market. The corresponding eight-firm, twenty-firm, and fifty-firm concentration ratios were 38, 50, and 62, respectively.[6]

It is clear that the definition decided upon for each market will have much to do with the concentration ratio derived. A broad market definition would ordinarily tend to reduce the computed concentration ratio, whereas a narrow market definition would usually have the opposite effect. The concentration ratios published by the Bureau of the Census are based upon market definitions that have been developed as a part of the Standard Industrial Classification (SIC) system. The SIC system utilizes numeric digits to label markets. (In the SIC system, markets are referred to as industries.) The economic activities of the nation are then classified in terms of the numeric digits. Thus, as Table 8.1 indicates, SIC Code 36 is termed a two-digit major industry group and represents electrical equipment and supplies. A three-digit industry represents a smaller industry group; hence, SIC Code 361 represents electrical and distributing equipment. In the same

[5]The reader is referred to Eugene M. Singer, *Antitrust Economics* (Englewood Cliffs, N.J.: Prentice-Hall, Inc., 1968), Chaps. 13 and 14, for a comprehensive and up-to-date discussion of concentration indexes.

[6]U.S. Department of Commerce, Bureau of the Census, *1967 Census of Manufactures: Concentration Ratios in Manufacturing*, Part I, MC67 (S)-2.1 (Washington, D.C.: U.S. Government Printing Office, 1970).

TABLE 8.1

The Standard Industrial Classification System: An Example

SIC Code	Name
36	Electrical equipment and supplies
361	Electrical and distributing equipment
3611	Electrical measuring instruments
36111	Electrical integrating instruments

fashion, SIC Code 3611 is still more refined and represents electrical measuring instruments. It is apparent that each additional numeric digit confers more specialized detail. The most recent SIC reclassification (undertaken in 1967) identified 73 two-digit industries, 372 three-digit industries, and 908 four-digit industries.[7] Further breakdowns of markets to five-, six-, and seven-digit levels of detail are available; however, the four-digit level of detail has come to be regarded by most economists as usually most representative of the economic concept of a market as it was developed in Chapter 2.

The SIC system was not constructed for the use of students of industrial organization. Certain of the markets identified by the system do not correspond to economic markets. An example in point is SIC Code 3711, motor vehicles and motor vehicle equipment. SIC Code 3711 includes the manufacture of not only passenger cars, but also semitrailer trucks and buses. Several distinct markets are included under this broad rubric. Thus, the resulting concentration ratios reported for SIC Code 3711 and similar markets may be inaccurate and misleading in a market sense.

Because concentration ratios are so often used in the analysis of industrial markets, it is important to be aware of their potential weaknesses. The most glaring possible weaknesses are the following:

1. The SIC system, upon which the concentration ratios are based, may not accurately reflect economic markets (as discussed above).

2. Concentration ratios do not reflect the presence or absence of potential entry of competitors.

3. Concentration ratios are based upon national figures and therefore ignore regional market power and regional concentration.[8]

4. Concentration ratios ignore the role of imports in domestic markets.

5. Concentration ratios ignore the export sales of domestic producers.

6. Concentration ratios do not describe the entire number and size distribution of firms, only a slice of it.

---

[7]Executive Office of the President, Bureau of the Budget, *Standard Industrial Classification Manual, 1967* (Washington, D.C.: U.S. Government Printing Office, 1967).

[8]The Bureau of the Census now publishes regional concentration ratios that can be used to reflect regional or local market power. However, a given regional concentration ratio imparts no information about other regions or about national market concentration.

7. Concentration ratios give no information about the relative size and position of the group of firms included in a ratio.

8. Concentration ratios fail to reflect "turnover" (changes in the position and ranking of given firms).

9. Concentration ratios are structural indicators that describe a given slice of the number and size distribution of firms in a given market; they do not necessarily imply certain types of conduct by firms in that market.

At this point, one might well ask why anyone bothers to use concentration ratios if they are potentially subject to so many failings. First, economic theory does predict that the exercise of monopoly power is more likely to occur in a highly concentrated market. Rosenbluth has stated, "Economic theory suggests that concentration as defined here is an important determinant of market behavior and market results. *Ceteris paribus,* monopolistic practices are more likely where a small number of the leading firms account for the bulk of any industry's output than where even the largest firms are of relatively small importance."[9]

Second, concentration ratios are a precise and easily understood indicator of a given slice of a market. When the four-firm concentration ratio for the electron-tubes industry (SIC Code 3673) is 94, this statistic means that the four largest firms account for 94 percent of the total value of shipments of electron tubes and that one of those four firms accounts for at least 23 to 24 percent of the total value of shipments in the market. Although further statements involving statistical precision are difficult to make, it is highly probable that such a market is characterized by oligopolistic interdependence mutually recognized, and/or that a dominant firm exists.

Third, and perhaps most important, concentration ratios are readily available for manufacturing markets, and alternative data sets describing this or other aspects of market structure are not widely available. Hence, concentration ratios are the most frequently used index of concentration, as well as the most frequently used indicator of general market structure. When used with discretion, concentration ratios can be a valuable aid to the analysis of industrial organization.

Summary Indexes

The differentiating feature of a summary index of concentration is that it takes into account all the firms in a market, rather than only a portion of them. There have been many attempts to construct an ideal summary concentration index. It would be too harsh to state that these attempts have failed, but each of the summary indexes contains its own biases and failings. The two most common are the Gini Coefficient and the Herfindahl Index. The Gini Coefficient is a statistical measure based upon the Lorenz

[9]Gideon Rosenbluth, "Measures of Concentration," in *Business Concentration and Price Policy,* ed. George J. Stigler (Princeton, N.J.: Princeton University Press, 1955), p. 57.

Curve, which is a familiar graphical tool to beginning economics students who are studying the distributions of income and wealth.[10] Figure 8.1 illustrates a Lorenz Curve for a hypothetical market X. Note that the Lorenz Curve, which is bowed outward toward the southeast when any inequality in firm sizes exists in a market, relates the percent of total market value of shipments to the percent of firms in the market, cumulated from the smallest to the largest. The diagonal line OC indicates what the Lorenz Curve would look like if the market's value of shipments were distributed with precise equality among all the firms in the market. It should be observed that the Lorenz Curve measures relative concentration rather than the absolute measure provided by a concentration ratio.

The Gini Coefficient for market X may be conceptualized visually as the darkened area inside triangle OCD in Figure 8.1, divided by the remaining undarkened area of that triangle. That is, it is the area labeled A divided by the area labeled B. The Gini Coefficient assumes a value of zero when the value of shipments of the market is distributed equally among all firms,[11] and approaches an infinitely large positive number as the value of

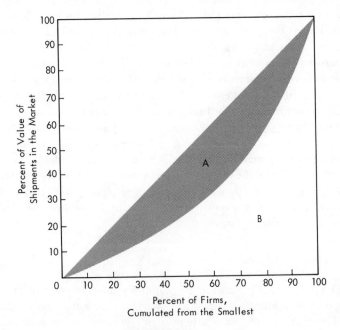

FIGURE 8.1

[10]The Gini Coefficient was originally developed by C. Gini, "Sulla Misure della Concentrazaione e della Variability die Carattere," *Atti del Reale Istituto Veneto di Scienze, Lettere e Arti*, Vol. 73 (1913–14), 1207ff.

[11]This causes problems for those who would use concentration indexes as a measure of monopoly power. Suppose a duopoly exists in which the two firms are of equal size. The Gini Coefficient for this market is zero even though it is likely that both duopolists possess substantial market power.

shipments of the market becomes more and more unequally distributed among the firms.

The primary problem associated with the Gini Coefficient is the same problem that confronts all summary concentration indexes: One needs to have accurate information about the market share of every firm in the market before one can construct a summary index. Such information is often not available, especially since the Bureau of the Census is prohibited by law from publishing any statistics that might disclose information about individual companies. Further, it is true that two entirely different Lorenz Curves can generate the same Gini Coefficient simply because they enclose the same relative areas. It is not clear what interpretation one should attach to two different Lorenz Curves that intersect and enclose different portions of the triangle, but that nevertheless have the same Gini Coefficient because the two curves enclose the same absolute area of the triangle. A Gini Coefficient, then, does not represent a unique distribution of firm sizes in a given market.

The Herfindahl Index is a measure of dispersion that can vary between zero and 1.[12] It is the sum of the squares of the relative sizes of the firms in the market, where the relative firm sizes are expressed as a percent of the total size of the market. That is,

$$\text{Herfindahl Index} = \sum_{i=1}^{N} \left(\frac{x_i}{T} \right)^2$$

where $N =$ number of firms
$x_i =$ absolute size of individual firm i
$T =$ total size of the market

Suppose that in a given market, the total value of shipments is 100, and three firms exist that have absolute sizes of 50, 30, and 20. The Herfindahl Index for this market is the sum of $(.5)^2$ plus $(.3)^2$ plus $(.2)^2$, or .38. The reader should be able to demonstrate that when all firms in a market are of equal size, the Herfindahl Index will be equal to the ratio $(1/N)$. When a large number of firms of equal size exist, the Herfindahl Index approaches a value of zero; when only one firm exists, it assumes a value of one.

The Herfindahl Index has a background in oligopoly theory, in that it measures changes in market shares.[13] Because it takes account of all firms in the market, and because it has some similarity to measures of monopoly power, it has attained some popularity of reputation, although not of use.

---

[12]The Herfindahl Index was originally suggested by O.C. Herfindahl, "Concentration in the Steel Industry" (Ph.D. dissertation, Columbia University, 1950). That this index is a measure of dispersion is apparent from the fact that the Herfindahl Index has been shown to be equal to $(V^2 + 1)/N$, where V is the coefficient of variation, and N is the number of firms in the market.

[13]See George J. Stigler, "The Measurement of Concentration," in *The Organization of Industry* (Homewood, Ill.: Richard D. Irwin, Inc., 1968), pp. 29–38.

The basic difficulty with the Herfindahl Index is, once again, the lack of data necessary to construct it.[14]

CONCENTRATION: PATTERNS AND TRENDS

How concentrated is the American economy? The answer to this question depends upon whether one wishes to examine the economy as a whole or to look only at specific SIC industries. "Overall" indexes of concentration measure concentration in the entire economy, without reference to SIC industry boundaries, whereas "intraindustry" indexes measure concentration inside given SIC industries. Both overall and intraindustry measures are partial rather than summary, and therefore do not take into account the entire size distribution of firms.

Overall Concentration

Considerable evidence now available points to a slight increase in overall concentration for the period 1909–47.[15] Since 1947, overall concentration has apparently increased sharply. The share of the 100 largest firms in the value added generated by manufacturing industries increased from 23 percent in 1947 to 33 percent in 1967.[16] Table 8.2 reveals the general upward trend in overall concentration for manufacturing corporations for the period 1925–68.

The rapid increase in overall concentration in the American economy since World War II has not gone without critical notice. Although some of the discussion surrounding this development has been alarmist and polemical, other discussion has been reasoned and cogent in pointing out the implications of such structural change in the economy. Willard Mueller, former Chief Economist of the Bureau of Economics of the Federal Trade Commission, has attributed most of the increase in overall concentration to corporate mergers.[17] Mueller has pointed out that in the year 1968 alone, the 200 largest manufacturing firms acquired $10 billion worth of assets via

[14]However, Nelson has constructed a fairly comprehensive, although now outdated, series of Herfindahl Indexes for much of American industry. See Ralph L. Nelson, *Concentration in the Manufacturing Industries of the United States* (New Haven, Conn.: Yale University Press, 1963).

[15]See, for example, A.D.H. Kaplan, *Big Enterprise in a Competitive System* (Washington, D.C.: The Brookings Institution, 1954); E.S. Mason, *Economic Concentration and the Monopoly Problem* (Cambridge, Mass.: Harvard University Press, 1957); M.A. Adelman, "The Measurement of Industrial Concentration," (November 1951), pp. 269–96; Norman R. Collins and Lee E. Preston, "The Size Structure of the Largest Industrial Firms, 1909–1958," *American Economic Review*, 51 (December 1961), 986–1003; and David Mermelstein, "Large Industrial Corporations and Asset Shares," *American Economic Review*, 59 (September 1969), 531–41.

[16]*1967 Census of Manufactures: Concentration Ratios in Manufacturing*, Part I, p. 5.

[17]Willard F. Mueller, "The Rising Economic Concentration in America: Reciprocity, Conglomeration and the New American 'Zaibatsu' System, Parts I and II," *Antitrust Law and Economics Review*, 4 (Spring 1971), 15–50, and 4 (Summer 1971), 91–104.

TABLE 8.2

Share of Manufacturing Assets Held by the 200 Largest Corporations, 1925–41 and 1947–68

Year	Shares Held by 100 Largest[a]		Shares Held by 200 Largest[a]	
	Total Assets	Corporate Assets	Total Assets	Corporate Assets
1925	34.5	36.1		
1927	34.4	36.0		
1929	38.2	39.7	45.8	47.7
1931	41.7	43.4	49.0	50.9
1933	42.5	44.2	49.5	51.4
1935	40.8	42.3	47.7	49.6
1937	42.1	43.7	49.1	50.9
1939	41.9	43.5	48.7	50.5
1941[b]	38.2	39.6	45.1	46.7
1947	37.4	39.3	45.0	47.2
1948	38.6	40.3	46.3	48.3
1949	39.5	41.1	47.1	49.0
1950	38.4	39.7	46.1	47.7
1951	38.1	39.4	46.1	47.7
1952	39.3	40.6	47.7	49.2
1953	40.3	41.7	48.7	50.4
1954	41.9	43.3	50.4	52.2
1955	43.0	44.3	51.6	53.1
1956	43.9	44.8	52.8	53.9
1957	45.2	46.3	54.3	55.6
1958	46.0	47.1	55.2	56.5
1959	45.4	46.3	54.8	56.0
1960	45.5	46.4	55.2	56.3
1961	45.8	46.6	55.4	56.3
1962	45.5	46.3	55.1	56.1
1963	45.7	46.5	55.5	56.4
1964	45.8	46.5	55.8	56.6
1965	45.9	46.5	55.9	56.7
1966	45.8	46.4	56.1	56.7
1967	47.6	48.1	58.7	59.4
1968	48.7	49.1	60.2	60.8

[a]Ranked according to asset size in each year.
[b]Data are not available for the years between 1941 and 1947 because some large corporations did not publish balance sheets for reasons of wartime security.
Source: *Bureau of Economics, Federal Trade Commission,* Economic Report on Corporate Mergers (*Washington, D.C.: U.S. Government Printing Office, 1969*), p. 173.

the merger route, and that this shift in assets represented about two thirds of the total shift in assets owing to merger. Further, the tendency has been for mergers affecting the 200 largest manufacturing firms to take place in markets that are already highly concentrated. Highly concentrated markets, as we shall soon see, typically afford those firms fortunate enough to operate in them higher profit rates on invested capital and higher price–cost margins.

Overall-concentration data do not permit the inference that competition is lacking in a given market. However, overall-concentration indexes may reflect (as Edwards has suggested) the brute economic strength and market power that results from large size.[18] Further, it has been argued that size-augmenting mergers that result in diversification across SIC industry lines will reduce risk for the new firm that emerges. Hence, smaller economic decision units are said to be at a disadvantage.[19] The evidence on this issue, however, is quite mixed.

Intraindustry Concentration

Most studies of intraindustry concentration have resulted in the conclusion that such concentration remained constant from 1900 to 1958.[20] Since 1958, it may have edged upward, particularly in consumer-goods-oriented industries.[21] The usual basis for such conclusions has been average concentration ratios, typically four-firm in nature, that have been weighted by some indicator of the relative sizes of the SIC industries involved in the sample.

Table 8.3 reveals that the average degree of concentration rose slightly, from 37.2 to 37.9, during the period 1958–66 in the manufacturing sector. The table also discloses that the share of total manufacturing value added accounted for by SIC industries with four-firm concentration ratios of 40 and higher edged upward from 38.0 to 39.7. Table 8.3 is highly aggregative in nature, however, and may hide particularly low or high levels of concentration in given areas of manufacturing. Table 8.4 disaggregates the manufacturing sector into 20 different SIC two-digit major areas and reports an average concentration ratio (four-firm) for the four-digit SIC industries within each two-digit area. A perusal of Table 8.4 reveals that while the average concentration ratio is found to be 39 in the year 1967, SIC Codes 23 (apparel and related products), 24 (lumber and wood products), and 25 (furniture and fixtures) had average concentration ratios of less than 20. On the other hand, SIC Code 21 (tobacco manufactures) had an average concentration ratio of 84.

Four-firm concentration ratios are not a precise indicator of market power. Therefore, the absolute level of concentration may be a datum that potentially hides more information than it reveals. Changes in the absolute

[18]Corwin D. Edwards, "Conglomerate Bigness as a Source of Power," in *Business Concentration and Price Policy*, ed. George J. Stigler (Princeton, N.J.: Princeton University Press, 1955), pp. 331–59.

[19]Mermelstein, "Large Industrial Corporations."

[20]See M.A. Adelman, "The Measurement of Industrial Concentration," (November, 1951) ; Solomon Fabricant, "Is Monopoly Increasing?" *Journal of Economic History*, 13 (Winter 1953), 89–94 ; G. Warren Nutter, "Is Competition Decreasing in Our Economy?" *Journal of Farm Economics*, 36 (December 1954), 751–59; and William G. Shepherd, "Trends of Concentration in American Manufacturing Industries, 1947–1958," *Review of Economics and Statistics*, 46 (May 1964), 200–212.

[21]Lee E. Preston, *The Industry and Enterprise Structure of the U.S. Economy* (Morristown, N.J.: General Learning Press, 1971).

TABLE 8.3

Percentage Shares of Total U.S. Manufacturing Value Added in 1967 that Occurred in Industries of Various Degrees of Concentration

Degree of Concentration in the 4 Largest Firms	Share of Value Added, According to:	
	Census Concentration Ratios, 1958	*Census Concentration Ratios, 1967*
90–100	2.1	4.8
80–89	2.0	2.7
70–79	9.4	7.0
60–69	4.1	4.2
50–59	13.1	7.7
40–49	7.3	13.3
30–39	13.0	13.2
20–29	22.5	24.7
10–19	19.0	16.9
0–9	7.5	5.6
70 and higher	13.5	14.5
40 and higher	38.0	39.7
"Average" degree of concentration	37.2	37.9

Source: *Calculated from data in U.S. Senate Subcommittee on Antitrust and Monopoly,* Concentration Ratios in Manufacturing Industry, 1963, Parts I and II *(Washington, D.C.: U.S. Government Printing Office, 1966); and U.S. Bureau of the Census,* 1967 Census of Manufactures, Special Report: Concentration Ratios in Manufacturing, Part 3 *(Washington, D.C.: U.S. Government Printing Office, 1971).*

level of concentration, however, are quite meaningful, since they indicate basic structural change in particular industries. Table 8.5 records changes in the level of four-firm concentration in 232 comparable industries for the period 1958–66. The reported four-firm concentration ratio increased in 134 (57.8 percent) of those industries and decreased in only 79 (34.1 percent). This confirms the results reported in Table 8.3, where we saw that intraindustry concentration rose during this period.

Certain markets, particularly those that are oligopolistic in nature, are of crucial importance to the functioning of the economy. Markets such as steel, motor vehicles, and petroleum refining have literally thousands of input and output connections with the remainder of the economy. Changes in market structure in such oligopolistic markets may affect competition and performance in those markets and can have significant effects upon other producing sectors of the economy, in addition to affecting consumer welfare. Therefore, the trend of concentration in oligopolistic industries is a matter of considerable importance in terms of prices, costs, and competitive effects throughout the economy.

An oligopolistic market is one in which there exist a few large sellers who jointly recognize the interdependence of their actions. Shepherd has suggested, as a first step in identifying such markets, that any four-digit SIC

TABLE 8.4

Distribution of Four-Firm Concentration Ratios by Major Industry Group for Manufacturing Industries, 1967

SIC CODE	Industry Group	Total		80 to 100		60 to 79		40 to 59		20 to 39		Less than 20		Weighted Average
		No. Industries	Value Added	No. Industries	Value Added	No. Industries	Value Added	No. Industries	Value Added	No. Industries	Value Added	No. Industries	Value Added	
20	Food and Kindred Products	43	25,184	3	859	9	3,174	7	2,440	20	15,589	4	3,122	37
21	Tobacco Manufactures	4	2,030	1	1,639	1	195	2	196	—	—	—	—	84
22	Textile Mill Products	29	8,139	1	91	3	247	6	1,642	15	4,344	4	1,815	30
23	Apparel and Related Products	33	9,900	—	—	—	—	3	502	11	2,604	19	6,884	17
24	Lumber and Wood Products	13	4,968	—	—	—	—	2	44	4	1,074	7	3,850	15
25	Furniture and Fixtures	12	4,164	—	—	—	—	1	122	6	1,377	5	2,665	18
26	Paper and Allied Products	17	9,751	—	—	2	637	5	1,931	8	5,893	2	1,290	34
27	Printing and Publishing	14	12,492	—	—	1	372	1	550	7	4,641	5	6,929	21
28	Chemicals and Allied Products	26	23,444	2	1,757	8	3,667	5	6,576	11	11,444	—	—	46
29	Petroleum and Coal Products	5	5,427	—	—	1	24	1	200	2	4,966	1	237	30
30	Rubber and Plastic Products n.e.c.	5	6,797	1	23	2	2,067	—	—	—	—	2	4,707	29
31	Leather and Leather Products	10	2,623	—	—	1	31	—	—	5	1,946	4	646	26
32	Stone, Clay, and Glass Products	27	8,320	2	647	6	1,947	5	1,137	9	2,039	5	2,550	41
33	Primary Metal Industries	23	19,921	1	811	6	1,805	3	9,557	11	7,152	2	596	45
34	Fabricated Metal Products	27	17,963	—	—	3	1,455	2	237	9	7,443	13	8,828	24
35	Machinery, Except Electrical	39	27,817	3	1,554	2	2,268	14	8,143	12	8,265	8	7,587	37

VALUE-ADDED CONCENTRATION RATIO FOR FOUR LARGEST COMPANIES

TABLE 8.4 (Cont.)

VALUE-ADDED CONCENTRATION RATIO FOR FOUR LARGEST COMPANIES

SIC CODE	Industry Group	Total No. Industries	Value Added	80 to 100 No. Industries	Value Added	60 to 79 No. Industries	Value Added	40 to 59 No. Industries	Value Added	20 to 39 No. Industries	Value Added	Less than 20 No. Industries	Value Added	Weighted Average
36	Electrical Machinery	33	24,392	9	3,732	6	2,918	9	6,600	8	8,530	1	2,612	47
37	Transportation Equipment	14	28,167	2	7,698	1	5,447	6	10,910	2	3,288	3	824	61
38	Instruments and Related Products	11	6,414	—	—	2	2,511	6	2,017	3	1,886	—	—	52
39	Miscellaneous Manufacturing	20	3,882	1	133	—	—	5	673	10	1,865	4	1,211	29
	Total, All Industries	405	251,885	26	18,944	54	28,765	83	53,477	153	94,346	89	56,353	39

Note: SIC industries 3332 and 3492 were not included in the computations because of insufficient data. Also, value-added data is stated in 000's.

Source: *U.S. Bureau of the Census, 1967 Census of Manufactures, Special Report: Concentration Ratios in Manufacturing, Part 3 (Washington, D.C.: U.S. Government Printing Office, 1971), Table 8.*

TABLE 8.5

Changes in Four-Firm Concentration, 232 Comparable Four-Digit SIC Industries, 1958–1966

Change in Four-Firm Concentration Ratio	Number of Industries	Percent of Industries	Percent Value of Shipments Accounted for by These Industries
Increase	134	57.8	46.7
Decrease	79	34.1	36.4
No Change	15	6.4	16.2
No Data	4	1.7	.7
Totals	232	100.0	100.0

Source: *U.S. Department of Commerce, Bureau of the Census,* Annual Survey of Manufactures, 1966 (*Washington, D.C.: U.S. Government Printing Office, 1969*), Chap. 9.

industry whose four-firm concentration ratio is 75 or greater might be usefully classified as being oligopolistic in nature.[22] Shepherd recognizes, of course, that this narrow definition of oligopoly is entirely structural in nature and does not depend upon behavior. No particular four-firm concentration ratio can be regarded as an absolute guide to oligopoly without reference to the behavior of the firms in that market. Nevertheless, such a classification is a useful starting point.

Table 8.6 indicates that 25 SIC manufacturing industries were characterized by a four-firm concentration ratio of 75 or greater in the year 1947. By 1967, the four-firm concentration ratio had increased in 8 of those 25 industries and had decreased in 14. (For 3 industries, data were available in 1947, but not in 1967.) The average change in concentration (unweighted by size) over the time period in question for the 22 industries was −5.4 percent.

The previous analysis is potentially defective in that many of the

TABLE 8.6

Changes in Concentration in 25 Comparable SIC Manufacturing Industries with Four-Firm Concentration ratios of 75 or Greater, 1947–1967

Total Number of Industries	25
Industries in Which Concentration Increased	8
Industries in Which Concentration Decreased	14
Industries in Which Data Are Not Complete	3
Average Percent Change in Concentration	−5.4%

Source: *U.S. Department of Commerce, Bureau of the Census,* 1967 Census of Manufactures: Concentration Ratios in Manufacturing, Part I, *MC67(S)-2.1* (*Washington, D.C.: U.S. Government Printing Office, 1970*).

[22]Shepherd, "Trends of Concentration."

SIC industries that are commonly regarded as being oligopolistic in nature are not included in the sample of industries found in Table 8.6. The requirement of a four-firm concentration ratio of 75 or higher in 1947 eliminates such industries as computers and related machinery, motor vehicles, steel mills, and primary zinc. Shepherd has once again come to the rescue by constructing a list of 35 "consensus" oligopolies for the year 1947.[23] These were suggested by either Stigler or Bain.[24]

Table 8.7 details the changes in four-firm concentration ratios that occurred in 18 of the 35 consensus oligopolies suggested by Stigler and Bain. Seventeen industries in the Stigler–Bain sample could not be included in Table 8.7; because of changes in their SIC definitions during the period 1947–67, the 1947 observation of the industry was not comparable to the 1967 version. In 8 of the 18 industries, concentration increased; in the remaining 10, it decreased. The average change in concentration (unweighted by size) over the time period was +1.0 percent.

TABLE 8.7

Changes in Concentration in 35 Consensus Oligopolies, 1947–1967

Total Number of Industries	35
Industries in Which Concentration Increased	8
Industries in Which Concentration Decreased	10
Industries in Which Data Are Not Comparable	17
Average Percent Change in Concentration	+1.0%

Source: *U.S. Department of Commerce, Bureau of the Census,* 1967 Census of Manufactures: Concentration Ratios in Manufacturing, Part I, *MC67(S)-2.1 (Washington, D.C.: U.S. Government Printing Office, 1970).*

Taken together, Tables 8.6 and 8.7 do not reveal any strong or important trend toward increased intraindustry concentration in oligopolistic markets. Indeed, one might argue that the data could be marshalled to support the opposite conclusion—namely, that concentration inside oligopolistic industries may have decreased slightly since World War II.

How, then, can we rationalize rapidly increasing overall concentration with our newest findings, from Tables 8.5 through 8.7, that intraindustry concentration has not increased rapidly and may actually have remained constant? Three particular reasons for this apparent contradiction have appeal. First, the frequency of conglomerate mergers across conventional SIC industry lines has increased significantly in recent years. The threat of antitrust action that hovers over mergers and growth of an intraindustry variety, and the possibility of increased growth, may have spurred firms to

[23]*Ibid.*

[24]George J. Stigler, "The Theory of Oligopoly," in *The Theory of Price,* rev. ed. (New York: The Macmillan Company, 1952), pp. 222–43; Stigler, "The Kinky Oligopoly Demand Curve and Rigid Prices," *Journal of Political Economy,* 55 (October 1947), 432–49; and Joe S. Bain, *Industrial Organization* (New York: John Wiley & Sons, Inc., 1958), pp. 410–39.

diversify across SIC industry lines. The result has been that the growth of large firms (which is captured by an overall-concentration index) has been dissipated among many SIC industries.

Second, one can argue strongly that SIC four-firm concentration ratios are biased downward, because of their failure to consider many important factors such as regional market power. Shepherd has attempted to adjust the published four-firm concentration ratios to take account of the numerous objections that have been levied against them.[25] Although he has not made explicit precisely how he made the adjustments, he has reported adjusted concentration ratios for every SIC four-digit industry for the year 1966. After adjustment, the average four-firm concentration ratio for 1966 rose from 39.0 (as reported in Table 8.3) to 60.3.[26] This is a highly significant difference. Even though it has not been firmly demonstrated, it is possible that adjusted intraindustry indexes of concentration would reveal important increases in intraindustry concentration that the unadjusted four-firm concentration ratios fail to reveal. If that were the case, then the true state of the world would be that both overall and intraindustry concentration are increasing.

Third, the largest firms are frequently in the most rapidly growing industries, and this fact by itself could account for the observed growth in the share of the largest firms.

NONMANUFACTURING CONCENTRATION: A BRIEF LOOK

All the concentration data we have reviewed thus far have described the manufacturing sector of the economy. This emphasis is not misplaced; about one third of the national income generated by the economy originates in the manufacturing sector.[27] Further, the purview of industrial organization has traditionally not included such other sectors of the economy as agriculture, finance, insurance, real estate, government, or most heavily regulated industries. Hence, manufacturing is the dominant sector insofar as the study of industrial organization is concerned. However, several other sectors of the economy that have not yet been considered are within the purview of industrial organization. Construction, services, and wholesale and retail trade are these sectors, and we will now briefly turn our attention to them.

The construction and services sectors of the economy account for about 15 percent of the national income.[28] These sectors are characterized by

[25]Shepherd, *Market Power and Economic Welfare,* especially Appendix Table 8, pp. 263–67.
[26]Shepherd, p. 106.
[27]*Survey of Current Business,* 51, No. 2 (February 1971), 10, Table 7.
[28]*Ibid.*

many small firms and low levels of market concentration, even in consideration of the regional and very local nature of the markets. A glance back at Table 7.3 (page 126) is instructive. In 1968, 65.0 percent of all construction firms possessed assets of $100,000 or less. The comparable statistic for the services sector was 74.9 percent. Almost 125,000 construction firms and about 227,000 firms providing services existed in 1968. The construction and the services sectors are apt examples of Chamberlinian monopolistic competition in the large-numbers case.

Much the same story characterizes the wholesale- and retail-trade sectors of the economy. Levels of concentration are low and the number of firms is large (476,000 in 1968). Table 7.3 reveals that 54.6 percent of all wholesale- and retail-trade firms possessed $100,000 or less of assets in 1968.

The wholesale- and retail-trade sector is not without its large firms, however. Retail chains such as J.C. Penney, Holiday Inn, Kentucky Fried Chicken, and Sears, Roebuck are large organizations in their own right. In 1970, Sears, Roebuck enjoyed sales of over $9 *billion*.[29] The franchising system, whereby a franchisor such as Holiday Inns sells to a franchisee the right (and perhaps the obligation) to use its name and methods, has grown by leaps and bounds and may now constitute as much as one quarter of all retail sales.[30]

CONCENTRATION AND THE PERFORMANCE OF THE FIRM

The static theories of competition and monopoly predict, *ceteris paribus,* that firms that have substantial monopoly power will tend to charge higher prices, produce and sell less output, earn higher rates of profit, and often successfully use their entrenched positions to resist the competitive thrusts and pressures emanating from other firms. Further, it has been argued that monopolists may be less progressive in the area of research and development.

On the presumption that concentration ratios are an appropriate proxy for monopoly power and/or restriction of competition, many researchers have attempted to verify the propositions above by studying the effects of concentration upon various aspects of performance. We will now examine the evidence that has been accumulated, as it pertains to (1) price–cost margins, (2) firm and market growth, (3) profit rates, (4) turnover, and (5) technological change.

---

[29]"The Fortune Directory," *Fortune,* 83 (May 1971), 196–97.
[30]Preston, *The Industry and Enterprise Structure of the U.S. Economy,* p. 16.

Concentration and Price–Cost Margins

Collins and Preston, in a series of three studies, have attempted to relate the average price–cost margin in a market to various indicators of market structure such as intraindustry concentration.[31] They utilized cross-sectional observations of SIC four-digit industries for the years 1958 and 1963 and found that average industry price–cost margins were strongly related to concentration (as measured by the four-firm concentration ratio), even when differences in capital intensity and geographic dispersion of the markets were taken into account.

It is apparently true that price–cost margins are higher in concentrated than in unconcentrated industries. The possibility exists, nevertheless, that concentration may not really be the causative influence at work; rather, it may be acting as a surrogate for other factors, which are truly causal in nature. Koch and Fenili, for example, found that concentration was no longer a significant predictor of price–cost margins when other relevant indicators of market structure, such as the rate of technological change and product differentiation, were also considered.[32]

Collins and Preston have intimated that price–cost margins may be regarded as profit rates. This is true, but only in a limited context. A price–cost margin is, as Benishay pointed out, a profit rate on the firm's sales, not on the firm's invested capital.[33] Inasmuch as economists and students of industrial organization are interested in the allocation of resources and the efficiency of use of those resources, the rate of profit on the firm's sales is irrelevant, and the rate of profit on invested capital is the rate of return that indicates misallocation of resources and inefficiency. Hence, although price–cost margins may indicate a firm's ability to raise its price over its costs of production, they do not provide direct evidence about resource misallocation and the amount of economic rents earned by firms with market power.[34]

[31] Norman R. Collins and Lee E. Preston, *Concentration and Price–Cost Margins in Manufacturing Industries* (Berkeley, Calif.: University of California Press, 1970); Collins and Preston, "Concentration and Price–Cost Margins in Food Manufacturing Industries," *Journal of Industrial Economics*, 14 (July 1966), 226–42; and Collins and Preston, Price–Cost Margins and Industry Structure," *Review of Economics and Statistics*, 51 (August 1969), 271–86.

[32] James V. Koch and Robert N. Fenili, "The Influence of Industry Market Structure upon Industry Price–Cost Margins," *Rivista Internazionale di Scienze Economiche e Commerciali*, 18 (November 1971), 1037–45.

[33] Haskel Benishay, "Concentration and Price–Cost Margins: Comment," *Journal of Industrial Economics*, 16 (November 1967), 73–74.

[34] The use of price–cost margins is also subject to attack on another count. Sherman and Tollison have pointed out that the price–cost margin, which is defined as $(P - MC)/P$, is equal to $(1/|\eta|)$, where $|\eta|$ is the absolute value of price elasticity of demand. [Roger Sherman and Robert Tollison, "Advertising and Profitability," *Review of Economics and Statistics*, 53 (November 1971), 397–407.] But Dorfman and Steiner have demonstrated that under reasonable conditions, the firm will be in equilibrium when the value of the marginal product of its advertising is equal to the absolute value of price elasticity of demand. [Robert Dorfman and Peter Steiner, "Optimal Advertising and Optimal Quality," *American Economic Review*, 44 (December 1954), 826–36.] This means that the size of the price–cost margin is related to the amount of advertising carried out. Hence, attempts to predict price–cost margins by means of indicators of market structure such as advertising intensity or price elasticity of demand may be circular and uninformative. Although Collins and Preston are not guilty of including such variables in their studies, they suggest that

Concentration and Growth

The static theory of the firm predicts that firms with monopoly power will engage in output restriction. The same theory does not, however, yield an unambiguous prediction about the effects of monopoly power upon the growth of an entire market. Several different predictions with respect to market growth are plausible when monopoly power exists. The firm with monopoly power must evaluate the various time streams of profit that are associated with alternative courses of action and, *ceteris paribus*, select the time stream of profits that has the highest expected present value. Depending upon the circumstances, the firm may choose to restrict or to stimulate market output. It may feel that the expected present value of the profit stream facing it is greatest when it pursues output-restricting activities. Such behavior might involve a high-price policy, which attracts eventual entry by other firms (and lower profits in the long run for the firm in question), but which is nevertheless optimal because it involves large short-run profits that are not discounted heavily, owing to their proximate nature in time.

Taking another view, the firm may optimize by stimulating industry growth, even though the firm in question may, as a result, accept a declining share of a growing industry.[35] A moderate pricing policy, designed both to discourage potential entry and to take advantage of any price elasticity of demand that might exist, is a probable result. Such a decision reflects the judgment that even though the monopoly power of the firm may be dissipated by this policy, the expected present value of the time stream of profits is still maximized.

Still another scenario exists in which the firm with market power chooses to stimulate industry output. In this version, the firm with market power may consistently anticipate future demand and may build plants that, creating excess productive capacity, will act to discourage entry and will preserve the firm's market power.

It is apparent that the static theory of the firm cannot provide a definite prediction about the effects of market power upon market growth. Unlike the question of the effects of market power upon the growth of a single firm, that of the effects of market power upon the growth of the entire market is primarily empirical, not theoretical, in nature.

We have already surveyed the evidence relating firm size to firm growth rates. Unfortunately, none of these studies specifically considered the role of concentration and other market-structure variables in the determina-

they should be included. Further, other studies, such as that performed by Koch and Fenili ("The Influence of Industry Market Structure"), have explicitly included such variables. They find, not surprisingly, that price–cost margins are strongly related to advertising expenditures. Therefore, price–cost-margin studies are incomplete when they omit relevant aspects of market structure, but are subject to criticism on the grounds of circularity of reasoning when variables such as advertising expenditures are included. The effects of concentration upon price–cost margins are, of course, difficult to ascertain in such a situation.

[35]This is the "open oligopoly" model suggested by George J. Stigler in *The Theory of Price*, Rev. Ed. (New York: Macmillan and Company, 1952), pp. 231–34.

tion of firm growth rates. Several studies have attacked the question of the effects of concentration upon *market* growth. The lessons that should be drawn from these studies do not leap out at the reader.

Nelson, Shepherd, Kamerschen, and Marcus have found an inverse relationship between initial market concentration and subsequent market growth.[36] A study by Phillips and other work by Hymer and Pashigian have suggested quite the opposite.[37] As in most issues of this type, the researchers were neither using the same sample of industries nor examining the same time period. Further, the units of measurement that were utilized to determine market size were frequently different among studies. Although it is almost an article of faith among certain economists that high levels of concentration retard growth, the available evidence is far from conclusive. The verdict remains open.[38] One of the major reasons that indicators of market structure such as intraindustry concentration have not been successfully tied to market growth is that it has proved to be almost impossible to sort out the effects of economy-wide and sector-wide growth upon the growth of a particular market. Additionally, defense purchases and the susceptibility of certain industries to cyclical business influences have also handicapped attempts to connect market structure to growth.[39]

Concentration and Profits

Studies connecting high levels of intraindustry concentration to high profit rates have become legion over the past few decades. Since the groundbreaking study by Bain,[40] at least 25 other studies have appeared, along with several lengthy critiques of the entire literature in the area.[41]

[36]Ralph L. Nelson, "Market Growth, Company Diversification and Product Concentration, 1947–1954," *Journal of the American Statistical Association,* 55 (December 1960), 640–49; Shepherd, "Trends of Concentration," *op. cit.*; David R. Kamerschen, "Market Growth and Industry Concentration," *Journal of the American Statistical Association,* 63 (March 1968), 228–41; and Matityahu Marcus, "Advertising and Changes in Concentration," *Southern Economic Journal,* 36 (October 1969), 117–21.

[37]Almarin Phillips, "Concentration, Scale and Technological Change in Selected Manufacturing Industries, 1899–1939," *Journal of Industrial Economics,* 4 (June 1956), 179–93; and Stephen Hymer and Peter Pashigian, "Turnover of Firms as a Measure of Market Behavior," *Review of Economics and Statistics,* 44 (February 1962), 82–87.

[38]An additional type of evidence not cited in the text above can be mustered in support of the output-restriction hypothesis. In the fashion of Chapter 4, one can attempt to measure the deadweight loss due to monopoly. The presumption is that in markets characterized by monopoly power, prices will be higher and quantity produced and sold lower. If the inflated price were reduced to competitive levels, more output would be sold. While the deadweight loss in consumer's surplus that results because of monopoly power is a dollar figure, it can also be used to determine exactly how much output restriction has occurred. The precise answer, however, will depend upon factors such as the degree of price elasticity of demand assumed, as well as the shape of the long-run cost curves.

[39]A thorough discussion of the monumental difficulties involved in attempting to predict market growth on the basis of market structure, and an empirical attempt to do so, may be found in James V. Koch, "The Effects of Market Structure upon Industry Growth," *Mississippi Valley Review of Business and Economics* (Fall, 1972), pp. 1–16.

[40]Joe S. Bain, "Relation of Profit Rate to Industry Concentration: American Manufacturing, 1936–1940," *Quarterly Journal of Economics,* (August 1951), 298–325.

[41]The reader is referred to a particularly interesting and cogently written volume by John S. McGee, *In Defense of Industrial Concentration* (New York: Praeger Publishers, Inc., 1971). McGee not only summarizes and criticizes the concentration–profit-rate literature, but also offers a reasoned defense of the benefits of concentration vis-à-vis competition, technological change, and other issues.

The implicit assumption underlying most of these studies has been that the continued and long-run ability of firms in certain markets to maintain higher-than-normal rates of profit is an indication that market power exists in those markets (*ceteris paribus,* of course). The conclusion of the studies has nearly always been that high levels of intraindustry concentration are representative of a type of market structure that permits firms in those markets to obtain persistently higher rates of profit than do firms competing in less concentrated markets.[42] The most sophisticated of these studies have controlled for multiple aspects of market structure rather than attempting to explain profit rates only by means of intraindustry concentration.[43]

The studies that seek to connect concentration and profit rates are burdened by several obvious weaknesses. First, concentration ratios, as we have seen, are not precise and unambiguous pieces of data, and the purist notion that concentration and market power are synonymous is not really subscribed to by any knowledgeable observer. Second, profit rates and profit-rate analysis in general are also saddled with difficulties. The profit rates computed for use in economic studies are invariably based upon accounting concepts and data. As a result, not only do such studies tend to ignore many costs attributable to the entrepreneurial factor of production, but also, the computed profit rate can be arbitrarily affected by differing valuations placed upon the firm's invested capital by the firm itself. Most profit-rate studies have also relied upon cross-sectional data; it is extremely hazardous to make long-run inferences about behavior on the basis of a snapshot view of a group of markets, many of which might be in a disequilibrium state. Further, most profit-rate studies have used mean profit rates as basic data without correcting them for differences in risk that might exist among firms or markets. Finally, it has been noted with some glee by critical observers that the more refined the market definition used (for example, four-digit rather than two-digit SIC detail), the weaker the observed relationship between concentration and profit rates. It is not surprising, then, that McGee has charged that "profits, even if measured, are irrelevant and misleading guides to either the existence or severity of allocation losses due to 'monopoly.' "[44]

---

[42]A notable exception is George J. Stigler, *Capital and Rates of Return in Manufacturing Industries,* Chap. 3. See, however, Robert W. Kilpatrick, "Stigler on the Relationship Between Industry Profit Rates and Market Concentration," *Journal of Political Economy,* 76 (May–June 1968), 479–88. Kilpatrick argues that Stigler consistently overestimated the amount of excess withdrawals of profits by officers of small corporations in unconcentrated industries. Stigler, in *Capital and Rates of Return,* pp. 67–68, had argued that the reported difference between profit rates in concentrated and unconcentrated industries would vanish if the excess withdrawals of officers in small corporations in unconcentrated industries were taken into account. Hence, contends Kilpatrick, the observed differential between profit rates in concentrated and unconcentrated industries remains.

[43]See, in particular, William S. Comanor and Thomas A. Wilson, "Advertising, Market Structure, and Performance," *Review of Economics and Statistics,* 49 (November 1967), 423–40.

[44]McGee, *In Defense of Industrial Concentration,* p. 94. For similar views, see Yale Brozen, "The Antitrust Task Force Deconcentration Recommendation," *Journal of Law and Economics,* 13 (October 1970), 293–306; and Yale Brozen, "The Significance of Profit Data for Antitrust Policy," in J. Fred Weston and Sam Peltzman, eds., *Public Policy Toward Mergers* (Pacific Palisades, Calif.: Goodyear Publishing Co., Inc., 1969), pp. 110–27.

The true nature of the relationship between profit rates and concentration has yet to be determined. Most economists are impressed with the massive outpouring of evidence that has linked them; yet, as our discussion has revealed, the impact of this evidence has been reduced by potential or real flaws in methodology. The oft-repeated statement that additional research is needed clearly applies in this case.

Concentration and Turnover

Much significance has been attached by some economists to the relationship between concentration and turnover.[45] The most common definition of turnover stresses a change in the size ranking of firms.

Turnover is a change in the size ranking of the largest firms in a given market.

The primary rationale for devoting attention to market turnover is that it is alleged to be a dynamic indicator of the intensity of competition. It is also said to be a useful supplement to the ordinary four-firm concentration ratio. Preston has argued that "in a game of chance and skill, it is unlikely that the same players will win, and win the same share of the pot, on every deal."[46] Lack of turnover may well mean a lack of competition, and possible tacit or outright collusion between supposed competitors.

Table 8.8 can be used to illustrate the contention that turnover information is a valuable addition to the information contained in the ordinary four-firm concentration ratio. Assume that only six firms exist in the widget

TABLE 8.8

Turnover in the Widget Industry

Firm	1950 Market Share		1970 Market Share	
A	50%	(1)	5%	(5)
B	20	(2)	2	(6)
C	13	(3)	45	(1)
D	7	(4)	30	(2)
E	6	(5)	8	(3)
F	4	(6)	7	(4)

Note: The number in parentheses is the size ranking of the firm in the year in question.

[45]Among the more recent contributions are A.D.H. Kaplan and A.E. Kahn, "Big Business in a Competitive Society," *Fortune,* 47 (February 1953), 10–14; Kaplan, *Big Enterprise in a Competitive System;* Hart and Prais, "Analysis of Business Concentration"; Herbert Simon and C.P. Bonini, "The Size Distribution of Business Firms," *American Economic Review,* 48 (September 1958), 607–17; Lee E. Preston, *Economic Concentration,* testimony in hearings before the Subcommittee on Antitrust and Monopoly, Committee on the Judiciary, U.S. Senate, 88th Cong., 2d Sess. (Washington, D.C.: U.S. Government Printing Office, 1964), pp. 56–76; Seymour Friedland, "Turnover and Growth of the Largest Industrial Firms, 1906–1950," *Review of Economics and Statistics,* 39 (February 1957), 79–83; and Collins and Preston, "The Size Structure of the Largest Industrial Firms, 1909–1958."

[46]Preston, *Economic Concentration,* p. 60.

market and that their percent shares of the market are those listed in Table 8.8. Note that the four-firm concentration ratio is 90 in both 1950 and 1970. This might lead one to conclude that the widget market is a stable oligopoly, possibly characterized by collusion. The four-firm concentration ratio succeeds in hiding the fact that not only has there been a change in the size ranking of the firms, but also that there has occurred a change in the identity of the four largest firms. Proponents of turnover indexes therefore claim that this particular statistic is an important supplement to concentration ratios, because it demonstrates clearly the vitality of competition.

No single datum can successfully represent all the complexities of market structure. So also it is with turnover. An obvious difficulty associated with the concept of turnover is definitional in nature. The most common definition of turnover stresses a change in the size ranking of the largest firms. However, the concept of turnover as a change in the identity of a group of firms (in addition to the change in size ranking, which must also take place when there is a change in identity) has also been used frequently.[47] The change-in-identity criterion is more demanding and represents a greater upheaval in the structure of a market. For example, in Table 8.8, all six firms changed size rankings during the period 1950–70, but only two of the four largest firms changed identity.

Turnover indexes are subject to the criticism that they ignore the possible existence of vertical and conglomerate power.[48] Further, mergers and even the progressive monopolization of an industry by one firm might lead to high, but quite deceptive, indexes of turnover. It is also possible that rather than turnover's reflecting vigorous competition, and a possible reduction in concentration as well, very high levels of turnover and market-share instability may actually be a cause of higher market concentration in the long run. Extremely rapid technological change may induce such a change.

Hymer and Pashigian, arguing that both changes in rank and changes in identity are potentially misleading measures, have proposed in their place a measure of the stability of market shares.[49] Figure 8.2 can be used to illustrate the dissatisfaction of Hymer and Pashigian with change in rank and identity. The figure records variations in the market shares of two firms, General Motors and Ford, during the period 1922–40. Three changes in size ranking are apparent, and no changes in identity occurred during that time period. Both the rank and identity changes ignore the obvious trends in market shares that occurred during the time period and the import of these trends for both concentration and competition. Hence, Hymer–Pashigian

[47]Friedland, "Turnover and Growth"; and Collins and Preston, "Size Structure."

[48]Telling criticisms of the use of turnover as an indication of the strength of competition have been made by George J. Stigler, "The Statistics of Monopoly and Merger," *Journal of Political Economy,* 64 (February 1956), 33; Jesse W. Markham, review of *Big Enterprise in a Competitive System* by A.D.H. Kaplan, *American Economic Review,* 45 (June 1955), 448; and M.A. Adelman, "A Note on Corporate Concentration and Turnover," *American Economic Review,* 44 (June 1954), 392.

[49]Hymer and Pashigian, "Turnover of Firms."

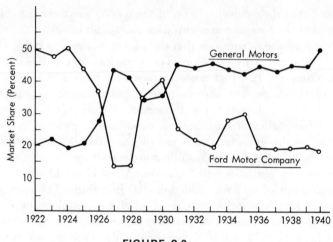

FIGURE 8.2

and others have insisted that a measure of market-share stability is of greater use than the typical measure of turnover.[50]

The basic causes of turnover or market-share instability are not controversial. Rapid changes in demand, changes in technology, low barriers to entry, and stochastic factors are the major determinants. Although high concentration may not be a cause of low turnover, Preston (among others) has asserted that "there is a weak, but apparently reliable association between higher concentration levels and the absence of change among the top four firms."[51] Conventional theories of oligopoly do predict that high levels of concentration will usually mean a higher probability of collusion, with the end result that turnover and market-share instability are reduced.

Nearly all economists who have researched the question assert that turnover has declined over time, both among all firms and inside individual markets.[52] Table 8.9 summarizes some of the results obtained by Collins and Preston concerning turnover among the 100 largest manufacturing, mining, and distribution companies from 1909 to 1958. The number of identity changes among the 100 largest companies declined noticeably during the period. More contemporary evidence, for the period 1958–66, indicates that this trend has continued.[53]

Gort has performed a definitive study that examined the stability of

[50]Michael Gort, "Analysis of Stability and Change in Market Shares," *Journal of Political Economy*, 71 (February 1963), 51–61; and Norman Schneider, "Product Differentiation, Oligopoly, and the Stability of Market Shares," *Western Economic Journal*, 5 (December 1966). 58–63.

[51]Preston, *Economic Concentration*, p. 61.

[52]Kaplan and Kahn, "Big Business"; Kaplan, *Big Enterprise*; Hart and Prais, "Analysis of Business Concentration"; Simon and Bonini, "Size Distribution"; Preston, *Economic Concentration*; Friedland, "Turnover and Growth"; Collins and Preston, "Size Structure"; and Hymer and Pashigian, "Turnover of Firms."

[53]U.S. Department of Commerce, Bureau of the Census, *Annual Survey of Manufactures, 1966* (Washington, D.C.: U.S. Government Printing Office, 1969), p. 446, Tables 2 and 3; and Stanley E. Boyle and Robert L. Sorensen, "Concentration and Mobility: Alternative Measures of Industry Structure," *Journal of Industrial Economics*, 19 (April 1971), 118–32.

TABLE 8.9

Entry and Exit of the 100 Largest Manufacturing, Mining, and Distribution Firms in the United States, 1909–1958

	Time Period				
Type of Movement	1909–1919	1919–1929	1929–1935	1935–1948	1948–1958
Exit from Top 100					
Number	40	31	16	20	16
Percent of All Assets	17.8%	19.0%	7.5%	7.8%	6.0%
Entry into Top 100					
Number	40	31	16	20	16
Percent of All Assets	31.3%	18.5%	5.6%	8.9%	8.2%

Source: *Norman R. Collins and Lee E. Preston, "The Size Structure of the Largest Industrial Firms, 1909–1958," American Economic Review, 51 (December 1961), 989, Table 1.*

market shares of the 15 largest firms in 205 SIC manufacturing industries for the period 1947–54.[54] The Gort study is unique in that it was based upon detailed market-share data for individual firms. Such information is ordinarily not available to the student of industrial organization because of disclosure rules. Gort correlated the 1947 market share of the 15 largest firms in each market with the corresponding 1954 market share of the same firms. In 152 of the 205 markets, the simple correlation coefficient was .8 or higher; in 111 markets, the correlation coefficient was .9 or higher. A correlation coefficient of about .8 between market shares implies perceptible, but minor, instability in market shares, whereas a correlation of .9 or more implies that virtually no disturbance has taken place in market shares.

One might attempt to explain the apparent decline in turnover by stating that the determinants of turnover (for example, technological change) diminished or were absent during the time period.[55] However, this explanation has little appeal, since there is no evidence that factors such as the rate of technological change have decreased. The most popular explanation of the decrease in turnover assigns the blame to rising concentration. Rising overall concentration and large firm size may confer sufficient market power on firms to immunize these firms against all but the most exceptional competitive thrusts. Another possibility is that the continued skewing of defense purchases by the federal government toward certain firms has reduced competition and lowered turnover.

Turnover indexes, particularly those reflecting changes in identity or

[54]Gort, "Analysis of Stability."

[55]Jules Backman, *Advertising and Competition* (New York: New York University Press, 1967), Chap. 3, introduces evidence purporting to demonstrate that product differentiation has increased turnover and market-share instability. However, this evidence is far from conclusive and can be interpreted to yield just the opposite conclusion. The recent study by Schneider, "Product Differentiation," is destructive of the Backman hypothesis; it resulted in the conclusion that the degree of product differentiation is unrelated to market-share stability.

stability of market shares, can be a valuable aid to the student of industrial organization in the evaluation of competition. Although low rates of turnover usually mean an absence of meaningful competition, the fact that turnover is great does not mean that competition is vigorous and healthy. Turnover succeeds in capturing only certain aspects of market structure and firm behavior and is not an all-inclusive summary index.

Concentration and Technological Change

Much of the evidence purportedly relating concentration and technological change is not that at all; rather, it is actually evidence seeking to relate firm size and technological change. Concentration and firm size may often be highly colinear with each other; however, they are not the same thing. Since Chapter 9 consists of a comprehensive treatment of the impact of technological change upon industrial organization, we shall limit our current discussion to the empirical evidence that specially relates concentration and technological change.

Productivity growth can occur for several reasons, one of which is technological change. Phillips and Stigler have attempted to ascertain if productivity growth is greater or less in highly concentrated industries.[56] Despite the fact that both economists examined the same time period (1899–1939) and used most of the same industries, they reached diametrically opposite conclusions. Phillips found that productivity increased most rapidly in highly concentrated industries, whereas Stigler's work supported the opposite inference.

One possible cause of the different results obtained by the two is the fact that Phillips utilized plant concentration ratios in his work, while Stigler relied upon firm concentration ratios. Firm concentration ratios are preferable to plant concentration ratios because many firms have multiple plants. In a market where many of the largest plants belong to the same firm, a plant concentration ratio may be quite deceptive. Unfortunately, firm concentration ratios are often less accurate than plant concentration ratios.

Two recent studies of the relationship between concentration and productivity changes have not dispelled the doubt originally created by the Phillips and Stigler studies.[57] Whether or not market power (for which concentration ratios are used as a proxy) promotes productivity growth is not clear. There is enough latitude in the empirical evidence to support nearly any preformed bias.

In a quite different type of study, Williamson relied upon a nonrandom

[56]Phillips, "Concentration, Scale and Technological Change"; and George J. Stigler, "Industrial Organization and Economic Progress," in L.D. White, ed., *The State of the Social Sciences* (Chicago: University of Chicago Press, 1960).

[57]Leonard Weiss, "Average Concentration Ratios and Industrial Performance," *Journal of Industrial Economics*, 11 (July 1963), 250–52; and Bruce T. Allen, "Concentration and Economic Progress: Note," *American Economic Review*, 59 (September 1969), 600–604.

sample of firms in the steel, petroleum, and bituminous-coal markets as a basis for a judgment about the effects of monopoly power upon technological change.[58] Williamson assumed that four-firm industry concentration ratios were an appropriate measure of monopoly power. He generated two separate estimates of the optimal concentration ratio—that is, the concentration ratio that in Williamson's models would maximize the number of innovations produced by the largest four firms in the three markets. One of Williamson's models yielded an optimal four-firm concentration ratio of 30, and the other an optimal four-firm concentration ratio of 5. Concentration ratios greater than these would decrease the number of innovations produced by the four largest firms, according to Williamson. The implication is that a general reduction in four-firm concentration ratios in these markets would have had beneficial effects upon technological change.

Scherer, in a series of studies, has produced results similar to Williamson's, bearing upon the relationship between concentration and technological change.[59] Scherer's estimate of the optimal four-firm concentration ratio that would maximize technological change was 50–55 for a large group of manufacturing markets. However, because of the difficulty he encountered in attempting to deal with intraindustry differences in the opportunities for technological advance, Scherer was not confident of his findings. The possibilities for technological change are greater in some industries (for example, electronic computing equipment) than in others (for example, meat packing).

Comanor attempted a multivariate study in which he sought to explain the employment of research and development personnel in a large number of three-digit SIC industries by means of factors such as the eight-firm concentration ratio, product differentiation, and barriers to entry.[60] The employment of research and development personnel was found to be negatively related to concentration and barriers to entry, but positively related to product differentiation. The use of research and development employment as a surrogate for the rate or importance of technological advance is, of course, subject to criticism. Also, intraindustry differences in technological opportunity could conceivably have washed out the Comanor results if they had been taken into account.

The studies cited all suffer from the common deficiencies of measuring and representing influences such as technological opportunity, and even from an inability to measure technological change itself. Further, intraindustry differences in opportunities to invent and innovate, and the checkered

[58]Oliver E. Williamson, Innovation and Market Structure," *Journal of Political Economy*, 73 (February 1965), 67–73.

[59]F.M. Scherer, "Firm Size, Market Structure, Opportunity, and the Output of Patented Inventions," *American Economic Review*, 55 (December 1965), 1097–1123; F.M. Scherer, "Market Structure and the Employment of Scientists and Engineers," *American Economic Review*, 57 (June 1967), 524–31.

[60]William S. Comanor, "Market Structure, Product Differentiation, and Industrial Research," *Quarterly Journal of Economics*, 81 (November 1967), 639–57.

availability of needed data, have cast clouds of doubt upon the studies just reviewed. It remains for Chapter 9 to give detailed consideration to the economics of technological change from a broader viewpoint than only that of concentration.

SUMMARY

Many economic sins have been laid at the doorstep of market concentration. Economic theory implies that highly concentrated markets are more likely to exhibit collusive, restrictive, oligopolistic behavior. This prediction, and the fact that the Bureau of the Census has made concentration ratios widely available, have led to a rash of empirical studies. These studies purport to demonstrate that highly concentrated markets (1) maintain higher price–cost margins, (2) restrict output, (3) earn higher-than-normal rates of profit, and (4) discourage technological change.

The sheer weight and amount of the evidence that condemns concentration should not be confused with the quality of that evidence. Much of the evidence is in dispute. There is no general agreement about how one should measure concentration, and the most frequently used index of concentration, the ubiquitous four-firm concentration ratio, has many admitted weaknesses. For example, the basic assumption that concentration might be related to market power is itself a point of contention. Further, the lack of data and occasional methodological carelessness and overstatement have rendered doubtful the conclusions of many of the studies that have found a link between concentration and undesirable market conduct and performance.

The fact that definitive answers cannot be provided with respect to the effects of concentration upon market conduct and performance should not be construed to mean that highly concentrated markets have received a clean bill of health. Nothing could be further from the truth. The impact of the mountains of evidence that have been accumulated concerning concentration is a strong indictment of concentration, and much of current public policy is based upon that indictment. As the studies examining concentration become increasingly sophisticated (because of both increased knowledge and the increased availability of data), we shall be better able to sort out and evaluate the role of concentration in market structures.

PROBLEMS

1. The Herfindahl Index of concentration can vary in value between zero and 1. However, it tends to produce values that are closer to zero than to 1. That is, the Herfindahl Index's values are skewed in the direction of zero. A typical Herfindahl Index value for a market might be .35. What difficulties might arise in connection with the use of an index of concentration that is skewed in this fashion?

2.   Appraise the following statement: "The lack of firm turnover in a market no more means that there is a lack of competition than the existence of a large amount of turnover means there is robust competition."

3.   Which is more important as a datum for use in public-policy formation—the absolute level of concentration, or the change in the level of concentration? Why?

4.   Is the growth of markets more likely to increase market concentration or to decrease it?

5.   The share of the 200 largest firms in the American economy has been growing in recent years. One hypothesized reason for this is that these firms have simply been operating in rapidly growing markets. Is this the case, or has the vitality of these firms made the markets grow rapidly?

9

Market Structure,
Technological Change,
and Competition

This chapter deals with technological change and how it affects, and is affected by, market structure. The nature and extent of the link between market structure and technological change is a perennial source of disagreement among certain groups of economists, primarily in terms of differences in opinion about the effects of market power upon technological change. We will tackle this controversy initially by indicating the nature and importance of the disagreement. Then, as is our fashion, we will survey the available empirical evidence on the issue. A detailed look at our current public policies toward technological change, especially the patent system, will serve as a natural conclusion to this chapter.

THE BASIC ISSUE AND ITS IMPORTANCE

Technological change has been occurring since the beginning of time, but only in recent decades has it garnered much attention from economists. Technological change can be visualized as a shift in the isoquants that represent the firm's production function. Isoquants are isoproduct curves that are the locus of all combinations of factor inputs generating given levels of output. This shift in isoquants is brought about by an advance in knowledge that has been implemented by the firm.

Technological change is a shift in the firm's production function caused by an advance in knowledge that has been implemented by the firm.

Students of the history of economic thought can, of course, point to early discussions of the economics of technological change in the works of Smith and Ricardo.[1] Nevertheless, the attention and research devoted to the area has increased at a geometric rate in recent years. The importance of technological change to the study of industrial organization should not be underestimated. One must understand the process of technological change in order to have a full understanding of competition in the market, for

[1] Adam Smith, *The Wealth of Nations* (Baltimore: Penguin Books, Inc., 1970); David Ricardo, *Principles of Political Economy and Taxation* (Baltimore: Penguin Books, Inc., 1971).

competition is often the direct result of technological change because of the introduction of new products or processes. The tremendous size of the new markets and the immensity of the changes in production functions that have been wrought by technological advances (for example, in electronic computers) can only be approximated. Terleckyj has estimated that in the year 1960, 10 percent of the sales accounted for by manufacturing firms were the result of new products developed between 1956 and 1960.[2] Solow has reached the astonishing conclusion that from 80 to 90 percent of the growth in productivity that has occurred in the United States has been due to technological change.[3]

The controversy surrounding technological change is not about its probable effects, however. Granted that technological change can be a source of short-run monopoly profits and that the patent system can substantially augment market power, it is generally agreed that the growing markets that result from technological change are of great assistance in the maintenance of competition and are destructive to collusive, restrictive practices. Rather, the controversy revolves primarily around the probable effects of market structure and market power upon inventive activity and the diffusion of technological advances. That is, what sorts of market structures are most conducive to the advent and diffusion of technological change; and will increased (decreased) market power stimulate technological change?

Schumpeter was perhaps the first economist to argue persuasively that technological advance requires the existence of large firms (some of which possess considerable market power) and that both the generation of innovations and rate of diffusion of those innovations will be increased if firms are given short-run protection and market power as a result of the innovation.[4]

An innovation is knowledge that has been applied for the first time, in the form of a productive process or product.

However, Schumpeter was not arguing for monopoly itself, only for a type of market structure and a legal–institutional framework that would in his eyes maximize technological advance. He also perceived technological change as an element of competition and spoke of perennial gales of "creative destruction," in which the market power of firms ebbed and flowed as changes in technology altered or rendered obsolete existing productive processes and products.[5] Schumpeter viewed the progress of capitalism as being spurred onward by technological change that was quickly diffused and

---

[2]Nestor Terleckyj, *Research and Development* (New York: National Industrial Conference Board, 1963).

[3]Robert Solow, "Technological Change and the Aggregate Production Function," *Review of Economics and Statistics*, 39 (August 1957), 312–20.

[4]Joseph A. Schumpeter, *Capitalism, Socialism, and Democracy* (New York: Harper & Row, Publishers, 1942), Part II.

[5]*Ibid.*, Chap. 7.

imitated. Thus, either the market power that stimulated technological change, or the momentary reward of market power that might have been necessary to spur innovations, would be transient in nature.

Schumpeter's view has been supported, amplified, and altered by several modern observers.[6] Foremost among these has been Professor Galbraith, who has argued that "a benign Providence...has made the modern industry of a few large firms an almost perfect instrument for inducing technical change. It is admirably equipped for financing technical development."[7] Galbraith has further argued that the competitive model almost precludes technological advance. In characteristically cutting prose, he concluded that "the foreign visitor, brought to the United States to study American production methods and associated marvels, visits the same firms as do the attorneys of the Department of Justice in their search for monopoly."[8]

Strong opposition to the Schumpeter–Galbraith hypotheses has arisen. Mason was among the first to reject or cast doubt upon the validity of the position.[9] The past few decades have witnessed an onslaught of empirical studies designed to shed light upon this difference of opinion. We shall shortly review these studies with great interest. However, justice requires that we first give greater attention to the *a priori* positions that have been staked out in the controversy.

The insistence of Galbraith et al. that large firms are the most efficient progenitors and transmitters of technological change is not based upon their collective imaginations. Five specific reasons have at various times been offered in support of such a conclusion. First, technological change does not occur in a vacuum. Resources must be devoted to the research and development (R&D) process if there is to be a continual expectation of technological change.[10] R&D expenditures, it can be argued, may be too costly for small firms to undertake. Second, economies of scale may exist in R&D that favor large research and development efforts. Third, R&D is a time-consuming process, and the possibility of deferred rewards for these activities may at the margin cause some small firms to forego any effort at all. Fourth, many R&D expenditures never pay off in terms of new productive processes or new products; hence, perhaps only a large firm can effectively spread the risk of many actual or anticipated failures over a sufficiently large

---

[6]For example, A.D.H. Kaplan, *Big Enterprise in a Competitive System* (Washington, D.C.: The Brookings Institution, 1954); David E. Lilienthal, *Big Business: A New Era* (New York: Harper & Row, Publishers, 1953); and Henry H. Villard, "Competition, Oligopoly and Research," *Journal of Political Economy*, 66 (December 1958), 483–97.

[7]J.K. Galbraith, *American Capitalism: The Concept of Countervailing Power* (Boston: Houghton Mifflin Company, 1952), p. 86.

[8]*Ibid.*, p. 91.

[9]Edward S. Mason, "Schumpeter on Monopoly and the Large Firm," *Review of Economics and Statistics*, 33 (May 1951), 139–44.

[10]Research activities are original studies that are aimed at the discovery of new knowledge, whereas development activities are designed to translate the existing fund of knowledge into productive processes and products.

number of projects. Fifth, it is possible that when R&D expenditures result in the discovery of important new knowledge, only the larger firms possess the necessary resources and expertise to exploit fully the advantages of the new productive processes and products that result.

On the other side of the coin, however, one can argue *a priori* that the forces of competition not only will stimulate technological change, but also will compel firms to adopt or imitate with the greatest possible speed any innovations that appear. Firms that fail to do so will be driven out of the market. A variant of the "sleepy monopolist" hypothesis is also offered here. Large firms with considerable market power, it is alleged, do not face the rigors of competition, and therefore have no stimulus to engage in extensive R&D or to adopt potentially risky productive processes or products. On this basis, then, one might expect less technological change in markets where market power exists, and the rate of diffusion of technological advance to be slower.

The preceding discussion reveals that it is impossible to settle the controversy on the basis of *a priori* considerations. Therefore, we must turn to empirical evidence in order to further our understanding of this crucial aspect of industrial organization.

WHO PERFORMS RESEARCH AND DEVELOPMENT?

Table 9.1 reports the dollar expenditures made for industrial R&D activities in the United States during the years 1953–67. The division of support for industrial R&D between the federal government and private companies is now about equal, although the share of the federal government in 1967 was 12 percent greater than its corresponding share in 1953. Table 9.2 breaks down the R&D expenditures in terms of the size of the company in which they were made. Companies that employed more than 10,000 individuals made 84 percent of all industrial R&D expenditures. Only 4 percent were made by firms employing less than 1,000 workers. Although the pattern is not uniform (for example, in SIC three-digit industry 283, drugs and medicines, only 35 percent of all R&D expenditures were made by companies that employed more than 10,000 workers), the impact of Table 9.2 is apparent. Large firms make most of the expenditures for industrial R&D in the United States. Indeed, a report from the early 1960's indicated that the top twenty industrial R&D firms (in terms of dollars spent) accounted for more than half of all R&D expenditures made.[11] Evidence exists indicating that small firms frequently do not even maintain an R&D establishment.[12] The threshold size for the establishment of an indus-

---

[11]Daniel Hamberg, *R&D: Essays on the Economics of Research and Development* (New York: Random House, Inc., 1966), p. 6.

[12]Richard Caves, *American Industry: Structure, Conduct, Performance*, 2nd ed. (Englewood Cliffs, N.J.: Prentice-Hall, Inc., 1967), pp. 100–104.

TABLE 9.1

Trends in Funds for Industrial R&D Performance, by Source, 1953–67

Year	Total R&D Amount	Total R&D Percent Change from Previous Year	Federal Amount	Federal Percent of Total	Company Amount	Company Percent of Total
1953	$3,630	—	$1,430	39	$2,200	61
1954	4,070	12	1,750	43	2,320	57
1955	4,640	14	2,180	47	2,460	53
1956	6,605	42	3,328	50	3,277	50
1957	7,731	17	4,335	56	3,396	44
1958	8,389	9	4,759	57	3,630	43
1959	9,618	15	5,635	59	3,983	41
1960	10,509	9	6,081	58	4,428	42
1961	10,908	4	6,240	57	4,668	43
1962	11,464	5	6,434	56	5,029	44
1963	12,630	10	7,270	58	5,360	42
1964	13,512	7	7,720	57	5,792	43
1965	14,185	5	7,740	55	6,445	45
1966	15,548	10	8,332	54	7,216	46
1967	16,420	6	8,388	51	8,032	49

Source: *National Science Foundation*, Research and Development in Industry, 1967 (*Washington, D.C.: U.S. Government Printing Office, 1969*), p. 26, Table 1.

trial R&D laboratory by a firm seems to be somewhere between 500 and 1,000 workers.

Several caveats must be issued at this point. It is clearly true that large firms typically expend more resources for R&D activities than do small firms. This does not, however, imply that the intensity of the R&D effort is greater in large firms. That is, one cannot conclude that large firms devote *proportionately* more resources to R&D activities than do small firms. The results of several studies, in fact, imply just the opposite. An example of such a study is that performed by Worley, who examined the number of R&D personnel employed by large firms in eight two-digit SIC industries.[13] Worley found that in only two such industries did the number of R&D personnel employed increase more than proportionately with size, where size was measured by the total number of employees. Hamberg undertook a similar study for a numerically larger group of two- and three-digit industries and confirmed Worley's findings.[14] Comanor has also attacked this question

[13] James S. Worley, "Industrial Research and the New Competition," *Journal of Political Economy,* 64 (April 1961), 183–86.

[14] Daniel Hamberg, "Size of Firm, Oligopoly, and Research: The Evidence," *The Canadian Journal of Economics and Political Science,* 30 (February 1964), 62–75.

TABLE 9.2

Funds for R&D Performance, by Industry and Size of Company, 1967

INDUSTRY	SIC CODE	MILLIONS OF DOLLARS					PERCENT DISTRIBUTION				
		Total	Companies with Total Employment of:				Total	Companies with Total Employment of:			
			Less than 1,000	1,000 to 4,999	5,000 to 9,999	10,000 or more		Less than 1,000	1,000 to 4,999	5,000 to 9,999	10,000 or more
Total	—	$16,420	$688	$1,111	$869	$13,752	100	4	7	5	84
Food and Kindred Products	20	168	3	30	25	110	100	2	18	15	65
Textiles and Apparel	22, 23	52	a*	11	a	a	100	a	22	a	a
Lumber, Wood Products, and Furniture	24, 25	14	a	4	a	a	100	a	31	a	a
Paper and Allied Products	26	94	a	23	12	55	100	a	24	13	59
Chemicals and Allied Products	28	1,565	76	196	175	1,118	100	5	13	11	71
Industrial Chemicals	281–82	1,006	17	45	29	914	100	2	4	3	91
Drugs and Medicines	283	354	a	100	104	125	100	a	28	29	35
Other Chemicals	284–87, 289	206	a	51	42	79	100	a	25	20	39
Petroleum Refining and Extraction	29, 13	469	a	9	19	431	100	a	2	4	92
Rubber Products	30	195	11	14	28	143	100	6	7	14	73
Stone, Clay, and Glass Products	32	152	a	10	14	113	100	a	7	9	74
Primary Metals	33	245	9	36	22	179	100	3	15	9	73
Ferrous Metals and Products	331–32, 3391, 3399	144	2	a	a	114	100	1	a	a	79
Nonferrous Metals and Products	Balance of 33	102	7	a	a	65	100	6	a	a	64

*"a" means not separately available but included in total.

TABLE 9.2 (Cont.)

| | | MILLIONS OF DOLLARS | | | | | PERCENT DISTRIBUTION | | | | |
| | | Companies with Total Employment of: | | | | | Companies with total Employment of: | | | | |
INDUSTRY	SIC CODE	Total	Less than 1,000	1,000 to 4,999	5,000 to 9,999	10,000 or more	Total	Less than 1,000	1,000 to 4,999	5,000 to 9,999	10,000 or more
Fabricated Metal Products	34	165	29	31	25	80	100	17	19	15	49
Machinery	35	1,478	96	119	89	1,174	100	7	8	6	79
Electrical Equipment and Communication	36, 48	3,806	101	217	218	3,270	100	3	5	6	86
Radio and TV Receiving Equipment	365	84	a	4	—	76	100	a	5	—	90
Communications Equipment and Electronic Components	366–67, 48	2,241	68	134	a	a	100	3	6	a	a
Other Electrical Equipment	361–64, 369	1,482	29	79	a	a	100	2	5	a	a
Motor Vehicles and Other Transportation Equipment	371 379 373–75	1,377	20	10	23	1,324	100	1	1	2	96
Aircraft and Missiles	372, 19	5,568	26	69	85	5,388	100	1	1	1	97
Professional and Scientific Instruments	38	464	32	69	64	298	100	7	15	14	64
Scientific and Mechanical Measuring Instruments	381–82	78	20	28	a	a	100	25	36	a	a
Optical, Surgical, Photographic, and Other Instruments	383–87	385	13	41	a	a	100	3	11	a	a
Other Manufacturing Industries	21, 27, 31, 39	70	a	19	12	28	100	a	27	17	40
Nonmanufacturing Industries	10–12, 14–17, 40–47, 49–67, 70–79, 89	540	233	243	44	20	100	43	45	8	4

Source: *National Science Foundation, Research and Development in Industry, 1967 (Washington D.C.: U.S. Government Printing Office, 1969), p. 28, Table 3.*

and has concluded that increases in firm size do not typically call forth more than proportionate increases in R&D employment by the firm.[15]

A second necessary caveat emphasizes the difference between the *inputs* to the process of technological change (for example, personnel) and the *outputs* of that process (as measured, perhaps, by the growth of productivity of some other index). Care must be taken that one does not confuse the number or intensity of usage of inputs with the efficiency of an economic enterprise by counting how many inputs are used.[16] Many otherwise sophisticated studies fail to mention that fact, perhaps because there exists a positive and significant correlation between R&D employment and R&D outputs such as patents.[17] The presumption underlying several studies has apparently been that R&D inputs are sufficiently related to R&D outputs to permit the substitution of inputs for outputs when needed. This, however, leaves much to be desired, because inputs such as R&D employment are capable of explaining only about 50 percent of the variance in R&D outputs such as patents.

MARKET STRUCTURE AND TECHNOLOGICAL CHANGE: THE EVIDENCE

A large body of evidence has been accumulated pertaining to the relationship between market structure and the results obtained from the R&D process. There is, unfortunately, no agreement about how one should measure the success of R&D efforts. The three most popular measures are (1) patents, (2) important innovations, and (3) productivity gains. None of these measures is without faults, however. Patents are a frequent end result of R&D; nevertheless, differences in the propensity to patent new advances, and differences in the technological opportunities available that might lead to a patent, make interindustry comparisons of patenting activity a perilous endeavor.[18] Further, the fact that an advance in knowledge has been pat-

---

[15]William S. Comanor, "Market Structure, Product Differentiation, and Industrial Research," *Quarterly Journal of Economics,* 81 (November 1967), 639–57.

[16]Worley, for example, in a study that postdates his work reported above, admitted that the "employment of research and development personnel is, therefore, not an accurate index of the rate of innovation." James S. Worley, "The Changing Direction of Research and Development Employment Among Firms," in *The Rate and Direction of Inventive Activity,* ed. Richard R. Nelson (Princeton, N.J.: Princeton University Press, 1962), p. 234.

[17]F.M. Scherer, "Market Structure and the Employment of Scientists and Engineers," *American Economic Review,* 57 (June 1967), 524–31; and Scherer, "Firm Size, Market Structure, Opportunity, and the Output of Patented Inventions," *American Economic Review,* 55 (December 1965), 1097–1123. Scherer reports a .72 simple correlation between the number of R&D employees for 352 firms in the year 1955 and the number of patents received in 1959 by the same firms.

[18]Scherer has pointed out that firms working under contract for the federal government may not patent otherwise patentable advances, either because the discovered knowledge automatically becomes public domain or because the firms must agree to grant royalty-free licenses to various users such as the government. This often typifies advances made in the aircraft or missile fields. Scherer, "Firm Size." Also, technological opportunity is not the same in all markets. Opportunities for technological advance in areas such as chemicals, plastics, and electronics are greater than those in markets revolving around lumber products. As a result, interindustry comparisons of patent activity may be invalid unless these differences in opportunity are taken into account.

ented does not necessarily mean that it is important, or even useful. As we shall see, patent standards are often low, and some firms engage in the process merely to frustrate and delay the advances or imitative activity of competitor firms.

The second popular measure of inventive success, the output of important innovations, is clearly a very useful measure if certain obvious obstacles can be overcome. Who is to decide what is an "important" innovation? Also, does one measure importance in terms of value to the firm, to the market, or to society? Does one ignore the process of the *diffusion* of innovations and instead ask only which firm originally developed the innovation?

We have already dealt with the question of the effects of market concentration upon the growth of productivity. Should the growth in productivity (the growth in labor productivity is the most popular measure) that results from a given firm's activities be used as an indicator of the success of that firm's R&D activities? One must be careful to sort out from the increased labor productivity the effects of increased capital per worker and such things as spillover effects from other markets. For example, continuous-casting machines were originally developed inside markets such as aluminum, and only much later were used in the production of steel. The productivity of steel workers rose as a result. It would be improper, however, to attribute this to the efficiency of R&D workers employed by steel firms. This type of growth in productivity relates to the diffusion of an innovation, rather than to its original development.[19]

MARKET STRUCTURE AND PATENTS

Patents, as we have seen, are an ambiguous measure either of technological change or of the success of R&D efforts. Nevertheless, the operation of the patent system in the United States has provided economists with a gold mine of data that, properly utilized, can be instructive. At the turn of the century, the large majority (over 80 percent) of patents were granted to individual inventors who were unassociated with any corporate laboratory. By 1957, however, the picture had changed substantially; only 36 percent of all patents granted were given to individuals, and 61 percent were given to corporations.[20] The role of the independent inventor, as measured by patent activities, clearly declined in an absolute sense.

Scherer has addressed himself to the relationships between patenting and firm size (as measured by total sales revenues).[21] As expected, he found

---

[19]Especially helpful discussions of spillover effects may be found in John Jewkes, David Sawers, and Richard Stillerman, *The Sources of Invention* (New York: St. Martin's Press, Inc., 1959), pp. 276–80; and Richard T. Nelson, Merton J. Peck, and Edward D. Kalachek, *Technology, Economic Growth, and Public Policy* (Washington, D.C.: The Brookings Institution, 1967), pp. 83–85.

[20]Hamberg, *R&D*, p. 17.

[21]Scherer, "Firm Size."

that large firms were responsible for more patents than were small firms; however, he also found diminishing returns to patenting with respect to firm size for all except the three largest firms in *Fortune's 500* in the year 1955. He concluded that "smallness is not necessarily an impediment to the creation of patentable inventions and may well be an advantage."[22]

Scherer also tested several other interesting hypotheses. He found some support for the contention that intermarket differences in technological opportunities and the propensity to patent are perhaps more important determinants of the output of patents than is firm size itself. The role of patenting vis-à-vis diversification was also considered. It has been argued that a diversified firm is better able to take advantage of the fruits of R&D activity, because the diversified firm has many potential outlets for the new processes and products that result. Consequently, diversified firms should tend to support R&D activities more heavily than nondiversified firms, and one might expect to find them obtaining more patents.[23] Scherer found no evidence of this, however. Rather, the important fact appeared to be that the firms in this sample tended to diversify into markets where technological opportunities were great.[24] The observed differences in the receipt of patents by diversified and nondiversified firms, therefore, could be accounted for by intermarket differences in technological opportunities.[25] Other tests performed by Scherer failed to reveal any statistically significant relationship between technological output (patents) and factors such as liquidity, profitability, and four-firm market concentration.[26]

[22]*Ibid.,* p. 1105.

[23]Richard R. Nelson, "The Simple Economics of Basic Scientific Research," *Journal of Political Economy,* 67 (June 1959), 297–306.

[24]The contention that firms tend to diversify into areas where technological change is rapid has been verified by Michael Gort, *Diversification and Integration in American Industry* (Princeton, N.J.: Princeton University Press, 1962).

[25]Two other studies have been performed that have considerable bearing on the diversification issue. Grabowski examined R&D expenditures during the period 1959–62 in the chemical, petroleum refining, and drug markets. He found that R&D expenditures were positively related to firm diversification. [Henry G. Grabowski, "The Determinants of Industrial Research and Development: A Study of the Chemical, Drug and Petroleum Industries," *Journal of Political Economy,* 76 (March–April 1968), 292–305.] Contrary results, however, have been reported by Comanor as a result of his study of 57 drug manufacturers. Comanor found R&D productivity, which he approximated by the total new drug sales generated by new products, to be inversely related to firm diversification, even after firm size and R&D intensity were held constant. [William S. Comanor, "Research and Technical Change in the Pharmaceutical Industry," *Review of Economics and Statistics,* 47 (May 1965), 182–91.] Although both studies are provocative and attack an important question, their meaning is in doubt. The Grabowski study emphasizes the inputs to the process of technological change rather than the outputs. The Comanor study fails to take account fully of the many disparate factors that might influence drug and pharmaceutical sales.

[26]It is possible to argue that the influence of market structure upon technological change is insignificant. Alternative hypotheses, which address themselves to the origin of and stimulus to technological change, frequently rely upon (1) a simple but strong relationship between technological change and the number and quality of inputs employed in R&D; and/or (2) exogenous bursts of scientific knowledge unrelated to market structure; and/or (3) the pull of demand. The last of these hypotheses has been given strong support by the findings of Schmookler, who has reported that the relative number of patents awarded for capital equipment in manufacturing markets is closely related to lagged expenditures on capital equipment in those same markets. Jacob Schmookler, *Invention and Economic Growth* (Cambridge, Mass.: Harvard University Press, 1966).

MARKET STRUCTURE AND IMPORTANT INNOVATIONS

The best measure of the success of inventive activity is the number of significant and important innovations generated by that activity. The shortcomings of this approach, however, are potentially numerous. It is obvious that one must be extremely knowledgeable about a market in order to be able to make the necessary judgments about innovative significance. Moreover, even assuming that the necessary expertise is available, several practical problems confront this approach to the measurement of the success of inventive activity. Among these problems are the difficulties in evaluating spillover effects into other markets, the possible dichotomy between the private importance and the social importance of an innovation, and the fact that the costs and benefits accruing to an innovation are spread out over time. The identification of important innovations, therefore, is both an art and a science, and the judgments of one evaluator are not always accepted with unanimity by other observers.

Jewkes, Sawers, and Stillerman, in a seminal study of twentieth-century inventive activity, compiled a list of the 61 most significant inventions during that time period.[27] Although an invention does not necessarily imply an innovation, the significance of inventions listed by the trio nearly always derived from the fact that the new knowledge had been profitably applied. Over one half (33) of the inventions were found to have been the result of individual inventive activity, whereas only 12 of them emanated from large corporate research laboratories.[28] Important inventions such as cellophane, the jet engine, and air conditioning were produced by private individuals. The implication of this evidence is that an environment of large firms in highly concentrated industries is not a necessary condition for significant changes in technology.

Mueller has studied the innovational activity of the du Pont Corporation from 1920 to 1950.[29] E.I. du Pont de Nemours is, of course, one of the twenty largest industrial corporations in the United States, in terms of either sales or assets.[30] It has traditionally devoted large amounts of resources to research and development activity. An example in point is the approximately $25 million du Pont is rumored to have expended on the development of Corfam, an artificial leather the company later regarded as a failure. Mueller's study revealed that the 25 most important product and process innovations produced by du Pont during the 1920–50 period were often not

---

[27]Jewkes, Sawers, and Stillerman, *The Sources of Invention.*

[28]*Ibid.*, Chap. 4.

[29]Willard F. Mueller, "The Origins of the Basic Inventions Underlying du Pont's Major Product and Process Innovations, 1920 to 1950," in *The Rate and Direction of Inventive Activity*, ed. Richard R. Nelson (Princeton, N.J.: Princeton University Press, 1962), pp. 323–46.

[30]"The Fortune Directory," *Fortune*, 83 (May 1971), 172.

discovered in the du Pont laboratories. In Mueller's judgment, 14 or 15 of the innovations were originally produced by independent researchers and were only later used by du Pont.[31]

Hamberg performed a similar study for the period 1946–55, examining 27 major inventions that appeared in the decade.[32] He concluded that only seven of these inventions were originally conceived in large corporate laboratories and that at least 12 were originally developed by individual inventors.

A much-quoted and emulated study performed by Mansfield is also relevant to our discussion.[33] Mansfield examined the innovational history of three markets: iron and steel, petroleum refining, and bituminous coal. He found that the four largest firms in the petroleum and coal markets carried out more than their share of the innovations produced in those markets, whereas the reverse was true in steel.[34] The critical features of the markets where the four largest firms produced more than their share of innovations were these: (1) The investment required for the typical innovation in that market was quite large in relation to the size of the firms in the market; (2) the minimum firm size in the market necessary for profitable use of the typical innovation was relatively large; and (3) the average size of the four largest firms in the market was much greater than the size of the typical potential user of the usual innovation.

Mansfield also addressed himself to an important question of public policy—namely, would the number of innovations produced in a given market be increased or decreased if the largest firms were broken up into several smaller firms? Mansfield concluded that in the petroleum and coal markets, a policy of dissolving large firms would be deleterious to the number of innovations produced if it were extended beyond the top few firms. In steel, however, he concluded that it was difficult to justify the existence of very large firms on the basis of their performance as innovators, and that a steel market composed of many smaller firms would probably be beneficial to technological change.[35] At the same time, Mansfield found evidence in all three markets that the smallest firms had done relatively less innovating in recent years than in the pre–World War II period.

Williamson, in a study previously reviewed, utilized the Mansfield

---

[31]Mueller, "Origins of the Basic Inventions."

[32]Daniel Hamberg, "Invention in the Industrial Research Laboratory," *Journal of Political Economy* 71 (April 1963), 95–115.

[33]Edwin Mansfield, "Size of Firm, Market Structure, and Innovation," *Journal of Political Economy*, 71 (December 1963), 556–76. The same information is also contained in Edwin Mansfield, *Industrial Research and Technological Innovation* (New York: W.W. Norton & Company, Inc., 1968), Chap. 5.

[34]The "share" of a firm was considered to be its share of the total market, where the size of the total market was variously measured as being ingot capacity in iron and steel, daily crude-oil capacity in petroleum, and yearly coal production in bituminous coal.

[35]This conclusion has been confirmed and elaborated upon by Walter Adams and Joel Dirlam, "Big Steel, Invention, and Innovation," *Quarterly Journal of Economics*, 80 (May 1966), 167–89. Adams and Dirlam traced the major innovations produced in steel in the last century, particularly the basic oxygen process, and concluded that the largest firms were almost uniformly the least likely to introduce innovations and the most tardy to adopt profitable innovations.

sample of markets in order to arrive at a guesstimate of the optimal level of four-firm concentration in terms of maximizing the output of innovations.[36] Williamson's two models yielded two different estimates, concentration ratios of 30 and of 5. These estimates are surprisingly low in view of the fact that all three of the Mansfield markets (coal, steel, and petroleum) have four-firm concentration ratios that exceed Williamson's higher estimate of optimality. Williamson admitted that although his results were indeed interesting, he did not think the study or the data to be of the strength and certainty necessary to support public policies designed to deconcentrate the three markets concerned.

MARKET STRUCTURE AND PRODUCTIVITY GROWTH

The inconclusive and contradictory findings concerning market structure and the growth of productivity have already been considered, in Chapter 8. That coverage will not be duplicated here. We shall use this opportunity, however, to levy at these studies a criticism that also applies to the empirical attempts to connect market structure with the output of patents or the generation of significant innovations. Such studies typically have emphasized the effects of concentration upon inventive and innovative output. The much-used concentration ratio is, however, only one aspect of market structure. Studies are needed that relate technological change to multiple aspects of market structure. Factors that must also be considered include economies of scale, product differentiation, capital requirements, demand characteristics, and import competition (to name several important features of market structure that one might identify, *a priori*, as being possible determinants of inventive and innovative output). This plea is best interpreted as an agenda for future research rather than a diminution of the groundbreaking importance of the studies that have been the center of our attention in our consideration of technological change.

MISCELLANEOUS ISSUES CONCERNING
TECHNOLOGICAL CHANGE

We now have a feel for the controversy surrounding the relationship between market structure and technological change, as well as some knowledge of the character of the empirical evidence that bears on the controversy. Several additional matters must be considered, however, before we may properly proceed with our work. Each of these topics relates to the subject at hand, although not in a coherent pattern. We shall give these topics their due in this section.

---

[36]Oliver E. Williamson, "Innovation and Market Structure," *Journal of Political Economy*, 73 (February 1965), 67–73.

The Task of Development

Whereas research is aimed at the creation of new knowledge, development involves the conversion of that knowledge into usable productive processes or products. The evidence of Jewkes et al., Hamberg, and Mueller indicates that small independent inventors and innovators have traditionally played a large role in technological change in major machinery and consumer-goods markets.[37] Nevertheless, there is considerable reason to believe that participation in the development process is heavily weighted in favor of large firms.

Crude evidence does exist to indicate that large firms spend proportionately more of their R&D budgets on development than do small firms. In 1967, manufacturing firms with 1,000 to 4,999 employees spent about 62 percent of their R&D budgets on development, whereas the comparable statistic for firms with 10,000 or more employees was 72 percent.[38] Several examples are also instructive: Brandenberger, the French chemist who invented cellophane, was unable to develop the new knowledge he had discovered, and ultimately allowed a large French firm to carry out the development process. Carlson, the inventor of the forerunner to the modern-day Xerox copying process, sold the rights to his knowledge to the Batelle Memorial Institute, a large R&D company. Batelle, in turn, licensed the Haloid (now Xerox) Corporation to develop and market the process commercially.

It is possible that the sheer magnitude of development expenditures discourages small firms from engaging in such work. Development expenditures made by manufacturing firms in the year 1967 were ten to fifteen times as large as expenditures made for basic research in most markets, and two to three times as large as those made for applied research.[39] There is also a good deal of risk and uncertainty attached to the payoff to development expenditures, as well as the prospect of deferred rewards for such work. Further, the fact that large firms frequently maintain extensive marketing networks not only may increase the visibility of any process or product developed, but also can mean that a large portion of the prospective market for it is already foreclosed and guaranteed. All of the factors above, if operational, tend to diminish the participation of small firms in the development portion of the R&D process.

The Diffusion of Innovations

The fact that new inventive knowledge has been translated into an innovation does not guarantee that the innovation will be immediately

[37]Jewkes, Sawers, and Stillerman, *The Sources of Invention;* Hamberg, "Invention in the Industrial Research Laboratory"; and Mueller, "Origins of the Basic Inventions."

[38]National Science Foundation, *Research and Development in Industry, 1967* (Washington, D.C.: U.S. Government Printing Office, 1969), p. 67, Table 46.

[39]*Ibid.*

adopted. The process of adoption of innovations is referred to as *diffusion*; the rate of diffusion is often slow.

The process of diffusion is appropriately viewed as a learning process. When an innovation initially appears, potential users may either be unaware of its existence or may doubt its usefulness or cost-effectiveness. Information about innovations often circulates slowly, and both the suppliers and the users of the innovation must often be a part of the learning process. Once an innovation has been applied, 25 or more years might be needed before all firms adopt it. Mansfield reports such a lag in the railroad industry for the adoption of centralized traffic control.[40] An early study performed by Jerome revealed that the process of diffusion of 23 innovative manufacturing machines lasted from 10 to 28 years.[41] Mansfield has examined the diffusion process in detail with respect to twelve major innovations in four markets—bituminous coal, iron and steel, brewing, and railroading. The number of years that elapsed before one half of all the firms in the appropriate market adopted an innovation ranged from 0.9 to 15.[42]

The time pattern of diffusion of a major innovation often approximates a logistic curve. Figure 9.1 illustrates several possible logistic curves. The factors determining the shape of the logistic curve (and the diffusion process upon which it is based) are many. Perhaps the most important factor

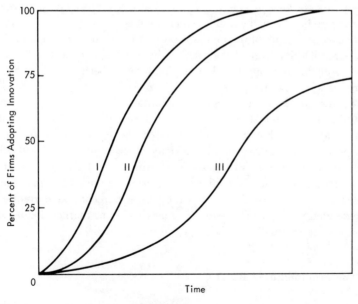

FIGURE 9.1

[40]Mansfield, *Industrial Research*, Chap. 7, p. 136.

[41]Harry Jerome, *Mechanization in Industry* (New York: National Bureau of Economic Research, 1934).

[42]Mansfield, *Industrial Research*, p. 136.

is expected profitability. The higher the expected profitability associated with an innovation, the more rapidly it will be adopted. Assume an increase in the expected profitability associated with a particular innovation. If the logistic curve associated with that innovation prior to the change in expectations was curve II, then the change in expected profitability is likely to shift curve II in the direction of curve I.

It is interesting to note that the major beneficiaries of a new process or product innovation are frequently not the firms that originally introduced it. Firms that climb on the bandwagon often reap disproportionate amounts of the profits from innovations. IBM's plunge into the electronic-computer field, after the pioneering work had already been performed by Remington Rand, is an instructive example. The latecomers often experience increased profitability because they avoid many of the blind alleys and costs experienced by the original innovator. Hence, it is not surprising that logistic curves I, II, and III in Figure 9.1 show in their initial stages rather slow acceptance of innovations, and also that such acceptance increases at an increasing rate. The greater the number of firms already using a potential innovation, the greater the probability that a nonusing firm will also adopt it.

In general, greater risk and uncertainty, higher initial investment cost, slow market growth, and low visibility for an innovation will tend to slow the diffusion process. Logistic curve III in Figure 9.1 represents a process of diffusion that has been delayed by such factors.

The relationship of market structure to diffusion is apparently not strong. Mansfield has argued that one might reasonably expect large firms to adopt an innovation more quickly than small firms, because large firms have greater financial resources, are more able to spread risk, have more opportunities to use an innovation, and may maintain closer ties with the vendors and producers of innovations.[43] The limited empirical evidence introduced by Mansfield for the four markets mentioned above gives lukewarm support to this proposition. He reports an elasticity of delay of -0.4 for the introduction of an innovation with respect to firm size.[44] This means that a 10 percent increase in firm size will, *ceteris paribus,* reduce the time the firm waits before initially using an innovation by 4 percent. Such results need to be extended to many innovations in many different markets before strong conclusions are merited.

The Profitability of R&D

Given that firms undertake expenditures on R&D, how profitable are those expenditures? Mansfield has once again provided the lion's share of

[43]Mansfield, *Industrial Research*, Chap. 7.
[44]*Ibid.*, p. 160.

the limited amount of evidence available.[45] He examined the R&D expenditures of five chemical firms and five petroleum firms, and found marginal rates of return on these expenditures that ranged from 7 to 30 percent in chemicals and from 40 to 60 percent in petroleum.[46] In chemicals, the profitability of R&D expenditures was directly related to firm size, whereas in petroleum, an inverse relationship obtained between the two. Mansfield also utilized a sample of ten manufacturing markets and found rates of return on R&D expenditures that exceeded 15 percent in the food, apparel, and furniture markets.[47]

Mansfield has cautioned that his results should not be taken as the last word on the subject, because of the strict assumptions required to generate the estimates, possible sampling errors, spillover effects among markets, and possible lags in the relationship between R&D expenditures and the rewards gained from them. Such caveats are well taken, particularly in view of the fact that very little concrete evidence is available concerning the profitability of R&D expenditures. The Mansfield rates of return are pleasantly high and imply possible underinvestment in R&D by manufacturing firms. It should be pointed out, however, that scraps of evidence do exist that support the opposite conclusion. Some manufacturing firms appear to have become disillusioned with R&D expenditures, on the ground that their contribution to profitability has not been demonstrated, and have either contracted their R&D establishment or even abolished it.[48]

Very little can be said about the relationship between the size of the firm and the profitability of its R&D establishment. Impressionistic evidence points to highly profitable R&D efforts by very small firms.[49] It is important that this evidence be placed in perspective. Many small firms do not maintain any R&D establishment. We have already observed that a certain minimum size of firm is necessary for an R&D effort to become worthwhile. Scherer, for example, has offered the ball-park guess that in most manufacturing industries, the minimum firm size consistent with the maintenance of an R&D establishment is $75 to $200 million worth of sales annually.[50] This, of course, is only a guess, and the precise size of the threshold varies greatly from market to market. It is commonly thought that except among the smallest firm sizes, where no R&D effort is supported, economies of scale and increased profitability with respect to R&D expenditures are minimal in nature.

[45]*Ibid.*, Chap. 4.

[46]*Ibid.*, p. 70.

[47]*Ibid.*, p. 71.

[48]See E.M. Kipp, "R&D: Corporate Profit Center or Philanthropy," *SAM Advanced Management Journal,* 35 (April 1970), 41–49; also, D. Cordtz, "Bringing the Laboratory Down to Earth," *Fortune,* 83 (January 1971), 106–8.

[49]"R&D Pays—Not Only in Big Firms," *International Management,* 24 (October 1969), 66–67; also, K.W. Bennett, "R&D is Small Firm's Secret Weapon," *Iron Age,* 204 (October 30 ,1969), 88–90.

[50]F.M. Scherer, *Industrial Market Structure and Economic Performance* (Skokie, Ill.: Rand McNally & Co., 1970), p. 361.

The Timing of Innovations

We have already noted that substantial lags in time often exist between the invention of new knowledge and the actual appearance of that knowledge in the form of a process or product innovation. Ten to 20 years is not an uncommon time lapse between invention and innovation.[51] The case of nylon is instructive. After the original discovery of the superpolymer upon which nylon is based, over 11 years passed before nylon was produced commercially. The time lapse between invention and innovation was approximately 14 years for the jet engine and over 22 years for television. The invention of the well-known Xerox copying process did not result in an actual productive innovation for over 20 years. The lag is often quite long in the field of electronics; 79 years lapsed between the invention of the fluorescent lamp by Bacquerel in 1859 and the subsequent innovation by General Electric and Westinghouse in 1938.

The length of the lag between invention and innovation is a function of factors such as expected profitability, demand conditions, capital costs, the state of existing technology, marketing sophistication, and the willingness to bear risk and uncertainty.[52] Lack of expected profitability, for example, has been cited by Brozen as the reason that transfer equipment was not used in the production of automobiles until the 1950's, even though it had been potentially available for over 30 years.[53]

From an *a priori* standpoint, the optimal time for an entrepreneur to introduce an innovation is that moment when the expected present discounted value of the prospective innovation is maximized. Unfortunately, this straightforward criterion typically cannot be applied by the prospective innovator because of the great risk and uncertainty associated with the future profit stream accruing to the innovation. Hence, the optimal point in time for the introduction of the innovation is more often than not unknown, and must therefore be approximated by whatever means are available.

The Role of Risk and Uncertainty

Risk and uncertainty permeate R&D and the process of innovation.[54] Mansfield has reported that over 60 percent of R&D projects initiated by

[51]See John L. Enos, "Invention and Innovation in the Petroleum Refining Industry," in *The Rate and Direction of Inventive Activity* (Princeton, N.J.: Princeton University Press, 1962), pp. 299–321, for a useful summary of the time lapses between invention and innovation for a large number of processes and products.

[52]Yoram Barzel, "Optimal Timing of Innovations," *Review of Economics and Statistics,* 50 (March 1968), 348–55.

[53]Yale Brozen, "The Economics of Automation," *American Economic Review,* 47 (May 1957), 339–50.

[54]Frank Knight has labeled a risky situation one in which a probability distribution can be attached to each of the possible outcomes of that situation; he describes a purely uncertain situation as one in which it is impossible to attach any probabilities to the possible outcomes. Frank H. Knight, *Risk, Uncertainty and Profit* (New York: Harper Torchbooks, 1965)

firms never resulted in a commercially used project or process.[55] This result should not, however, be accorded exaggerated importance. A more detailed examination of the R&D activities of a large firm, by Mansfield and Brandeburg, revealed that the estimated predicted success (ex ante) of R&D projects undertaken by the firm was 0.8.[56] While the ex post success ratio was only 0.5, about two thirds of the failures of the projects initiated were due to changed objectives on the part of the firm and/or transfer of vital personnel involved in the projects.

Galbraith and others have suggested that the ability of the large firm to bear risk and uncertainty and to spread them over a large number of R&D projects has conferred an obvious advantage upon large firms.[57] Like many appealing Galbraithian assertions, however, this particular hypothesis would not seem to be given great support by available empirical evidence. The work of Jewkes et al., Hamberg, and Mueller suggests that small, independent inventors and innovators have been frequent and prosperous participants in the process of technological change.[58] Indeed, if anything, the evidence points to a reluctance on the part of many large firms to tackle risky or radically different projects. Large firms often opt for smaller, safer, short-run projects that promise more immediate payoffs.

The Patent System

Earlier discussion in this chapter resulted in three specific variables being suggested as possible proxies for the rate of technological change: (1) patents, (2) important innovations, and (3) productivity growth. Although each of this triad of variables is susceptible to the ebb and flow of public policy, the impact of public policy and law upon patents is most noticeable. A patent is in fact a creature of law and public policy, and exists only within the legal–institutional framework designed by Congress and the judicial system. Hence, public policy is vitally intertwined with the patent system.

A patent is a legal grant of monopoly implying exclusive control, which is given to an inventor or an innovator who has developed a process or product that is original and nonobvious in nature.

The definition above is deserving of additional attention. A patent is a grant of monopoly power given by the public to an individual for a given time period, typically 17 years. Under certain circumstances, patents may be renewed. A patent makes it illegal for another entrepreneur or individual

---

[55]Edwin A. Mansfield, *The Economics of Technological Change* (New York: W.W. Norton & Company, Inc., 1968), p. 68.

[56]Mansfield, *Industrial Research*, Chap. 3.

[57]See, for example, J.K. Galbraith, *The New Industrial State* (Boston: Houghton Mifflin Company, 1967).

[58]Jewkes, Sawers, and Stillerman, *The Sources of Invention;* Hamberg, "Invention"; and Mueller, "Origins of the Basic Inventions."

to utilize the patented process or product without the express permission of the holder of the patent. It is possible for a patent holder to license prospective users of the process or product and to charge them fees that reflect either the amount of use made of the license or other considerations. Indeed, the Supreme Court has suggested that "a patent empowers the owner to exact royalties as high as he can negotiate with the leverage of that monopoly."[59]

Although the U.S. Patent Office's standards for granting patents have often been criticized as being too low,[60] it is nonetheless true that not every random brainstorm or permutation of existing processes and products may be patented. A patent should represent "the creation of something that did not exist before,"[61] and a patent should *not* be granted "if the subject matter as a whole would have been obvious at the time the invention was made to a person having ordinary skill in the art to which said subject matter applies."[62] Abstract philosophical principles, which may or may not in the future be translated into a process or product, cannot be patented.

Machlup has skillfully pointed out that defenders of the current patent system typically base their defense upon one or all of the following four arguments: (1) the contention that natural law assumes that a man has the property rights to his own ideas, and that in the absence of patents, these property rights might be violated or denied; (2) the reward-by-monopoly position, which assumes that society should reward inventiveness by a grant of monopoly; (3) the incentive argument, which is based upon the assumption that technological change would not occur unless a patent incentive were provided; and (4) the exchange-for-secrets thesis, which presumes that the inventor surrenders his secret knowledge in exchange for patent protection.[63]

The incentive argument and the secrecy argument are of most concern to the economist. The incentive rationale for the existence of patents has always found favor. The President's Commission on the Patent System based much of its 1966 report upon the need for the system to provide and act as an incentive for technological change.[64] Many observers have argued, however, that such large incentives are unneeded if competition exists in the market. Hamberg has become identified with this viewpoint.[65] He argues that competition forces firms to undertake R&D activity, and that the firm

[59]*Brulotte et al.* v. *Thys Co.*, 379 U.S. 29 (1964), p. 33.

[60]See, among many, Carl Kaysen and Donald F. Turner, *Antitrust Policy: An Economic and Legal Analysis* (Cambridge, Mass.: Harvard University Press, 1965), p. 171ff.

[61]*Pyrene Mfg. Co.* v. *Boyce*, C.C.A.N.J., 292 F. 480.

[62]*Graham et al.* v. *John Deere Co. of Kansas City et al.*, 383 U.S. 1 (1966).

[63]Fritz Machlup, *An Economic Review of the Patent System*, Study Number 15 of the Subcommittee on Patents, Trademarks, and Copyrights of the Senate Judiciary Committee, 85th Cong., 2d sess. (Washington, D.C.: U.S. Government Printing Office, 1958), pp. 3–5.

[64]*To Promote Progress of the Useful Arts*, A Report of the President's Commission on the Patent System (Washington, D.C.: U.S. Government Printing Office, 1966).

[65]Hamberg, R&D, pp. 26–27.

that fails to undertake it will be disciplined by the market. It is widely recognized that R&D rivalry exists, particularly among large firms.[66] It is not known, however, what would be the precise effect upon technological change of lowering the patent incentive.

The secrecy argument finds its theoretical roots in the area of information theory. The marginal social cost of using information that has already been discovered is zero. Proponents of the secrecy hypothesis contend that inventors will be unwilling to price their newly discovered information equal to marginal social cost. That is, inventors will refuse to supply the information at a zero price. Hence, it is necessary for society to purchase via the patent system information that might otherwise remain undisclosed. The purchase price of the information contained in the patent is the cost to society of the grant of monopoly power that allows the inventor to charge prospective users of the invention for the right to use it. This approach comes perilously close to begging several important questions, the most important of which is whether society should purchase newly discovered information with cash rather than a grant of monopoly power. The grant of a patent may create monopoly power, but may also force other firms and competitors to waste resources in order to "invent around" or "differentiate around" the patented product.

The potential for abuse of the patent system is widespread. Patent licensing agreements, as the Supreme Court noted long ago in the *General Electric Case,* can closely approximate price fixing, market sharing, and cartelization.[67] General Electric once maintained an agreement with Westinghouse that Westinghouse was also allowed to produce light bulbs. However, Westinghouse was forced to pay a 2 percent royalty on sales to General Electric, up to 25.2441 percent of the two firms' combined sales, and a 30 percent royalty above the 25.2441 percent figure.[68] The power of firms to fix prices via the patent route has since been restricted but not eliminated.

The extent of the monopoly grant associated with a patent has often been whatever the firm owning the patent made of its opportunities. Patent pooling has been used on occasion with great success by firms in order to suppress competition. The classic example is the case involving the Hartford Empire Company.[69] Hartford Empire accumulated a pool of more than 800 patents by means of licensing, cross-licensing, and outright purchase, then used this power over techniques and production to allocate production within the market as a whole. This arrangement was held by the Supreme Court to be too restrictive of competition.

[66]See, for example, F.M. Scherer, "Research and Development Resource Allocation Under Rivalry," *Quarterly Journal of Economics,* 81 (August 1967), 359–94.

[67]*United States* v. *General Electric Co. et al.,* 272 U.S. 476 (1926).

[68]G.W. Stocking and M.W. Watkins, *Cartels in Action* (New York: Twentieth Century Fund, 1946), pp. 304–62; also, H.C. Passer, *The Electrical Manufacturers* (Cambridge, Mass.: Harvard University Press, 1953), pp. 161–64.

[69]*Hartford Empire Co. et al.* v. *United States,* 323 U.S. 386 (1945).

It is also possible that the patent system might encourage firms to patent individual processes or products that they have no intention of utilizing, in order to prevent their use by competitors. The Supreme Court has typically refused to void patents, even when there existed obvious intent on the part of the recipient of the patent to suppress the information patented.[70] Such judicial attitudes retard rather than promote technological change, and distort the basic intent of the patent system.

The current low standards of patentability maintained by the U.S. Patent Office (typically lower than those insisted upon by the courts) also encourage the practice of "snowballing." Snowballing is the practice of patenting innumerable items or pieces of information connected with a given process or product. The existence of so many patents may act as a protective barrier against competition for the firm that engages in this practice. Indeed, the intent of snowballing is to delineate clearly large areas of technology as being off limits to prospective competitors.

Few authorities in the area of patents would suggest the total abolition of the patent system. Nevertheless, proposals for the reform of the system as it now stands have been frequent and forceful. It has been suggested that the typical 17-year length of a patent is too extensive a time period, except for truly significant breakthroughs in technology. The concept has been suggested of "petty" patents, granted for time periods of less than 17 years. The major problem with a policy that seeks to match the length of a patent grant with the significance of the patent is that it is the most significant patents that would (when made readily available) cause the greatest changes in technology and impact upon efficiency. The effect of such a policy, therefore, would be to deny the social benefits that are greatest.

Systems of compulsory licensing have also drawn favor in some quarters. That is, the recipient of a patent would be forced to share the patented knowledge with the rest of society by means of the licensing procedure. It can easily be seen that this solution contains within it elements of trouble. Company X may be forced to license Company Y; however, the amount of the royalty must necessarily vary among patents. The "reasonableness" of the royalty for each patent must therefore be judged, and a new wave of business for the already inundated judicial system will have been created.

Those economists who subscribe to the incentive or secrecy approaches to patenting are insistent that some reward must be paid to inventors and innovators, in order that (1) inventing and innovating take place, and (2) the results of such activity be made public. A frequent suggestion in this regard is to replace the patent system with a program of public purchase of new inventions. The new inventions would then be made available to the public at very minimal or no cost. Such a policy would reward inventiveness

---

[70]An example in point is *Special Equipment Co. v. Coe, Commissioner of Patents,* 324 U.S. 370 (1945).

and discourage secrecy, while at the same time recognizing that the marginal social cost of using already-discovered information is zero. The problem of valuation of an invention is clearly the primary obstacle to the implementation of such a policy. One can easily imagine the emergence of a new regulatory body charged with deciding such questions, and a welter of lawsuits concerning the rules, regulations, and implementation of such a policy.

Government-sponsored research and development is yet another alternative deserving of attention. It is possible for government to finance research performed in private laboratories, or even to operate its own laboratories. The output of the government R&D laboratories would presumably enter the public domain. Both the amount of resources to be devoted to such an arrangement and the selection of R&D projects would be subjects of potential controversy. With regard to the latter consideration, it is not clear whether equity and economic-efficiency criteria would result in the selection of the same projects for government R&D. The basic risk and uncertainty involved in R&D would render difficult the systematic evaluation of projects even if the political process did not have to be taken into account.

One final set of reforms has been suggested to take place within the current patent system. The President's Commission on the Patent System, which, when the verbiage of its report is stripped away, recommended an essentially status quo approach to the patent system, has called for an upgrading of minimum standards for patentability.[71] Further, the commission decried the long delay that now often exists between the filing of a patent request and the action upon that request. Both the low standards of patentability and the delay (an average of 3.5 years)[72] have caused the judicial system to be flooded with cases based upon patent infringement and similar charges. The present system unnecessarily promotes judicial action; and long, involved judicial actions may strain the resources of small firms and play into the hands of large firms.

Although the preceding paragraphs have implied that the present patent system leaves much to be desired, they have also noted that the various alternatives proposed are not without fault. The central question, still unanswered, is how much protection is needed by inventor, developer, and innovator alike in order to maximize the societal benefits obtained from the societal resources expended.

SUMMARY

In this chapter, we have examined the economics of technological change. Particular emphasis has been given to the effects of market structure upon technological change. Technological change has the potential both to

---

[71] *To Promote Progress of the Useful Arts.*
[72] Mansfield, *The Economics of Technological Change,* p. 211.

spur and to limit competition. Controversies abound in this area. Schumpeter and Galbraith have staked out the position that large firms, high market concentration, and some degree of monopoly power are part and parcel of modern-day technological change and are necessary prerequisites or results of it. Others, notably Mansfield and Scherer, have challenged this assertion with a large volume of research. This latter group of economists contends that a wide range of optimal firm sizes exists with respect to technological change and that small firms are often more efficient vehicles for technological advance than are large firms.

It is clear that large firms expend more resources on R&D than do small firms; it is not clear, however, that large firms devote proportionately more resources to R&D than do small ones. In any case, it is probably not appropriate to judge the efficiency of R&D efforts by counting the magnitude of inputs used; it is necessary to look at the outputs that result from the R&D process. The three major alternative measures of R&D output include patents, important innovations, and productivity growth. The evidence concerning these three outputs with respect to market structure is mixed. Nonetheless, the evidence gives one little reason to believe that the Schumpeter–Galbraith hypothesis is valid in any more than a few markets. At the same time, there does exist evidence that large firms dominate the development portion of the R&D process. Further, large firms tend to adopt new innovations more quickly than do small firms.

The major determinant of the amount and direction of R&D activity is the expected profitability of that activity. Since considerable risk and uncertainty is involved in the R&D process, many mistakes are made by firms in assessing expected profitability.

The most noticeable public policies with respect to technological change are found in the patent system. A patent is a monopoly grant that may be used by the recipient in a wide range of ways to limit competition or imitation by competitors. Many alternatives to the present patent system have been proposed. The more serious suggestions include reducing the length of the typical patent below 17 years, compulsory licensing of certain patents, government purchase of new inventions for the public domain, and government sponsorship of R&D. Structural reform of the current patent system has also been suggested. Such reforms are typically aimed at increasing standards for patentability and reducing the delays inherent in the current system.

PROBLEMS

1. Indicate the difference between the generation of innovations and the diffusion and acceptance of those innovations. Is it possible for a firm to excel in one of these areas and not the other?

2.   An attorney for a large chemical firm recently stated that it was more profitable for his firm to pirate the inventions and technical knowledge of other firms (and then to fight any court actions that might result) than it was for them to engage in original research and development in their own laboratories. Comment on this in the light of current patent law, and indicate any resolutions to the problem, if you consider it to be one.

3.   Most studies of the economics of technological change state that an important determinant of the rate of diffusion of an innovation is the expected profitability of that innovation. What influence, if any, does the variance of the expected profitability have upon the rate of diffusion?

4.   Firm X, a small manufacturing firm, has just developed a new and profitable productive process. Which of the following strategies is likely to be most profitable for Firm X to pursue? (a) Sell the development rights to the innovation to a larger firm; (b) patent the innovation and refuse to license any interested parties; (c) patent the innovation and attempt to realize substantial revenues by means of licensing other interested parties; (d) do not publicize the innovation, but attempt to use it secretly inside the firm.

5.   There is strong evidence that many small firms do not even maintain formal research and development establishments. Is this evidence that diseconomies of scale in research and development apparently exist at this size of firm, which are dissipated as the firm grows?

6.   Assume that you are Commissioner of Technology, and you have been directed to use your newly acquired powers of eminent domain in the area of technology to purchase for the public a new invention from an inventor. This invention promises to yield returns of about $10,000 per year to the inventor for a period of 20 years if the inventor controls it. The social worth of this innovation, if widely publicized and used, is estimated at $20,000 per year for a period of 20 years. What is the appropriate payment for you to make to the inventor?

10

Integration, Diversification,
and Merger

Rare is the firm that truly produces only one product. Most firms, even those commonly thought of as producing only one product, actually produce many. For example, the Ford Motor Company produces automobiles, to be sure. But Ford has also at one time or another been involved in the production of items such as spark plugs, paint, and car wax. Ford is also involved in the sale of automobiles at the retail level, and attempts to vend a huge variety of other goods and services that ordinarily accompany the sale of new and used automobiles.

The subject matter of this chapter concerns the logic behind integration and diversification, the extent and economic effect of these activities, and the appropriate posture that public policy should assume with respect to such activities. We will deal first with some important definitional distinctions that relate to integration and diversification, and then will document the motivation, extent, and effects of integration, diversification, and merger. In view of the recent wave of mergers, we will consider in some detail the economics of mergers between firms.

DEFINITIONAL MATTERS

Integration and *diversification* are terms that are used to describe the organizational characteristics of production. These terms are used in two different ways. First, one can speak of the existing state or degree of integration and diversification. In this case, the discussion refers to the organizational characteristics of production at a given point in time. The second way of using the terms is to signify the *act* of integrating or diversifying. That is, this second usage highlights *changes* in the organizational characteristics of production.

Two basic kinds of integration exist: horizontal and vertical.

Horizontal integration is the combination or merger of two or more firms that are at the same stage of the same productive process.

Vertical integration is the combination or merger of two or more firms that are at separable stages of the same productive process.

Although our definitions of integration have emphasized the act of integrating, it should be borne in mind that *integration* may also refer to a particular state of the organization of firms in a market.

Horizontal integration is conceptually easy to visualize; it involves the combination or merger of two firms that are producing the same product. The proposed merger of the Bethlehem Steel Corporation and the Youngstown Sheet and Tube Company during the 1950's is an example of horizontal integration.[1] Vertical integration is more versatile in nature. Table 10.1

TABLE 10.1

The Process of Steelmaking

Step	Process	Materials Involved
1	Mining	Coal, iron ore, limestone
2	Input preparation	Coke, ore concentrates
3	Smelting	Pig iron
4	Refining	Ingot steel
5	Rolling	Semifinished steel (e.g., rods)
6	Finishing	Finished steel products (e.g., pipe)
7	Fabrication	Manufactured steel products (e.g., buildings)
8	Distribution	

illustrates the productive process commonly referred to as steelmaking. The steelmaking productive process can be viewed as consisting of at least eight separate steps. Many steel firms (for example, U.S. Steel) have combined into one firm many of the early stages of the process. U.S. Steel owns and controls substantial iron-ore deposits and also the means to transport such ore to other locations. This type of vertical integration, which is in the direction of the factor supplies, is referred to as "upstream" vertical integration. Integration of a "downstream" nature, which is also commonplace in the steel market, could involve a steel company's acquiring its own facilities for rolling, finishing, fabricating, and perhaps even distributing. Downstream vertical integration involves the acquisition of a stage of the productive process that is closer to the final consumer market.

Contemporary examples of integration abound. The petroleum market is vertically integrated in both an upstream and a downstream fashion. Major petroleum refiners own oil reserves (upstream) and retail gas stations (downstream). Automobile manufacturers, as it was pointed out earlier, now produce many of the inputs used to make automobiles, and

[1]The Bethlehem–Youngstown merger resulted in a suit being brought by the Antitrust Division of the Department of Justice. The intent of the suit was to disallow the merger, and the district court concurred. *United States* v. *Bethlehem Steel Corp.*, 168 F. Supp. 576 (1958).

at the same time own and control many retail sales outlets and agencies for automobiles.[2]

Diversification is a concept that is inclusive of, but not limited to, vertical integration.

> *Diversification is the combination or merger of one firm with one or more other firms that are either at different stages in the same productive process or in totally different productive processes.*

Diversification has taken place when one firm acquires another firm that is not producing the same product. The acquired firm may be at a different stage of the same productive process (vertical integration); however, it might also be producing in an entirely different and unrelated productive process ("conglomerate" diversification).

Diversification, particularly diversification of a conglomerate nature, has become a very frequent occurrence. Conglomerates such as Gulf & Western, ITT, Litton Industries, and Ling-Temco-Vaught (LTV) have experienced dizzying rates of increase in size via the conglomerate-diversification route. Gulf & Western, for example, has acquired firms as disparate as Paramount Pictures and New Jersey Zinc. Gulf & Western began the 1960's as a manufacturer of automobile bumpers, with sales of $8.4 million. In 1968, after some 80 acquisitions, Gulf & Western's sales exceeded $1.3 billion.[3]

A STATISTICAL LOOK AT INTEGRATION, DIVERSIFICATION, AND MERGER

The common thread that unites integration and diversification is merger. Integration and diversification are accomplished by means of the combination and merger of firms. Sometimes the act of merger is hardly noticeable, in that the merged firms retain their separate identities and, often, their independence of action. In other cases, one of the firms (usually the acquired firm) passes out of existence as a legal entity. It is generally accepted that the American economy has experienced three distinct waves of mergers during the twentieth century. The first wave, which might be dated approximately 1895–1905, attained its peak at the turn of the century and resulted in the formation of many large firms and concentrated markets. Firms such as U.S. Steel, U.S. Rubber, AT&T, and American Tobacco were

---

[2]An informative discussion of the augmentation of the market power of the large producers of automobiles by means of their control of the market for repair parts may be found in Robert Crandall, "Vertical Integration and the Market for Repair Parts in the United States Automobile Industry," *Journal of Industrial Economics*, 16 (July 1968), 212–34.

[3]Arthur M. Louis, "Ten Conglomerates and How They Grew," *Fortune*, 74 (May 1969), 218.

products of this wave of mergers. The origins of many of the most highly concentrated markets are to be found in this time period.[4]

The second merger wave can be dated approximately 1920–33, with its peak during the last years of the 1920's. Eis has demonstrated that this wave was characterized primarily by horizontal mergers.[5] Particularly significant mergers took place in petroleum, primary metals, and food products. For example, National Dairy Products acquired 331 separate dairy firms between 1923 and 1932.[6]

The third wave of mergers, which began in approximately 1950, is perhaps still upon us as this book is being written. This wave of mergers has clearly dwarfed the others in terms of the number of mergers recorded. From 1950 through 1970, 25,475 mergers were recorded. The number in 1969 alone was 4,542,[7] which far exceeded the total number that occurred during the merger wave at the turn of the century, and was about two thirds of the total number recorded during the wave of the 1920's.

Horizontal mergers are once again prominent in the current merger wave. However, horizontal mergers involving firms that possess large proportions of their markets have virtually disappeared; instead, the horizontal mergers have involved small firms, frequently those operating only in local or regional markets. The outstanding feature of the current wave has been the frequency of mergers that diversify the activities of the acquiring firm. Conglomerate mergers, in particular, have increased in frequency. Table 10.2 reveals the strength of this trend. Whereas only 19.3 percent of all mergers were of a conglomerate nature during the 1926–30 time period, 81.6 percent were conglomerate in 1966–68. The meteoric rise of conglomerate firms such as Gulf & Western, LTV, Textron, and Litton Industries during the 1960's is clearly reflected in Table 10.2.

The amount of vertical integration already existent in the economy is neither well known nor easily measured. One of the few attempts to measure it was made by Gort.[8] In a classic study of integration and diversification, he examined a sample of 111 large firms during the period 1947–54. He determined the major product produced by each firm and classed all other products produced by the firm as "auxiliary" in nature. An admittedly imperfect measure of the integration of each firm was then constructed, consisting of the ratio of each firm's employment in auxiliary activities to the total employment of the firm. The assumption was that a

[4]The foremost historian of merger activity in American markets has been Ralph L. Nelson, *Merger Movements in American Industry, 1895–1956* (Princeton, N.J.: Princeton University Press, 1959).

[5]Carl Eis, "The 1919–1930 Merger Movement in American Industry," *Journal of Law and Economics*, 12 (October 1969), 267–96.

[6]A.C. Hoffman, *Large Scale Organization in the Food Industries* (Washington, D.C.: U.S. Government Printing Office, 1940), pp. 27–28.

[7]Bureau of Economics, Federal Trade Commission, *Current Trends in Merger Activity, 1970*, R 6–15–10 (Washington, D.C.: U.S. Government Printing Office, 1971), p. 8.

[8]Michael Gort, *Diversification and Integration in American Industry* (Princeton, N.J.: Princeton University Press, 1962).

TABLE 10.2

The Changing Character of Mergers, 1926–1968

Type of Merger	Time Period					
	1926–1930	1940–1947	1951–1955	1956–1960	1961–1965	1966–1968
Horizontal	75.9%	62.0%	39.2%	30.1%	22.5%	8.6%
Vertical	4.8%	17.0%	12.2%	14.9%	17.5%	9.8%
Conglomerate	19.3%	21.0%	48.6%	55.0%	60.0%	81.6%
Total	100.0%	100.0%	100.0%	100.0%	100.0%	100.0%

Source: *Federal Trade Commission*, Economic Report on Corporate Mergers, *Hearings on Economic Concentration, Subcommittee on Antitrust and Monopoly, U.S. Senate, 91st Cong., 1st sess. (Washington, D.C.: U.S. Government Printing Office, 1969), p. 63.*

high ratio of auxiliary to total employment represented a greater amount of vertical integration. Gort's estimates ranged from a low of 9.7 percent in transportation to 67.3 percent in petroleum. The average for 13 broad market groups similar to two-digit SIC industries was 25.2 percent.[9]

Adelman has addressed himself to the question of whether the degree of vertical integration of economic activity has been increasing or decreasing.[10] He concluded from a study of the period 1849–1951 that there had been no recognizable change in the degree of vertical integration. A more recent study conducted by Laffer for the period 1929–65 resulted in the same conclusion.[11] Laffer also found the degree of vertical integration to be unrelated to the business cycle. Other researchers have failed to find a significant connection between the degree of vertical integration and either the amount of market concentration[12] or firm size.[13]

Robinson has coined the term "vertical disintegration" to label the phenomenon of firms voluntarily divesting themselves of the ownership and control of other firms at different stages of the same productive process.[14] Robinson was not impressed with the empirical importance of this possibility, and there is little evidence of the pervasiveness of such a development in the United States, except where it has been hastened by antitrust pressures. Heflebower, however, has concluded that the efforts of General

[9]*Ibid.*, pp. 79–81.

[10]M.A. Adelman, "Concept and Statistical Measurement of Vertical Integration," in *Business Concentration and Price Policy*, George J. Stigler, ed. (Princeton, N.J.: Princeton University Press, 1955), pp. 281–322.

[11]Arthur B. Laffer, "Vertical Integration by Corporations, 1929–1965," *Review of Economics and Statistics*, 51 (February 1969), 91–93.

[12]Nelson, *Merger Movements.*

[13]Gort, *Diversification and Integration.*

[14]E.A.G. Robinson, *The Structure of Competitive Industry* (Chicago: University of Chicago Press, 1958), p. 20.

Motors after World War II to strip itself of some firms that maintained a vertical relationship to GM, and GM's general attempts to decentralize, were in fact vertical disintegration in action.[15]

The degree of vertical integration in the American economy may be changing only imperceptibly, but the same is not true of the degree of diversification. Available evidence indicates that both the total amount and the rate of diversification have increased since World War II. It should be remembered that vertical integration is but one possible avenue for the diversification of the firm. Another possible means is conglomerate diversification by the firm into productive processes that are unrelated to the firm's previous activities. Table 10.2 emphasized the fact that conglomerate mergers now account for over four-fifths of all recorded mergers. It is the rising tide of conglomerate mergers, and not increased vertical integration, that is responsible for the rising tide of diversification in the American economy.

Two methods have been used to measure the degree of diversification. The first is based upon employment and is the ratio of a firm's "primary" employment to its total employment. A firm's primary employment consists of those employees whose work activities are substantially involved in the production of the product that accounts for the greatest proportion of the firm's employment. The primary-employment ratio may vary between zero and 1, with values near zero indicative of extreme diversification, and values near 1 indicative of the absence of diversification. Gort's work with primary-employment ratios is the best known. Gort found that the primary-employment ratio for his 111 manufacturing firms fell from .69 to .64 between 1947 and 1954.[16] Other, more recent information compiled by Koch, from data made available by the Federal Trade Commission, indicates that during the period 1947–63, the primary-product specialization ratio fell in 84 SIC four-digit industries, rose in 61, and remained constant in 27.[17] Changing industry definitions and lack of data prevented an extension of the comparison to the more than 200 other four-digit industries.

The second measure of diversification involves nothing more than a simple count of the number of SIC industries in which firms are involved. Gort found that 7 of his 111 firms were involved in more than 40 different four-digit SIC industries in the year 1954.[18] General Electric alone was involved in 74 out of the 430 possible four-digit SIC industries. Houghton examined the 1,000 largest industrial firms in the year 1962. Only 49 of these 1,000 firms were active in only one SIC industry at the five-digit level

[15]Richard B. Heflebower, "Observations on Decentralization in Large Enterprises, *Journal of Industrial Economics*, 9 (November 1960), 7–22.

[16]Gort, *Diversification and Integration*, p. 61, Table 23.

[17]Bureau of Economics, Federal Trade Commission, *Industry Classification and Concentration* (Washington, D.C.: U.S. Government Printing Office, 1967). The primary-product specialization ratios reported here are strictly analogous to primary-employment ratios. The sole difference is that the primary-product specialization ratios were based upon value-of-shipments data rather than employment.

[18]Gort, *Diversification and Integration*, pp. 155–57, Table B-1.

of detail. Fifteen of the firms maintained activities in more than 50 of the five-digit SIC classifications.[19] In a study that relied upon a much broader definition of markets, O'Hanlon found that Litton Industries was a participant in 18 of 54 possible market categories in 1967.[20]

There is little doubt that diversification has increased. How much is not clear. Berry, for example, has argued that the true increase in diversification from 1960 to 1965 was only 3 to 5 percent, not 40 percent as would be suggested by simple counts of the number of markets in which firms are involved.[21] It is apparent that such arithmetic counts can overemphasize very casual participation in a given market by a firm. On the other hand, primary-employment ratios, the other major alternative measure of diversification, ignore the numerical diversity of markets in which a firm is involved and are very sensitive to substantial diversification into a market. Both measures, however, point to increased firm diversification in the American economy.

THE MOTIVATIONS FOR MERGER

The static theory of the firm (portions of which were reviewed in Chapter 2) deals with a single-product, single-plant firm. Indeed, mergers, diversification, and integration are seldom if ever mentioned when the theory of the firm is considered. It is hardly surprising, then, that the static theory of the firm is an inadequate means of explaining the accelerated merger activities of firms in recent years. It is correct to state that no single theory of mergers is accepted by most observers of the merger scene. There exist many competing theories that incorporate many different explanatory factors. Although not all these theories are equally useful, the root cause of the recent wave of mergers is probably an amalgam of many of them.

Merger for Profits

The most frequently implied cause of merger is the increased profitability that is said to result. A great number of other hypotheses seeking to explain merger (for example, the contention that firms merge in order to attain market power) are ultimately explainable in terms of the increased profits that will be generated if the goal concerned (market power) is achieved. It is altogether remarkable, therefore, that virtually no modern

[19]Harrison F. Houghton, Testimony in U.S. Senate, Committee on the Judiciary, Subcommittee on Antitrust and Monopoly, Hearings, *Economic Concentration, Part 1* (Washington, D.C.: U.S. Government Printing Office, 1964), pp. 155–58.

[20]Thomas O'Hanlon, "The Odd News About Conglomerates," *Fortune,* 79 (June 15, 1967), 175–77.

[21]Charles H. Berry, *Corporate Bigness and Diversification in Manufacturing* (Washington, Brookings Institution, 1967).

evidence exists that points to increased profitability on the part of merged firms. Hogarty, an informed observer of the recent wave of mergers, has commented that "no one who has undertaken a major empirical study of mergers has concluded that mergers are profitable, i.e., profitable in the sense of being 'more profitable' than alternative forms of investment."[22]

Three major studies performed since World War II have examined the relationship between profitability and merger. These studies furnish a strong basis for the conclusion that the net effect of merger upon profitability is at the very least neutral, and may even be negative. Kelly selected two samples of 21 firms from the list of *Fortune*'s 500 largest industrial companies and 50 largest merchandisers. The first sample of firms included only those whose merger activity has been great. The second group of firms was characterized by little or no merger activity and served as a control group. Kelly utilized five different measures of profitability during the period 1946–60 and concluded that mergers had no perceptible effect upon profitability.[23]

Whereas the sample used by Kelly was somewhat arbitrarily chosen, as well as being deficient in size, the same criticism does not apply to work performed by Reid.[24] Reid examined the profitability of 478 firms among *Fortune*'s largest 500 firms for the year 1961. In an analysis incorporating three different measures of profitability, he found a weak, but negative, relationship between profitability and merger activity.

Hogarty performed a careful study of the profitability–merger relationship.[25] His sample consisted of 43 firms randomly selected from *Moody's Industrial Manual* for the year 1965. Hogarty recognized that the motives of managers for mergers (increased growth and size) might be different from the motives of stockholders (increased profitability). However, neither growth nor profitability proved to be valid explanations of the mergers observed. Having taken into account the fact that the adding together of two firms' sales via merger would create a new firm with the sum of these sales, Hogarty found that in well over half the cases, profitability did not increase beyond the level that would have been expected given the previous profitability of the merging firms.

Table 10.3 provides a crude but useful look at the comparative profitability of conglomerate firms vis-à-vis firms in other broad market groups. The profit rates of conglomerate firms are quite close to the average profit rate for firms in all market groups. Further, conglomerates showed no

[22]Thomas F. Hogarty, "Profits from Merger: The Evidence of Fifty Years, *St. John's Law Review*, 44 (Spring 1970), 378–91.

[23]Eamon Kelly, *The Profitability of Growth Through Mergers* (Thesis, Columbia University 1965).

[24]Samuel R. Reid, *Mergers, Managers, and the Economy* (New York: McGraw-Hill Book Company, 1968), Chap. 8, pp. 153–75.

[25]Portions of Hogarty's work have been reported in three places: Hogarty, "Profits from Merger"; Thomas F. Hogarty, "The Profitability of Corporate Mergers," *Journal of Business*, 43 (July 1970), 317–27; and Michael Gort and Thomas F. Hogarty, "New Evidence on Mergers," *Journal of Law and Economics*, 13 (April 1970), 167–84.

TABLE 10.3

Comparative Performance of Selected Industry Groups and Conglomerate Companies

Group	Average 5-Year Return on Equity	Average 5-Year Return on Total Capital	Average Return on Equity, 1970
Nonferrous Metals	15.2%	12.3%	12.7%
Electronics	13.5%	11.3%	12.3%
Energy	12.9%	9.5%	10.7%
Chemicals	11.3%	8.7%	9.5%
Automotive	10.8%	8.9%	8.7%
Steel	8.1%	6.6%	5.3%
Average of 27 Broad Industry Groups	12.4%	9.5%	10.4%
Conglomerates	14.0%	9.9%	10.4%

Source: *Adapted from "Who's Where Within the Industry Groups?"* Forbes, *107 (January 1, 1971), 66.*

greater ability to defend their profitability in the face of slackened business conditions than did other firms.

Merger to Reduce Risk

The fact that there is little evidence of increased mean profitability on the part of merged firms does not exclude the possibility that merger might reduce instability of profits and general risk associated with profitability for firms involved. Reduced risk (risk typically being approximated by the variance or standard deviation of profit rates) is a common explanation of merger, and particularly of diversification. The old adage that advises against carrying all one's eggs in a single basket is a manifestation of some statistical principles upon which some mergers may be based. We will briefly examine those principles before evaluating the empirical evidence concerning merger and risk.

Variability with reference to the mean or average of a group of numbers is often adopted as a measure of risk and instability. A very common statistical measure of variability about the mean is a statistic known as the standard deviation. Standard deviation is a popular statistic largely because it possesses many desirable statistical properties. For example, under certain circumstances, the standard deviation of a group of numbers can be used to make a definite statement about the likelihood of a given occurrence, such as the probability of a certain rate of profit being earned. *Ceteris paribus,* the higher the standard deviation, the greater is variability and risk.

We will now demonstrate what diversification (via merger) can and cannot do with respect to the variability of profit rates. Assume the existence of a firm (Firm A) that earns the rates of profit on invested capital indicated in Table 10.4a during each of four years.[26] Firm A's mean profit rate during the four years is 6.5 percent. The standard deviation of those profit rates is 1.12, and is computed by means of the following formula:

$$\text{S.D.} = \sqrt{\sum_{i=1}^{N} (x_i - \bar{x})^2 / N}$$

Each profit rate is considered to be a particular x_i; the mean profit rate is labeled $\bar{x}$. $\sum_{i=1}^{N}$ indicates that the squared differences between each x_i and $\bar{x}$ should be summed. N is the number of years profit rates were earned.

Next, assume another firm of exactly the same size, Firm B, whose profit experience over the same four-year period is indicated in Table 10.4b. Is it possible that a merger of firms A and B could result in a greater stability of profit rates than was experienced by either Firm A or Firm B? That is, if instability of profit rates is regarded as evidence of risk, is it possible for merger to reduce such risk? It is clear from Table 10.4b that this is possible. The merged firm, Firm A-B, has a standard deviation of profit rates less than that of either of the individual firms. Diversification, therefore, has the potential to reduce risk.

It is often true that when two firms merge whose profit rates move in opposite directions during the same time period (that is, whose profit rates are negatively correlated), the variability of the merged firm's profit rate will be less than the variability of the profit rates of either of the merging firms. But more than simple negative correlation of firms' profit rates is needed in order to ensure that a merger will reduce risk. Consider Table 10.4c, which describes a merger between Firms A and C. The profit rates of Firm A and C are negatively correlated; that is, their profit rates generally move in opposite directions as time passes. Note that when Firms A and C merge into Firm A-C, the standard deviation of the merged firm's profits is larger than that of Firm A's profits prior to merger. Such a merger, therefore, would increase rather than decrease risk from Firm A's standpoint. This occurs because the standard deviation of Firm C's profit rates is so large relative to the standard deviation of Firm A's profits. Firm C's profit-rate variability is so large that a merger between Firms A and C would not reduce the risk faced by Firm A.

Hence, both the correlation between profit rates and the absolute size of the variability of each firm's profit rate influence the variability of the merged firm's profit rate. The precise statistical relationship among correlation, size of variability, and the standard deviation of the profit rate of a merged firm is beyond the scope of this volume. The reader is referred to Alberts for a rigorous discussion of the principles involved.[27] It suffices for

[26]We simplify the example for purposes of clarity of exposition by using an example based upon only a four-year time period. There is nothing magic about four years, and longer time periods are generally desirable.

[27]William W. Alberts, "The Profitability of Growth by Merger," in William W. Alberts and Joel E. Segall, eds., The Corporate Merger (Chicago: University of Chicago Press, 1966), pp. 262–72.

TABLE 10.4a

Profit Characteristics of Firm A

Year	Profit Rate (%)
1	6.0
2	7.0
3	8.0
4	5.0
Mean = 6.5	
S.D. = 1.12	

TABLE 10.4b

Profit Characteristics of Merged Firms A and B

Firm A		Firm B		Merged Firm A-B	
Year	Profit Rate (%)	Year	Profit Rate (%)	Year	Profit Rate (%)
1	6.0	1	6.0	1	6.0
2	7.0	2	3.0	2	5.0
3	8.0	3	2.0	3	5.0
4	5.0	4	7.0	4	6.0
Mean = 6.5		Mean = 4.5		Mean = 5.5	
S.D. = 1.12		S.D. = 2.06		S.D. = .50	

TABLE 10.4c

Profit Characteristics of Merged Firms A and C

Firm A		Firm C		Merged Firm A-C	
Year	Profit Rate (%)	Year	Profit Rate (%)	Year	Profit Rate (%)
1	6.0	1	6.0	1	6.0
2	7.0	2	1.0	2	4.0
3	8.0	3	0.0	3	4.0
4	5.0	4	11.0	4	8.0
Mean = 6.5		Mean = 4.5		Mean = 5.5	
S.D. = 1.12		S.D. = 4.39		S.D. = 1.66	

our purposes to have demonstrated that there are many instances in which diversification via merger can indeed reduce the variability of the profit rate of the merged firm below that of any of the firms that were involved in the merger.

The preceding examples reveal that reduced variability is a possible, not a necessary outcome of merger. Yet another point must also be stressed in this respect. The variability or risk associated with any firm is typically calculated on the basis of past performance. There is no guarantee, of course, that the future performance of the firms involved will be the same. A merger that is expected to reduce the variability that the merged firm's profits have shown in the past may actually increase the variability of its profits in the future, if the past profit behavior of the firms involved in the merger is not duplicated in the future.

The paucity of empirical evidence concerning merger and risk is a reflection of the recent nature of the conglomerate-merger phenomenon. The evidence that is available provides no support for the conclusion that acquiring firms successfully reduce their risk (as measured by instability of earnings) by means of merger.[28] This is somewhat shocking in view of the widespread lip service paid diversification as a principle of portfolio management.[29]

It will be remembered that in Chapter 7, evidence was introduced indicating that the variability of large firms' profit rates was less than the variability of small firms' profit rates.[30] We have just stated that size-increasing mergers apparently do not decrease the variability of firms' profit rates. Are these two findings contradictory? The answer is, not necessarily. Hall and Weiss did find that firm size and profit-rate variability were inversely related; however, their evidence pertains only to firms within *Fortune*'s 500 largest industrial firms and is cross-sectional in nature. Growth in firm size via the merger route, particularly when across conventional market lines, need not affect the firm's profitability in the same fashion that observed differences in firm size apparently affect firms in a cross-sectional snapshot of the economy.

Merger Because of Stock-Market Effects

Waves of merger activity have been historically associated with periods of active trading and rising prices in the stock market. Nelson found stock prices and the number of mergers consummated to be positively correlated ($+.47$) between 1895 and 1954.[31] The reasons for this are not clear; however, the expectations of both buyers and sellers may have been responsible.

---

[28]See, for example, Hogarty, "Profits from Merger."

[29]It has been argued, however, that since individual investors can diversify their own portfolios and do not need firms to do that for them, there is no need for firms to diversify. Hence, diversified firms will not be better buys in the market, and pleasing investors is not a stimulus for diversification. An early statement of this view may be found in Malcolm R. Fisher, "Toward a Theory of Diversification," *Oxford Economic Papers*, n.s. 13 (October 1961), 293–311. A more recent discussion is contained in William W. Alberts, "Profitability of Growth," pp. 271–72.

[30]Marshall Hall and Leonard Weiss, "Firm Size and Profitability," *Review of Economics and statistics*, 49 (August 1967), 319–31.

[31]Nelson, *Merger Movements*, p. 118.

Much ado has been made in recent years about the pure stock-market manipulative effects that have become possible via the conglomerate-merger route, based upon the expectations of investors in the stock market. A conglomerate firm can experience growth in its earnings, by means of the merger process if investors' expectations can be maintained in a certain fashion. A much-quoted scenario for such a situation is the following.[32]

Suppose that two firms exist. One is a conglomerate named International Everything, the other a one-product firm named One Product. International Everything has 1,000,000 shares outstanding and has annual net profits of $1,000,000—one dollar per share. International Everything, however, is a glamorous growth company and is selling for a 30:1 price–earnings ratio—that is, $30 per share. One Product also has 1,000,000 shares outstanding and $1,000,000 per year in net profits, but is priced at only a 10:1 ratio and, therefore, sells for $10 per share. International Everything, a rapidly growing conglomerate, proposes to buy One Product, offering a one-half share of newly issued stock in International Everything to each holder of one share of One Product stock. Since half a share of International Everything is worth $15 at current market prices, it is an offer of $15 for $10. The owners of One Product find this offer irresistible and sell One Product to International Everything. After the merger, International Everything has 1,500,000 shares of stock outstanding and $2,000,000 of earnings. International Everything's earnings per share are now $1.33 instead of the premerger $1.00. If investors continue to regard International Everything as a 30:1 buy in terms of price–earnings ratio (a crucial assumption), the price of International Everything will rise from $30 to $40 per share. Everybody, it seems, is happy, and everyone, it seems, has gained. As long as International Everything acquires firms that have lower price–earnings ratios than it has, it can increase its earnings per share by means of merger. And its price per share in the market will rise as long as investors continue to maintain the same price–earnings expectations about International Everything.

These manipulative effects, where obtainable, would clearly be a stimulus to merger. It would be incorrect, nevertheless, to ascribe a large proportion of mergers to this motive. Many of the largest conglomerate firms do not have high price–earnings ratios. Moreover, these same large conglomerate firms often acquire firms with price–earnings ratios greater than their own. For example, Textron, a high-flying conglomerate in the 1960's, had a price–earnings ratio of 13:1 in 1961 when it acquired Spencer Kellogg and Sons, a firm with a 22:1 price–earnings ratio.[33]

In sum, stock-market effects are a possible cause of mergers, but certainly not a demonstrably important cause. We must look elsewhere in order to explain the many mergers that do not correspond to the scenario above.

[32]Adapted from "The Conglomerates," *Wall Street Journal,* 172 (July 25, 1968), 18.
[33]*Fortune,* 74 (May 15, 1969), p. 208.

Merger Because of Valuation Discrepancies

In the context of mergers, valuation discrepancies exist when circumstances cause Firm A to be willing to pay a price for Firm B that is greater than the price Firm B itself feels it is worth. In such a circumstance, a sale resulting in merger is likely to occur. Such a valuation discrepancy could have its origins in the stock-market effects described earlier; however, such phenomena are not the only potential cause. Gort has pointed out that when changes in technology are rapid and price fluctuations are frequent, valuation discrepancies can arise because of differences in how firms perceive events and form their expectations.[34] Rapid market growth can also encourage valuation discrepancies.

Another possible source of valuation discrepancies can be found in the tax laws. Tax laws that favor income deferral and encourage the taking of tax losses may stimulate mergers even if the acquired firm is a "loser" in terms of profitability.[35] Differing accounting procedures can also result in vastly different views about the worth of a firm.

Lack of management succession is another possible source of valuation discrepancies. If a firm has been owner-managed, and the elderly owner anticipates possible death or retirement, which would leave the firm without a family member to manage and run it, he may choose to sell the firm. In this case, the owner's valuation of the worth of the firm is affected by the lack of immediate family to succeed him in the management process. A related development sometimes occurs when the elderly owner of a firm needs to establish a valuation for his firm for tax purposes. He knows that if he dies, his estate, including the firm, must be so evaluated. The Internal Revenue Service, while not completely lacking in charity, may tend to overvalue the firm so that more taxes are paid. If, however, the firm is sold before the owner's death, then a market valuation of some sort has been placed on the firm for estate purposes. In both the preceding examples, the mere aging of management can alter the valuation placed upon a firm.

A classic example of an apparent valuation discrepancy was disclosed by the officials of the Falstaff Brewing Company when they asserted that they could acquire brewing capacity via the merger route at about one half the cost per barrel of building new capacity from scratch.[36] *Ceteris paribus,* if markets are operating competitively and efficiently, the cost per barrel of

---

[34]Michael Gort, "An Economic Disturbance Theory of Mergers," *Quarterly Journal of Economics,* 83 (November 1969), 624–42.

[35]Dewey has argued that many mergers occur because the tax laws encourage firms to acquire unprofitable firms in order to obtain a tax write-off. [Donald J. Dewey, "Mergers and Cartels: Some Reservations About Policy," *American Economic Review,* 51 (May 1961), 255–62.] Boyle, however, has performed statistical tests that give little support to this hypothesis. [Stanley E. Boyle, "Pre-Merger Growth and Profit Characteristics of Large Conglomerate Mergers in the United States," *St. John's Law Review,* 44 (Spring 1970), 152–70.]

[36]"How Falstaff Brews New Markets," *Business Week,* No. 1926 (July 30, 1966), 46.

acquiring capacity through merger should tend to be the same as the cost of building new capacity. This, however, was clearly not the case.

Gort has tested a form of the valuation-discrepancies hypothesis by means of a sample of 5,534 mergers recorded by the Federal Trade Commission during the years 1951 through 1959. He found strong evidence that the rate of merger is positively influenced by the rate of technological change and industry growth. Gort argues that this evidence supports the valuation-discrepancies hypothesis because valuation discrepancies most often occur during periods of rapid flux and change.[37]

Merger to Gain Efficiency

It is possible that mergers can result in the realization of economies of scale. Nearly all the possible causes of economies of scale inside a single firm are also applicable to the merger of firms. Among the more obvious possible causes of economies of scale are reductions in inventory needs, lowered transportation and distribution costs, technical propinquity that eliminates duplicative research and results in complementary R&D, cheaper input prices owing to increased size of purchase, and the combination of two firms that were individually suboptimal in size.[38] Coase has suggested that firms that merge and integrate do so in order to supersede the price system; use of the price system entails costs, and merger eliminates some of those costs.[39]

The entire argument in support of the realization of scale economies because of merger relies upon the presumption that the joint operation of two otherwise separate firms will somehow result in lower per-unit costs of production and distribution. It will be recalled, however, that the evidence surveyed in Chapter 6 lends very little encouragement to the expectation of significant multiplant economies of scale. Further, many of the alleged benefits of merger (for example, the reduction of transportation costs via the elimination of cross-hauling) apply primarily to horizontal mergers and not to vertical and conglomerate mergers. Since the large majority of mergers are now of a conglomerate variety (see Table 10.2), the possible economies of scale accruing from mergers are reduced.

No empirical evidence based on a substantial number of mergers points to the realization of economies of scale via the merger route. Gort has attempted to test the hypothesis that economies of scale are an important incentive for (and result of) merger; he concluded that the evidence encouraged the opposite conclusion.[40] It appears that many of the econo-

---

[37]Gort, "Economic Disturbance Theory."

[38]Weiss has argued that many mergers involve the acquisition of suboptimal capacity by the acquiring firm. Leonard W. Weiss, "An Evaluation of Mergers in Six Industries," *Review of Economics and Statistics,* 47 (May 1965), 172–81.

[39]Ronald H. Coase, "The Nature of the Firm," *Economica,* n.s., 4 (November 1937), 386–405.

[40]Gort, "Economic Disturbance Theory."

mies of scale mistakenly attributed to mergers are in fact the result of the exercise of market power that can result from mergers.[41] We will, therefore, turn our attention to the question of whether the pursuit of market power is a basic motivation for merger.

Merger to Attain Market Power

The potential for growth in market power by means of merger cannot be ignored. Thomas Edison admitted that a prime motive behind the formation of General Electric was the desire to establish formidable market power.[42] Horizontal mergers, in particular, can produce firms that possess considerable market power. The previously cited merger wave at the turn of the twentieth century produced industrial titans such as U.S. Steel. Although there has been little attempt to specify exactly how much or in what ways market power is enhanced by horizontal mergers, the spectre of increased market power and lessened competition because of them has resulted in what amounts to a judicially imposed prohibition against horizontal mergers involving or creating firms that are even a modest proportion of a local or national market.

Whether or not the market power of a newly formed firm can be greater than the sum of the market power of the firms that merged to form it is a matter of controversy. Weston has suggested that synergy (a circumstance in which the whole exceeds the sum of the parts) is a possible outcome of merger:

> Another type of general theory for diversification, internal and external, is synergy. This aspect embraces a very wide range of elements which ultimately result in a $2 + 2 =$ more than 4 effect. Synergy results from complementary activities or from the carryover of managerial capabilities. . . . One firm may have a strong research organization, while the other may excel in production and marketing; joining the two renders both firms more effective. Similarly, one firm may possess good product lines but lack the requisite marketing organization; the former's combination with the firm having the strong marketing organization of the type required benefits both firms. . .appropriate merger combinations will achieve the requisite balance throughout the operation.[43]

Stigler, among others, has voiced doubts that synergistic market power does result from mergers; however, Stigler also says that if it does, the purchase price of the acquired firm will be bid up to reflect this synergistic

[41]The theoretical tradeoff between scale economies and market power resulting from merger was discussed in Chapter 6.

[42]H.C. Passer, *The Electrical Manufacturers: 1875–1900* (Cambridge, Mass.: Harvard University Press, 1953), p. 326.

[43]J. Fred Weston, "The Nature and Significance of Conglomerate Firms," *St. John's Law Review*, 44 (Spring 1970), 70.

value.[44] "Bargains" owing to synergy, therefore, are not to be expected. An attempt has been made to determine if bargains or premiums are paid by acquiring firms to the acquired firm in the merger process. Reilly found that "in nearly 88 percent of the mergers examined...the surviving corporation paid a premium to the stockholders of the acquired firm of about 7 percent."[45] Weston has suggested that the premium may be as high as 50 percent in some cases.[46] Of course, any study of the size of premiums paid must necessarily be based upon some notion of what the ordinary value of the firm would be in the absence of synergy. This is not easily ascertained. As a result, the Reilly evidence on purchase-price premiums must be regarded as a promising start to the analysis of bargains and premiums, and not the last word on the issue.

Vertical mergers in either a downstream or an upstream direction can increase market power. Downstream mergers often involve the acquisition of retail outlets, which can have the effect of foreclosing substantial portions of retail markets from competition. Examples are not difficult to find: Automobile manufacturers own retail automobile sales agencies that are not allowed to sell the automobiles produced by competing manufacturers. The well-known *Brown Shoe Case* was notable for the attention it gave to the retail shoe outlets owned by Brown and Kinney.[47] Similar considerations underlay the enforced divestiture of the General Motors stock owned by du Pont.[48]

In cases of upstream vertical integration, particularly where it is aimed at control of factor supplies, the owners of the factor inputs may force competitors to dance to strange tunes in order to earn the privilege of buying factor inputs. During the early 1940's, when Alcoa was virtually the sole producer and source of virgin aluminum ingot in the United States, Alcoa and several competing firms were engaged in the fabrication of aluminum ingots into sheet aluminum. Alcoa charged its competitor firms exceptionally high prices for their ingot purchases until judicial action forced a change in behavior.[49] A recent example of upstream vertical integration that has been frowned upon by the courts is Ford Motor Company's ownership of Autolite, a producer of automobile spark plugs.[50] The effects

[44]George J. Stigler, "Mergers and Preventive Antitrust Policy," *University of Pennsylvania Law Review*, 104 (November 1955), 178–84. Stigler comments (p. 184), "I must confess that the exact mechanics by which the total power possessed by firms gets larger than the sum of the parts escapes me."

[45]Frank K. Reilly, "What Determines the Ratio of Exchange in Corporate Mergers?" *Financial Analysts Journal*, 18 (November–December 1962), 47–50. Gort and Hogarty, "New Evidence on Mergers," also found similar evidence.

[46]J. Fred Weston, "The Determination of Share Exchange Ratios in Mergers," in William W. Alberts and Joel E. Segall, eds., *The Corporate Merger* (Chicago: University of Chicago Press, 1966), pp. 131–38.

[47]*Brown Shoe Company, Inc. v. United States,* 370 U.S. 294 (1962).

[48]*United States v. E.I. du Pont de Nemours and Company et al.,* 353 U.S. 586 (1957); 366 U.S. 316 (1961).

[49]*United States v. Aluminum Company of America et al.,* 44 F. Supp. 97 (1941); 148 F. 2d 416 (1945).

[50]As reported in "Supreme Court Rules Ford Can't Make Spark Plugs for 10 Years, Must Sell Line," *Wall Street Journal,* 52 (Thursday, March 30, 1972), 3ff.

of market foreclosure, in spark plugs or elsewhere, depend greatly upon the number of alternative suppliers or demanders and upon price elasticities of supply and demand.

Conglomerate mergers offer less opportunity for the enhancement of market power of the acquiring firm. The possible exercise of already-existing market power by the acquiring firm is a more important factor in a conglomerate merger than the possible augmentation of that market power by the merger.[51] The possibility that a large conglomerate firm will engage in cross-subsidization of its various branches has been suggested by several writers.[52] The core of this thesis is that a large conglomerate firm will engage in price discrimination in one market in order to monopolize that market while maintaining its prices in all other markets. Very few actual cases of such behavior have ever been documented, despite the insistence by the Federal Trade Commission and others that "predatory pricing is a fact of industrial life."[53] The enhancement of market power by means of conglomerate merger is not an empirical reality.

Mergers, especially conglomerate mergers, are frequently criticized on the basis of the possible buying reciprocity that might result.[54] Reciprocity is the practice of one firm's stating to another, "I will buy from you if you will buy from me." Reciprocity can, and does upon occasion, involve open coercion and the absence of meaningful price competition.[55] It is admittedly an important determinant of the identity of buyers and sellers in the chemical, petroleum, and steel markets.[56] The impact of reciprocity is likely to be small and the duration short if the reciprocal prices charged are not competitive in nature. The competitive level of the prices charged in a reciprocal agreement is not, however, the important issue. As the court noted in the *Consolidated Foods Case,* reciprocity can destroy price competition.[57] To the extent that conglomerate mergers reduce the number of independent decision points in the economy, they may be a cause of reciprocity and reduced price competition. Nevertheless, in the absence of evidence that conglomerate firms exercise monopsonistic power in order to

[51]*Federal Trade Commission* v. *The Proctor and Gamble Co. et al.,* 87 S. Ct. 1224, 1231 (1967), is an example.

[52]Early note of predatory pricing by conglomerate firms was made by Fritz Machlup, "Characteristics and Types of Price Discrimination," in *Business Concentration and Price Policy,* George J. Stigler, ed. (Princeton, N.J.: Princeton University Press, 1955), pp. 397–435; and Robert C. Brooks, Jr., "Price Cutting and Monopoly Power," *Journal of Marketing,* 25 (July 1961), 44–49.

[53]John R. Reilly, "Conglomerate Mergers—An Argument for Action," *Northwestern Law Review* 61 (September–October 1966), 534.

[54]Notable among these criticisms is that of the former head of the Bureau of Economics of the Federal Trade Commission, Willard F. Mueller, in *A Primer on Monopoly and Competition* (New York: Random House, Inc., 1970), pp. 94–97.

[55]For example, in the mid-1960's, General Dynamics Corporation openly acknowledged the fact that it maintained a trade-relations department to extract sales from those firms from whom it made purchases. See Mueller, *A Primer on Monopoly and Competition,* p. 96.

[56]Leonard Sloane, "Reciprocity: Where Does the P.A. Stand?" *Purchasing,* 51 (November 20, 1961), 70–71.

[57]*Federal Trade Commission* v. *Consolidated Foods Corporation,* 380 U.S. 592 (1964).

command lower input prices, reciprocity would not appear to be an important stimulus to merger.

Merger for Growth

Growth is intimately related to merger. Except in very unusual circumstances, the merger of two or more firms will result in a firm that is larger in size than any of the individual firms. Hence, growth is an important outcome of most mergers. Gort's frequently cited study of diversification and integration revealed that the most frequently entered markets were those characterized by rapid growth rates and high rates of technological change. He also observed that the growth rates of markets entered by diversifying firms were often higher than the growth rates of the markets in which the firms already participated.[58] The question therefore arises, Is a fundamental motive for merger on the part of acquiring firms a simple desire to maximize growth, given some minimum profit constraint? The evidence on this issue is, as usual, limited in amount and mixed in terms of results. It is consequently well worth our while to precede our discussion of that evidence by a clarification of the basic issues surrounding growth maximization.

Our work in Chapter 3 revealed that the underlying basis for many non-profit-maximizing theories of the firm was the concept of the separation of ownership and management. That is, much is attributed in these theories to the fact that large corporations are typically not managed by their large stockholders. Separation of ownership and management was alleged to cause a divergence of interest between the two, such that stockholders are primarily interested in the current and future size of their dividends, whereas managers are more interested in the size of the firm, its growth, and their own prerogatives, prestige, and salary. Dennis Mueller has suggested that these differences in motivation may be expressed in terms of the differing rates of discount applied by stockholders and by management to the time stream of profits facing them.[59] Stockholders are most concerned with the immediate, and therefore have high rates of discount. Managers are more inclined to sacrifice current profits in search of growth, and therefore have lower rates of discount. In any case, this divergence of interest could plausibly be evidence of the motivation of managers in parting with current profits in order to experience the rapid growth that is a consequence of an aggressive merger policy.

The preceding argument fails to recognize that what is ostensibly a growth-maximizing policy in the short run can also be a profit-maximizing policy in the long run, because it maximizes the present discounted value

---

[58]Gort, *Diversification and Integration,* Chap. 4.

[59]Dennis C. Mueller, "A Theory of Conglomerate Mergers," *Quarterly Journal of Economics,* 83 (November 1969), 643–59.

of the time stream of profits as seen from the vantage point of the current period. Major differences in behavior are implied by short-run and long-run maximization of profits. Because of this, Mueller has commented that it is virtually impossible to construct a rigorous and discriminating empirical test of the growth-maximization hypothesis with respect to mergers, since such a test must rely upon future developments that are unknown in the current period.[60]

Reid has tested a hypothesis that is closely related to the growth-maximization hypothesis.[61] Rather than testing the proposition that the differing interests of stockholders and managers cause mergers for the purpose of growth, Reid examined the hypothesis that frequent mergers will transform a firm into one that is more oriented to managers' interests than to stockholders' interests. His sample consisted of 478 large industrial firms during the period 1951–61. These firms acquired over 3,300 other firms by means of merger during this time. Reid found that the intensity of merger activity on the part of a firm was positively related to firm-size variables such as assets, sales, and employees, but often negatively related to stockholder-interest variables such as market price per share and profitability. He concluded that mergers did benefit managers more than stockholders. From this finding, we might infer that the wise manager is aware of such results from merger and that this awareness therefore becomes a cause of merger as well as a result.

A more demanding test has been performed by Hogarty.[62] Hogarty attempted to ascertain whether the sales of newly merged firms were greater or less than the aggregate sales that could reasonably have been expected from the individual firms in the absence of merger. In only 15 of the 41 cases Hogarty examined did he find that the sales of the newly merged firm were greater than the sum of the expected sales of the individual firms. He therefore concluded that sales were not pursued at the expense of profits. It should be noted, however, that Hogarty's evidence does not imply that the acquiring firms in a merger did not grow as a result of merger; rather, the evidence indicates that more often than not, the newly merged firm's sales simply did not grow faster than might have been expected. If an absolutely large firm size brings large managerial salaries and favorable non-monetary inducements with it, then managers may seek to merge with other firms regardless of whether the sales of the newly merged firm will grow faster than might have been predicted.

The growth-maximization explanation for merger activity is intuitively appealing. Nevertheless, both the lack of definitive empirical evidence in support of it and the uncertain empirical validity of the many alleged behavioral implications of the separation of ownership and management

[60]*Ibid.*
[61]Reid, *Mergers, Managers, and the Economy,* Chap. 8.
[62]Hogarty, "Profits from Merger."

seriously undermine its status as an explanation. Of course, the same standards, when applied to the other major hypotheses seeking to explain recent merger activity, also result in a verdict of no support or outright rejection with respect to those hypotheses. A theoretically satisfying and empirically valid theorem has not yet been devised to explain the merger phenomenon. Economic theory remains unexpectedly primitive in this area.

POLICY ASPECTS OF MERGERS

The mainspring of public policy with respect to mergers is encased primarily within Section Seven of the Clayton Act, as amended in 1951. Section Seven has been labeled an "antimerger" law by some;[63] however, it has done little to stem the rising tide of mergers in the post–World War II period. The enforcement of Section Seven, it can be argued, has influenced the mixture of mergers so that horizontal mergers are no longer prevalent and conglomerate mergers are now pervasive. Amended Section Seven is sufficiently vague in language (mergers that could create a "substantial lessening of competition" or a "tendency to monopoly" are frowned upon)[64] that its meaning and application have been developed by the judicial system.

The major impetus for passage of amended Section Seven was the large number of horizontal mergers that were taking place. One particular merger focused attention upon the impotence of the pre-1951 Section Seven with respect to horizontal mergers. This merger, between U.S. Steel and Columbia Steel, resulted in the *Columbia Steel Case*.[65] The Justice Department sought to halt the merger, but the Supreme Court did not honor that request, on the ground that the pre-1951 Section Seven did not cover the situation at hand.[66]

Congressional intent in amending Section Seven was to lessen the number of mergers, particularly those between large firms. There is also some evidence that certain of the congressional supporters of amended Section Seven viewed it as applying to (and limiting) all mergers, including those of a conglomerate variety.[67] This intent and application has brought

[63]An example of such a view is David D. Martin, "The Brown Shoe Case and the New Antimerger Policy," *American Economic Review*, 53 (June 1963), 340–58.

[64]These passages are taken from amended Section Seven, also known as the Celler-Kefauver Act, Dec. 20, 1950, 64 Stat. 1125; 15 U.S.C. 18; Public Law 899, 81st Cong.

[65]*United States* v. *Columbia Steel Co. et al.*, 334 U.S. 495, 524, 525, 527 (1948).

[66]More specifically, pre-1951 Section Seven prohibited the acquisition of the *stock* of another firm where the effects might be to lessen competition or create a tendency to monopoly; however, the law did not prohibit the acquisition of the *assets* of the firm, even though the effects might be the same. This loophole was often used by merging firms and was a centerpiece of the defense's argument in the *Columbia Steel Case*. Amended Section Seven covers both stock and asset acquisitions.

[67]Richard A. Miller, "Conglomerate Mergers: A Monopoly Problem?" *St. John's Law Review*, 44 (Spring 1970), 221.

cries of "Foul!" from other authorities on the ground that amended Section Seven was never meant to apply to conglomerate mergers.

What must be considered a prohibition per se against many horizontal mergers has been developed by the courts. Horizontal mergers involving one or more large firms have consistently been disallowed. In the *Brown Shoe Case,* the merger of Brown and Kinney would have resulted in a firm that controlled only 5 percent of the national shoe market, even though in specific cities their combined share of the market would have approached 25 percent. This merger was not allowed. The *Von Grocery Case* resulted in an even more stringent guide being developed vis-à-vis horizontal mergers.[68] Von's Grocery Co. and Shopping Bag Stores, two competing Los Angeles area grocers, sought to merge. Their combined share of the area market was 7.5 percent. In disallowing the merger, the Supreme Court placed heavy emphasis upon the decreasing number of grocery stores in the Los Angeles area.

The *Von Grocery Case* is an excellent illustration of an apparent misconception that has repeatedly plagued judicial decisions in the area of mergers. The majority opinion in the case seemed to equate a reduced number of competitors with a necessary reduction in competition. Numbers of competitors, however, and the tenor and strength of competition are not synonymous. It is possible that a merger that strengthens one competitor but reduces the total number of competitors could increase competition. A simple count of firms in the market has particularly sharp limitations as a guide to the strength of competition when basic structural change is sweeping a market. The disappearance of the corner grocery store is such an example. It should not be the function or result of public policy to discourage basic structural or technological change that results in increased efficiency.

It is necessary from an economic standpoint to define the market or markets in which firms are competing, in order to evaluate the possible competitive impact of a merger. We pointed out in Chapter 2 that markets have three dimensions: product, geography, and time. The courts have traditionally had difficulty in determining the markets that pertain to a merger. The Supreme Court has recently held, in the *Pabst Case,* that no specific market need be defined in order to demonstrate a violation of amended Section Seven.[69] The *Pabst Case* is illustrative of the confusion that has permeated market definitions under amended Section Seven. The Department of Justice prosecuted the case, which involved a proposed merger between the brewing companies Pabst and Blatz. The Justice Department alternatively spoke of the State of Wisconsin and of the entire United States as the relevant market where competition might be endangered by the merger. Pabst and Blatz attacked these market definitions on the grounds

[68]*United States* v. *Von's Grocery Co. et al.,* 384 U.S. 270 (1966).
[69]*United States* v. *Pabst Brewing Co. et al.,* 384 U.S. 547 (1966).

that the State of Wisconsin is an arbitrarily chosen market that does not correspond to actual marketing patterns. Further, the defendants argued that if the entire United States were the relevant market, then it was virtually impossible to show that competition would be lessened materially in this large market. The Supreme Court, however, held that no specific market need be demonstrated that is satisfying from either a logical or an economic standpoint.

The Pabst Case is an unfortunate precedent not only because it represents a failure to define rigorously the relevant market but also because it represents an implicit rejection of the possible contributions of economic analysis to merger problems. Precise definition of a market is, of course, a difficult and inexact task; however, the failure to specify any market where competition is said to be altered introduces an undesirable lack of precision into merger cases and opens the door to judicial subjectivity with respect to an essentially economic phenomenon. Economic analysis is not capable of answering all questions of import relating to mergers; nevertheless, the applicability of economic analysis and accompanying empirical evidence cannot be denied. The intelligent use of economic principles and empirical evidence can only upgrade and rationalize public policy in the area of mergers.

The legal stance of the courts with respect to vertical mergers has been more relaxed and less rigid than the corresponding attitude with respect to horizontal mergers. This statement does not mean that a vertical merger that results in the foreclosure of a significant portion of a market is likely to be approved. Just the opposite is the case. The *du Pont—GM Case* is instructive in this area.[70] During the years 1917–19, du Pont acquired a 23 percent share of the stock of General Motors. Du Pont viewed GM as an attractive, growth-oriented investment opportunity, but was more notably interested in the market for its own products that GM might afford. Du Pont subsequently became a very important supplier of fabrics, plastics, paints, and other products to GM. The Justice Department, after waiting over thirty years, brought suit, charging that du Pont's entrenched market position as a supplier to General Motors had not been obtained on the basis of "competitive merit." Subsequently, du Pont was ordered by the court to divest itself of its General Motors stock.[71]

There is little sign that the Department of Justice and the Federal Trade Commission, which are responsible for administering the merger statutes, have decided to be more lenient with respect to vertical mergers. For example, throughout the 1960's, the Federal Trade Commission filed over twenty complaints that sought to halt an obvious trend toward down-

---

[70]*United States* v. *E.I. du Pont de Nemours and Co. et al.*, 353 U.S. 586 (1957).

[71]The *du Pont–GM Case* raised some legal eyebrows, in that it forced du Pont to divest itself of stock it had acquired more than thirty years prior to the passage of amended Section Seven of the Clayton Act, upon which the divestiture was based. Further, the formal suit against du Pont was filed prior to the passage of amended Section Seven, even though amended Section Seven was used to obtain the conviction.

stream vertical integration in the cement market.[72] And upstream integration is faring no better, as is illustrated by the recently announced Supreme Court decision that ordered Ford Motor Company to divest itself of Autolite.

It is generally agreed that vertical mergers do have the potential to increase market power; however, there is no unanimity with respect to either how harmful vertical mergers are or how frequently harmful vertical mergers occur. Bork and others have argued that vertical integration will seldom harm competition, and that it (1) will often result in the achievement of economies of scale, and (2) will often increase competition because it enables firms to bypass monopolistic suppliers.[73] Others, notably Mueller, counter this *a priori* defense of vertical integration by asserting that the determination of the effects of vertical integration is an empirical question that cannot be settled by means of the static theory of the firm.[74] The static theory of the firm, it will be remembered, does not specifically treat the case of vertically integrated firms.

The intent and effects of upstream and downstream vertical integration need not be the same. The classic example of vertical integration as an element of market power is the previously discussed *Alcoa Case*.[75] Alcoa used its control over factor supplies to bludgeon competitors and to prevent entry into the aluminum ingot market for more than thirty years during the first half of the century. Upstream vertical integration, therefore, can be used to increase entry barriers and place competitors at a disadvantage. Both upstream and downstream vertical integration can have the effect of reducing transactions costs and uncertainty. Downstream vertical integration, on the other hand, is most often directed at ensuring a market for the final product of the firm. A recent example is instructive.

The aforementioned developments in the cement market during the 1960's illustrate downstream vertical integration used both offensively and defensively. During the period 1959–67, a total of 65 cement users were acquired by cement manufacturers.[76] The mergers typically involved a large cement producer, such as Ideal or Lehigh Portland, that acquired ready-mixed-concrete or concrete-product firms. The effect of the initial acquisitions in this series was to strip some of the cement manufacturers of established customers; they reacted by attempting to foreclose a portion of the market for their own by also acquiring cement users. Hence, the initial

[72]Willard F. Mueller, "Public Policy Toward Vertical Mergers," in J. Fred Weston and Sam Peltzman, eds., *Public Policy Toward Mergers* (Pacific Palisades, Calif.: Goodyear Publishing Co., Inc., 1969), p. 159.

[73]Robert H. Bork and Ward S. Bowman, "The Crisis in Antitrust," *Columbia Law Review*, 65 (March 1965), 363–76; Robert H. Bork, "Vertical Integration and Competitive Processes," in Weston and Peltzman, eds., *Public Policy Toward Mergers*, pp. 139–49; J.J. Spengler, "Vertical Integration and Antitrust Policy," *Journal of Political Economy*, 58 (August 1950), 347–52; and Fritz Machlup and Martha Taber, "Bilateral Monopoly, Successive Monopoly, and Vertical Integration," *Economica*, 27 (May 1960), 101–17.

[74]Mueller, "Public Policy Toward Vertical Mergers," pp. 150–66.

[75]See also Merton J. Peck, *Competition in the Aluminum Industry* (Cambridge, Mass.: Harvard University Press, 1961).

[76]Mueller, "Public Policy Toward Vertical Mergers," p. 159.

downstream vertical integration in the cement market was aggressively offensive in nature, whereas the subsequent reaction of competitors to this development was primarily defensive.[77]

The numeric predominance of conglomerate mergers in recent years has confronted antitrust authorities and the courts with a phenomenon not specifically mentioned in amended Section Seven of the Clayton Act, or in the broadly worded Section Two of the Sherman Act and Section Five of the Federal Trade Commission Act. Hence, the application of antitrust statutes to conglomerate mergers has been slow and at times uncertain. The *Procter & Gamble–Clorox Case,* which involved the first substantial conglomerate merger that was challenged under amended Section Seven, was therefore groundbreaking in nature.[78] Procter & Gamble, the largest single producer of detergents, sought to acquire Clorox, the largest single producer of bleach. Since P&G operated in essentially unrelated markets (although such a merger is sometimes referred to as a "product extension" merger), the merger had no obvious effects upon frequently cited elements of market structure such as concentration or the number of competitors. This seemed to leave little room in which the Federal Trade Commission (which sought to halt the merger) could operate, because past judicial decisions had placed heavy emphasis upon the observable effects of a merger upon such market-structure variables. The Federal Trade Commission, however, chose to emphasize what it thought were the probable consequences for conduct and performance in the bleach market as a result of the merger. The commission maintained that P&G's huge resources could be used to injure or destroy Clorox's competitors. Specifically, the commission noted the fact that P&G was the nation's largest single advertiser and contended that Clorox would therefore benefit from this by means of discounts in price obtained for advertising and because of possible economies of scale in advertising.[79] The commission was also impressed by what is known as the "deep pocket" argument—that is, that P&G could engage in cross-subsidization and predatory pricing because of its large size. Further, the commission also argued that P&G's acquisition of Clorox would raise barriers to entry in the bleach market because other prospective new competitors would not be able to match the resources that P&G would devote to activities such as advertising.

The Supreme Court agreed with the Federal Trade Commission and asserted that it is not necessary under amended Section Seven to prove that a merger would lessen competition or tend to create a monopoly. Rather, the Court stated, only a possibility of such results need be demonstrated in order for a merger to be invalidated. The Court also reinforced its already

[77]Bureau of Economics, Federal Trade Commission, *Economic Report on Mergers and Vertical Integration in the Cement Industry* (Washington, D.C.: U.S. Government Printing Office, 1966).

[78]*Federal Trade Commission* v. *Procter & Gamble Co.,* 386 U.S. 568 (1967).

[79]This contention has been decisively refuted by John L. Peterman, "The Clorox Case and Television Rate Structures," *Journal of Law and Economics,* 10 (October 1968), 321–422.

negative view toward a possible tradeoff between economies of scale that might result from a merger and the enhanced market power that might also result.[80] (This tradeoff, suggested by Williamson, was described in Chapter 6.)[81] The Court stated that economies of scale "cannot be used as a defense to illegality."[82]

The judgment of economists with respect to conglomerate mergers is hardly unanimous. The precise competitive effects of conglomerate mergers are not well known and can only be guessed at. Because the observable effects of conglomerate mergers on market structure are limited, some observers (including a recent presidential commission chaired by Stigler)[83] argue that nothing should be done to severely curtail such mergers at this time. At the same time, it has been pointed out with great gusto by Heflebower that once a merger has been consummated, it is difficult or even impossible to reverse that result or to accomplish a divestiture. Consequently, Heflebower argues, public policy should err in the direction of not permitting mergers when the benefits of such a merger do not clearly outweigh the costs. Where structural considerations also indicate a substantial probability that a merger will result in a lessening of competition, then the merger should not be allowed.[84]

A common thread in the judicial enforcement of amended Section Seven has been the emergence of an apparent judicial prohibition per se against mergers involving large firms. Such a development has frequently been suggested by those concerned with merger policy.[85] The most influential guidelines, summarized in Table 10.5, have been offered by the Antitrust Division of the Department of Justice. The department served notice with these guidelines that it would ordinarily challenge any merger that violated them, unless clearly important extenuating circumstances existed.

The appearance of the merger guidelines and the increasing tendency of the courts to rule against certain classes of mergers seem to signify a rejection of the "rule-of-reason" criterion that typified merger decisions for decades.[86] The rule-of-reason approach to antitrust-law enforcement

---

[80]The Supreme Court had earlier rejected any scale-economies defense in *Brown Shoe Co.* v. *United States*, 370 U.S. 294 (1962), and in *United States* v. *Philadelphia National Bank*, 374 U.S. 321 (1963).

[81]O.E. Williamson, "Economies as an Antitrust Defense: The Welfare Tradeoffs," *American Economic Review*, 58 (March 1968), 18–36.

[82]*Federal Trade Commission* v. *Procter & Gamble Co.*, 386 U. S. 568 (1967), p. 580.

[83]*Report of the Task Force on Productivity and Competition*, as reprinted in *Antitrust Law and Economics Review*, 2 (Spring 1969), 13–36.

[84]Richard B. Heflebower, "Corporate Mergers: Policy and Economic Analysis," *Quarterly Journal of Economics*, 77 (November 1963), 537–58.

[85]Stigler, "Mergers and Preventive Antitrust Policy"; Carl Kaysen and Donald F. Turner, *Antitrust Policy: An Economic and Legal Analysis* (Cambridge, Mass.: Harvard University Press, 1965), p. 133; and *Report of the White House Task Force on Antitrust Policy* ("Neal Report") as reprinted in *Antitrust Law Review*, 2 (Winter 1968–69), 11–52.

[86]The rule-of-reason approach is generally agreed to have been a practical result of the majority opinion of the Supreme Court in *Standard Oil Co. of New Jersey* v. *United States*, 221 U.S. 1 (1911).

TABLE 10.5

Department of Justice Merger Guidelines

HORIZONTAL MERGERS

(1) Where the four-firm concentration ratio is 75 or more, a merger will ordinarily be challenged if the firms involved possess the following market shares:

Acquiring Firm		Acquired Firm
4% or more	AND	4% or more
10% or more	AND	2% or more
15% or more	AND	1% or more

(2) Where the four-firm concentration ratio is less than 75, a merger will ordinarily be challenged if the firms involved possess the following market shares:

Acquiring Firm		Acquired Firm
5% or more	AND	5% or more
10% or more	AND	4% or more
15% or more	AND	3% or more
20% or more	AND	2% or more
25% or more	AND	1% or more

(3) Other mergers may be challenged, especially those where the acquired firm has at least 2% of the market, if either the acquiring firm or the acquired firm is among the eight largest firms in that market and the market share of the eight largest firms has increased 7% or more in the ten years preceding the merger.

VERTICAL MERGERS

(1) Mergers will be ordinarily challenged where the firm supplying inputs accounts for 10% or more of sales in its market and the purchasing firm accounts for 6% or more of the purchases in the same market.

(2) Mergers will ordinarily be challenged where the firm which is purchasing inputs accounts for 6% or more of purchases in the market and the supplying firm accounts for 10% or more of the sales in the same market.

(3) Other mergers may be challenged outside of the above limits.

CONGLOMERATE MERGERS

(1) Mergers will ordinarily be challenged where: (a) the acquired firm has 25% of the market; (b) the acquired firm is one of the two largest firms in the market and the top two firms have at least 50% of the market; (c) the acquired firm is one of the four largest firms in the market and the top eight firms in the market have at least 75% of the market and the acquired firm at least 10% of the market; (d) the acquired firm is among the largest eight firms in a market where the largest eight firms have at least 75% of the market.

(2) Mergers will ordinarily be challenged where a danger of reciprocal buying might result.

(3) Mergers will ordinarily be challenged where the acquisition might increase the acquiring firm's market power or raise barriers to entry.

Source: *"Merger Guidelines," U.S. Department of Justice, May 30, 1968, Commerce Clearing House, Trade Regulation Reporter, 1, Paragraph 4430.*

emphasizes the examination of each merger case on its own merits and allows for the consideration of the reasonability or workability of a particular situation. It emphasizes actual performance rather than *a priori* reasoning in arriving at judgments about the desirability of a given situation.

The merger guidelines of the Department of Justice represent a victory for those who emphasize a structural approach to merger policy. The structuralists argue that certain types of market structures typically produce undesirable conduct and performance.[87] The twin bases for this conclusion are empirical evidence and the static theories of monopoly and competition. In Adams' eyes, conventional price theory predicts undesirable behavior in market structures characterized by monopoly power and few sellers; further, empirical evidence, much of which we have already surveyed, also points to the frequent occurrence of undesirable performance in monopolistic markets. The moral of all this, according to the structuralists, is that undesirable market structures should not be permitted to develop by means of merger.

Implicit within the structuralist argument is the assertion that the structure–conduct–performance link is empirically valid. Few serious students of industrial organization would deny the occasional or even frequent validity of the structure–conduct–performance triad. Nevertheless, even Mason, who is primarily responsible for current emphasis upon this relationship, saw interaction and joint causation inside it. Mason opted for an antitrust policy that combined the structuralist viewpoint with a healthy emphasis upon the rule of reason in the form of attention to the peculiar circumstances of each particular case.[88]

A strict case-by-case performance standard for the evaluation of mergers has not attained great popularity among economists.[89] One probable reason is that one may easily infer from a performance standard that the conventional economic theory of market structures is irrelevant and useless. However, a more powerful objection to a pure performance standard is the fact that few mergers ever involve totally good or totally bad performance. As a result, normative judgments must be made about the reasonableness of a given action or a given circumstance. Mason has pointed out that the application of a pure performance standard would necessitate such long and complex investigations of performance that the antitrust laws would atrophy as a result.[90]

---

[87]A strong case for the structuralist position has been made by Walter Adams, "The Case for Structural Tests," in Weston and Peltzman, eds., *Public Policy Toward Mergers*, pp. 13–26; see also Walter Adams, *The Structure of American Industry*, 3rd ed. (New York: Macmillan and Company, 1961), pp. 554–60.

[88]Edward S. Mason, "The Current State of the Monopoly Problem in the United States," *Harvard Law Review*, 62 (June 1949), 1265–85.

[89]A well-known example of a suggested performance standard is S. Chesterfield Oppenheim, "Federal Antitrust Legislation: Guideposts to a Revised Antitrust Policy," *Michigan Law Review*, 50 (June 1952), 1158–61.

[90]E.S. Mason, *Economic Concentration and the Monopoly Problem* (Cambridge, Mass.: Harvard University Press, 1957), p. 398.

SUMMARY

We are currently in the midst of the third major wave of mergers that has swept the economy during the twentieth century. The first two waves were smaller than the current one and, particularly the first, involved more horizontal mergers. The first merger wave was responsible for the creation of many of the modern industrial giants such as U.S. Steel. The current wave is dominated by mergers of a conglomerate nature across conventional market lines; over four-fifths of current mergers are of a conglomerate variety.

Despite the number and significance of the mergers that have occurred in recent years, neither economic theory nor empirical evidence offers a firm explanation for mergers. The persistence of conglomerate mergers is particularly baffling. Corwin Edwards neatly summarized the situation when he observed that "conglomerate enterprise does not have a well-defined place either in public policy or in economic theory."[91] Popular explanations attributing mergers to factors such as increased profitability or reduced risk find little empirical support. A promising hypothesis, which needs additional testing, has been offered by Gort. He suggests that valuation discrepancies lead to mergers and that valuation discrepancies proliferate when change and growth are rapid.

Public policy in the area of mergers has drifted in the direction of informal prohibitions per se against many types of mergers, particularly those of a horizontal nature, or those that involve firms of even medium size. The Department of Justice has published recommended guidelines for mergers, which largely eliminate rule-of-reason arguments favoring a given merger on the basis of performance. The courts have also consistently held that economies of scale may not be utilized as a defense against a charge of possible monopolization.

All things considered, it is fair to say that both public policy and economic analysis are in a transitional state with respect to mergers.

PROBLEMS

1. No single theory that has been offered seems able to explain the wave of mergers that began in the decade of the 1950's. Does this inability to explain firm mergers represent a failure of economic theory? Is it possible for a given economic phenomenon to possess such complexity that ordinary static price theory is unable to explain it?

2. The stock-market-effects theory of mergers relies upon investors' maintaining a certain price–earnings ratio for a firm's stock, even when changes occur in that firm's circumstances. Do investors pay attention to price–earnings ratios in purchasing stocks,

---

[91]Testimony of Corwin D. Edwards before the Subcommittee on Antitrust and Monopoly, Committee on the Judiciary, U.S. Senate, *Economic Concentration* (Washington, D.C.: U.S. Government Printing Office, 1964), p. 37.

and if so, do such investors maintain such ratio expectations regardless of the changing circumstances of the firm?

3. The text of this chapter mentions a statement by managers of the Falstaff Brewing Company indicating that Falstaff was able to purchase already-existing brewing capacity from other brewers more cheaply than it could have built the same capacity. Hence, Falstaff possessed a major motive for merger. Is this due to a market imperfection and/or valuation discrepancy? Could valuation discrepancies ever retard mergers?

4. "Vertical integration is an example of diversification. The reverse is not always true. Horizontal integration is neither vertical integration nor is it diversification." Comment.

5. What meaning can you attribute to the terms *defensive diversification* and *offensive diversification*?

6. During the period 1951–65, about 85 percent of all merger cases brought by the Antitrust Division of the Department of Justice involved horizontal mergers. Does this preponderance reflect (a) the proportion of all mergers that are of this type; (b) the clearer statements of economic theory with respect to horizontal mergers than with respect to other types of mergers; or (c) other factors?

11

Product Differentiation
and Advertising

Product differentiation is a pervasive characteristic of goods and services of all kinds in the American economy. Millions of differentiated products exist in both consumer- and producer-goods markets. Most consumers are readily able to identify differentiated consumer products such as Coca-Cola and Kleenex. Producer goods such as Boeing 747 airplanes and IBM computers are also familiar. Connoisseurs of a particular line of products can speak knowledgeably of Datsun 240-Z sports cars, Nabisco Triangle Thins crackers, Revlon Blush On, Caterpillar D-9 tractors, and even LaFayette LR-1500TA deluxe stereo receivers.

This chapter deals with the complex phenomenon of product differentiation as an element of market structure. The structure–conduct–performance triad is evident throughout the analysis. The extent of product differentiation and nonprice competition, including advertising, its probable competitive effects, and public-policy alternatives, garner the majority of our attention in our study.

PRODUCT DIFFERENTIATION: ITS MANY ASPECTS

Our first need is to be more precise about the term *product differentiation*. The most popular view of what constitutes product differentiation is still that rendered by Chamberlin in his classic work, *The Theory of Monopolistic Competition*.

> A general class of product is differentiated if any significant basis exists for distinguishing the goods (or services) of one seller from those of another. Such a basis may be real or fancied, so long as it is of any importance whatever to buyers, and leads to a preference for one variety of the product over another.[1]

Chamberlin correctly observed that much of product differentiation is perceived rather than actual in nature. That is, goods A and B may be tech-

[1]E.H. Chamberlin, *The Theory of Monopolistic Competition* (Cambridge, Mass.: Harvard University Press, 1933), p. 56.

nically similar in that they perform and operate identically, and they may be priced the same. However, consumers may perceive a difference between goods A and B because of other factors, not the least of which might be a carefully fostered image perpetuated by the producer of one or both of the goods. For example, when we purchase Pepsi-Cola, we also purchase membership in the Pepsi Generation, which (Pepsi-Cola would have us believe) is populated by the beautiful people everywhere. The carefully nurtured image associated with Pepsi-Cola is therefore one of dashing vitality, youthful form and thoughts, interesting activities, and friendly people. The company makes a deliberate effort to lead the public to believe that much of that image rubs off on them when they join the Pepsi Generation by purchasing Pepsi-Cola.

Despite the nonconcrete nature of much of product differentiation, objective bases for it do exist. Among these are patented features; trademarks and copyrights; differences in product quality; variations in design, style, and color; conditions surrounding the sale, such as convenience, courtesy, and even such comfort factors as air conditioning; the service promised; warranties and guarantees; credit or payment terms; and method, time, and cost of delivery. Product differentiation has so many aspects that it is an elusive and perhaps unquantifiable concept. Some would argue that it is an unusable concept.

Product differentiation is not achieved without cost to the firm. Its major cost is advertising. The 100 largest domestic advertisers spent $4.67 billion on advertising in 1970; Procter & Gamble alone was estimated to have spent $265 million of that amount.[2] Table 11.1 summarizes portions of the annual report on advertising expenditures made by the trade journal *Advertising Age*. Advertising expenditures and advertising-to-sales ratios are particularly high in the soaps and cleansers, drugs and cosmetics, and food markets.

Advertising expenditures are often used as a proxy for the Chamberlinian concept of "selling costs." Selling costs, according to Chamberlin, are costs incurred in order to alter the position or the shape of the demand curve for the product. They include not only those costs incurred in order to persuade buyers to purchase a good from one supplier rather than another, but also those incurred to convince the buyer to make a purchase in the first instance and to persuade a given seller to stock a given good and then to push its sale. The typical empirical study involving advertising variables depends upon advertising data that are some hybrid of Chamberlin's concept of selling costs.[3] Advertising expenditures are nearly always used as a surrogate for selling costs, because selling-cost data are generally unavailable.

[2]*Advertising Age*, 42 (August 30, 1971), 22.

[3]By way of contrast, Chamberlin considered production costs to be all costs that do *not* result in a change in the shape or the position of the demand curve. Production costs are therefore a residual item, in his eyes. See Chamberlin, *The Theory of Monopolistic Competition*, Chap. 6.

TABLE 11.1

Selected Advertising-Dollar Volumes, 1970

Rank in Terms of Dollars Spent	Firm	Market Area	Millions of Dollars Spent	Advertising as a Percent of Sales
1	Procter & Gamble	Soaps	265	8.3
2	General Foods	Foods	170	8.6
3	Sears	Merchandising	130	1.4
4	General Motors	Autos	129	0.7
5	Warner-Lambert	Drugs	126	15.6
6	Colgate	Soaps	121	22.4
7	Bristol-Myers	Drugs	117	11.9
8	American Home	Drugs	100	9.5
9	Ford	Autos	90	0.6
10	AT&T	Telephone	86	0.5
13	Sterling	Drugs	76	19.0
27	Richardson	Drugs	57	15.0
33	Alberto-Culver	Drugs	52	30.6
56	Carter-Wallace	Drugs	30	23.7
65	J.B. Williams	Drugs	27	36.0
78	Block	Drugs	23	30.4
88	Noxell	Drugs	19	29.6

Source: *Reprinted with permission from the August 30, 1971 issue of* Advertising Age. *Copyright 1971 by Crain Communications, Inc.*

Qualitative statements concerning the degree of product differentiation are easier to make than are precise quantitative statements about it. The most ubiquitous measure of the degree of product differentiation is the advertising-to-sales ratio. Yet, as we have seen, advertising expenditures are not coincident with selling costs, and many nonadvertising selling costs visibly differentiate products (for example, a change in the wrapper of a candy bar). Further, market-level advertising and sales data are usually available only at the two- or three-digit SIC level of detail. That is, market studies that incorporate advertising and sales information often deal with market definitions that are too broad. Firm-level advertising and sales data are generally unavailable except for the largest firms and advertisers, and therefore seldom form the basis for a wide-ranging study.

The coefficient of cross-elasticity of demand is another possible measure of the degree of product differentiation. For example, if a change in the price of Magnavox television sets elicits little or no reaction in the quantity demanded of SONY television sets, then (*ceteris paribus*) one might conclude that a considerable degree of product differentiation is present. Such a measure must be carefully employed, however. The coefficient of cross-elasticity of demand between wheat and aluminum ingots probably approaches zero, yet such a number implies nothing about the degree of product differentiation. The measure is also dependent upon the occurrence of price changes of measurable significance; otherwise no coefficient can be computed. The rigid demands for data that the coefficient of cross-elasticity, of demand presents have militated against its frequent use.

An entropy-based measure of the degree of product differentiation has also been suggested.[4] *Entropy* is a term drawn from communications theory and refers to the degree of randomness of a given arrangement. In the current context, an entropy-based measure of the degree of product differentiation highlights the extent to which customers in a given market make their purchases from the same seller. At one extreme, customers always make their purchases from the same sellers and the degree of product differentiation is said to be quite high. The opposite extreme is the case where customers distribute their purchases throughout the market so that each seller receives a proportion of each customer's purchases that is equal to that seller's market share. One suggested entropy measure of the degree of product differentiation assumes values between zero and 1, with the value of zero reflecting limited product differentiation and the value of 1 representing a high degree of product differentiation.[5]

Still another approach to the measurement of the degree of product differentiation is that originally utilized by Bain and since imitated frequently.[6] Bain, in his well-known study of barriers to entry, classified twenty industrial markets as exhibiting low, medium, or high product-differentiation barriers. He did not base his classification upon any single statistic, such as advertising-to-sales ratios. Rather, his own knowledge and expertise were the primary basis for placement of a market in one category rather than another. This approach clearly allows a knowledgeable observer to take into account facets of product differentiation not always captured by advertising-to-sales ratios (for example, rivalry by means of product shape or color). On the other hand, the method may allow arbitrary groupings, and the classification scheme that results can be no better than the quality of the information possessed by the classifier. The user of any such scheme is dependent upon the skill of the classifier, since the basis for the grouping is sometimes unknown.[7]

However measured, product differentiation and nonprice competition are not simple extensions of price competition. Product differentiation can accomplish the same ends as price competition, but can do so in a much more subtle way. The reaction by competitors to product-differentiation activities, including advertising, is usually slower than their reactions to price changes. Grabowski and Mueller have demonstrated that in the cigarette market, changes in product differentiation are hard to detect and, once detected,

[4]Irwin Bernhardt and K.D. Mackenzie, "Measuring Seller Unconcentration, Segmentation, and Product Differentiation," *Western Economic Journal,* 6 (December 1968), 395–403.

[5]*Ibid.*

[6]Joe S. Bain, *Barriers to New Competition* (Cambridge, Mass.: Harvard University Press, 1965).

[7]See, for example, Bureau of Economics, Federal Trade Commission, *Industry Classification and Concentration* (Washington, D.C.: U.S. Government Printing Office, 1967).

more difficult to counter than price competition.[8] The obvious competitive reaction of a firm to price competition from other firms is to match the price cuts. The appropriate reaction to competitive product differentiation is often not clear and can seldom be immediate. The automobile market is illustrative. A price cut on Ford automobiles can be quickly detected and easily matched by Chevrolet. The introduction of an entirely new Ford automobile, such as the Mustang, may not be detected until it is well along in development, and perhaps cannot be countered or imitated (the Camaro?) for a year or more.

Most firms operating in markets where products are differentiated will exhibit more independence in their product policies than in their pricing policies. The aforementioned factors of delayed detection and lagged response to new product differentiation are partially responsible for this greater independence. However, product-differentiation activities and nonprice competition in general are not usually considered to be as warlike and aggressive in intent as price-cutting policies. Firms that do not wish to provoke bitter intramarket fights (but still wish to increase market penetration) may therefore opt for product-differentiating tactics instead of price-cutting tactics.

THE THEORY OF PRODUCT DIFFERENTIATION

Most firms have at least some control over product price, product-differentiation activities such as advertising, and product characteristics such as quality.[9] The profit-maximizing firm will wish to use each of its available market tactics (price cuts, advertising expenditures, and quality variations) in such a fashion that profits are indeed maximized. Hence, the firm must apply a variant of the Marshallian Principle of Substitution in order to ascertain the most profitable combination of price cuts, advertising expenditures, and quality variations. That is, in equilibrium, a dollar spent on any of these three action variables (or on any other available tactic) should garner the same incremental profit no matter where that dollar is employed. A dollar spent on advertising should result in the same amount of profit as a dollar spent on quality variations or a dollar spent on price cuts, if the profit-maximizing firm is in equilibrium.[10] More rigorously, the

---

[8]Henry G. Grabowski and Dennis C. Mueller, "Imitative Advertising in the Cigarette Industry," *The Antitrust Bulletin,* 16 (Summer 1971), 257–92.

[9]Much of the work in this section follows closely the groundbreaking work of Robert Dorfman and Peter O. Steiner, "Optimal Advertising and Optimal Quality," *American Economic Review,* 44 (December 1954), 826–36. See also later work by Lester Telser, "How Much Does It Pay Whom to Advertise," *American Economic Review,* 51 (May 1961), 194–205.

[10]The cost of a price cut is the sales revenue lost because of the price cut that would have been earned had the price not been cut on the units previously sold at a higher price.

profit-maximizing rule is as follows:

$$\frac{M\pi_{PC}}{C_{PC}} = \frac{M\pi_{ADV}}{C_{ADV}} = \frac{M\pi_Q}{C_Q} = \cdots = \frac{M\pi_N}{C_N}$$

where $M\pi_i$ = marginal profit attained due to undertaking action i
$\qquad$ C_i = cost of undertaking action i

It is possible to make more explicit the relationship between product price and advertising expenditures. Dorfman and Steiner have demonstrated (holding the quality dimension of products constant) that a profit-maximizing firm's advertising-to-sales ratio will be the following:

$$A/S = \frac{P - MC}{P} \cdot \eta_{Q,A}$$

where A/S = advertising-to-sales ratio
$\qquad$ $\dfrac{P - MC}{P}$ = Lerner Index of monopoly power

$\qquad$ $\eta_{Q,A}$ = elasticity of output with respect to advertising expenditures

The equation above is interesting for several reasons. First, it asserts that the higher the degree of a firm's monopoly power, the higher will be that firm's advertising-to-sales ratio. That is, monopoly power is associated with a high degree of product differentiation. Second, the equation also relates the effects of advertising expenditures upon product price to the firm's advertising-to-sales ratio. This latter point can be demonstrated algebraically:

(1) $\quad A/S = \dfrac{P - MC}{P} \cdot \eta_{Q,A}$

(2) $\quad A/S = \dfrac{1}{\eta_{Q,P}} \cdot \eta_{Q,A}$ $\qquad\qquad$ Lerner Index equal to reciprocal of price elasticity of demand.

(3) $\quad A/S = \dfrac{1}{\frac{\%\Delta \text{ in } Q}{\%\Delta \text{ in } P}} \cdot \dfrac{\frac{\%\Delta \text{ in } Q}{\%\Delta \text{ in } A}}{1}$ $\quad$ Definition of elasticity.

(4) $\quad A/S = \dfrac{\%\Delta \text{ in } P}{\%\Delta \text{ in } Q} \cdot \dfrac{\%\Delta \text{ in } Q}{\%\Delta \text{ in } A}$ $\quad$ Multiply first term in (3) by second term, rearrange terms.

(5) $\quad A/S = \dfrac{\%\Delta \text{ in } P}{\%\Delta \text{ in } A} = \eta_{P,A}$ $\qquad$ Right-hand term in (4) is the elasticity of output with respect to advertising.

Equation (5) above indicates that the greater the sensitivity of product price to advertising expenditures, the greater will be the advertising-to-sales ratio of the profit-maximizing firm.

Our theoretical work has thus far ignored the passage of time. Product differentiation and advertising are appropriately viewed as constituting investments that yield returns both currently and in the future. Heflebower has suggested that product differentiation and advertising expenditures are to the firm as expenditures upon a fruit orchard are to a farmer. Just as the fruit-growing farmer does not receive an output of fruit instantaneously with the planting of fruit trees, and just as he must continually tend and care for the orchard each year lest it deteriorate and become less productive, so also the firm slowly develops its own position with respect to product differentiation and advertising.[11] The fact that profitability does not instantly follow advertising expenditures means that the firm must compare profits earned at different points in time. Profits that are not earned until several years after today's advertising expenditures are worth less to the firm than the same amount of profits earned today. In general, the farther in the future the profits are, the less they are worth to the firm today, since profits earned by the firm today are available for investment opportunities that will earn positive rates of return.

The problem the profit-maximizing firm faces with respect to its expenditures upon product differentiation, therefore, is one of maximizing the present discounted value of the time stream of the firm's profits by means of such expenditures.[12] Let S_i represent the sales revenues of the firm in year i, and C_i the cost of manufacturing and selling in year i. In any given year i, the positive difference between S_i and C_i is profit. Hence the task of the firm is to maximize

$$PDV = \sum_{i=1}^{N} \frac{(S_i - C_i)}{(1 + r)^i}$$
$$= \sum_{i=1}^{N} \frac{\pi_i}{(1 + r)^i}$$

where r = rate of discount
   π_i = profit in year i

Assuming that the costs of manufacturing have already been met, the firm need only decide whether or not advertising expenditures in year i, which we shall designate A_i, are worthwhile from a benefit–cost standpoint, given the next-best alternative of the firm, which is represented by the rate of discount. That is, the firm will compute an internal rate of return on the advertising expenditures by means of the formula indicated below, and

[11] Richard B. Heflebower, "The Theory and Effects of Nonprice Competition," in Robert E. Kuenne, ed., *Monopolistic Competition: Studies in Impact* (New York: John Wiley & Sons, Inc., 1967), pp. 177–201.

[12] Much of the following analysis is similar to that presented by Hans Brems, *Product Equilibrium Under Monopolistic Competition* (Cambridge, Mass.: Harvard University Press, 1951), pp. 116–31.

will then compare that internal rate of return to other available alternatives it faces.[13]

$$0 = \sum_{i=1}^{N} \frac{\pi_i^a}{(1 + IRR)^i}$$

where IRR = internal rate of return
  π_i^a = profits owing to advertising expenditures in year i

If the rate of discount is represented by r, then the firm will undertake the expenditure on product differentiation and advertising when the expected IRR due to such expenditures is greater than r.

Although advertising expenditures have the properties of an investment, most firms do not treat them as investments when constructing their balance sheets. Advertising expenditures are often charged totally to the year in which they are incurred, and no allowance is made for the image, goodwill, and future-profit prospects that are being created. Hence, the book value of many firms' assets will be understated, because they do not adjust their balance sheets to take account of the greater amount of capital they have available as a result of their advertising expenditures. The empirical consequences of this are not trivial. Profit-rate studies often discover disproportionately high profit rates being earned by firms that spend large sums on product differentiation. Since they are typically computed on the basis of invested capital possessed by the firm, the profit rates are unrealistically high, because the value of the capital possessed by the firm is actually higher than stated. If advertising and other product-differentiating expenditures were viewed as investments yielding depreciable assets similar to the investment in physical capital, then much of the higher reported profit rates for firms that spend large sums on product-differentiation activities might disappear.

Let us take a brief look at some empirical evidence that relates to the investment properties of advertising. Palda examined the advertising expenditures and the sales of the Lydia Pinkham Medicine Company for the period 1908–60.[14] He found that only when advertising was viewed as an investment could one infer profit maximization from the Pinkham Company's behavior. Specifically, he estimated that it took almost seven years for the company's advertising dollars to achieve 95 percent of their sales-generating effects. A similarly lengthy lag between advertising expenditures and sales was discovered in the cigarette market by Telser.[15] He estimated

---

[13]We choose to skirt the involved theoretical discussion over the merits of the present-discounted-value criterion versus the internal-rate-of-return criterion.

[14]Kristian S. Palda, "The Measurement of Cumulative Advertising Effects," *Journal of Business,* 38 (April 1965), 162–79; see also Palda, *The Measurement of Cumulative Advertising Effects* (Englewood Cliffs, N.J.: Prentice-Hall, Inc., 1964).

[15]Lester Telser, "Advertising and Cigarettes," *Journal of Political Economy,* 70 (October 1962), 471–99.

that advertising expenditures built up a fund of goodwill that depreciated at a rate varying between 15 and 20 percent per year.

THE WELFARE ECONOMICS OF NONPRICE COMPETITION

The effects of product differentiation and advertising upon economic welfare have long been debated. The 988-page length of Borden's classic work, *The Economics of Advertising,* is visible testimony to the fact that the issues are not yet resolved.[16] Clear thinking is needed to separate the fatuous arguments concerning product differentiation from the substantive arguments. We shall consider a multitude of these arguments in turn.

Information vs. Image

Advertising, the main cost of product differentiation, can increase consumer information by describing and identifying goods and services. The theory of information tells us that advertising can reduce buyer and seller search costs.[17] Hence, advertising can be an economic good that serves a positive and beneficial economic purpose.

Some of the confusion surrounding the welfare economics of advertising expenditures is the result of unrealistic applications of the received economic theory of market structures. The perfectly competitive market structure assumes perfect information on the part of buyers and sellers (see Chapter 2). Therefore, in such a market, no advertising need be done, particularly by sellers, since they are able to sell all they desire at the going market price. Knowledge of these facts has led to the conclusion that advertising expenditures are a sign of market imperfection, since they do not exist in a perfectly competitive world. Consequently, the more advertising that exists, the more imperfect and monopolistic the situation.

It is, of course, true that there is no need for advertising expenditures in a perfectly competitive world. It does not follow, however, that advertising expenditures cannot be economically efficient in nature. At the root of the problem is the distinction between "perfect" competition and "pure" competition. Whereas perfect competition assumes perfect information (as well as homogeneous products, an absence of entry barriers, and so forth), pure competition drops the assumption of perfect information while retaining all the remaining attributes of perfect competition. In pure competition, then, both buyers and sellers are to various degrees ignorant of pertinent market facts. As a result, both buyers and sellers may find it worthwhile at the margin to invest resources in information-acquiring or information-

[16]Neil H. Borden, *The Economics of Advertising* (Homewood, Ill.: Richard D. Irwin, Inc., 1944).

[17]A debt is owed by economists to George J. Stigler for his "Economics of Information," *Journal of Political Economy,* 64 (June 1961), 213–25.

disseminating activities. Viewed in this context, resources expended upon advertising can be economically efficient expenditures that increase information and reduce search costs.

Because ignorance of market characteristics such as price, service, quality, durability, and location does exist in the real world, the purely competitive market structure is a more useful vehicle for examining advertising expenditures than is the perfectly competitive market structure.[18] In pure competition, an advertising expenditure is socially desirable if the marginal social benefit that accrues from it exceeds the marginal social cost of the same expenditure. The social benefit is the reduced costs of search owing to the advertising, and the consequent improved allocation of resources; the social cost is the value to all individuals in society of the alternatives foregone when resources were used for the purpose of advertising.

It is probably uneconomic in most situations to eliminate all ignorance of market characteristics, for, as Stigler has noted, "Ignorance is like subzero weather: by a sufficient expenditure its effects upon people can be kept within tolerable or even comfortable bounds, but it would be wholly uneconomic entirely to eliminate all its effects."[19] Advertising can therefore be an economically efficient means of perfecting the operation of a market and should not be considered prima facie evidence of the existence of resource misallocation, the existence of monopoly power, or the impairment of welfare.

Although much product differentiation and advertising is desirable from a welfare standpoint because of its informative characteristics, a considerable amount of product differentiation by means of advertising expenditures is uninformative, deceptive, and even untruthful. That is, advertising has both the potential to perfect the marketplace and the potential to delay and disrupt its functioning. Advertisements that seldom mention product prices or traits and instead stress the merits of Dodge Fever or the social stigma of having a ring around one's shirt collar are of doubtful usefulness. Providing precious little to increase the consumer's knowledge about key economic-decision variables such as price, quality, location, service, and durability, such advertising is aimed almost solely at altering the shape and position of the demand curve and confers only small social benefit while expending large amounts of resources.[20]

Still other advertisements are blatantly deceptive and fallacious. The well-known pain reliever Bufferin has been advertised as acting twice as fast as aspirin. However, a drug-efficacy study conducted jointly by the National Academy of Sciences and the National Research Council labeled this

---

[18]See David R. Kamerschen, "The Statistics of Advertising," *Rivista Internazionale di Scienze Economiche e Commerciali*, 19 (January 1972), 1–25, for a more complete discussion of this point.

[19]Stigler, "Economics of Information," p. 224.

[20]See, however, George J. Stigler, "Price and Non-Price Competition," *Journal of Political Economy*, 76 (February 1968), 149–54, concerning the relative efficiency of price and nonprice competition.

claim "ambiguous and misleading."[21] Testimony presented to the Select Subcommittee on Small Business of the U.S. Senate in 1971 concerning the advertising of proprietary medicines revealed that there was no evidence to support the claims of Anacin concerning its effectiveness and speed of pain relief.[22] The same hearings resulted in the statement that there was no known evidence that Miles Nervine, advertised as a sleep aid and sedative, was effective as either.[23] The Federal Trade Commission has recently begun to require certain firms to run "corrective" advertisements, modifying or altering previous advertising claims. In one case, the FTC forced the ITT Continental Baking Company to run advertisements explaining that the reason slices of its Profile Bread have fewer calories than those of other, competing breads is that Profile Bread is sliced thinner.[24] Such corrective actions are seldom accomplished quickly; it took fully sixteen years for the FTC to get the word "Liver" taken out of the name of Carter's Little Liver Pills.[25]

Few advertisements are ever clearly false or totally uninformative. As little as one-quarter or as much as three-quarters of all advertising expenditures may be primarily of an informative nature, rather than being directed at creating imagery designed to woo consumers' dollars away from alternative expenditures. Therein lies the difficulty with product differentiation in general and advertising expenditures in particular. Despite the claims of many vocal observers, product differentiation and advertising are neither all good nor all evil from a welfare standpoint.

The Scale-Economies Issue

One additional argument in favor of advertising is based upon the alleged realization of economies of scale by the firm that advertises.[26] Advertising, it is claimed, will expand existing markets and create new ones as well; firms can therefore grow larger and realize economies of scale. The empirical evidence on this issue is quite mixed and fails to affirm or discredit the hypothesis. Nevertheless, it should be pointed out that the circumstances necessary for the realization of production economies of scale because of advertising are limited in nature. The scale-economies argument assumes that all output expansion in a market is attained by the expansion of existing firms rather than by the appearance of independent new com-

[21]Testimony in hearings before the Subcommittee on Monopoly, Select Committee on Small Business, U.S. Senate, 92d Cong., 1st sess., *Advertising of Proprietary Medicines* (Washington, D.C.: U.S. Government Printing Office, 1971), Part I, p. 96.

[22]*Ibid.*, Part I, pp. 119–20.

[23]*Ibid.*, Part II, p. 442.

[24]Ocean Spray Consents to Ads Clarifying Drink Claims, in Second Such FTC Accord," *Wall Street Journal*, 52 (Monday, May 8, 1972), 5.

[25]*Advertising of Proprietary Medicines,* Part I, p. 214.

[26]Jules Backman, *Advertising and Competition* (New York: New York University Press, 1967).

petitors. The implication is that substantial barriers to entry exist. Further, if expansion of output is to result in the realization of economies of scale, then the firm must have been operating somewhere above and to the left of the lowest point of its long-run average-cost curve prior to the expansion of output. Also, although it is true that one firm in a market can expand its output at the expense of other firms at a given point in time, a fallacy of composition is clearly involved if it is implied that all firms can simultaneously expand their outputs at the same time. Finally, the idea of realization of economies of scale in advertising is not encouraged by the strong evidence that no overall firm- or plant-level economies of scale ordinarily exist.

Encouragement of Innovation

Advertising has also been touted as providing encouragement and promise to firms that they will be able to extract the maximum amount of benefits from any new product or process that they develop. The contention is that firms know that the process of advertising will bring their new product or process to the attention of prospective users and that they will therefore reap the benefits. This argument may have some merit in markets such as drugs, notions, and cosmetics. It seems to have much less validity in producer-goods markets. Objectively, one can ask whether or not a new product or process materially increases productivity; subjectively, one can ask if it really incorporates something new, or whether it is merely old wine in new bottles. A large number of the new products that are developed in highly differentiated and heavily advertised markets such as drugs would indeed seem to fit the description of old wine in new bottles. One after another new toothpastes and mouthwashes are placed on the market. The technical similarity of such goods (which is quite apart from the perceived image of the goods maintained by consumers) is difficult to escape. The overall force of the stimulation argument, therefore, is considerably diluted, since high degrees of product differentiation and advertising do not seem to have been important motivating forces for many of our most important technological advances.

Wider Choice of Goods and Services

It is asserted that advertising and product differentiation give consumers a much wider choice of goods and services than they would otherwise have. As an empirical proposition, this is unarguable. However, it largely evades the crucial consideration: Do we as a result have an excessive amount of advertising and product differentiation? Although it is difficult to apply the rigor of economic analysis to this issue, we are nevertheless prepared to state that economic welfare might be increased by a reduction in both the amount of product differentiation and the total expenditures made upon advertising, even though consumers may have a taste for variety. The primary basis for this educated hunch is the feeling that a substantial portion of current-day advertising expenditures is aimed at image making and the rearrangement of consumer expenditures, rather than at providing consumers with concrete information about the product and conditions of sale.

Support of Communications

The communications argument in favor of advertising is also perplexing to the economist, since it is grounded in sociopolitical considerations. Advertising, it is said, is not a net cost to society, because it supports and is responsible for the continued existence of independent radio, television, magazines, and newspapers. One despairs at evaluating this argument analytically, since it is impossible to know which of these outlets would be supported (and to what degree) in the absence of advertising. The theory of information instructs us that information and news are marketable commodities; hence, it would be incorrect to forecast the demise of all independent communications outlets. The theory of information does not, however, provide an operational basis for establishing the type or quantity of information that will be bought and sold.

Advertising and Monopoly Power

Over two decades ago, in a survey article about the economics of advertising, Nicholas Kaldor suggested that product differentiation is a cause of monopoly power.[27] This thesis has been argued and tested numerous times since then. One of the major difficulties in attempts to test it is the fear that the direction of causation is not one-way in nature. That is, advertising may promote monopoly power, but cannot monopoly power also stimulate product differentiation and advertising? An additional pragmatic difficulty is that, as our work in Chapter 4 indicated, no accepted measure of monopoly power exists. Kaldor himself suggested the Lerner Index as the measure,[28] but that suggestion has not been followed in subsequent tests of the monopoly-power hypothesis.

Telser was the first to test the Kaldor hypothesis.[29] He examined 42 consumer-goods markets at approximately the three-digit level of detail

[27]Nicholas Kaldor, "The Economic Aspects of Advertising," *Review of Economic Studies,* 18 (No. 1, 1950), 20.

[28]*Ibid.*

[29]Lester G. Telser, "Advertising and Competition," *Journal of Political Economy,* 72 (December 1964), 537–62.

during the years 1947, 1954, and 1958. Telser found simple correlations between the average market advertising-to-sales ratio and the market four-firm concentration ratio of .163, .165, and .160, respectively, in the three years. Contending that the four-firm concentration ratio is a "widely accepted" measure of monopoly power, Telser concluded that the relationship between advertising and monopoly power was "unimpressive.[30]

Three main grounds exist for questioning the Telser study. First, the propriety of using concentration ratios as a proxy for monopoly power is a matter of dispute. Second, the broad market definitions utilized by Telser may disguise important relationships. Third, Telser's data set contains a few extreme observations in which low concentration ratios are matched with quite high advertising-to-sales ratios. When the effect of these disparate observations is minimized by computing a rank correlation coefficient between advertising and concentration, the correlations rise to .292, .362, and .300, respectively. Each of these correlation coefficients is statistically significant at the 5 percent level, whereas none of Telser's simple correlation coefficients achieved statistical significance at that level.[31] The rank correlations were carried out by the team of Mann, Henning, and Meehan,[32] who later conducted further work in which they found strong and statistically significant correlations between concentration and advertising for leading firms in 14 four-digit markets.

In the November 1969 issue of the *Journal of Industrial Economics,* a symposium was conducted on the advertising-and-concentration question.[33] The symposium was not notable for resolving the issues involved. Rather, the discussion centered upon the appropriateness of the studies by Telser and Mann et al. in terms of market definition, sample size, and sample selection. Also, two subsequent studies by Ekelund and Gramm, on the one hand, and Marcus, on the other, reached quite opposite conclusions concerning the effects of advertising upon monopoly power while using quite different samples and techniques.[34]

The most interesting piece of recent evidence concerning advertising and concentration has been contributed by Greer.[35] According to Greer,

---

[30]*Ibid.*

[31]As reported in the statement of H. Michael Mann, Director, Bureau of Economics, Federal Trade Commission, before the Subcommittee on Activities of Regulatory Agencies Relating to Small Business, Select Committee on Small Business, U.S. House of Representatives, Washington, D.C., June 25, 1971, p. 4.

[32]H. Michael Mann, J.A. Henning, and J.W. Meehan, Jr., "Advertising and Concentration: An Empirical Investigation," *Journal of Industrial Economics,* 16 (November 1967), 34–39.

[33]Robert B. Ekelund, Jr., and Charles Maurice, "An Empirical Investigation of Advertising and Concentration: Comment," *Journal of Industrial Economics,* 18 (November 1969), 76–84; see also articles in the same issue: H. Michael Mann, J.A. Henning, and J.W. Meehan, Jr., "Testing Hypotheses in Industrial Economics: A Reply," pp. 81–84; Lester Telser, "Another Look at Advertising and Concentration," pp. 85–94; H. Michael Mann, J.A. Henning, and J.W. Meehan, Jr., "Statistical Testing in Industrial Economics: A Reply on Measurement Error and Sampling Procedure," pp. 95–199.

[34]Robert B. Ekelund, Jr., and William P. Gramm, "Advertising and Concentration: Some New Evidence," *The Antitrust Bulletin,* 15 (Summer 1970), 243–49; and Matityahu Marcus, "Advertising and Changes in Concentration," *Southern Economic Journal,* 36 (October 1969), 117–21.

[35]Douglas F. Greer, "Advertising and Market Concentration," *Southern Economic Journal,* 38 (July 1971), 19–32.

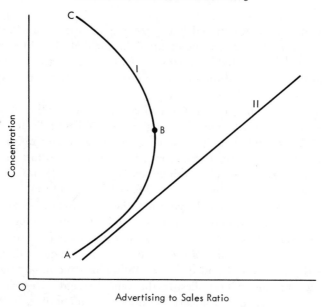

Figure 11.1

the relationship between advertising and concentration is not linear, as all previous studies have assumed, but is quadratic in nature. Figure 11.1 illustrates this distinction. Function I is quadratic, whereas function II is linear. The quadratic form, according to Greer, implies dual causality. Section *AB* of function I illustrates the possibility that advertising can create monopoly power (the Kaldor–Mann–et al. thesis) ; however, there is also a feedback effect of monopoly power upon advertising. This later feedback (section *BC* of function I) occurs because of tacit collusion between oligopolists, which reduces the amount of advertising expenditures. Greer cited Fellner's celebrated work on oligopoly, *Competition Among the Few,* as the theoretic basis for such tacit collusion.[36] Greer additionally provided regression results that lent support to the quadratic conjecture.

Both the theoretical basis and the empirical evidence for Greer's interesting hypothesis are subject to qualifications. Fellner did indeed foresee the possibility of tacit collusion between oligopolists, where nonprice variables were concerned. Such collusion could be evidenced by joint agreement to lower advertising expenditures. However, he foresaw that particular scenario only in what he termed "completely mature" oligopolies.[37] In other circumstances, there would be no agreement over nonprice variables, and competitive advertising might be the result. Since Greer's sample of 41 three-digit markets contains few if any completely mature oligopolies, the theoretical underpinnings for his work may not be applicable. Further, Mann, Henning,

[36]William Fellner, *Competition Among the Few* (Clifton, N.J.: Augustus M. Kelley, Publishers 1965).

[37]*Ibid.*, p. 188.

and Meehan have demonstrated that Greer's quadratic form depends upon the existence of one extreme observation in each of the three classes of markets that Greer tested.[38] Removal of that one extreme observation resulted in the rejection of the quadratic form (and instead, the assumption of a linear form) in six of nine cases.

The relationship between advertising and concentration has perhaps been given excessive attention. Although most studies indicate a positive, usually significant, relationship between advertising-to-sales ratios and concentration ratios, this verdict is far from unanimous. It is fair to comment that even if the relationship is positive and significant, the meaning of this fact is still not clear. Concentration ratios have been found wanting numerous times as measures of monopoly power. Other empirical studies have also suggested that concentration may act as a proxy for other, more important facets of market structure.[39] When other indicators of market structure (for example, economies of scale, rate of technological change, and the rate of growth of demand) are included, concentration loses the importance it ordinarily achieves in bivariate studies. In this vein, a recent advertising–concentration study concluded that advertising does not profoundly affect four-firm concentration; rather, it actually has greater effect upon the size structure of the entire market as represented by a Lorenz Curve.[40]

A final point needs to be made about the advertising component of the advertising–concentration studies. Product differentiation, like monopoly power, is an intricate and sophisticated phenomenon. It cannot be represented fully and accurately by a single variable. As Simon has commented, "Advertising ratio data alone are not competent to serve as the basis for any general investigation of the economics of advertising."[41]

Advertising and Prices

Little reputable evidence indicates that product differentiation and advertising cause lower retail prices. On the other hand, a rather large number of studies (many of which could hardly be termed rigorous) have pointed to their causing higher prices. Notable among these is the report made by the National Committee on Food Marketing, which found prices to be 4 to 35 percent higher on nationally advertised goods than on private or local branded goods.[42] Adams reports that during the decade of the 1950's, unbranded muslin sheets sold for 25 percent less than branded sheets

[38]H. Michael Mann, J.A. Henning, and J.W. Meehan, Jr., "On the Quadratic Relation Between Advertising and Concentration," mimeographed (1972).

[39]James V. Koch, "Industry Market Structure and Industry Price–Cost Margins" (unpublished manuscript).

[40]Louis A. Guth, "Advertising and Market Structure Revisited," Journal of Industrial Economics, 19 (April 1971), 179–98.

[41]Julian Simon, Issues in the Economics of Advertising (Urbana, Ill.: University of Illinois Press, 1970), p. 110.

[42]U.S. National Commission on Food Marketing, Special Studies in Food Marketing, Special Study No. 10 (Washington, D.C.: U.S. Government Printing Office, 1966), p. 65.

of the same quality.[43] And it is well known that in the area of ethical drugs, one generally pays a premium for the privilege of purchasing technically similar advertised preparations instead of unadvertised drugs that are known only by their generic chemical names. H. Michael Mann, the director of the Bureau of Economics of the Federal Trade Commission, presented evidence to a Senate subcommittee in 1971 that the suggested retail price for 100 aspirin tablets was 1.7 times as high for the heavily advertised Bayer brand than it was for the lightly advertised St. Joseph's brand. However, in the area of children's aspirin, where both brands were advertised equally, the suggested retail prices were identical.[44] Table 11.2 summarizes these findings.

TABLE 11.2

Retail Aspirin Prices and Advertising

	Advertising Expenditures by Manufacturer	Suggested Retail Price per Container
Bayer's:		
5-grain	$15.6 million	
50 tablets		$0.63
100 tablets		$0.98
200 tablets		$1.73
Children's		
36 tablets	$2.3 million	$0.39
St. Joseph's:		
5-grain	$.7 million	
50 tablets		$0.39
100 tablets		$0.59
200 tablets		$0.98
Children's		
36 tablets	$2.1 million	$0.39

Source: *Testimony in hearings before the Subcommittee on Monopoly, Select Committee on Small Business, U.S. Senate, 92d Cong., 1st sess.,* Advertising of Proprietary Medicines (*Washington, D.C.: U.S. Government Printing Office, 1971), Part I, p. 271.*

The evidence quoted here is insufficient for conviction. Controlled studies of pricing are difficult to carry out because of the many nonprice elements that almost insidiously insert themselves into the analysis. It is not surprising, therefore, that Kamerschen has charged that "part of the higher price of advertised over non-advertised goods may be accounted for by the higher level of quality and smaller variance of the advertised merchandise."[45] This view has been echoed by Johnson, Telser, and Stigler.[46] Hence,

[43]Walter Adams, *The Structure of American Industry*, 3rd ed. (New York: Macmillan and Company' 1961), p. 56.

[44]*Advertising of Proprietary Medicines*, Part I, p. 52.

[45]Kamerschen, "The Statistics of Advertising," p. 5.

[46]Harry G. Johnson, "The Economics of Advertising," *The Advertising Quarterly*, 1 (Autumn 1964), 9–14; Telser, "Advertising and Competition"; and Stigler, "Price and Non-Price Competition."

caution is called for in our conclusions about the effects of advertising upon prices. While existing evidence points to higher prices as a result of advertising (hardly surprising, since economic theory does predict that price will reflect all long-run average costs of production when competition exists), more sophisticated evidence is badly needed.

Competitive Advertising: The Prisoner's Dilemma

There is considerable evidence that in many markets, the total dollar amount of advertising undertaken by all firms is greater than the dollar amount of advertising would be in the same market if a single-firm monopolist existed. In the jargon of the theory of games, a "prisoner's dilemma" may have developed. Assume that one or more firms have increased their advertising expenditures in an effort to defend or increase their market shares. Faced with declining market shares, these firms' rivals are gradually forced into similar behavior, unless they wish to compete on the basis of price. Soon all firms in the market have increased their budgets for advertising. When all is said and done, market shares may have changed but little, because each firm's increased advertising expenditures are cancelled by the similar efforts of its rivals. A vicious circle may develop. The individual firm must increase its advertising expenditures in order to defend or increase its market share; however, in the absence of collusion, it can never decrease its advertising expenditures once they have been increased. To decrease them would be to invite a declining market share. If the firms in the market engaged in collusion (legal or otherwise), they would all decrease their advertising expenditures simultaneously and thereby avoid the self-defeating and futilely high levels of advertising expenditures that have been engendered by competition.

The most outstanding examples of the prisoner's dilemma in advertising are to be found in the cigarette market. Schoenberg, Borden, Basmann, Weiss, Shubik, Simon, and Grabowski and Mueller have all contributed evidence in this area.[47] Basmann, for instance, found that a $2.2 million decrease in advertising expenditures in the cigarette market would have decreased sales by only $1.25 million.[48] Recent evidence contributed by Grabowski and Mueller points to a strong reaction by one cigarette manufacturer to increases in advertising by others; a 1 percent increase in advertising by a particular competitor was found to provoke an average increase in advertising of 1.12 percent for the typical firm in the market.[49]

[47]E.H. Schoenberg, "The Demand Curve for Cigarettes," *Journal of Business*, 6 (January 1933), 15–35; Borden, *The Economics of Advertising*; Robert L. Basmann, "An Application of Several Econometric Techniques to a Theory of Demand with Variable Tastes" (Ph.D. diss., Iowa State University, 1955); Leonard W. Weiss, *Case Studies in American Industry* (New York: John Wiley & Sons, Inc., 1967); Martin Shubik, *Strategy and Market Structure* (New York: John Wiley & Sons, Inc., 1959); Julian L. Simon, "The Effect of the Competitive Structure upon Expenditures for Advertising," *Quarterly Journal of Economics* 18 (November 1967), 610–27; and Grabowski and Mueller, "Imitative Advertising."

[48]Basmann, "An Application of Several Econometric Techniques."

[49]Grabowski and Mueller, "Imitative Advertising," p. 275.

The type of collusion in which the firms in a market arrive at a joint-profit-maximizing agreement that entails lower advertising expenditures does not often occur. Both antitrust pressures and the lure of self-interest militate against such a solution in all but the most mature oligopolies. The cigarette manufacturers have achieved only short-run success in proscribing or eliminating particular varieties of advertising. Trade associations internal to a given market might ordinarily be expected to attempt to find joint-profit-maximizing arrangements concerning advertising; however, such associations have been largely impotent in this area—although they have upon occasion been successful in eliminating false or misleading advertising. Indeed, except for the documented case involving British soap manufacturers whose agreement reduced overall advertising expenditures,[50] there is little evidence that the prisoner's-dilemma situation has been avoided by collusive understandings among producers.

The circumstance that often emerges in markets where the degree of product differentiation is high (see Table 11.1) is long periods of stability with respect to total advertising dollar volumes, interspersed with competitive hassles in which nearly all firms in the market ultimately increase their advertising expenditures. The initial causes for such battles are not clear, but may include a declining share for one or more firms in the market, newly devised advertising campaigns or products, or perhaps new personnel. When the dust has settled, nevertheless, the postconflict market shares of individual firms often closely approximate their preconflict shares.[51] Such escalation of advertising expenditures and use of resources is futile and a social waste.[52]

Welfare Economics of Trading Stamps, Games, and Contests

The economics of trading stamps, games, and contests is strikingly similar to the prisoner's-dilemma possibility discussed in the last section. When one firm dispenses trading stamps or allows customers to play seemingly lucrative games and contests, that firm can conceivably increase its market share at the expense of other firms that do not choose to engage in similar nonprice competition. However, just as in the case of advertising expenditures, one must guard against the fallacy of composition. Trading stamps, games, and contests will ordinarily exercise a cancelling effect upon each other when adopted by most or all firms in a given market. Hence, no firm will increase its market share, consumers may pay higher prices for

---

[50]This agreement has been reported in P. Leslie Cook, *Effects of Mergers* (London : George Allen & Unwin, 1958).

[51]More complete explanations of this phenomenon may be found in Roy W. Jastram, "Advertising Outlays Under Oligopoly," *Review of Economics and Statistics,* 31 (May 1949), 106–9; see also James V. Koch, "The Concept of a Plateau of Selling and Product Variation Costs," *Economic and Business Bulletin* 22 (Winter 1970), 31–36.

[52]Thorstein Veblen was one of the first to make this observation in his *Theory of the Leisure Class* (New York : Modern Library, Inc., 1934).

goods and services, and only the stamp, game, and contest manufacturers themselves benefit. In response to the rhetorical question, "Who wins marketing promotion games?" O'Hanlon concluded, "Nobody, really, but the promoters themselves, if you take the testimony of food-chain managers, gasoline dealers, and disillusioned players."[53]

The use of trading stamps dates back to the early 1890's, when Schuster's Department Store in Milwaukee began to issue stamps to its customers. Approximately 250 trading-stamp companies currently exist. The largest, Sperry and Hutchison (S&H), controls about 40 percent of the market. Trading stamps must be viewed as a distinct market, since the individual firm that dispenses these stamps at the retail level must first buy them from supplying firms such as S&H. The stamps may ultimately be redeemable by the consumer in terms of merchandise at a redemption store, or may occasionally be translated into cash.

Vendors of trading stamps tout them to prospective retail users as primarily a means of increasing their sales volumes. Increased sales volumes, it is added, can lead to lower per-unit costs of production and consequently to lower prices. However, this contention is valid only under very narrow conditions. First, one firm can increase its market share at a given point in time only at the expense of other firms. When all firms in a given market are giving stamps to customers, increased sales for all the dispensing firms are not likely.[54] Second, even if increased sales are realized by firms that award stamps to their customers, it does not follow that lower per-unit costs of production will be realized. Increased firm size could actually result in diseconomies of scale. The fact that the stamp-using firm must buy the stamps it dispenses means that it has assumed an additional cost of production. Economies of scale resulting in lower prices is neither an *a priori* prediction concerning the use of trading stamps, nor a verified empirical proposition.

In a circumstance where all firms in a given market are dispensing trading stamps or offering games and contests, the only certain winner appears to be the manufacturer of the stamps, games, or contests. A trading-stamp company such as S&H benefits because the stamps it sells to using firms are priced higher than the value of the merchandise the stamps can be used to redeem. Further, many of the stamps dispensed by using firms such as grocery stores are never redeemed by consumers. The unredeemed portion of trading stamps varies from a low of about 5 percent for companies such as S&H to a high of about 40 to 50 percent for less well-

---

[53]Thomas O'Hanlon, "Who Wins Marketing Promotion Games?" *Fortune*, 74 (February 1969), 104–8ff. This sentiment was also voiced in the *Wall Street Journal*, 157 (September 17, 1963), 24: "Who pays the costs of stamps when everyone is using them and there can be no gain in sales?"

[54]Sales may grow owing to the general growth of the market; however, this is not attributable to trading stamps. Sales might also grow because this particular market takes sales away from other markets for different types of goods and services. This possibility, however, assumes that these other markets are not also dispensing trading stamps.

established companies.[55] Additionally, there is a lag in time between the purchase of stamps by a using firm and the possible redemption of merchandise by consumers. This lag provides the trading-stamp manufacturer with an interest-free loan for that period of time.

Retailers may attempt to cover the cost of the stamps they have purchased by raising prices. This is quite unlikely to be a profitable action if undertaken on all merchandise sold by the retailer. More typical is a policy of selective price increases on items whose price elasticity of demand is inelastic and unresponsive. Yet a selective policy of price increases, if profitably pursued, implies that the retailer in question was not maximizing profits in his previous situation. By implication, if no circumstances have changed other than the fact that trading stamps are now being used, then the previous pricing position of the retailer was non-optimal with respect to profitability.

The empirical evidence concerning the effects of trading stamps, games, and contests upon prices is spotty. A large portion of the evidence has been contributed by individuals who have more than a casual vocational interest in the conclusions reached from their research. The most reliable evidence indicates that trading stamps do indeed lead to higher prices being charged at retail stores that dispense them. Bromley and Wallace found an increase in store prices of about 2 percent when a specific store adopted trading stamps and its competitors were already using them.[56] But that is not the whole story. When some firms utilize trading stamps, the pricing behavior of firms that do not use them may be affected.[57] Since stamp-using firms apparently charge higher prices, the nonusing stores may also charge higher prices without suffering the effects of competition. A study by Rothwell indicated that the introduction of trading stamps raised prices in both trading-stamp-using and nonusing retail outlets; the increase in the stamp-using stores, however, was .6 percent higher than the increase in the non-stamp-using stores.[58]

Bell and Sherman have demonstrated that the use of trading stamps also has allocative implications.[59] Some consumers benefit at the expense of other consumers when trading stamps are used. Further, even if trading stamps are regarded as just another good or service that consumers purchase, it is a limiting good in the sense that the stamps cannot typically be redeemed for cash and because the choice of merchandise available to stamp

---

[55]The estimates reported here are based upon conversations with individuals from trading-stamp manufacturing firms.

[56]J.D. Bromley and W.H. Wallace, "The Effect of Trading Stamps on Retail Food Prices," Rhode Island Agricultural Experiment Station, Contribution Number 1091 (Kingston, R.I., 1965).

[57]This point has been made with clarity by Robert H. Strotz, "On Being Fooled by Figures: The Case of Trading Stamps," *Journal of Business*, 31 (October 1958), 304–10.

[58]Doris P. Rothwell, "Impact of Trading Stamps on Food Prices," *Monthly Labor Review*, 82 (March 1959), 276–78.

[59]Carolyn Shaw Bell, "Liberty and Property, and No Stamps," *Journal of Business*, 40 (April 1967) 194–202; and Roger Sherman, "Trading Stamps and Consumer Welfare," *Journal of Industrial Economics* 17 (November 1968), 29–40.

holders for redemption purposes is not complete. Trading-stamp redemption stores are inefficient distributors of goods and services, not only because their merchandise selection is limited, but also because of the increased transport costs and loss of time the stores typically inflict upon consumers.

It is not difficult to extend our analysis of trading stamps to the phenomenon of games and contests. The high-water mark of games and contests such as the Mr. President Coin Game, Mr. and Mrs. N.F.L., and Let's Go to the Races was the year 1968, when enterprising game manufacturers sold over $200 million worth of such games to retail firms.[60] Since that time, the use of games and contests has declined, to a great degree because of pressure from the Federal Trade Commission. The FTC disclosed that many of the games and contests were rigged in terms of the distribution of prizes, and that in many cases the promoters of games and contests knew in advance that it would be made impossible for most or all of the advertised prizes to be awarded.

The analytical similarity of the case of games and contests with that of trading stamps is striking. When most or all gasoline stations or supermarkets are using some combination of games and contests, the potential is great for a prisoner's dilemma situation to arise. Further, economic theory suggests that where competition exists, the prices of goods and services will in the long run reflect all the costs of production. Since the games and contests adopted by firms represent a cost of production to those firms, it is probable that the prices consumers pay for the goods and services marketed by those firms will rise. The desire of some consumers to gamble and play games that are rigged is crude evidence that the nonprice aspects of the games and contests are apparently quite attractive in many cases.

Rivalry on the Basis of Style

Few individuals consciously opt for behavior that deliberately makes them "out of style." Although what is stylish varies considerably among individuals and groups—whether the current fad is large automobile tail fins or hula hoops, chocolate fondue or bleached blue jeans and bare feet—the mass of the consuming body politic endeavors to stay abreast of current styles by ordering their purchases appropriately. Unfortunately, style changes are not accomplished without cost. Also, the effects of style rivalry among firms upon the competitive process is not trivial. The welfare effects of style rivalry are therefore worthy of additional attention.

The automobile market is the most frequently cited example of the high cost and the possible adverse competitive impact of style rivalry. Fisher, Griliches, and Kaysen, in an article now regarded as a classic, attempted to ascertain the costs of automobile model changes between 1949

[60]*Fortune*, 74, p. 107.

and 1960.[61] The trio looked at 1949 automobiles and asked what magnitude of resources would have been saved during the 1949–60 period if the automobile producers had continued to use the 1949-model automobile lengths, weights, horsepowers, transmissions, and so forth to produce each new year's automobiles. In the conceptual experiment, allowance was made for the producers to utilize new and better technology as it developed; however, the producers were constrained to use the superior technology to produce the 1949 model automobile. The empirical results were eye-opening. The three researchers estimated that $454 per newly produced automobile would have been saved (constant prices) if sizes and horsepowers had not been augmented during the time period in question. The saving would have been $116 per car if additional optional equipment had not been added during the time period, and $99 per car would have been saved because the automobile makers would not have been forced to retool each year in order to produce newly styled cars. The 1960 automobiles were also found to give significantly worse gasoline mileage, the cost being estimated at $968 million per year. The investigators ignored possible complementary costs such as new and better roads, bigger garages, more policemen, and the like, which might have been required by the 1960 automobiles.

It should be emphasized that Fisher, Griliches, and Kaysen did not contend that the 1960 automobiles were not better in many substantive respects. Rather, they performed a study in the tradition of positive economics and provided information about what actually *is*. The reader may exercise his own judgment concerning whether or not the "better" automobile merited the higher costs necessary to produce it. A definitive societal conclusion cannot be reached on this issue with the theoretical tools at our disposal. The point, nevertheless, has been forcefully made: Style changes, particularly in the automobile market, are a costly matter and require considerable amounts of society's resources each year to accomplish.

Reliable estimates of the cost of style changes in other markets are not available, but it is nonetheless apparent that the frequent style changes occurring in certain markets may render the existing capital stock artificially obsolescent. That is, certain items in the capital stock, whether automobiles, houses, or other durables, may be impatiently discarded in favor of newer, more stylish (although technically similar) models. Hence, the growth of the stock of capital is retarded. Similar patterns appear in the consumer-goods market. Who would seriously contend that men's ties six inches wide should be regarded as anything but technically similar to men's ties three inches wide? The problems associated with such speculation are twofold: (1) Society's preferences (its social-welfare function) are unknown, and there-

---

[61] Franklin Fisher, Zvi Griliches, and Carl Kaysen, "The Costs of Automobile Style Changes since 1949," *American Economic Review*, 52 (May 1962), 259–61; see also the more comprehensive article by the same authors, "The Cost of Automobile Model Changes since 1949," *Journal of Political Economy*, 70 (October 1962), 433–51.

fore the "best" mixture of goods, services, and capital stock is unknown; and (2) even if the tastes and preferences of society were known, the difficulties associated with measurement of any social loss involved might well be insurmountable.

Style rivalry has also had profound effects upon the number of competitors in the automobile market. Beginning in the 1920's, rapid style changes became the accepted mode of behavior here. Menge has pointed out that rapid style changes work to the detriment of small firms in the automobile market, because only the largest firms are able to utilize newly installed production equipment sufficiently during a production year to wear it out and thereby reduce unit produciton costs per automobile.[62] More concretely, every time an automobile is substantially restyled, new tools and dies must be installed on the large stamping presses that mold such items as automobile fenders and hoods. At the end of the model year, if restyling is to take place, the tools, and especially the dies, must be replaced. The dies are quite expensive pieces of equipment, and it takes a great deal of time and rather large amounts of production to reduce this considerable expense by spreading it over many automobiles. Small automobile manufacturers such as Hudson and Packard did not produce a sufficient number of units to approach wearing out their tools and dies; hence, when the new model year arrived, they were forced by styling competition to invest in new tools and dies even though their existing equipment was still usable. Menge contends that styling rivalry promoted by the "Big Three" automobile makers was responsible for the demise of producers such as Hudson, Packard, and Studebaker. American Motors briefly broke the annual restyling custom and prospered, despite the fact that its levels of production were so low that fully thirteen years would have been required for it to wear out the die it used to produce deck lids. Changing consumer tastes in favor of larger automobiles ended American Motors' challenge in this area. In the early 1970's, American Motors was still producing fewer automobiles annually than its former chief executive, George Romney, had suggested some fifteen years previously was the minimum optimal scale in the automobile market.[63]

The most significant example of an automobile producer that is able to avoid the annual restyling rites is Volkswagen. The producers of the "Beetle" have intentionally shaped their advertising to point out to prospective customers the fact that the basic style of the Volkswagen changes but little from year to year. Customers are told that technological improvements are made, but that the basic body style will not be altered. Volkswagen has

---

[62]John Menge, "Style Change Costs as a Market Weapon," *Quarterly Journal of Economics*, 76 (November 1962), 632–47.

[63]Romney suggested that economies of scale in automobile production might be realized up to about 400,000 automobiles per year. Report, together with individual views of Subcommittee on Antitrust and Monopoly, Committee of the Judiciary, U.S. Senate, *Administered Prices: Automobiles*, 85th Cong., 2d sess. (Washington, D.C.: U.S. Government Printing Office, 1958), pp. 13–16.

had considerable success in transmitting this advertising message. As a result, the production costs of Volkswagens have been reduced, and many customers have purchased Volkswagens rather than annually restyled automobiles for both price and style reasons.

THE PROFITABILITY OF NONPRICE COMPETITION

How profitable is nonprice competition? If firms regard expenditures upon nonprice competition as investments, then (*ceteris paribus*) the rate of return on such an investment should closely approximate the rates of return obtained on other types of capital, assuming the absence of barriers to entry. Barriers to entry are commonplace, however, in markets where the degree of product differentiation is high and profit rates are greater than average. Hence, while Weiss has observed that "some of the highest profit rates appear in industries which advertise heavily,"[64] it is not certain whether the supranormal profit rates are due to nonprice competition in the form of advertising, or to other factors.

The methodological problems associated with any study attempting to answer this question are immense. Any such study must take into consideration multiple sources of market power, rather than only one possible source such as advertising. Such a study must also come to grips with the fact that the tax laws do not view advertising as an investment. This, as we have seen, may bias upward the profit rates that are used in advertising studies. Finally, cross-sectional profit-rate studies are subject to a host of criticisms quite independent of those stated here. These objections have been discussed in Chapter 8 in some detail.

No study that has attempted to unravel the relationship between advertising and profitability is methodologically flawless. The one that represents the most reasoned approach to the problem (it has since been frequently imitated) was performed by Comanor and Wilson.[65] These two researchers attempted to explain market profit rates by means of multiple indicators of market structure. One such indicator was the average market advertising-to-sales ratio. This variable proved to be a highly significant predictor of market profit rates, even when a host of other relevant aspects of market structure were also included in the analysis. Comanor and Wilson found that although the average market profit rate in their study was 8 percent, the average profit rate earned in heavily advertised markets was 12 percent.[66] They attributed this to the product-differentiation barrier created and maintained by advertising expenditures.

---

[64]Leonard W. Weiss, "Advertising, Profits, and Corporate Taxes," *Review of Economics and Statistics*, 51 (November 1969), 421–30.

[65]William S. Comanor and Thomas A. Wilson, "Advertising, Market Structure, and Performance,' *Review of Economics and Statistics*, 49 (November 1967), 423–40.

[66]*Ibid.*, p. 437.

The Comanor–Wilson results have since been verified in several studies.[67] The supporting studies, however, are subject to the same methodological criticisms as is the Comanor–Wilson study—namely, they are cross-sectional profit rate studies, and the profit rates utilized may be exaggerated in markets where advertising expenditures are high because of the tax laws. Nonetheless, the Comanor–Wilson study and the subsequent efforts in its mold clearly point to the viability of advertising in terms of profitability. Those who scoff at the connection between advertising and profitability are reduced to the position of making methodological criticisms of existing studies, since contrary evidence is not common.[68]

SUMMARY

Nonprice competition and product differentiation are pervasive characteristics of the American economy. Advertising, the most common form of nonprice competition, is not a penny-ante activity. Some individual firms spend more than a quarter of a billion dollars annually upon advertising.

The purpose of advertising is to alter the shape and position of the consumer's demand curve. This activity may not always be consistent with the economically efficient provision of information. Information is an economic good. Since we live in an imperfect world in terms of knowledge, advertising can be an economically efficient activity that increases knowledge and information. Alternatively, it can fail to impart knowledge and instead be designed only to create images in the consumer's mind.

Advertising is but one possible avenue that nonprice competition can take. Nonprice competition may emphasize product characteristics and quality, service, conditions of sale, style, trading stamps given with the sale, or credit, to name a few possibilities. The imagination of the entrepreneur is exceedingly fertile where product differentiation and nonprice competition are concerned.

Nonprice competition is typically not perceived as quickly by competing firms, and is not reacted to as rapidly or as fiercely, as is price competition. It is often viewed as being less threatening than price competition. The fact that nonprice competition of a sophisticated variety is not developed overnight may also slow reactions to it when it is discovered.

[67]Among the studies in the Comanor–Wilson genre are Roger Sherman and Robert Tollison "Advertising and Profitability," *Review of Economics and Statistics,* 53 (November 1971), 397–407; Louis Esposito and Frances Ferguson Esposito, "Foreign Competition and Domestic Industry Profitability," *Review of Economics and Statistics,* 53 (November 1971), 343–53; and William G. Shepherd, "The Elements of Market Structure," *Review of Economics and Statistics,* 54 (February 1972), 25–37.

[68]One of the more vehement critics of studies that allege to find a connection between advertising and profitability is Jules Backman. Backman, in *Advertising and Competition,* a study sponsored by the Association of National Advertisers, attacked on methodological grounds the statistical relationship between advertising and profitability but failed to produce empirical evidence to the contrary. Backman's statistical interpretations of the results he surveyed and his sample selection leave much to be desired.

The competitive aspects of nonprice competition should not be glossed over. Continually escalating advertising battles can lead to socially non-optimal and privately inefficient levels of advertising in some cases. The cigarette market is an apt illustration of futilely high advertising levels. Nevertheless, there is considerable evidence pointing to better-than-average profitability for advertising expenditures in many industrial markets.

PROBLEMS

1. Precisely how differentiated can products be and still be considered to be in the same market? Is it actually possible to measure product differentiation, or is it, as some contend, a meaningless term?

2. It is often charged that much of the product differentiation observed in markets is socially wasteful, in that consumers would be equally satisfied with less differentiated products. Do consumers have a taste for differentiated products that is legitimate and satisfiable? Can producers create a demand for differentiated products that would otherwise not have been present?

3. "The Madison Avenue admen cannot create a demand for transportation; they can only cause me to purchase a Ford rather than a Plymouth." Comment.

4. Some advertising is directed mostly at current-period sales—for example, the supermarket's weekly ad promoting the weekend's sale items. Other advertising—for example, automobile advertising that fails to mention price—is probably aimed at sales over several periods. What is the appropriate rate of discount to apply to advertising expenditures and the profits that result, in view of the fact that both expenditures and profits are spread through time?

5. Some observers of the so-called prisoner's-dilemma circumstance in competitive advertising argue that it is necessary to permit some degree of collusion between firms in order to avoid the social waste of resources that results from such a situation. What is the appropriate methodology to use to weigh the benefits that might arise from permitting collusion between and among firms against the costs that might also accrue because of such collusion?

6. Stigler says many economists believe that price competition is much more effective than nonprice competition in increasing output and reducing profits and prices. Are they right?

12

Oligopoly Behavior
and Pricing: Theory

The term *oligopoly* is typically applied to a market characterized by the existence of a few large firms. Some of the key industrial markets in the American economy, such as automobiles, steel, copper, and aluminum, are commonly labeled oligopolies. Slightly less than 22 percent of the value added produced in the American manufacturing markets in 1966 was generated in markets where the four-firm concentration ratio was 60 or higher.[1] William Baumol, always a knowledgeable observer of economic phenomena, has observed, "Perhaps the most remarkable failure of modern value theory is its inability to explain the pricing, output, and other related decisions of the large, not quite monopolistic firms which account for so large a proportion of our output."[2] Because of the importance of oligopoly, and because of our imperfect understanding of oligopolistic markets, Chapters 12 and 13 must be considered among the most important in this book.

The purpose of these two chapters is to examine oligopolistic market behavior, with the twin aims of furthering our understanding of that behavior and clarifying the inability of economic theory to deal successfully with certain aspects of it. Our analysis will emphasize the pricing process, not only because an understanding of oligopolistic pricing is central to the overall understanding of oligopoly, but also because most of the unresolved controversies concerning oligopoly behavior revolve around the pricing process.

The roadmap we will follow in this chapter will lead us first to a critical examination of the major modern theories of oligopoly behavior. These theoretical formulations will provide the skeleton necessary for our subsequent analysis of particular topics and issues of special interest concerning oligopoly, such as price flexibility, price discrimination, and cartel behavior. Chapter 12 will emphasize theoretical approaches to oligopoly, whereas Chapter 13 will be devoted primarily to applied problems that are suggested by oligopoly theory.

[1]U.S. Bureau of the Census, "Value-of-Shipment Concentration Ratios by Industry," *Annual Survey of Manufactures, 1966*, M66 (AS)-8 (Washington, D.C.: U.S. Government Printing Office, 1968).
[2]William Baumol, *Business Behavior, Value and Growth* (New York: Harcourt Brace Jovanovich, 1967), p. 13.

MODERN THEORIES OF OLIGOPOLISTIC
BEHAVIOR AND PRICING

There is no accepted theory of oligopoly. Many competing theories exist, each of which typically highlights one or more critical aspects of certain oligopolistic markets, while at the same time making only casual mention of, or completely ignoring, other possibly important aspects of the same markets. The incredibly large number of theoretical explanations of oligopoly that are available is a direct result of the diversity of the oligopoly phenomenon itself. One set of assumptions concerning oligopolistic behavior (for example, the assumptions of homogeneous products and entry-excluding pricing behavior) may be broadly representative of, say, the motor-carriers market at a given point in time, but may fail to represent adequately other markets (for example, cigarettes), or even fail to do justice to the motor carriers at a different point in time.

Suffice it to say that there is no generally acknowledged explanation of oligopoly behavior. So many different (although plausible) combinations of behavioral assumptions for oligopoly exist that newly proposed combinations and permutations of these assumptions could fill the available space in economic journals many times over. They are not, however, totally dissimilar. The assumption that unifies nearly all oligopoly models is that the number of sellers in the market is sufficiently small that they recognize the joint mutual interdependence of their activities. One seller recognizes the fact that his actions affect other sellers and that other sellers are likely to react in some fashion to his activities. The type of reaction and the timing of the reaction are often not predictable *a priori*.

Oligopolistic competition can be usefully likened to a neighborhood poker game.[3] Each player in the game has a past history of which the other players are to some degree aware. The probable strategy of a particular player and his usual tactics are therefore not a complete mystery, even though his precise behavior is perhaps not predictable ex ante. Each player in the poker game realizes the interdependence of his fortunes with those of the other players. The two aces that are already on the table in front of player X clearly influence the behavior of the other players, as does the likelihood that player X will win the hand in question. The number of players who are still "in" on a given hand and the order in which they play are also relevant factors. The list of possible influencing factors is endless. Each player nevertheless assimilates this mass of information along with his own hunches and intuition and decides upon an action, knowing well that his action will inspire reactions.[4]

[3]Richard B. Heflebower, "Stability in Oligopoly," *The Manchester School*, 29 (January 1961) 79–93.

[4]The essence of oligopoly is often conflict. Rothschild has contended that oligopoly theory should borrow considerably from sources such as Von Clausewitz' *Principles of War*. K.W. Rothschild, "Price Theory and Oligopoly," *Economic Journal*, 57 (September 1947), 299–320.

The precise outcome of a poker hand cannot be predicted even when the distribution and the identity of the cards in each player's hand are known. Much depends upon how the cards are played. So also it is with oligopoly. Many models of oligopoly yield indeterminate solutions.[5] Indeterminacy does not mean that no solution exists; rather, it means that sufficient information is not at hand for the model to yield a unique prediction. Instead, the model may well generate a range of feasible solutions to the problem in question. A reduction in the number of feasible outcomes is, however, a valuable piece of information. Given appropriate additional information, perhaps in the form of institutional knowledge,[6] an observer might be able to select a unique solution from among the range of feasible solutions suggested by the general theory. Hence, a general theory of oligopoly can be tailored for use in a particular situation. "Indeterminate" need not be synonymous with "vague" or "useless."

An unconstrained claim upon the resources of a very large publishing house would be needed in order to cover adequately all the oligopoly models that have been proposed. Our discussion of oligopoly models will be limited in nature and will focus upon five modern theoretical contributions that have considerable appeal, owing either to their predictive validity or to the fact that they raise or dispose of important issues. These five models are (1) Chamberlin's small-group case, (2) kinked demand curve, (3) entry-limit pricing, (4) "open" oligopoly, and (5) cost-plus-markup pricing. We will ignore duopoly models, such as those proposed in the nineteenth century by Cournot, Bertrand, and Edgeworth, as well as Hotelling's interesting and more modern discussion of location in duopoly.[7] Duopoly models add little if anything to the explanation of behavior in oligopolistic markets that cannot also be gained by examination of conventional models of oligopoly. The theory of games, a comparatively recent contribution to oligopoly theory, will also be passed over. Game-theoretical models have typically been long on promise and short on fulfillment. That is, the theory of games appears to hold within it many useful insights and applications to oligopoly. It is consternating that useful and predictively valid applications of it have been few in number, although aficionados of the theory, such as Shubik, foresee a reversal of this history in the near future.[8] In any case, the reader has already been given a taste of the theory of games in Chapter 3.

[5] Heflebower, "Stability in Oligopoly."

[6] This has been suggested by Edward S. Mason in *Economic Concentration and the Monopoly Problem* (Cambridge, Mass.: Harvard University Press, 1957).

[7] Augustin Cournot, *Researches into the Mathematical Principles of the Theory of Wealth* (New York: The Macmillan Company, 1927); Joseph Bertrand, "Théorie Mathématique de la Richesse Sociale," *Journal des Savants*, September 1883, pp. 499–508; also, Bertrand, *Bulletin des Sciences Mathématiques et Astronomiques*, 7 (November 1883); F.Y. Edgeworth, "Le Teoria Pura del Monopòlio," *Giornale degli Economísti*, 15 (1897); and Harold Hotelling, "Stability in Competition," *Economic Journal*, 39 (March 1929), 41–57.

[8] Martin Shubik, "A Curmudgeon's Guide to Microeconomics," *Journal of Economic Literature*, 8 (June 1970), 405–34.

Chamberlin's Small-Group Case

Edward Chamberlin, along with Joan Robinson, made groundbreaking advances in economic theory dealing with imperfectly competitive markets during the 1920's and 1930's.[9] Chamberlin is best known for his large-group case, commonly referred to as monopolistic competition. Monopolistic competition as a market structure can be modified to cover more explicitly oligopolistic circumstances where the number of firms involved in a market is small.[10] Assume the existence of a small group of oligopolistic firms, producing differentiated products that are close substitutes for each other. Consider the circumstance of a particular firm in that market. That firm has expectations concerning what would happen to its sales in the market if it altered its price but all of its competitors did not change their prices. The demand curve that reflects such expectations is *dd* in Figure 12.1a. P_1 is the price that other firms maintain despite changes in price of the firm in question. Alternatively, the firm might speculate about what would happen to its sales if all other firms in the market always matched any price change inaugurated by itself. Demand curve *DD* in Figure 12.1a illustrates such expectations on the part of the individual firm.

Figure 12.1a reveals that pure profits (economic rents) are being earned by the firm in question. Given the absence of substantial barriers to entry (a Chamberlinian assumption), new entrants will be attracted into the market by supranormal profits. The effect of entry upon the *dd* and *DD* demand curves is illustrated in Figure 12.1b. The total sales in the market are divided by more firms; this causes both the *dd* and the *DD* demand curves to shift in a southwesterly direction.[11] The shift in both the *dd* and the *DD* demand curves will continue until there are no more rents to be earned in this market. Figure 12.1c illustrates this situation. It should be noted that this figure represents the long-run equilibrium solution for the typical firm. As Chamberlin pointed out, this long-run solution will obtain only if (1) there is freedom of entry, (2) the market and sales of each firm are the same size, (3) the cost conditions of each firm are identical, and (4) the price elasticity of demand facing each firm is the same.

Such a long-run solution is one possible outcome in an oligopolistic market. It may be an infrequent occurrence, however. Most oligopolistic markets are characterized by the existence of barriers to entry. If these are present, then the long-run equilibrium described in Figure 12.1c where all pure profits have been driven out will not occur. Pure profits (economic

---

[9]E.H. Chamberlin, *The Theory of Monopolistic Competition* (Cambridge, Mass.: Harvard University Press, 1933) ; and Joan Robinson, *The Economics of Imperfect Competition* (London: Macmillan and Company, Ltd., 1934).

[10]See Chamberlin, *The Theory of Monopolistic Competition*, especially Chap. 5.

[11]When new competitors enter the market, both the amount the individual firm thinks it could sell if all other firms in the market failed to match any price changes it made, and the amount the same firm thinks it would sell if all other firms in the market constantly matched any price changes it made, will decline at each and every price because of the increased competition for each sale.

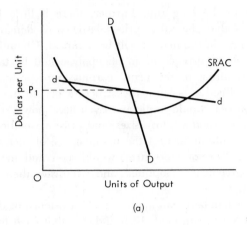

(a)

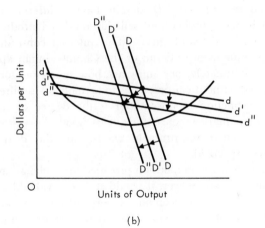

(b)

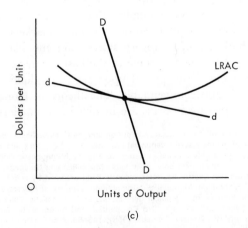

(c)

Figure 12.1

rents) will remain in the long run. Further, there is little likelihood in oligopolistic markets that the sales, price elasticity of demand, and cost conditions of each firm in the market will be identical. Chamberlin himself thought a more likely occurrence in an oligopoly would be tacit collusion among the firms, resulting in the firms' earning pure profits. Such tacit collusion might be effective because the structure of the market and the existence of entry barriers would so dictate. Even here, however, it is probable that differing cost structures, firm sizes, and price elasticities of demand for each firm would militate against the maintenance of such collusion for long periods of time. One or more firms would soon find the joint-profit-maximizing tacit agreement suboptimal and withdraw their consent via some aggressive action.

A keystone of Chamberlinian analysis is the existence of differentiated products. Yet Figures 12.1a through 12.1c indicate that each firm faces the same demand curves, *dd* and *DD,* despite having differentiated products. If the firms do in fact produce and sell differentiated products, then they should face dissimilar demand curves. This internal contradiction has resulted in a large amount of criticism of the Chamberlinian apparatus from many quarters.[12] Ultimately, one must ask how much product differentiation can be allowed without causing firms to actually be in different markets. The important distinction in this matter is the degree of substitutability. The Chamberlinian market concept depends upon the existence of firms producing differentiated substitutable goods, but the degree of substitutability is never specified.

Even if monopolistic competition provided an explanation of economic activity in no markets whatsoever, it would still be a valuable, although not earthshaking, contribution to economic theory in that it succeeds in transferring the attention of many economists to market problems not typified by the extremes of perfect competition and pure monopoly. Monopolistic competition, however, does occasionally afford insights about the nature of nonprice competition and its operation in many markets, such as retail gasoline stations, barber shops, grocery stores, and the like. This is true despite the theoretical fuzziness of some of the basic elements of the theory. The emphasis that Chamberlin placed upon excess productive capacity for the individual firm is also commendable. The theory of monopolistic competition serves best when many firms are involved and barriers to entry are

---

[12]Although the doctrine of monopolistic competition and the Chamberlinian apparatus have never been short of critics, some of the most severe denunciations have come from the so-called Chicago School economists. An early indication of this is found in George J. Stigler, "Monopolistic Competition in Retrospect," in *Five Lectures on Economic Problems* (New York: Macmillan and Company, 1949), pp. 12–24. The burden of criticism from this quarter has more recently been assumed by Harold Demsetz, in three articles: "The Nature of Equilibrium in Monopolistic Competition," *Journal of Political Economy*, 67 (February 1959), 21–30; "The Welfare and Empirical Implications of Monopolistic Competition," *Economic Journal*, 74 (September 1964), 623–41; and "Do Competition and Monopolistic Competition Differ?" *Journal of Political Economy*, 76 (January–February 1968), 146–68. A summary of many views may be found in Robert E. Kuenne, ed., *Monopolistic Competition: Studies in Impact.* (New York: John Wiley and Sons, Inc., 1967), The Chicagoite evaluation of this is found in Lester G. Telser, "Monopolistic Competition: Any Impact Yet?" *Journal of Political Economy*, 76 (March–April 1968), 312–15.

minimal. It works less well as an explanation of many oligopolistic markets where the number of firms is small and barriers to entry are moderate to substantial.

The Kinked Demand Curve

The kinked demand curve of economic literature is one that consists of two connected linear segments. Figure 12.2 illustrates two possible varieties of kinked demand curves. The existence of a kinked demand (which is a matter of dispute) depends upon particular types of expectations by individual firms in a given market about the probable reactions of their

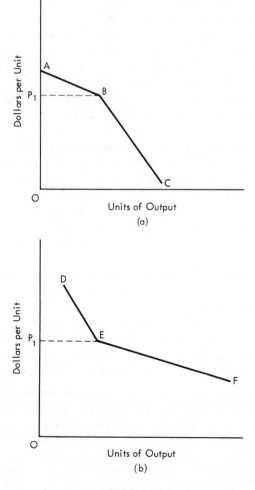

Figure 12.2

competitors to price changes. In the best-known version of the kink, it is assumed that individual firms feel that no competitor would match a price increase, whereas all firms in the market would match a price cut. Figure 12.2a illustrates a demand curve that reflects such expectations. Price P_1 is assumed to already exist. This circumstance may be typical of a recession period, when sales are depressed below normal levels and excess productive capacity exists in the market. The less-famous version of the kinked demand curve is based upon the assumption that the individual firm feels that all its competitors would match a price increase, but that none would match a price cut. Figure 12.2b illustrates this possibility, with the assumption that price P_1 already exists. An inflationary situation where sales are brisk and little excess productive capacity exists is most likely to produce such expectations. The result of the expectations that cause a kinked demand curve is said to be rigid, inflexible prices. Since it is widely believed that price changes occur less frequently in oligopolistic markets, the kinked demand curve has achieved some notoriety as an explanation for that rigidity.[13]

The kinked demand curve was proposed almost simultaneously by Sweezy and by Hall and Hitch, even though the analytical tools and premises supporting each explanation were quite different.[14] It is interesting to observe the close dependence of the Sweezy explanation of the kink on the Chamberlinian dd and DD demand curves. The recession version of the kinked demand curve proposes that firms do not expect their price increases to be matched by competitors. This section of the kinked demand curve (section AB in Figure 12.2a) therefore conveys the same information as the dd demand curve of Chamberlin. Likewise, when firms are of the opinion that their price cuts will always be matched (as in section BC of the kinked demand curve in Figure 12.2a), they operate as if they were on the DD demand curve of Chamberlin.[15] The kinked demand curve, then, is a combination of the dd and DD demand curves of Chamberlin.

The kink in the demand curve causes the marginal-revenue curve corresponding to the kinked demand curve to be discontinuous. Consider kinked demand curve ABC in Figure 12.3. Corresponding to Chamberlin's dd demand curve (labeled ABI here) is marginal-revenue curve ADE. Since segment BI of demand curve ABI is assumed not to exist in the most common version of the kinked demand curve, so also segment DE of marginal-revenue curve ADE does not exist. A similar argument disposes of segment FB of demand curve FBC (Chamberlin's DD demand curve) and

[13]This popular thesis has many proponents. One of the most recent and extensive sorties in support of this hypothesis is John M. Blair, *Economic Concentration: Structure, Behavior and Public Policy* (New York: Harcourt Brace Jovanovich, 1972), especially Chaps. 16 through 19.

[14]Paul M. Sweezy, "Demand Under Conditions of Oligopoly," *Journal of Political Economy*, 47 (August 1939), 568–73; and R.L. Hall and C.J. Hitch, "Price Theory and Business Behavior," *Oxford Economic Papers*, 2 (May 1939), 12–45.

[15]Analogously, the reverse or inflationary version of the kinked demand curve combines Chamberlin's dd demand curve in section DE of the demand curve in 12.2b and Chamberlin's DD demand curve in section EF of the same demand curve.

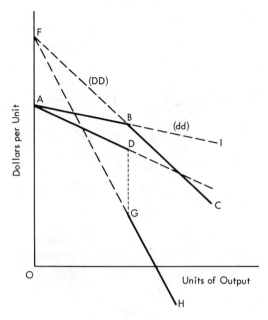

Figure 12.3

corresponding segment *FG* of marginal-revenue curve *FGH*. We are left with only demand curve *ABC* and discontinuous marginal-revenue curve *ADGH,* both of which are drawn with solid lines in Figure 12.3. The dotted line *DG* is the discontinuous portion of the marginal-revenue curve. The dashed lines represent segments of demand curves and marginal-revenue curves that do not represent the particular assumptions being made in this instance about how firms expect their competitors to react to price changes.

It is the discontinuity in the marginal-revenue curve corresponding to the kinked demand curve that enables the kinked-demand-curve formulation to explain and predict price rigidity in oligopoly. Assume that the oligopolistic firm represented in Figure 12.4 faces demand curve *ABC* and possesses marginal-cost function MC_1. The firm equates marginal revenue and marginal cost in order to maximize profits. The profit-maximizing price and quantity are P_E and Q_E, respectively. Suppose that the firm now experiences an increase in costs, perhaps owing to the negotiation of more expensive labor contracts. An increase in costs will shift MC_1 upward toward MC_2 and MC_3. Whether the marginal-cost curve is MC_1, MC_2, or MC_3, the equilibrium price and quantity combination for the firm will still be P_E, Q_E. A rise in costs will not cause an immediate rise in prices, because the firm fears that its competitors would not match that price increase and it would therefore lose much of its market share. By the same token, should a decrease in costs occur, as long as the new intersection of marginal revenue

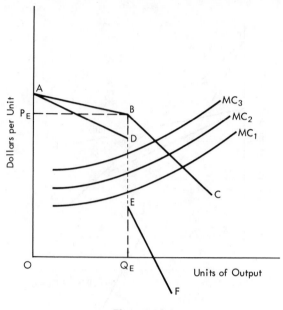

Figure 12.4

and marginal cost occurs somewhere inside the discontinuity, no decrease in prices will take place either. Price rigidity is the result.

Presumably, price rigidity in a circumstance such as that illustrated by Figure 12.4 will continue until there is general agreement among the firms in the market that a change in price is necessary. At that time, according to the kinked-demand-curve theorists, most or all of the firms in the market will change prices in rapid order. Both the prediction of price rigidity and the prediction that infrequent price changes will be quickly adhered to by all firms in the market are testable propositions. Casual empirical observations form the basis of most of the supportive evidence for the first hypothesis, and the second hypothesis—concerning prices being changed in unison—is also supported mainly by casual empirical generalizations. The worth of this evidence about price rigidity has frequently been disputed, however, and we shall evaluate these arguments in some detail later in this chapter. We would be derelict at this point, however, not to mention a seminal study performed by Stigler concerning the empirical validity of the kink.[16] Stigler examined the price behavior in seven oligopolistic markets during the late 1920's and early 1930's and concluded that there was no evidence in support of the kink. Price increases by one firm were not always eschewed by other firms, and price cuts were not always

[16]George J. Stigler, "The Kinky Oligopoly Demand Curve and Rigid Prices," *Journal of Political Economy*, 55 (October 1947), 432–49. See also recent work by Julian Simon, "Another Test of the Kinky Oligopoly Demand Curve," *American Economic Review*, 59 (December 1969), 971–75.

followed. Unanimity of action among the firms concerning price changes did not exist. Further, prices in the markets did not appear inflexible.

Stigler's work has been criticized in many quarters as incorrectly interpreting the kinked-demand-curve explanation. Heflebower and Efroymson, among others, have pointed out that Stigler assumes that the kink can be observed by watching the actual conduct of firms.[17] This, however, assumes that the kink always exists and is of the same sharpness at any point in time. Supporters of the kinked-demand-curve explanation contend that the kink may occasionally lessen or even disappear, and that Stigler's evidence merely confirms that fact. Heflebower has observed that when price increases by one firm are followed by other firms, this may mean nothing more than that "they occur only when the kink is eliminated by collusion, by orders above capacity, or by substantial increases in factor prices, influences not considered in this test by Stigler."[18] Although this may be true, the logical difficulty associated with such an argument is evident: When the evidence is supportive, the kink is there; when the evidence does not support the kink, it is not there. The circularity of this argument would invalidate any empirical test unfavorable to the kink explanation, on the ground that the kink was not there at that point in time.

The empirical validity and even the testability of the kinked-demand-curve theory depend substantially upon the sharpness and duration of any kink that might exist. It is of value, therefore, to examine the conditions that determine the sharpness and duration of the kink.[19] The single condition necessary for the existence of a kinked demand curve is that a firm expects its competitors to behave in an asymmetric fashion in their responses to price increases and decreases. The kink in the demand curve will be sharper (and therefore the discontinuity in the marginal-revenue curve greater) when (1) few competitor firms exist, (2) the size of the most important firms in the market is about the same, (3) products are relatively homogeneous, and (4) there is an absence of collusion.

These conditions are deserving of greater attention. The more competitors that exist in a market, the more likelihood there is that some firms will pursue independent pricing policies. Hence, when many competitors exist, it is less probable that any given firm will either increase or decrease prices in the manner posited by the kinked demand curve. When one firm is very large relative to the other firms in a market, it may dominate that market and force other firms to follow its pricing initiatives. As a result, no kink will exist, because smaller firms can neither raise nor lower their prices successfully unless the act is validated by the dominant firm. The

[17]Richard B. Heflebower, "Full Costs, Cost Changes, and Prices," in *Business Concentration and Price Policy*, ed. George J. Stigler, pp. 361–91; and Clarence W. Efroymson, "The Kinked Oligopoly Curve Reconsidered," *Quarterly Journal of Economics*, 69 (February 1955), 119–36.

[18]Heflebower, "Full Costs," p. 388.

[19]Stigler has done so in "The Kinky Oligopoly Demand Curve."

more homogeneous the products in oligopolistic markets, the more likelihood there is of a large kink. If one oligopolist raises his price, customers will rapidly shift to other suppliers if the product being supplied is homogeneous within the entire market. This will accentuate the kink in the demand curve. Finally, when either tacit or outright collusion exists among the firms in an oligopolistic market, the kink in the demand curve will be small or even nonexistent, because effective collusion eliminates any possibility of independent pricing policies by a particular firm. Instead, all firms act in concert and the possibility of a price change not being matched disappears.

Although it is far from being universal in application and cannot deal with many observed circumstances in oligopolistic markets, the kinked oligopoly demand curve is properly viewed as an explanation of the price rigidity that is found in some oligopolistic markets. It should be noted, nevertheless, that the kink explanation does not indicate either how the current price was formed or why the kink has any given location. The existing market price is taken for granted. Other facets of oligopolistic behavior, such as warfare and retaliation, are also not treated by the theory. Therefore, despite the popularity of the kink explanation (it is sometimes presented as if it were *the* theory of oligopoly), it is appropriately viewed as being a nongeneral theory that provides insights into limited aspects of oligopoly behavior.

Entry-Limit Pricing

Entry-limit pricing theories assume that the pricing behavior of the firms existing in a market will be directed at either discouraging or completely eliminating entry into that market by new competitors. Although one can find hints of entry-limit modeling in the work of Kaldor and of Clark,[20] and even before, the credit for the innovation is properly attributed to Bain.[21] Sylos-Labini and Modigliani have also figured prominently in the development of entry-limit pricing theory.[22]

The entry-limit pricing models assume long-run profit-maximizing desires by the firms already in a given market. The distinctiveness of entry-limit models is that they assume that existing firms achieve profit maximization by limiting or preventing entry by new competitors. The key decision variable for the existing firms is the market price. The existing firms will collusively choose to set the existing market price at a level that will retard

---

[20]Nicholas Kaldor, "Market Imperfection and Excess Capacity," *Economica*, n.s., 2 (February 1935), 33–50; and John M. Clark, "Toward a Concept of Workable Competition," *American Economic Review*, 30 (June 1940), 241–56.

[21]Joe S. Bain, "A Note on Pricing in Monopoly and Oligopoly," *American Economic Review*, 39 (March 1949), 448–64.

[22]Paolo Sylos-Labini, *Oligopoly and Technical Progress*, rev. ed. (Cambridge, Mass.: Harvard University Press, 1969); and Franco Modigliani, "New Developments on the Oligopoly Front," *Journal of Political Economy*, 76 (June 1958), 215–32.

or even eliminate the entry of new firms. Such a result, which is designed to maximize the present discounted value of the time stream of profits facing the firms, may result in the sacrifice of short-run profits. The entry-forestalling price will nearly always be less than the joint-profit-maximizing price for the market as a whole in the short run. Therein, of course, lies the dilemma facing the entry-limit-practicing firms: A price that is too low will be self-injurious, and a price that is too high will attract new entrants into the market.[23]

Bain has suggested six possible scenarios describing how existing firms will react in an oligopolistic market when a new entrant appears.[24] Possibilities include lowering price, lowering output, keeping output constant, and so forth. By far the most commonly assumed pattern of reaction in entry-limit pricing models has become known as Sylos' Postulate. Sylos' Postulate assumes that existing firms react to the new entrant by holding their outputs constant, and as a result allow the market price to fall because of the increased market output being produced. If such a reaction resulted in the market prices falling below the entrant's average costs per unit of output, then the entrant might be forced to leave the market. If some degree of knowledge and foresight is presumed on the part of prospective entrants, then entry may not occur at all, because entry will drive market price down to levels that inflict losses on the entrant.

The prospective entrant must weigh carefully the effect of large outputs that reduce average unit costs of production, against the price-depressing effects of that same output. The shape of the entrant's long-run average-cost curve is therefore a matter of more than casual interest, because it reflects the cost efficiencies the entrant can realize by producing larger outputs. Figure 12.5 illustrates one possible cost–revenue circumstance that could face an entrant. The entrant's minimum optimal scale (MOS) is output X_3. If the entrant produces output X_3, however, he will drive market price down to P_3, which is less than his long-run average unit costs of production. Entry at output X_1 (one quarter of MOS) or at output X_2 (one half of MOS) is a possibility. Whether in fact the entrant does enter at output X_1 or X_2 may depend upon at least three factors. First, the existing firms in the market may already be maintaining the market price at a level that is below the long-run average-cost curve of the entrant. Such a price is entry-deterring in nature. Second, even when the existing firms have not maintained an entry-deterring price structure, their actions subsequent to entry may have the same effect. They may attempt to pick on an entrant and drive him out of the market by predatory pricing tactics. Finally, the fact that an entrant might find it possible to enter a market at a given scale

[23]This point has been made by Fritz Machlup in his *Economics of Sellers' Competition* (Baltimore: Johns Hopkins Press, 1952), p. 537.

[24]Joe S. Bain, *Barriers to New Competition* (Cambridge, Mass.: Harvard University Press, 1965), pp. 97ff.

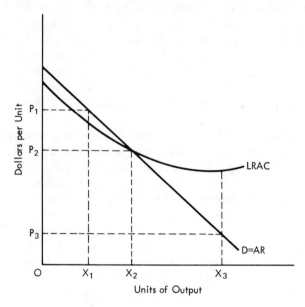

Figure 12.5

does not mean that he will choose to do so. Such entry may be less profitable than the prospective entrant's other alternative uses of capital. Hence,
existing firms need not make entry altogether unprofitable to avoid entry;
they need only make it less profitable than the investment alternatives that
confront the typical entrant.

The critical nature of the tradeoff between cost advantages gained
by producing larger outputs and the price disadvantages also caused by
increased outputs can be further illuminated by means of an example. We
will assume that we are dealing with an oligopoly that is characterized by
(1) homogeneous products; (2) a single common market price for all
firms; (3) price elasticity of demand equal to unity;[25] (4) identical per-unit
costs of production for all firms in the market at any given level of output;
(5) the ability of any entrant to enter the market at his own MOS, or at
one half, one quarter, or one tenth of his MOS; (6) a cost disadvantage
associated with less than MOS entry for any entrant that is equal to 2
percent of minimum average unit costs at one-half MOS; (7) current total
production of 100 units; (8) current price per unit in the market of $1.00;
and (9) minimum average cost per unit of $1.00 for all firms in the market.

The reader is invited to visualize the plight of a prospective entrant
into this market by means of Table 12.1. Column 2 of Table 12.1 records
the cost disadvantage that accrues to the entrant when he enters at scales

[25]Note that since price elasticity of demand is assumed to be unity, total sales revenue in the market
will always remain constant. That is, total sales revenue will always be 100 × $1.00 = $100, regardless of
the price per unit charged for output in the market.

TABLE 12.1

An Entry-Limit Pricing Model

Output of Entrant (Units)	Cost Disadvantage (percent)	$I =$ $[(N/O)(100)]$ Price Disadvantage (percent)	Maximum Price Elevation— Sum of Columns 1 and 2 (percent)
MOS = 20	0	20	20
One-Half MOS = 10	2	10	12
One-Quarter MOS = 5	4	5	9
One-Tenth MOS = 2	8	2	10

other than MOS. Existing firms in the market are well aware of this possible disadvantage and will exploit it by raising their own prices above the $1.00 level by a percent equal to the cost disadvantage should the entrant choose to enter at a scale less than MOS. They can do this with impunity, since any cost disadvantage realized by a prospective entrant will raise his costs of production accordingly and will enable the existing firms to do likewise without fear of price undercutting by the entrant. The entrant is also plagued by the fact that his output will depress market prices below current levels. The precise percent amount of price depression (which we shall signify by the letter R) is equal to $[(N/N+O)\ (100)]$, where N is the output in units of the entrant at whatever scale he enters, and O is the output of the entire market in units prior to any entry.[26] The firms already in the market are aware of the fact that entry depresses market price; hence, they know that they can raise the existing market price above the minimum average unit-cost level (which is $1.00) without provoking entry. Entry would drive the market price below $1.00 and be self-defeating for the entrant. The maximum percent that market price can be increased above minimum average unit costs (this we label I) is equal to $[(N/O)(100)]$. Column 3 of Table 12.1 records values of I for the various outputs the entrant can produce.[27]

[26]Assume that market output is 500 units and market price is $1.20 per unit. Total sales revenue in the market is therefore 500 × $1.20 = $600. If an entrant joins the market and adds 100 units to market output, then price will fall to $1.00 per unit. This follows from the fact that price elasticity of demand is equal to unity, and 600 × $1.00 = $600. Also, applying the appropriate formula, $R = [(N/N + O)(100)] = [(100/100 + 500)(100)] = [(.167)(100)] = 16.7$ percent reduction in price owing to the entrant's producing 100 units of output. 16.7 percent of $1.20 is $.20; $1.20 − $.20 = $1.00.

[27]Assume that market output is 200 units, and market price and minimum average unit costs are $1.00. Further assume that the entrant can enter only at his MOS, which is one tenth of market output and yields no cost disadvantage. If the entrant does join the market at his MOS, then he will drive market price down by 9.1 percent, to $.909 per unit ($R = [(20/20 + 200)(100)] = 9.1$). Knowing this, existing firms will be able to raise their prices by 10.0 percent above minimum average unit costs—that is, to $1.10 per unit—without attracting entry. This follows from the fact that $I = [(N/O)(100)] = [(20/200)(100)] = 10.0$. Also, it can be observed that when market price is $1.10 per unit, then market output must be 181.8 units, because 181.8 × $1.10 = $200. If the entrant joins the market at a scale equal to one tenth of total market output, then the entrant will add 18.2 units of output to the market, for a total of 200. When market output is 200 units, market price will once again be $1.00. Hence, the $1.10 market price is the highest possible price that existing firms can maintain without attracting entry by new firms.

The total disadvantage faced by a prospective entrant is represented by the cost disadvantage and the price disadvantage. Existing firms can therefore raise their prices above minimum average costs per unit (above $1.00) by the sum of the cost disadvantage and the price disadvantage. As column 4 of Table 12.1 reveals, this sum varies according to the output being produced by the entrant. Since the entrant can threaten entry at any scale, the entry-forestalling market price will be driven down to the smallest attainable sum of the cost and price disadvantages. As column 3 indicates, the smallest attainable sum is found to be 9 percent at an output equal to one quarter of the entrant's MOS. The entry-limit pricing model developed here would therefore predict that market price will closely approximate $1.09 per unit and that this price will not encourage entry. A price lower than $1.09 per unit would obviously place a very great damper upon entry.[28]

It is apparent that the shape of the long-run average-cost curve facing the typical firm is a matter of crucial importance in entry-limit pricing theories. If the long-run average-cost curve for the typical firm (entrant or otherwise) declines only briefly and is flat over broad ranges of outputs, then, Bain, Sylos-Labini, and others would contend, the "scale-economies barrier" is minimal, because there is little cost disadvantage accruing to any entrant at any scale. A steeply sloping long-run average-cost curve, however, which does not reach its minimum point until very large outputs have been produced, constitutes a large "scale-economies barrier" in the eyes of entry-limit pricing theorists. In this latter case, they would predict that existing firms will successfully establish the market price at a level substantially above minimum average unit costs without provoking entry. We place the phrase "scale-economies barrier" inside quotation marks because our discussion of entry barriers in Chapter 5 resulted in the conclusion that economies of scale were not a barrier to the entry of new firms, since the same economies of scale are potentially available to all firms, existing and entrant alike. This is particularly true in entry-limit pricing models that assume that the cost structure of all firms is identical.

The simple entry-limit pricing model that has been developed here can easily be complicated by deviating from restrictive assumptions concerning product homogeneity, unit-price elasticity of demand, and the rate of entry.[29] Certain desirable refinements, however, substantially alter the substance of the entry-limit pricing models. For example, the assumption that all firms possess the same cost structure is quite limiting in nature. However, if one assumes that each firm faces a different cost structure, then it is likely that the outright or tacit collusion necessary to produce

---

[28]The assumptions underlying the entry-limit pricing models developed here are typical of models in that area. See, for example, Bain, *Barriers to New Competition*, Chap. 3. The author appreciates the insights afforded him about entry-limit pricing models by a colleague, Robert Fenili.

[29]Pashigian has theorized that the rate of entry into a market is not only a function of the size of the gap between the market price and the entry-forestalling price, but also a function of the length of time that the gap is observed. B.P. Pashigian, "Limit Price and the Market Share of the Leading Firm," *Journal of Industrial Economics*, 16 (July 1968), 165–77.

entry-forestalling pricing behavior will be impossible to achieve. Different cost structures for each firm will probably make it profitable for one firm to pursue a price-cutting strategy.

The matter of the amount of collusion assumed by the entry-limit pricing models is also bothersome. Such extensive collusion is not often observed in American markets. It is not surprising, therefore, that successful attempts to apply entry-limit pricing models to oligopolistic markets have been few in number.[30]

The concept of an entry-forestalling price is also questionable in some markets. Successful entry often occurs even in markets that have been classified as completely blockaded because of very high barriers to entry. Further, Wenders has demonstrated that the assumption of output maintenance in the face of enry is not ordinarily a profit-maximizing strategy.[31]

Stigler, a vocal critic of entry-limit pricing theories, has concluded that the "theory raises questions faster than it answers them."[32] While substantially accurate, this judgment is perhaps too harsh. Entry-limit pricing tactics are observed in real-world markets, although the duration and breadth of such behavior have not yet been established. The crucial test of a theory must be its ability to explain and predict the phenomena toward which it is directed. It is here that the entry-limit pricing theories have yet to succeed in any great degree.

"Open" Oligopoly

The so-called "open"-oligopoly model was originally suggested by Stigler in his well-known text, *The Theory of Price*.[33] The open-oligopoly model predicts that oligopolists may maximize the present discounted value of their profit stream by gradually yielding up part of the market to new rivals. That is, the prediction of the open-oligopoly model is that the existing firms in a market will not choose to price in an entry-deterring fashion; rather, they will set prices that are often higher than the entry-deterring price. These prices will, however, maximize the present value of their profit stream.

The open-oligopoly model and the entry-limit pricing model are similar in that both assume long-run profit maximization as the goal of the firms in a market. However, where the entry-limit theories suggest that this will be attained by preventing entry into the market, the open-oligopoly

[30]Roger D. Blackwell, "Price Levels in the Funeral Industry," *Quarterly Review of Economics and Business*, 7 (Winter 1967), 75–84; Bernard J. McCarney, "ICC Rate Regulation and Rail-Motor Carrier Pricing Behavior: A Reappraisal," *ICC Practitioners Journal*, 25 (July–August 1968), pp. 707–18; see also McCarney, "Oligopoly Theory and Intermodal Transport Price Competition: Some Empirical Findings," *Land Economics*, 46 (November 1970), 474–78.

[31]John T. Wenders, "Collusion and Entry," *Journal of Political Economy*, 79 (November–December 1971), 1258–77.

[32]George Stigler, *The Organization of Industry* (Homewood, Ill.: Richard D. Irwin, Inc., 1968), p. 21.

[33]George J. Stigler, *The Theory of Price* (New York: The Macmillan Company, 1952), Chap. 13.

theory suggests that it may be more profitable to set higher prices today even though this attracts entrants as time passes. Where entry-limit theories predict collusion in order to prevent entry, the open-oligopoly model predicts an absence of collusion and the existence of substantially independent behavior on the part of each firm in the market.

Stigler has argued that the open-oligopoly model correctly describes twentieth-century developments in the steel, tin-can, and corn-product markets, as well as others.[34] For example, U.S. Steel was for many years the dominant firm in the steel market. Nevertheless, it accepted a declining share of a growing market instead of expending great amounts of time and resources upon preventing the entry of new firms. Of course, it could be argued here that this was not a free choice on the part of U.S. Steel, because the result of the *Steel Case* in 1920 was effectively to bar the growth of the market share of U.S. Steel from that point on.[35]

Since the open-oligopoly model and the entry-limit pricing model both assume long-run profit-maximizing intent on the part of oligopolists, only appropriate empirical evidence can settle the issue of the relative usefulness and validity of these competing models. Stigler neatly framed the issue at hand when he stated that "the present value of a series of declining profits...may exceed the present value of a perpetual profit rate...."[36] Figure 12.6 translates the controversy into geometric terms. It contains the graph of two alternative streams of profit as they vary through time. Profit

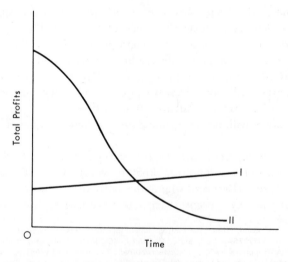

Figure 12.6

[34]*Ibid.*, p. 233.
[35]*United States* v. *United States Steel Corporation et al.*, 251 U.S. 417 (1920)
[36]Stigler, *The Theory of Price*, p. 234.

stream I is a steady profit rate that grows only slightly as time passes. Profit stream II represents the earning of very high profits in the near future, followed by sharply declining profits as time passes. Either profit stream could have the higher present value, depending upon the rate of discount chosen. If the rate of discount is very high, then the value of profits earned far in the future will be very minimal. This will cause the present value of profit stream II to exceed that of profit stream I. If, on the other hand, the rate of discount is very low, then the worth of a steady and slowly increasing profit stream such as I is accentuated. Hence, in this case, the present value of profit stream I would exceed that of II.

The question of the relative validity of the models, then, actually amounts to one of what rate of discount oligopolists use, because that rate of discount will clearly influence what strategy they follow when they seek to maximize the present value of their profit streams.[37] Fog has argued that large, oligopolistic firms will ordinarily have low rates of discount (which implies a long time horizon), whereas small firms will have higher rates of discount and shorter time horizons.[38] Although it is legitimate to ask, "How high is 'high'?" the question is, of course, unanswerable. We must therefore move to other forms of evidence on the issue.

Kamerschen has performed tests based upon concentration ratios and the number of firms entering markets, in an attempt to ascertain the empirical validity of the two competing models.[39] If concentration ratios are generally falling in oligopolistic markets, and the number of firms is continually growing, then this would constitute evidence in favor of the open-oligopoly model. If the contrary is found, then the evidence would favor the entry-limit explanations. Kamerschen looked at two separate samples of oligopolistic markets during the time period 1947–63. One sample consisted of those markets whose four-firm concentration ratios were greater than 75 in 1947. Changing market definitions reduced the size of this sample to 22 in number. By 1963, only 12 of these markets were still oligopolies, if a four-firm concentration ratio of 75 is the criterion. The unweighted mean change in the four-firm concentration ratio in these markets was −4.4 percent, even though for all markets the same statistic was +2.2 percent. In 12 of the 22 markets, the number of firms increased. Kamerschen's other sample of oligopolies consisted of a list of "consensus" oligopolies suggested by Bain, Shepherd, and Stigler.[40] Although 35 such oligopolistic markets were suggested by the three, comparable data for the period 1947–63 was available for only 26 of the markets. In 12 of them, the four-firm concen-

---

[37]Shepherd was one of the first to point this out, in "Trends of Concentration in American Manufacturing Industries, 1947–1958," *Review of Economics and Statistics,* 46 (May 1964), 200–212.

[38]Bjarke Fog, "How Are Cartel Prices Determined?" *Journal of Industrial Economics,* 5 (November 1956), 16–23.

[39]David R. Kamerschen, "An Empirical Test of Oligopoly Theories," *Journal of Political Economy,* 76 (July 1968), 615–34.

[40]Joe S. Bain, *Industrial Organization* (New York: John Wiley & Sons, Inc., 1958), p. 279; Shepherd, "Trends of Concentration"; and Stigler, *The Theory of Price,* Chap. 13.

tration ratio decreased during the time period in question; it increased in 10 markets, and was constant in 4.

The Kamerschen results, while crude, cast doubt upon the empirical validity of the entry-limit pricing models as a general explanation of oligopolistic markets. The same results give some encouragement to the open-oligopoly hypothesis. The results are subject to qualifications, however, as Kamerschen himself has pointed out. Declining concentration might be due to influences such as diversification and antitrust pressures, such as those brought upon U.S. Steel. Further, sampling of the oligopolistic markets could be a source of bias. The sample sizes are small, but even more important, markets whose SIC market definition changed between 1947 and 1963 could not be used because of data unavailability. It is not farfetched to hypothesize that it is precisely these markets (which are changing rapidly, owing to technological change and the introduction of new products and processes) in which quite different results might be found. The Kamerschen empirical results therefore qualify as interesting, but hardly conclusive.

Cost-Plus-Markup Pricing

Cost-plus-markup pricing is an intuitively appealing explanation of oligopolistic pricing and behavior, which in actual practice turns out to be a variant of the marginal-revenue-equals-marginal-cost pricing that conventional economic theory predicts. Cost-plus-markup pricing assumes that the firm sets its price only with regard to the average costs of production plus some profit markup. Price is said to be set equal to the "full" average costs of production plus some "reasonable" profit markup. Hence, cost-plus-markup pricing is also known by names such as average-cost pricing and full-cost pricing. Cost-plus-markup pricing models have been used to explain both the level of prices and the conditions and determinants of price change.

The modern enthusiasm for cost-plus-markup pricing theories can be traced to the work of Hall and Hitch, whose influential study of the pricing behavior of 38 British firms was published in 1939.[41] Hall and Hitch concluded that most firms do set their prices according to some average-cost-plus-profit-markup rule; only 8 of the 38 firms in their sample indicated otherwise.[42] Subsequent work performed by Saxton, Dean, Lester, and Oxenfeldt was also supportive of the cost-plus-markup notion.[43]

The popularity of the cost-plus-markup pricing models with economist and layman alike is primarily due to the fact that cost-plus-markup pricing

---

[41] Hall and Hitch, "Price Theory and Business Behavior."

[42] Similar evidence of the widespread usage of cost-plus-markup pricing rules has been contributed by W.W. Haynes, "Pricing Practices in Small Firms," *Southern Economic Journal,* 31 (April 1964), 318–20.

[43] C.C. Saxton, *The Economics of Price Determination* (Cambridge, England: Oxford University Press, 1942); Joel Dean, *Managerial Economics* (Englewood Cliffs, N.J.: Prentice-Hall, Inc., 1951); Richard A. Lester, "Shortcomings of Marginal Analysis for Wage–Employment Problems, *American Economic Review,* 36 (March 1946), 63–82; and Alfred R. Oxenfeldt, *Industrial Pricing and Market Practices* (Englewood Cliffs, N.J.: Prentice-Hall, Inc., 1951).

is descriptively accurate. It is what businessmen say they use; further, it seems to be an equitable way of doing things, because average costs of production are covered and a reasonable markup is added to those costs. Few businessmen wish to be accused of charging all that the market will bear. Such tactics evoke frowns and stimulate talk about business not fulfilling its social responsibilities. Hence, the businessman who explains to the public that his pricing is based upon a cost-plus-markup formula seems to be acting in a responsible fashion.

Cost-plus-markup pricing involves considerably more than a first glance might indicate, however. The concept of average costs per unit includes both fixed and variable costs. The average fixed costs per unit will vary inversely with the level of output being produced. Consequently, any cost-plus-markup rule must necessarily assume that a given level of output is being produced. This assumption typically takes the form of a statement about how much of the firm's productive capacity is being utilized, a figure known as the "standard" volume of production. For example, for many years, General Motors used 80 percent of its capacity as its standard-volume assumption.[44]

Given a standard-volume assumption, the invested capital of the firm, a target rate of return on that invested capital, the expected sales of the firm, and the costs of production, both a product price and the markup over costs within that price can be computed. The target rate of return is simply the rate of return on invested capital that the firm wishes to realize during a given time period. There is considerable evidence that firms think at least superficially in terms of target rates of return.[45] Again taking General Motors as an example, GM apparently attempted to realize a 15 to 20 percent rate of return on invested capital for many years.[46] In years when its actual sales exceeded the standard volume, GM's profit rate on invested capital tended to be about 20 percent, whereas the same profit rate was only about 15 percent in years when actual sales fell short of standard volume.[47]

In its purest form, cost-plus-markup pricing appears to directly challenge two basic parts of economic theory.[48] First, it denies that demand has anything to do with the setting of prices; this is equivalent to rejecting the

---

[44]Testimony of Frederic Donner et al., in *Study of Antitrust Laws*, hearings before Subcommittee on Antitrust and Monopoly, U.S. Senate, 84th Cong., 1st sess., November 23, 1955–December 9, 1955 (Washington, D.C.: U.S. Government Printing Office, 1956).

[45]Homer B. Vanderblue, "Pricing Policies in the Automobile Industry," *Harvard Business Review* 18 (Autumn 1939), 64–81 ; A.D.H. Kaplan, Joel B. Dirlam, and Robert F. Lanzilotti, *Pricing in Big Business: A Case Approach* (Washington, D.C.: The Brookings Institution, 1958); Robert F. Lanzilotti, "Pricing Objectives in Large Companies," *American Economic Review*, 48 (December 1958), 921–40; and A.D.H. Kaplan, Joel B. Dirlam, and Robert F. Lanzilotti, "Pricing Objectives in Large Companies: Reply," *American Economic Review*, 49 (September 1959), 679–86.

[46]Testimony of Donner et al., in *Study of Antitrust Laws*.

[47]The reader is referred to Marshall R. Colberg, Dascomb R. Forbush, and Gilbert R. Whitaker, Jr., *Business Economics: Principles and Cases*, 4th ed. (Homewood, Ill.: Richard D. Irwin, Inc., 1970), pp. 462–67, for a more detailed discussion of target-rate-of-return pricing as practiced by GM.

[48]See Heflebower, "Full Costs," for an excellent survey of the cost-plus-markup literature and its implications.

Marshallian scissors-cross geometry on the ground that the demand curve does not belong in the analysis. Second, cost-plus-markup pricing insists that the marginal-revenue-equals-marginal-cost guideline to pricing is incorrect.

The key to the conflict between cost-plus-markup pricing and conventional $MR = MC$ pricing is the size of the markup. Coase has commented that what the typical businessman believes to be a "reasonable" markup is in fact what he thinks the market will bear most profitably.[49] That is, the size of the markup is in the long run determined by cost and demand factors, as conventional theory predicts. In particular, price elasticity of demand is an important determinant of the size of the markup utilized. The following brief exercise is helpful in demonstrating that point. We begin with a well-known equation, which we have used before, in Chapter 4:

(1) $MR = P(1 + 1/\eta)$

(2) $MC = P(1 + 1/\eta)$ Assume profit maximization and replace MR by MC.

(3) $MC/(1 + 1/\eta) = P$ Divide both sides by $(1 + 1/\eta)$.

(4) $MC/(\eta + 1/\eta) = P$ η is common denominator in $(1 = 1/\eta)$ term in (3).

(5) $MC/(\eta/\eta + 1) = P$ Invert $(\eta + 1/\eta)$.

(6) $LRAC\left(\dfrac{\eta}{\eta + 1}\right) = P$ In the long run, given constant costs, $MC = LRAC$.

Equation (6) above indicates that price is determined by the joint interaction of the supply (cost) factor and the demand (price elasticity) factor. Equation (6) is also a close representation of cost-plus-markup pricing. Price is long-run average costs of production multiplied by a markup factor based upon price elasticity of demand. Assume that price elasticity of demand is equal to -2.00 and the long-run average costs of production are $1.00 per unit. The markup factor will be equal to $[(\eta/\eta + 1) - 1]$, or $[(-2/-2+1) - 1]$, or 1.00. That is, the markup will be 100 percent above the long-run average unit costs of production. Price will therefore be $2.00 per unit. If price elasticity of demand were equal to -7.00, and long-run average costs per unit were once again $1.00, then the markup would be 16 2/3 percent above long-run average unit costs, and price would be $1.17 per unit. Note that the more elastic and responsive price elasticity of demand is, the smaller the markup over costs and the lower the price.[50]

The markup in cost-plus-markup pricing therefore emerges as a representation of the firm's "feel for the market." Casual empirical analysis con-

---

[49]Ronald Coase, "Comment," in Stigler, ed., *Business Concentration and Price Policy*, pp. 392–94.
[50]The reader should also be aware that equation (6) is not defined when $-1 \leq \eta \leq 0$.

firms this. Businessmen seldom choose exceptionally high markups, because such markups are known to be unprofitable from the businessmen's past experience. Likewise, very low markups can also be non-profit-maximizing when demand is inelastic and unresponsive. Although businessmen may never have heard of price elasticity of demand, they act as if they are quite familiar with it when they choose a markup over costs. The correct markup is arrived at only by trial and error and will in the long run tend to approximate the results that would have been obtained had marginal-revenue-equals-marginal-cost pricing been followed.

Cost-plus-markup pricing is a means for firms to introduce stability into their pricing patterns; such stability, however, is seldom purchased at the expense of long-run profit maximization. Cost-plus-markup pricing as practiced by most firms appears to be a means to the end of long-run profit maximization. The fatal flaw in the Hall–Hitch genre of study is that it presumes that what firms say they are doing about pricing is what they are actually doing. As Weston, who has recently undertaken substantive research into oligopoly pricing, has commented, "What businessmen formally say about their pricing and what they do about it are often very different. And their action is more consistent with classical theory than their talk."[51]

SUMMARY

The work of this chapter has been devoted to oligopoly theory. It is apparent that no single oligopoly theory is able to represent the diversity of oligopoly behavior that appears in the world. Each theory highlights a different facet of oligopoly markets, primarily because each theory makes differing assumptions about the behavior and interrelationships among oligopolists. While few common threads exist among oligopoly models, nearly all models stress the mutual interdependence of firms. This typically means that the number of sellers is few, and the presumption often is that the number of sellers and the strength of competition are related.[52]

Each of the models that was considered in this chapter focused on a particular aspect of oligopolistic markets. The Chamberlinian model emphasized the expectations of sellers with respect to the reaction of their competitors when a price change was initiated. The kinked-demand-curve models seized upon the Chamberlinian expectations and utilized them as an explanation of price rigidity in oligopoly. The desire of existing firms

---

[51]As reported in Gilbert Burck, "The Myths and Realities of Corporate Pricing," *Fortune*, 85 (April 1972), 88.

[52]Fama and Laffer have shown, however, that the relationship between the strength of competition and the number of firms may well disappear in a general-equilibrium context. Eugene F. Fama and Arthur B. Laffer, "The Number of Firms and Competition," *American Economic Review*, 62 (September 1972), 670–74.

to price in such a way that they limit entry into the market was the focus of the entry-limit pricing model presented. Diametrically opposed was the open-oligopoly model, which predicted that existing firms would find it most profitable to price in a fashion that might attract entry. Finally, the cost-plus-markup model suggested that firms set their prices by computing average costs of production and then adding to that a "fair" markup.

Relatively little empirical evidence is available in the area of oligopoly models. The scanty evidence has cast doubt upon the kinked-demand-curve explanation and the entry-limit pricing model. The cost-plus-markup pricing model, on the other hand, appears to have great accuracy in terms of describing how businessmen set their prices; however, a closer look at it reveals that in actuality it does not conflict with conventional marginal pricing models.

The theory of oligopoly has yet to be developed. Existing theories are capable of dealing with some observed phenomena, but not with others. Nearly all the oligopoly models are indeterminate in certain circumstances and cannot always yield a definitive prediction. For all their inadequacies, however, the existing theories of oligopoly do broach interesting questions and conjectures about how oligopolists actually do behave. In Chapter 13, we shall investigate further several of these matters.

PROBLEMS

1. Keeping in mind the ideal attributes of a theory, which Chapter 1 discussed, is it possible to argue that the kinked-oligopoly-demand-curve theory is not really a theory at all?

2. "The ultimate form of collusion is merger. Many economists forget that fact when they place their stamp of approval upon mergers that create oligopoly." Comment.

3. Consider an entry-limit pricing model. Assume that market demand is growing over time. Will it be possible for existing firms to convince prospective entrants that the entrants will be unable to garner any of that increased demand?

4. Fellner and others have argued that there exists a tendency in oligopoly for all the firms in a market to maximize the total profits realizable in that market. If true, is this consistent with, or in opposition to, the conventional theory of the firm, which assumes that individual firms maximize profits?

5. It has been argued that in many oligopolistic markets, the frequency of price cuts is greater when those price cuts are directed at firms not in a position to retaliate. Is it possible to express such a condition in the form of a price elasticity?

13

Oligopolistic Behavior

and Pricing: Applied Topics

Our attention will now shift from the theoretical aspects of oligopolistic behavior to a more intense study of particular applied aspects. The theoretic models of Chapter 12 lead directly to these issues, which are applied and often empirical in nature. As usual, the pricing process will garner the lion's share of our attentoin. The subjects of our scrutiny will be (1) price flexibility; (2) price leadership; (3) basing-point pricing; (4) price discrimination; (5) resale-price maintenance; (6) tying contracts, requirements contracts, and exclusive dealing; and (7) cartelization.

PRICE FLEXIBILITY

The economic models we surveyed in Chapter 12 often predicted that price changes in oligopolistic markets would be less frequent than price changes in other markets. Certain of these models—for example, the kinked-demand-curve hypothesis—maintained that oligopolistic prices might remain rigid even when substantial cost and demand changes occurred. The empirical interest of economists in price rigidity and flexibility has been enduring in nature, but recent interest is primarily due to the work initiated by Means during the 1930's. Means charged that many oligopolistic prices showed little sensitivity to cost or demand changes. He termed such sticky prices "administered" in nature.[1] That is, the price was set by oligopolistic fiat rather than by the forces of supply and demand.

The evidence produced by Means in support of his hypothesis was the result of a tabulation of the frequency of recorded price changes for 747 of the commodities included in the Bureau of Labor Statistics' wholesale price index over a 95-month period from 1926 through 1933. What Means found was a bimodal frequency distribution not unlike Figure 13.1. Some prices were found to change very frequently, whereas others were

[1]Gardiner C. Means, *Industrial Prices and Their Relative Flexibility*, 74th Cong., 1st sess., Senate Document Number 13 (Washington, D.C.: U.S. Government Printing Office, 1935), p. 1. See also Means, "Price Inflexibility and Requirements of a Stabilizing Monetary Policy," *Journal of the American Statistical Association*, 30 (June 1935), 401–13; and A.A. Berle and Gardiner C. Means, *The Modern Corporation and Private Property* (New York: Commerce Clearing House, Inc., 1932).

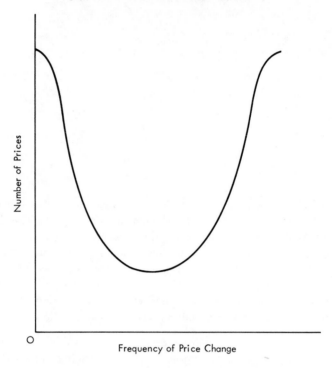

Figure 13.1

found to change infrequently. Means interpreted this to mean that two substantially different groups of prices existed in the American economy. One group was highly flexible and was determined by supply-and-demand factors; the other group was inflexible and "administered" in nature. In all cases, the frequency of the recorded price changes was taken to represent the degree of flexibility in the prices.

Means's contribution caused a flurry of activity on the price-flexibility issue in the economics profession, and a sharp increase occurred in the number of papers devoted to the issue. Critics of Means argued that (1) the frequency of the price changes was largely irrelevant if their direction and amplitude were not also known;[2] (2) reported list prices of oligopolistic firms might frequently differ from the prices actually charged by the same firms;[3] and (3) Means's data did not permit any inference about whether more prices were shifting from the competitively determined group to the administered group, or vice versa.

With regard to the first point above, it is hardly comforting to know that a price has changed if it has changed in the "wrong" direction or in

---

[2]The amplitude of a price change is its total size—that is, the highest price minus the lowest price.

[3]This has been a recurring point of controversy between Means and his detractors. For example, the recent work of Stigler and Kindahl was specifically directed at measuring price flexibility on the basis of prices actually charged rather than prices reported by firms. George J. Stigler and James K. Kindahl, *The Behavior of Industrial Prices* (New York: National Bureau of Economic Research, 1970).

the "wrong" amount. For example, assume that a given firm experiences an increase of the cost of the factors of production that it has been hiring. If no substitution of cheap for expensive factors can take place, then this is a cost of production that must ultimately be reflected in the price of the firm's product if competition exists in the market in which the firm operates. It would be disconcerting to find, however, that the change in product prices observed because of the increase in factor prices was either very small or in fact a decrease. Finished-product price changes that are disproportionate in size to changes in the prices of factor inputs, and/or product price changes that go in one direction when logic would dictate a change in the opposite direction—both would be evidence of administered prices. The Means measure of price flexibility was not sensitive to such possibilities, however.

Objection number 2 above is essentially a statement that the Bureau of Labor Statistics' wholesale price index is inaccurate, the inaccuracy in this case being attributed to secret price chiseling undertaken by oligopolists (which they would never admit to) via change in their published price list.[4] If the prices quoted by oligopolistic firms are not actually the prices at which sales are made, but rather list prices perhaps generated by some method such as cost-plus-markup pricing, then there may exist considerably more price flexibility than has been found by Means and others. The problem is that such a contention is extremely difficult to subject to testing, because secret price cuts are, by definition, secret and ordinarily not available for the scrutiny of economists.

The third objection to the work of Means et al. deals with the fact that Means's empirical results do not permit any inference about whether more prices are edging into the administratively determined category from the competitive category than vice versa. The implication is clear in the work of Means, Berle and Means, Galbraith, and others that fundamental changes occurring in the economy are reducing both the number of competitively determined prices and the amount of their flexibility.[5] The available empirical evidence is not kind to that conjecture, however.[6] There is little evidence that a greater proportion of prices are administered than are competitive, whatever the definition of *administered*.

---

[4]This point was first made by Willard L. Thorp, "Price Theories and Market Realities," *American Economic Review*, 26 (March 1936), 15–22. It has since been repeated many times, most recently in the Stigler–Kindahl volume, *The Behavior of Industrial Prices*.

[5]Means, *Industrial Prices* and "Price Inflexibility"; Berle and Means, *The Modern Corporation*; John Kenneth Galbraith, "Monopoly Power and Price Rigidities," *Quarterly Journal of Economics*, 50 (May 1936), 456–75; and testimony offered in *Administered Prices: A Compendium on Public Policy*, Subcommittee on Antitrust and Monopoly, U.S. Senate, 88th Cong., 1st sess. (Washington, D.C.: U.S Government Printing Office, 1963); also, testimony offered earlier before the same committee in *Administered Prices*, Volumes 1–32 (Washington, D.C.: U.S. Government Printing Office, 1957–1961).

[6]Don D. Humphrey, "The Nature and Meaning of Rigid Prices, 1890–1933," *Journal of Political Economy*, 45 (October 1937), 651–61; Rufus S. Tucker, "The Reasons for Price Rigidity," *American Economic Review*, 28 (March 1938), 41–54; Edward S. Mason, "Price Inflexibility," *Review of Economics and Statistics*, 20 (May 1938), 53–64; Jules Backman, "Price Inflexibility—War and Post-War," *Journal of Political Economy*, 56 (October 1948), 428–37.

The ideal measure of price flexibility has yet to be developed. The most tenable measure, however, is based upon a well-known equation that is closely related to Lerner's index of monopoly power. Lerner's index was long ago proposed by Dunlop as an appropriate measure of price flexibility, because it is sensitive to both costs and demand, and implicitly sensitive to output and employment.[7] The variant of the equation that we shall use is $MC = P(1 + 1/\eta)$.

Ruggles has expressed with precision how this measure is to be used: "Prices will be considered flexible if they react as would be expected in response to changes in cost and demand conditions, inflexible if they do not change as much as would be expected, and perverse if they move in the direction opposite from that expected."[8] For example, assume that the coefficient of price elasticity of demand is -2.00, and the marginal cost per unit is \$1.50. Price would therefore be \$3.00 per unit. If the marginal cost per unit falls to \$1.00, then price should fall to \$2.00 per unit if price elasticity of demand does not change. If price does not change in the required direction and by the required amount, then prices are deemed inflexible. Similar expected price changes may be generated by assuming changes in the coefficient of price elasticity of demand.

The Ruggles measure of price flexibility has not proved popular wtih researchers, primarily because it imposes upon the researcher great demands for data. Nevertheless, supporters of the administered-pricing thesis have attempted to buttress their case with less-demanding tests, patterned after the suggestions of Ruggles. The relationship of price changes to the business cycle has received a great deal of attention in recent years by such protagonists of the administered-pricing hypothesis as Blair and Means.[9] When the economy is contracting and demand for the products of a particular market or firm are weak, one might predict considerable downward pressure on prices. Instead, the evidence often shows price increases during such time periods in concentrated markets.

The administered-pricing controversy has been remarkably durable. The recent Stigler–Kindahl study, performed under the auspices of the National Bureau of Economic Research, represents an admirable attempt to use survey data on the actual sales prices of commodities rather than on posted list prices.[10] The success of this particular part of the Stigler–Kindahl

[7]John T. Dunlop, "Price Flexibility and the Degree of Monopoly," *Quarterly Journal of Economics*, 53 (August 1939), 522–34.

[8]Richard Ruggles, "The Nature of Price Flexibility and the Determinants of Relative Price Changes in the Economy," in George Stigler, ed., *Business Concentration and Price Policy* (Princeton, N.J.: Princeton University Press, 1955), pp. 441–95.

[9]John M. Blair, *Economic Concentration: Structure, Behavior and Public Policy* (New York: Harcourt Brace Jovanovich, 1972), especially Chaps. 16–19; and Gardner C. Means, "The Administered-Price Thesis Confirmed," *American Economic Review*, 62 (June 1972), 292–306. It is worth noting that Blair was an important advisory cog in the administered-pricing hearings carried out by the U.S. Senate Subcommittee on Antitrust and Monopoly during the 1950's.

[10]Stigler and Kindahl, *The Behavior of Industrial Prices*.

enterprise cannot be properly judged, since only the firms surveyed truly know whether they have accurately reported the actual prices at which sales were made. Stigler and Kindahl concluded that (particularly during the 1961–66 period) prices were considerably more flexible in highly concentrated markets than administered-pricing proponents had previously suggested. Means, who is as durable as his administered-pricing hypothesis, has severely criticized the Stigler–Kindahl research.[11] Means places great emphasis upon the fact that the cyclical behavior of prices is different in some markets from what it is in others. Specifically, he has argued that the Stigler–Kindahl data do show that prices fall less often during recessions (and rise less rapidly in expansions) in oligopolistic markets than in competitive markets. The Stigler–Kindahl conclusion, using the same data, is that prices tend to follow the business cycle in a flexible fashion much as competitive theory would predict.

Evidence points toward the conclusion that prices in oligopolistic markets may not be as flexible as those determined in more competitive markets. (This could, however, be due to the fact that input prices fluctuate less in oligopolistic markets also.) Further, Stigler and Kindahl notwithstanding, the weight of empirical evidence does indicate that oligopolistic prices change less than competitive prices, during both upswings and downswings of the business cycle. Unfortunately, the methodological weaknesses of the empirical work offered by the administered-pricing advocates vitiates much of the effect of the conclusions based upon that empirical evidence. The secrecy and subtleties of price competition in an oligopolistic market make questionable any piece of empirical research in the area.

Flexible prices are needed in order to allocate resources correctly. By the same token, some stability in prices is necessary, and stability will actually reduce uncertainty and costs. Despite the argument of the last four decades, however, the precise amount of price flexibility present in oligopolistic markets is still in doubt.

PRICE LEADERSHIP

To the extent that collusion between firms does exist in the market, it need not be of a formalized nature. Collusion can also be tacit and can be based upon long-standing custom and habit. Price leadership is often of this variety. Open or even tacit collusion among firms is usually a cause for antitrust action. Price leadership, however, is seldom the target of antitrust action, perhaps because it is so common. Price leadership also need not have bad allocative consequences. The price leader may choose prices that assist and improve the resource-allocation process. Of course, the op-

---

[11] Means, "The Administered-Price Thesis Confirmed."

posite circumstance may also be true. In order to maintain the price set
by the leader, firms may be forced to adjust their outputs, and this adjustment might have undesirable allocative consequences.[12]

Three distinct types of price leadership are common in industrial
markets: (1) dominant firm, (2) collusive, and (3) barometric firm. Dominant-firm price leadership is the easiest to comprehend, even though its
importance may be overdone.[13] The dominant firm is often the largest firm
in the market. The other firms follow the pricing lead of the dominant firm
because they fear large-scale price cutting if they do not. U.S. Steel was
for many years the dominant firm in the steel market, and its price initiatives were typically followed by the other firms in the market. Figure 13.2
illustrates a possible dominant-firm price-leadership situation. The dominant firm faces the demand curve labeled d_{dom}, and its marginal-revenue
curve is mr_{dom}. The remaining firms in the market, all of which are small,
collectively have the marginal-revenue curve P_1X. The demand curve for
the entire market is D_{mkt}. The dominant firm maximizes its profits by
equating its marginal cost to its marginal revenue and therefore decides to

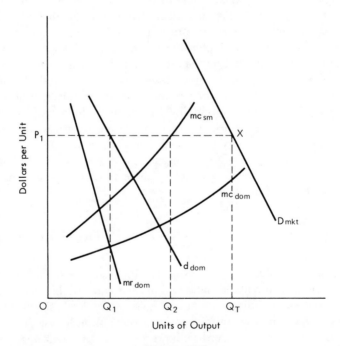

Figure 13.2

[12]George P. Comer, "Price Leadership," *Law and Contemporary Problems*, 7 (Winter 1940), 61–73.

[13]Baumol, for example, has argued that many large firms tend to ignore the consequences of their
pricing, and that they pay little attention to the pricing actions of other firms except when long-term decisions
are involved. William Baumol, *Business Behavior, Value and Growth* (New York : Harcourt Brace Jovanovich,
1967), Chap. 4.

sell output Q_1 at price P_1. The small firms in the market accept this dictum in a fashion similar to perfect competitors: The price is given to them and they need only decide how much they will produce at that price. Price P_1 appears to the small firms as a horizontal demand curve. Hence, they will equate their marginal cost with their marginal revenue and decide to produce output Q_2. Output Q_1 plus output Q_2 is the total output produced in the entire market—namely, Q_T. The dominant-firm price-leadership model can be modified to allow for differentiated products, transport costs, and even for more than one dominant firm.

Where a dominant firm exists for a long period of time, that firm is often the most efficient in the market. Markham, in his well-known article on price leadership, has labeled this type of price leadership *low-cost firm leadership*.[14] The dominant firm described in Figure 13.2 is also the most efficient firm and can produce nearly any output more cheaply than its rivals can. Presumably, the reason that the dominant firm does not drive its competitors out of the market via price-cutting techniques that it could easily sustain is the threat of antitrust action. The growth of markets, technological change, and the entry of new firms typically erode the position of even the most deeply entrenched dominant firm. Examples of this include the dethronement of Firestone in the rubber market and Bird's Eye in the concentrated frozen orange juice market.

Collusive price leadership is relatively common in situations where the mutual interdependence of the oligopolists in a market is recognized by the oligopolists themselves. As Markham has pointed out, collusive price leadership works best when the products produced by each firm in the market are highly substitutable and are amenable to a single price policy.[15] The collusion over price need not be formal; it may involve mutual "understandings" that certain types of price competition are to be avoided. Tacit understandings can easily be obtained that prices will ordinarily be changed only at certain times during the year (the automobile market often illustrates this), or that prospective price changes will be announced well in advance of their implementation so that all the other firms in the market have ample opportunity to decide whether to follow the price change or to fight it.

Markham has offered the tobacco market as the prime example of what we have termed collusive price leadership.[16] During the 1920's and 1930's, the "Big Three" among the tobacco producers (Reynolds, American, and Liggett & Myers) followed what must be termed a unified pricing policy, since their price structures were rarely in disagreement. The initiator of a price change in a collusive price-leadership arrangement need not al-

[14]Jesse W. Markham, "The Nature and Significance of Price Leadership," *American Economic Review*, 41 (December 1951), 891–905.

[15]*Ibid.*

[16]The checkered pricing history of the cigarette producers was a major basis for the decision against the "Big Three" producers in *American Tobacco Co. v. United States*, 328 U.S. 781, 813–15 (1946).

ways be the same firm. Each of the "Big Three" cigarette manufacturers has initiated price changes, with Reynolds and American most often commencing a movement in the price structure of the market.

It is often difficult to distinguish barometric-firm price leadership from the dominant-firm and collusive types. Several of the more obvious cases of price leadership could easily be included in any of the classifications made by Markham. General Motors is the dominant firm in the automobile market; nevertheless, GM has not been the only initiator of price changes in the market, and generally there has been widespread agreement when price changes have been initiated. Hence, the barometric firm—the firm that initiates the proper price change at the proper moment—could also be the dominant firm. In other cases—for example, the price changes led by Bethlehem Steel in the late 1960's—the firm that initiates the price change is not the dominant firm.

The barometric firm will remain the barometric firm only as long as the price changes it proposes are agreeable to the remainder of the firms in the market. No particular gains accrue to the firm that is barometric in nature; therefore, there is seldom a struggle over which firm assumes the barometric role. Indeed, in certain cases, the barometric firm may have become that for strange reasons. In the early 1960's, U.S. Steel announced an increase in steel prices that was opposed furiously by President Kennedy. Most of the major steel producers followed U.S. Steel's lead and raised their prices. Inland Steel, however, did not choose to increase its prices and instead announced, amid great publicity, that it did not feel the price increase was in the best interests of the steel market. Inland's perception was undoubtedly influenced by the fact that the U.S. government threatened to, and did, shift some steel purchases away from firms that had gone along with the price increase. The immense public pressure generated by the White House made Inland Steel's noncompliance with the price hike the prudent course of action, and the other steel firms, including U.S. Steel, followed Inland in short order.

The system of categorizing price leadership is not nearly as important as the phenomenon itself. Price leadership, however labeled, does occur. As the president of one small firm testified, "The price schedules issued by the ———— Company are contingent upon the prices published by the larger units of the industry. From time to time these larger units publish their scale of prices, and our company has no alternative except to meet such published prices in order to compete."[17]

Price leadership does decrease the flexibility of prices. It has the clear potential to impair the allocation of resources if prices do not shift at the appropriate time or by the appropriate amount. Unless the cost and demand conditions facing every firm in a market are identical, it is doubtful that

[17]Testimony of H.L. Randall in *Temporary National Economic Commission Hearings,* Part Five, 76th Cong., 1st sess. (Washington, D.C.: U.S. Government Printing Office, 1939).

the price imposed by a leadership situation will be completely appropriate. If the price is not appropriate to the cost and demand conditions facing the individual firm, then the firm will be forced to adjust its own output so that it can meet the established price. More often than not, this will mean output restriction in response to a high price. An example in point is the action of the steel firms during the late 1950's. Even though demand was falling as a consequence of the 1958 recession and the big steel firms were operating at less than half their productive capacity, they nevertheless increased prices. Such price leadership—and followership—results in an inefficient allocation of resources.

A major difficulty associated with public policy toward price leadership, and price inflexibility in general, resides in the fact that most leader–follower arrangements do not emanate from formal collusion. Firms may be pricing in a totally similar fashion and altering their prices by the same amounts at the same points in time, but still have never consulted each other. This is the essence of tacit collusion, where price and output coordination in a market are completely voluntary and informal in nature. Price fixing itself is illegal per se; that is, no defense of reasonableness is permitted once the charge of price fixing has been established.[18] Where tacit collusion is present, however, no price-fixing agreement can be established, since none has ever been made. The effects of tacit collusion may nevertheless closely approximate the pricing arrangements observed in cases involving outright collusion. Turner has argued that "any economist worthy of the name would immediately brand this price behavior as noncompetitive."[19] The quandary is that quite different forms of conduct in the market can lead to identical results.

The response of the courts to tacit collusion resulted in the enunciation of the doctrine of "conscious parallelism" in the late 1940's. Beginning with the *Tobacco Case*,[20] and especially in the *Rigid Steel Conduit Case*,[21] the courts ruled that even though there was no evidence of collusion or conspiracy concerning prices, the firms' behavior was no different from what would have been observed if open collusion and cartelization had occurred. The courts held that the Sherman Act had therefore been violated.

---

[18]A long line of judicial decisions have resulted in the development of the "per se" prohibition against price fixing. Among the more important cases in this area are *Addyston Pipe and Steel Company v. United States*, 175 U.S. 211 (1899); *United States* v. *Trenton Potteries Co. et al.*, 273 U.S. 392 (1927), where the "per se" rule was really formulated; and *United States* v. *Socony-Vacuum Oil Co.*, 310 U.S. 150 (1940), where Justice Douglas stated that "ruinous competition, financial disaster, evils of price cutting, and the like appear throughout our history as ostensible justifications for price fixing. If the so-called competitive abuses were to be appraised here, the reasonableness of prices would necessarily become an issue in every price-fixing case. In that event, the Sherman Act would be emasculated. . . ."

[19]Donald F. Turner, "The Definition of Agreement Under the Sherman Act: Conscious Parallelism and Refusals to Deal," *Harvard Law Review*, 25 (February 1962), 655–706.

[20]*American Tobacco Co.* v. *United States*, 328 U.S. 781 (1946).

[21]*Triangle Conduit and Cable Company et al.*, v. *Federal Trade Commission*, 162 F. 2nd, 175 (1948).

Conscious parallelism is a judicially unenforceable doctrine unless modified. Thousands, if not millions, of examples of parallel pricing are observed each day in every town (for example, the retail pricing of gasoline).[22] Moreover, the firms involved in this parallel pricing are aware of their behavior, even though no agreement of any kind has been made. The law cannot and should not prohibit noncollusive parallel pricing per se, even if the participants are aware of their activities. Rather, the law and judicial decisions should be directed at halting parallel pricing where such pricing is apparently against the best interests of the parties concerned. Identical prices can be consistent with independent competitive decisions, depending upon cost and demand conditions facing each firm. However, if firms keep prices rigid even when demand declines or prices change, or if prices rise in the face of large amounts of excess productive capacity, or if identical prices and price bids surface when large amounts of excess productive capacity are present, then in these cases, legal action should be considered. The courts have in any case backed away from the strong positions taken against conscious parallelism in the 1940's. Recent circumstances that violate even the relaxed guidelines proposed here (for example, steel price increases in the face of falling demand and chronic excess capacity) have escaped untouched.

BASING-POINT PRICING

Because basing-point pricing appears in so many different forms, it is difficult to pin down precisely what it is and is not. Basing-point pricing usually implies a pricing system by which the delivered price paid by the purchaser is the sum of some mill price plus freight costs from some basing point to the customer. The mill price is the f.o.b. (free on board) price at the firm's plant location and does not include any transport or delivery costs. The location of the mill, used to determine the mill price, and the location of the basing point, used to compute transport costs, need not be the same, although they usually are. Multiple mill prices and basing points can be utilized in sophisticated basing-point pricing schemes.

The classic example of basing-point pricing is the "Pittsburgh-plus-freight" system, which operated in the steel market until at least the year 1924.[23] Except in rare instances, the delivered price of steel at any location

---

[22]A phenomenon that has become known as "focal-point pricing" can also be responsible for the existence of consciously parallel price structures. Even when firms behave independently, there will often be a tendency for their decisions to converge upon some focal point. Schelling has pointed out that retail gasoline prices converge upon prices such as 32.9 cents per gallon, not 32.4 cents per gallon. This is the result of custom and not necessarily of collusion. Schelling has developed many examples of focal-point pricing in Thomas Schelling, *The Strategy of Conflict* (Cambridge, Mass.: Harvard University Press, 1960).

[23]Action by the Federal Trade Commission in 1924 forced the steel producers to abandon the single-basing-point pricing system they had theretofore followed. [8 F.T.C. (December 1, 1924).] It is probable that the single-basing-point system would not have lasted indefinitely anyway, since in the early 1920's, Chicago-based steel firms were attempting to be considered as basing points.

in the country was the Pittsburgh mill price plus freight costs from Pittsburgh to the customer's location.[24] The Pittsburgh-plus-freight price would be quoted by any steel manufacturer, regardless of his location. For example, steel produced in Chicago and sold to customers in Minneapolis would nevertheless be priced at the Pittsburgh mill price plus transport costs from Pittsburgh to Minneapolis, even though a large portion of the transport costs were never really incurred by the Chicago steel producer. Such unincurred transport costs have often been labeled "phantom freight," because the customer pays for freight never used.

Freight costs in the Pittsburgh-plus-freight pricing system assumed that rail transportation was being used. An enterprising firm could further increase the amount of phantom freight it was earning by delivering the steel to its customers by some alternative form of transportation that was cheaper than rail. On the other hand, a Chicago steel producer who wished to sell steel to a customer in Wheeling would have to charge the Pittsburgh-plus-freight price, which would involve a considerably smaller allowance for freight costs than he would actually incur. Hence, the Chicago steel producer would in this case be forced to "absorb freight."

Figure 13.3 illustrates a single-basing-point pricing system in which both phantom freight and freight absorption can occur. Assume that the basing point is a firm located at point BP, that all firms in the market are producing homogeneous products, and that transport costs are uniform in all directions from the basing point. The concentric rings around the basing-point firm indicate points of equal delivered prices, regardless of the identity of the selling firm or of the customer. If Firm 1 (F_1) sells to Customer 1 (C_1), then F_1 will realize phantom freight, since the delivered price paid by C_1 will be the mill price at BP plus five units of freight costs from BP to C_1, even though only two units of freight costs were actually incurred. If, however, F_1 wishes to sell to C_2, then F_1 must absorb three units of freight, since the freight costs amount to six units and he is permitted to charge C_2 for only three units.

The phenomenon of "cross-hauling" may also rear its head in basing-point pricing schemes. In Figure 13.3, firm F_2 will find it profitable to sell to customer C_1, because he will realize phantom freight by so doing. He will therefore sell in territory that is F_1's from the standpoint of economic efficiency. This is cross-hauling. F_1, in turn, may also find cross-hauling profitable; he can sell to C_3 more profitably than can F_2, despite the fact that F_2 is actually next door to C_3. This is because F_1 will realize phantom freight by selling to C_3, whereas F_2 receives no phantom freight for selling to such nearby customers. What frequently emerges in such a situation is the wasteful possibility that the shipments of F_1 and F_2 to their respective

[24]The reign of the single-point pricing system was not complete. The appearance of large and important customers often forced an abandonment of this mode of pricing. An example is the case of Detroit where the steel-using automobile firms were able to modify the single-basing-point pricing system.

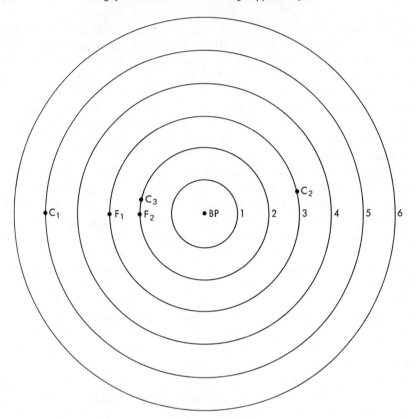

Figure 13.3

customers may actually pass each other going in opposite directions because it is profitable for each firm to ship into the other firm's natural territory.

The potential economic evils of basing-point pricing are many.[25] First and foremost is the fact that it eliminates all but secret, under-the-table price competition. A "one price in any location" basing-point pricing system confronts the consumer with a circumstance remarkably similar to the one that results from pure monopoly. It is deceptively true (as some of its defenders have hastened to point out) that basing-point pricing yields the same solution as perfect competition—namely, a single price. This argument, however, is a gross misrepresentation of price formation in perfect competition. The single-market-price result of perfect competition does not mean that transport or any other costs are ignored in the final market price. Further, the single-price result of perfect competition is the direct result of the competitive process rather than of the elimination of competition. The elimination of price competition in a basing-point pricing system often occurs in the most obvious fashion. Machlup has reported that in response to a government request for cement bids in the State of New Mexico, eleven cement companies submitted identical bids of $3.286854 per barrel.[26] Moreover, such parallel behavior was hardly an accident, for Loescher has quoted an official of the Cement Institute, a trade association of cement producers, as saying that "ours is an industry that cannot stand free competition. . . . [We must] systematically restrain competition or be ruined."[27]

Rigid prices that have no necessary relation to the true economic costs of production and distribution are inefficient prices. They impede the movement of resources to the locations where they are needed. It is worth noting that the economic rationale for a market system is severely damaged if there is no opportunity for firms to compete by means of price.

A second major inefficiency associated with basing-point pricing is that it promotes improper usage of resources and encourages firms and customers to choose what would otherwise be economically inefficient locations. Customers in particular are encouraged to locate near a basing point even if the actual source of the inputs they purchase is located elsewhere. Also, an inauspiciously located firm might be forced to absorb freight continually in order to sell to customers that it could serve expeditiously and efficiently if basing-point pricing were not used.

It is also possible that basing-point pricing schemes promote market concentration and retard the entry of new firms. A firm entering a market dominated by basing-point pricing cannot gain new customers by offering lower prices; hence, it will be difficult for new firms to enter the market against already-established rivals. Also, since the basing-point pricing system will sometimes arbitrarily make certain plant locations bad ones, some firms may leave the market. As a consequence, concentration in the market might rise.

Single-basing-point pricing systems were effectively discouraged by two decisions handed down by the Supreme Court on the same day in 1945. These two decisions, in the *Corn Products Case* and the *Staley Case,* overruled the "Chicago-plus-freight" pricing system followed by both Corn Products and Staley, primarily because neither producer was located solely in the city of Chicago.[28] The "Big Three" automobile companies and others continue to use individualized single-basing-point pricing systems in many instances, however. The prices of the "Big Three" are often quoted "Detroit

[26]Machlup, *The Basing-Point Pricing System,* p. 99.

[27]Samuel M. Loescher, *Imperfect Collusion in the Cement Industry* (Cambridge, Mass. : Harvard University Press, 1959), p. 85.

[28]*Corn Products Refining Company* v. *Federal Trade Commission,* 324 U.S. 726 (1945); and *Federal Trade Commission* v. *A.E. Staley Manufacturing Company,* 324 U.S. 726 (1945). Corn Products was located in both Chicago and Kansas City ; Staley, which typically followed Corn Products' price leadership, was located in Decatur, Illinois.

plus freight," even though the firms have many plants outside the Detroit area. The major difference between automobile pricing of this type and the Pittsburgh-plus-freight steel pricing examined earlier is that there does not exist in the automobile market one uniform basing-point pricing system; rather, each firm maintains its own. One reason is the obvious differentiation of the automobiles sold by these firms. One pricing system would not be viable, given that diversity. From an economic standpoint, of course, most of the inefficiencies of single-basing-point pricing remain when each firm separately maintains its own basing-point pricing system. Although there is more opportunity for price competition, pricing and locational inequities continue to persist.

Most basing-point pricing systems that exist today are some variant of a multiple-basing-point pricing system in which all or nearly all plants in a market are regarded as basing points. The delivered price in such a world is usually the mill price of the plant nearest the customer plus the freight costs from the mill to the customer. Phantom freight and cross-hauling are largely eliminated. The cement producers have for many years followed a multiple-basing-point pricing system. Even though such a system is preferable to a single-basing-point pricing system, it still suffers from the fact that it eliminates all price competition except secret price chiseling. Multiple-basing-point pricing is responsible for the cement producers' bids referred to above, which were identical to the nearest ten-thousandth of a cent. Indeed, in the *Cement Case*, evidence showed that the cement producers, through their trade association, the Cement Institute, forced wavering firms to submit to the discipline of a multiple-basing-point pricing system by encouraging pricing reprisals and boycotts.[29]

Basing-point pricing is not the worst economic evil that can befall a market. It is a recurring phenomenon in markets characterized by high transport costs, relatively homogeneous products, and geographically unstable demand. Firms within a market often practice basing-point pricing in much the same fashion as that in which Sears, Roebuck catalog sales have been carried out for years: To an f.o.b. price, existing at the location of the catalog house, is added freight transportation, perhaps based upon the location of the customer in one of various freight zones around the catalog-house location. The delivered price is therefore the result of an individualized basing-point pricing system. Basing-point pricing has the advantage of introducing stability and certainty into a market; for example, the catalog customer can ordinarily rely upon the prices quoted in the catalog. Such basing-point pricing is relatively harmless, however, when compared to the impact of basing-point pricing as it takes place in large industrial markets. Price stability and certainty are admirable goals, but should not be purchased at too high a cost. The costs of stability and cer-

---

[29]*Federal Trade Commission* v. *Cement Institute,* 333 U.S. 683 (1948).

tainty via basing-point pricing can include an absence of price competition and locational distortion. It is for this reason that most economists regard most basing-point pricing systems as not being beneficial to competition or welfare.

PRICE DISCRIMINATION

Price discrimination is one of the most widespread of all economic practices. It occurs daily in nearly all markets and can either help or hinder the competitive process. Our analysis of price discrimination begins with a definition.

Price discrimination is the sale of technically similar goods at prices that are not proportional to the marginal costs of manufacture, sale, and delivery, with due allowance for risk and uncertainty.

This definition states that price discrimination has occurred if $P_1/MC_1 \neq P_2/MC_2$, where 1 and 2 denote sales of technically similar goods. Note that the role of technically similar goods is emphasized. The mere appearance of a different label or the changing of a decorative color (a mattress manufacturer was once found to be selling the identical mattress at a wide of prices under a series of labels that implied vastly differing levels of quality) has no bearing on whether price discrimination exists, if the goods in question remain technically similar. The definition also emphasizes the delivered price to the purchaser, rather than the mill price. Costs surrounding the sale, including such things as the risk of the seller's not being paid, are included. Not stated, but implied, is the fact that we must ordinarily be talking about a given short-run time period in which a *ceteris paribus* assumption is appropriate.[30] Finally, it should be recognized that a seller can be guilty of economic price discrimination even if he charges two customers the same price for the identical good or service. If the marginal costs of manufacturing and selling to the two customers differ, then it is economic price discrimination to charge each customer the same price.

Price discrimination can occur only in an imperfect market. Either the seller who discriminates in price must have monopoly power, or the buyer who forces the seller to discriminate in the buyer's favor must have monopsony power. Consider the seller who has no monopoly power and who attempts to discriminate in price between customers. The customers will get together and agree to have the low-price customer purchase any units needed by the high-price customer. Only if the price-discriminating firm

[30]Some price discrimination, of course, occurs on the basis of time. The price for a ticket to a matinee theater performance is typically less than the price for the same show performed at night. In this case different time periods can be involved.

can keep the two customers separate will price discrimination be successful. The ability to keep markets separate necessitates monopoly power.[31] It should be noted that the source of the firm's monopoly power may in fact be consumer ignorance.

Much of the price discrimination we observe is systematic in nature and is based upon a consistent separation of markets and prices on the basis of differences in factors such as income, location, and the like. Other price discrimination is unsystematic in nature and fails to exhibit any consistency. The haggling between buyer and seller over the price of an automobile is typically unsystematic in character. Whether systematic or unsystematic in nature, price discrimination will not be a profitable endeavor for a firm unless the firm is able to separate its total market into at least two distinct parts. Although monopoly is a necessary condition for the firm to be able to subdivide profitably the market it faces, it is not a sufficient condition. Each market subdivision must also possess a different price elasticity of demand. For example, a textbook publisher may possess some degree of monopoly power owing to product differentiation and other factors. Suppose the publisher attempts to subdivide the market it faces on the basis of whether the book purchaser is left-handed or right-handed. Since the publisher has some monopoly power, he may well be able to subdivide the market in this fashion. However, such a subdivision will probably not be profitable, since there is no reason to believe that the price elasticities of demand of southpaws and right-handers are different. Only if price elasticities of demand differ in the market subdivisions will the firm find it possible to increase its profits by means of price discrimination.

The most common reason for a firm to engage in price discrimination is the desire to increase its profits. Price discrimination can be profitable if the conditions cited above can be met. Nevertheless, the motive of increased profits may occasionally take a back seat when the firm wishes to pursue other goals—for example, the introduction of a new product, the penetration of a market, or the disciplining and/or destruction of a rival firm. These motives will be discussed shortly. In the interim, we shall assume that the motivation for the price discrimination is the desire of the firm to increase its profits.

It has long been customary to speak of three distinct degrees of price discrimination: first, second, and third.[32] First-degree price discrimination is rare; conceptually, it involves the firm's selling each unit to the customer

---

[31]The college bookstore that charges lower prices to faculty members than to students for the same merchandise will soon find such a price structure untenable if students find some way to take advantage of the faculty price discount—for example, by using a faculty member's identification, or having faculty members purchase all the books needed by students. The bookstore that increases its profits by means of such a discriminatory price structure must also have the ability to keep the faculty and student markets separate.

[32]A.C. Pigou, *The Economics of Welfare* (London: Macmillan and Company, Ltd. 1920), pp. 240–56, was the first to make this distinction.

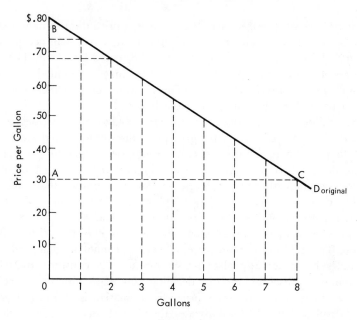

Figure 13.4

at the highest possible price that the customer will pay for that single unit. This results in a large portion of the purchaser's consumer's surplus being taken away by the firm. Figure 13.4 illustrates such a possibility. The consumer would, in the absence of first-degree price discrimination, pay the sum of $2.40 ($.30 per gallon) if he wished to purchase eight gallons of gasoline. Instead, he is forced to pay $4.16 for the eight gallons. He must pay $.75 for the first gallon, and $.68 for the second gallon.[33] Unless he pays these prices, he will not be able to buy more gallons. Each of the separate prices per gallon paid by the consumer is the highest possible price that he would pay for that individual gallon. His consumer's surplus, which would be approximated by the area of triangle *ABC* in the absence of first-degree price discrimination, is reduced almost to zero. First-degree price discrimination is sometimes called "perfect" price discrimination, and it is indeed perfect from the seller's viewpoint. The seller succeeds in making the consumer pay the highest possible price for each unit that he purchases. The net effect of this is to make the original demand curve (*BCD*) the new marginal-revenue curve for the firm.[34] A new demand curve must now be drawn to represent accurately the consumer's recorded willingness to purchase

[33]He will pay (in order) $.75, $.68, $.62, $.55, $.48, $.42, $.36, and $.30 for the single gallons he purchases.

[34]Marginal revenue is the addition to total revenue derived from the sale of an extra unit. The dollar values found on the original demand curve *BCD* for each gallon purchased give that information. For example, the marginal revenue derived from the sale of the second gallon of gasoline is $.68.

gasoline at various *average* prices.[35] First-degree price discrimination seldom occurs, because few consumers are so impotent that they will accept such a solution and few firms are so powerful that they could impose it. The actual incidence of first-degree price discrimination may be limited to esoteric cases such as the traveler without sufficient water or gasoline, the patient sorely in need of medical help, and the like.

Second-degree price discrimination is a pedigree of first-degree price discrimination. Whereas in first-degree price discrimination, the buyer was forced to pay the maximum price he would be willing to pay for each separate unit, in second-degree price discrimination, the same type of phenomenon occurs with respect to groups of units, rather than individual ones. For example, a user of a pay telephone might talk for the first three minutes for a cost of $.90 ($.30 per minute). The second three minutes may cost $.75 ($.25 per minute) and the next six minutes $1.20 ($.20 per minute). The $.20-per-minute price, of course, cannot be achieved by the buyer unless he has already talked for six minutes. The consumer himself performs the act of discrimination by deciding how many minutes he will talk.

The effect of second-degree price discrimination is also to reduce consumer's surplus. Figure 13.5 illustrates this fact. Instead of demand curve *ACEHI,* which could be the consumer's demand curve in the absence of price discrimination, we now find discontinuous demand curve *BCDEGH* as a result of the exercise of second-degree discrimination. In the absence of price discrimination, consumer's surplus is approximated by the area

---

[35]Price is the average revenue derived from the sale of a given number of units. In the case described above, total revenue from the sale of eight gallons of gasoline was $4.16; hence, average revenue (price) for eight gallons was $4.16/8 = $.52. One point on the new demand curve would therefore have the coordinates of $.52 per gallon and 8 gallons. The graphical relationship between the old and the new demand curves is the following:

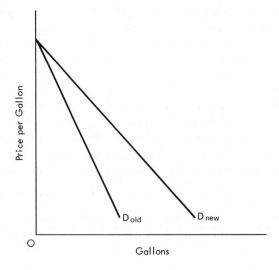

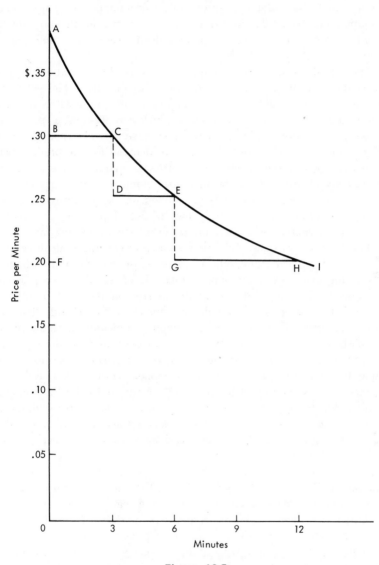

Figure 13.5

inside *AFH,* but second-degree price discrimination reduces that surplus by an amount equal to the area of hexagon *FBCDEG* (which is darkened in Figure 13.5).

The reader is probably aware that second-degree price discrimination is apparently practiced not only in many public-utility markets, but also in the private sector in many different forms, one example being the conferral of quantity discounts. I say "apparently" because what may at first glance appear to be a blatant case of price discrimination may upon closer examination not be so considered if there is a cost justification for the observed price differential. This is potentially the case where any quantity discount is offered by a seller.[36]

The conditions that are prerequisite to successful second-degree price discrimination are the same as for any price discrimination. The seller must be able to segment the market (for example, he must be able to keep pay-telephone users from paying the successively lower per-minute prices that accompany long conversations, unless they have already talked a given number of minutes). The price elasticities of demand for the product being sold must also be different in each segment of the market (for example, the price elasticity of demand for the first three minutes of conversation must be different from the price elasticity of demand for the next three minutes). These two conditions are frequently met in actual practice, and second-degree price discrimination is therefore a fairly common pricing tactic.

Third-degree price discrimination is the most general of all three types, since from a technical standpoint it must be present for either first- or second-degree price discrimination to take place. Third-degree price discrimination involves segmentation of the market on the basis of differing price elasticities of demand. It will be remembered that both first- and second-degree price discrimination also involve segmentation of the market on the basis of price elasticities. In these two cases, however, the segmentation is performed upon the units purchased by one particular customer (for example, the first three minutes of a pay-telephone conversation, as opposed to the second three minutes of the same conversation). In third-degree price discrimination, the market is segmented on the basis of the price elasticities of demand of *different* purchasers. Third-degree price discrimination, then, groups customers, not the units purchased by a single customer, by price elasticities of demand.

Figure 13.6 provides a graphical illustration of third-degree price discrimination. The firm described in Figure 13.6 faces demand curve ABC in an unsegmented market. The market can be segmented on the basis of price elasticities of demand, however, and demand curves D_1 and D_2 represent each market segment. In the absence of price discrimination, the firm would equate marginal cost with marginal revenue in the entire market (MR_M) and produce output Q_T at nondiscriminatory price P_{ND}. The essence of third-degree price discrimination is the setting of separate prices in each market segment so that the marginal revenue obtainable from the sale of a unit in any segment is identical. Hence, we must amend our previous nondiscriminatory profit-maximization criterion $(MC = MR_M)$ to include

---

[36]The question of whether the quantity discounts granted by the Morton Salt Company to its larger customers were justified on a cost basis was an issue at stake in *Federal Trade Commission* v. *Morton Salt Company*, 334 U.S. 37 (1948). Morton's pricing schedule offered both quantity discounts for a particular purchase and cumulative volume discounts in favor of those customers who accumulated a large volume of purchases in a given time period. Morton contended that its prices could be justified on a cost basis, but the Supreme Court did not accept Morton's argument.

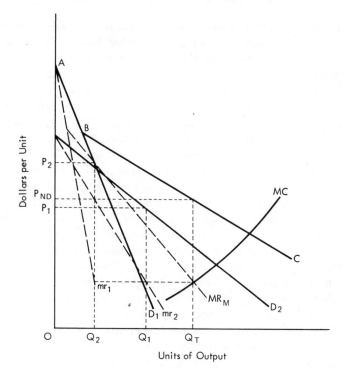

Figure 13.6

the fact that the marginal revenue obtained from each market must also be equal to marginal cost. That is, the profit-maximizing criterion under third-degree price discrimination is that $MC = MR_M = mr_1 = mr_2$. Exercising this rule, the firm will sell Q_2 units to market segment 2 at price P_2; it will sell Q_1 units to market segment 1 at price P_1. The sum of the sales to each market segment $(Q_1 + Q_2)$ will equal total market sales, Q_T.

As Figure 13.6 indicates, the higher price is charged in that market segment where demand is least price-elastic, and the lower price is charged in that market segment where demand is more price-elastic.[37] This is an intuitively sensible result. Price increases in a price-inelastic market will not lower total sales revenue, whereas price increases in price-elastic markets will lower total sales revenue. Hence, price will be higher in the price-inelastic market than in the price-elastic market.[38]

Examples of third-degree price discrimination abound. Airlines, amusement parks, theaters, and the like offer lower prices to the young than to adults. Commercial users of electrical power are charged lower

[37]Demand curves are ordinarily both price-elastic and -inelastic, depending upon the point selected on the demand curve. In this case, the point referred to on each demand curve is that place where price is P_{ND}.

[38]This can also be confirmed as follows : We know that $MR = P(1 + 1/\eta)$. When two segmented markets exist, profit maximization requires that $MR_M = mr_1 = P_1(1 + 1/\eta_1) = mr_2 = P_2(1 + 1/\eta_2)$. Suppose that $MR_M = mr_1 = mr_2 = \$1.00$, and that $\eta_1 = -10$, while $\eta_2 = -5$. Then, $P_1 = \$1.11$, and $P_2 = \$1.25$.

rates than are individual homeowners. Medical doctors sometimes size up the incomes of their patients and charge higher fees to those with high incomes than to those with lower incomes.[39] The per-gallon price of the same gasoline is often higher at stations on a tollway than at stations that are in the driver's vision but not located on the tollway.

Within the broad rubric of the three degrees of price discrimination, an almost infinite variety of variations exists. Machlup, for example, has catalogued 22 distinct types of price discrimination.[40] Although a complete discussion of each of the 22 types exceeds our need for detail, it is nevertheless beneficial to examine several of the most common bases for price discrimination. The time of the purchase is often an important basis; resorts, theaters, and utilities all vary their rates at the expense of the peak-time user. The quantity purchased by the consumer, the use to which the purchased good is put, the location of the consumer, his age or income, his newness as a customer, and the quality of the item he wishes to purchase—all are means that firms might use to identify differences in price elasticity of demand among consumers. It can also be noted now that basing-point pricing is discriminatory, since it establishes price structures that are unrelated to costs of production and distribution.

A comprehensive system that labels each and every type of price discrimination is of less value to us than is an understanding of the effects of price discrimination upon economic welfare. We have previously stated that monopoly power is a prerequisite for the existence of price discrimination. Price discrimination would not exist in a perfectly competitive economy. The truth of this statement has unfortunately led to the conclusion that price discrimination is therefore an economic evil. Such is not the case. Given the imperfections in the economy, price discrimination may improve the allocation of resources, provide an indispensable element of price competition, and sometimes actually be necessary for the survival or rational operation of essential firms.[41] That is, given that the welfare optimum entailed by perfect competition is not attainable, price discrimination may assist us in reaching a "second-best" or constrained optimum solution.[42]

---

[39]Income in this case is a determinant of price elasticity of demand. Increases in income generally reduce price elasticity of demand for medical services, although they may increase price elasticity of demand for other goods (for example, consumer durables such as refrigerators).

[40]Fritz Machlup, "Characteristics and Types of Price Discrimination," in Stigler, ed., *Business Concentration and Price Policy*, pp. 397–435.

[41]The discussion concerning the welfare economics of price discrimination is patterned after the author's work in "A Closer Look at Price Discrimination in an Imperfect World," *Mississippi Valley Review of Business and Economics,* 5 (Spring 1970), 11-23.

[42]The theory of the second best has received a great deal of attention in the economic literature of the past two decades. Seminal articles include Kevin Lancaster and R.G. Lipsey, "The General Theory of the Second Best," *Review of Economic Studies,* 24 (December 1956), 11–32; M. McManus, "Comments on the General Theory of Second Best," *Review of Economic Studies,* 26 (June 1959), 209–24; and E.J. Mishan, "Second Thoughts on Second Best," *Oxford Economic Papers,* n.s., 14 (October 1962), 205–17. Two earlier articles that hinted at the principles at stake are John M. Clark, "Toward a Concept of Workable Competition," *American Economic Review,* 30 (June 1940), 241–56; and L.W. McKenzie, "Ideal Output and the Interdependence of Firms," *Economic Journal,* 56 (December 1951), 785–803.

Price discrimination can result in increased output, although the conditions under which this will happen are limited. Figure 13.7 demonstrates a circumstance in which price discrimination does increase output. Joan Robinson has shown that price discrimination will increase output in the two-market case if the more-elastic demand curve is more convex to the

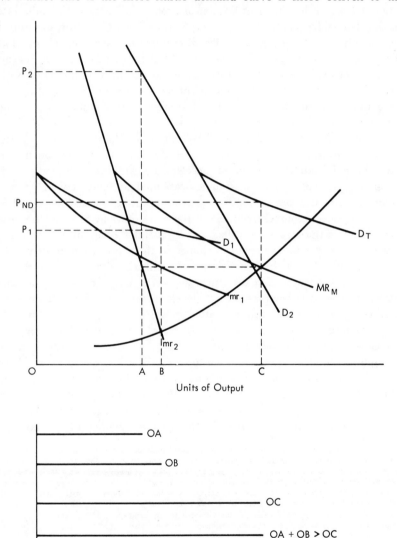

OA = output in market one with price discrimination
OB = output in market two with price discrimination
OC = output in markets one and two in the absence of
     price discrimination

Figure 13.7

origin than is the less-elastic demand curve.[43] The amount by which output has increased in Figure 13.7 because of price discrimination is only about 2 percent; however, even such a small increase in output is over $20 billion in terms of current gross national product.

Price discrimination may also increase the efficiency of resource allocation, by permitting fuller utilization of productive capacity.[44] Public rate-making bodies frequently sanction this result when they allow the utilities they watch over to engage in price discrimination based upon peak-load charges or customer status.[45] It can be argued that as long as the revenue the firm derives from the low-price market covers the variable costs associated with that market as well as some of the fixed costs of the entire firm, price discrimination is merely of a loss-minimization nature and is not predatory.[46]

When viewed from a static viewpoint, price discrimination is a sign that resources have been allocated incorrectly. Price discrimination may be the vehicle initiating, forcing, or accelerating structural changes in the economy that will correct this misallocation. The favored firms prosper while the firms that are discriminated against shrink in size. The net effect is to make more resources available to the more efficient firms in the economy. Three major structural difficulties surround this argument: (1) It is difficult to identify basic structural change in the economy until after it has already occurred; (2) the beneficiaries of such price discrimination may be large firms, some of which are integrated on a large scale, and law and public opinion may frown on such a development; and (3) such price discrimination may be blatantly predatory in nature.

The first and second *Standard Oil Cases* pose many of the problems associated with the preceding argument.[47] Like other large sellers, Standard Oil sold gasoline to large jobber customers in the Detroit area at a lower price than it sold the same gas to smaller, retail service-station customers. The FTC sought to halt this practice on the ground that it destroyed competition at both the wholesale and retail levels. It is probable that basic structural change was occurring in the gasoline market in question and

---

[43]Joan Robinson's exposition of this point makes reference to concavity of demand functions rather than to convexity, as stated here. This difference is consistent with a long-standing difference in usage between mathematicians and economists. *Convex to origin,* as used here, has the same meaning as Robinson's *concavity.* Both imply that the demand curve is bowed in toward the origin, rather than bowed outward away from the origin. Robinson, *The Economics of Imperfect Competition* (London: Macmillan and Company, Ltd., 1934), pp. 188–208, 193, and 201, specifically.

[44]The excess productive capacity might be due to the geographic configuration of demand, a temporary decline in demand, the shape of demand over time, seasonal demands and prices, increased productivity, or expectations.

[45]J.M. Clark long ago pointed out that the possibility of price discrimination's reducing excess capacity is not limited to public utilities. John M. Clark, *Studies in the Economics of Overhead Costs* (Chicago: University of Chicago Press, 1923), p. 10.

[46]Of course, if the resulting price charged in the high-price market is greater than previously, the argument loses its force. The social opportunity cost of reducing excess capacity could, however, be greater than the benefits derived from reducing that excess capacity.

[47]*Standard Oil Company* v. *Federal Trade Commission,* 340 U.S. 231 (1951), is the "first" *Standard Oil Case;* the "second" is *Federal Trade Commission* v. *Standard Oil Company,* 355 U.S. 396 (1958).

that the price discount afforded the jobber customers by Standard Oil accelerated the demise of smaller customers, who could not purchase gasoline in such large quantities as tank-car loads. Yet the disappearance of competitors, particularly small competitors, has always been mourned by the courts, almost regardless of the magnitude of the alleged efficiencies involved. In the first *Standard Oil Case*, the FTC was upheld, and in the second case it was overruled, but evidence concerning economic efficiency was not the basis for either decision.

Attention should also be given to the potential role of price discrimination as an indispensable element of price competition. In a market characterized by fewness of sellers, vigorous and open price discrimination may sometimes be the exception rather than the rule. The secret price cutting and chiseling that are a vital source of price flexibility in such markets will nearly always be discriminatory in nature.[48] Hence, once again, given the imperfections already existing in the market, price discrimination may be desirable.

Price discrimination may in some cases be necessary for the survival of some firms. If firms operating in transportation or communications are not allowed to engage in price discrimination, they might well disappear, unless subsidies are forthcoming from public coffers. Such a possibility is presented in Figure 13.8. P_{ND} represents the price the firm would charge in the absence of price discrimination. P_{ND} is everywhere below the average-cost curve of the firm, and therefore the firm is sustaining per-unit losses. Price discrimination will allow the firm to survive, however. The weighted average of discriminatory prices P_1 and P_2 (the prices that will be charged by the firm to its respective market segments) is P_W. P_W is greater than the average cost per unit of the firm at output T, and therefore the firm will be able ot survive. Railroads and airlines frequently argue that their continued existence depends upon their ability to discriminate in terms of price in the fashion outlined in Figure 13.8. The survival of essential firms is, of course, something to be valued; however, the social opportunity cost of the resources used to ensure that survival may be excessive. Further, public ownership of the firms is another alternative for consideration.

The apparatuses of welfare economics and the theory of the second best are not yet sufficiently refined to enable us to make a precise determination about the desirability of every instance of price discrimination in an imperfectly competitive world. The examples cited should, however, dispose the reader not to conclude hastily that price discrimination is of necessity an economic evil.

Public policy toward price discrimination is in a state of disarray, primarily because of the language and intent of the Robinson-Patman Act,

---

[48]Not all observers agree that the ability to discriminate in price is necessary in order to obtain price flexibility in oligopoly situations. Indeed, Blair has led a caustic attack on both the need for such price behavior and its probable frequency of appearance in an oligopolistic market. Blair, *Economic Concentration,* pp. 342–44.

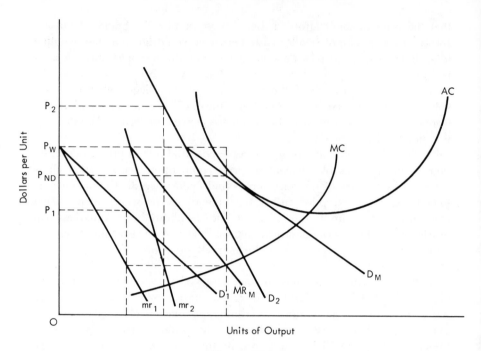

Figure 13.8

which is the major piece of legislation concerned with price discrimination.[49] The Robinson-Patman Act was passed in 1936 as an amendment to Section Two of the Clayton Act. The impetus for its passage was almost certainly the encroachment of large chain stores, such as A&P and Sears, Roebuck, upon smaller, independent retailers. The act was designed to eliminate alleged discriminatory pricing practices carried out by the retailing chains, as well as to eliminate discriminatory pricing concessions that the chains were thought to receive.[50]

Price discrimination in the context of the Robinson-Patman Act is not the same thing as economic price discrimination as we have defined it. In the legal view, price discrimination exists when differing prices are charged to two or more customers for goods that are of "like grade and quality." Such action is declared to be illegal if it might have the effect of lessening competition or if it might tend to create a monopoly or to destroy competition. Three exceptions to this broad dictum are allowed: First, "legal" price discrimination is permissible if a cost justification for it can be shown. Second, it is allowable if it is undertaken in order to meet com-

---

[49]Comprehensive studies of the Robinson-Patman Act include Corwin D. Edwards, *The Price Discrimination Law* (Washington, D.C.: The Brookings Institution, 1959); and Frederick M. Rowe, *Price Discrimination Under the Robinson-Patman Act* (Boston: Little, Brown and Company, 1962).

[50]Adelman has cast considerable doubt upon the validity of the abuses attributed to chain retailers such as A&P. M.A. Adelman, *A&P: A Study in Price–Cost Behavior and Public Policy* (Cambridge, Mass.: Harvard University Press, 1959).

petition "in good faith." Third, the discrimination is tolerated if it is undertaken in order to dispose of goods that might otherwise deteriorate (as in the case of produce) or become obsolescent (as in the case of out-of-style clothes or automobiles).

The Robinson-Patman Act has proved to be laced with problems and operational contradictions.[51] The determination of what comprises goods of like grade and quality has been a continual matter of dispute, for even if two units of a good are technically similar in a manufacturing sense, the conditions surrounding the sale can alter that technical similiarity beyond recognition. Hence, in order for the Robinson-Patman Act to operate as intended, one must take into account the nonprice aspects of each sale and attempt to place a monetary value upon those conditions.[52] The cost-defense provision is also a source of difficulty. Whereas it is the marginal cost of a sale that is the centerpiece of the economic definition of price discrimination, the legal examination of price discrimination has centered upon average costs. Further, the burden of proof has been placed upon the firms involved. The firm that discriminates in price must be able to demonstrate any cost justification that it says exists; on the other hand, the government need not show that no cost justification exists.[53]

The "meeting competition in good faith" clause has also developed into a legal can of worms. A firm must have precise knowledge about the actions and price structure of its competitors if it wishes to plead that its own prices are necessary in order to meet the rigors of competition. Further, the firm may not meet another firm's illegal price in good faith, as the Staley Company was informed in one of the basing-point-pricing cases discussed earlier.[54] So in order for a firm to defend itself successfully against a charge of price discrimination under the Robinson-Patman Act, that firm must have intimate knowledge of the costs and prices of its competitors, and the legality of those competitor firms' activities. Not altogether facetiously, one might inquire if indeed the firm that had all this information might not also be subject to prosecution under the provisions of the Sherman Act, for engaging in collusion.

---

[51]The substantial criticisms of the Robinson-Patman Act that are voiced here are generally subscribed to by most economists. For a contrary view, see Robert C. Brooks, Jr., "Injury to Competition under the Robinson-Patman Act," *University of Pennsylvania Law Review*, 109 (April 1961), 777ff.; see also Brooks, "Price Cutting and Monopoly Power," *Journal of Marketing*, 25 (July 1961), 44–49.

[52]An interesting example of the courts' dabbling in the nonprice aspects of transactions is found in *Federal Trade Commission* v. *Borden Company*, 383 U.S. 637 (1966), as later remanded to an appeals court in *Borden Company* v. *Federal Trade Commission*, 381 F. 2d 175, 181 (1967). One of the major issues in the cases was whether Borden should be allowed to sell technically similar canned milk at different prices under different labels. A similar case, which has raised eyebrows, was *Federal Trade Commission* v. *Anheuser-Busch, Inc.*, in which the court ruled that premium beers that were technically similar to regional beers except for advertising and imagery were nevertheless not to be considered goods of like grade and quality.

[53]In the *Morton Salt Case*, Morton alleged that cost justifications existed for its differential pricing structure. The Supreme Court, however, rejected this contention, and in so doing stated that the entire burden of proof rested with the Morton Salt Company. *Federal Trade Commission* v. *Morton Salt Company*, 334 U.S. 37 (1948).

[54]*Federal Trade Commission* v. *A.E. Staley Manufacturing Company*, 324 U.S. 726 (1945).

An important and economically inefficient result of the Robinson-Patman Act has been to discourage price flexibility. As Kaysen and Turner have commented, "The manufacturer who sells at the same price in train-load lots and in cases may be violating the prescriptions of common sense, but he is not violating the Robinson-Patman Act."[55] The Robinson-Patman Act encourages firms to ignore cost differences and competition, because the burden of proof in a legal battle will fall upon the firm to substantiate its case. The anticipation of this possibility is hardly conducive to price competition.

A confusion concerning injury to competition and injury to specific competitors has also been present in many cases involving the Robinson-Patman Act. An injury to a specific competitor, or even a reduction in the absolute number of competitors, does not, per se, indicate a reduction in competition. Rather, this may be a desirable evidence of competition. To be sure, a reduction in the number of competitors that resulted from a predatory pricing campaign aimed by one firm at another specific firm is ordinarily undesirable. The so-called "power of the long purse" could be used by a large firm to drive small firms out of its market. The potential for cross-subsidization between the branches of a large firm in order to finance predatory pricing in one particular area is also a possibility.[56]

The estimated frequency of predatory pricing behavior has, however, become the basis for a long and recurring dispute. The dispute has often centered upon the interpretation placed on the activities of the Standard Oil Company during the late 1800's and early 1900's. McGee and others have challenged the conventional wisdom that the Standard Oil Company forced many of its competitors to the wall by means of predatory pricing techniques.[57] The conclusion of Adelman that A&P not only was not often guilty of predatory pricing, but also that A&P did not receive substantial discriminatory price discounts, strengthened the position of those who contend that predatory pricing practices are not an important problem.[58] Recent work by Blair has once again thrown down the gauntlet on the issue, however; he has compiled a long and detailed list of instances where predatory pricing is said to have occurred.[59]

The identification of predatory pricing is not an easy job. The fact that one or more competitors of a price-cutting firm are suffering declining

---

[55]Carl Kaysen and Donald F. Turner, *Antitrust Policy: An Economic and Legal Analysis* (Cambridge Mass.: Harvard University Press, 1965), p. 181.

[56]IBM was accused of predatory pricing in the 1960's, when it priced its computer models in response to how much competitive pressure it was receiving in the market for each model. Thus, certain "fighting machines" may have been sold at prices that forced a per-unit loss on IBM, while other machines were sold at high per-unit profits. The possibility of cross-subsidization among models is apparent here and is currently the subject of several different antitrust actions.

[57]John S. McGee, "Price Discrimination and Competitive Effects: Standard Oil of Indiana Case," *University of Chicago Law Review*, 23 (Spring 1956), 398ff.; also, McGee, "Predatory Price Cutting: The Standard Oil (N.J.) Case," *Journal of Law and Economics*, 1 (October 1958), 137–69.

[58]Adelman, *A&P: A Study.*

[59]Blair, *Economic Concentration*, p. 341.

market shares is not evidence of predatory pricing. Evidences of predatory pricing *might* include some or all of the following: (1) The alleged predator is undertaking his price cuts in hopes of injuring specific, identifiable competitors, rather than simply to increase his overall market share regardless of the identity of the losing firms; (2) the product whose price is cut is being sold at a price that is less than long-run average variable costs, and that product is not being newly introduced, nor has it recently undergone substantial alterations; (3) the firm that is cutting prices is recouping its revenue losses by raising prices in other markets; and (4) the past history of the market has not been characterized by price cutting and by fluctuating market shares.

The criteria above are in no sense binding. Consider the frequently chronicled story of Bethlehem Steel in 1968, when it introduced and later retracted price cuts in order to induce U.S. Steel to adhere more rigorously to its published prices instead of engaging in secret price cutting. Bethlehem's price cuts were clearly aimed at U.S. Steel; however, they were hardly predatory in nature and were designed to increase price discipline in the steel market.

An assessment of whether predatory pricing has occurred has particularly bedeviled the courts when no firm is driven from the market as a result of the price cuts. An instructive example is the *Anheuser-Busch Case*.[60] During the mid-1950's, Anheuser-Busch, brewer of the premium-grade beer Budweiser, lowered the price of Budweiser to the level of regional and local brews not ordinarily considered to be premium beers. The share of Anheuser-Busch in the St. Louis market, where it undertook the price cuts, tripled within a two-year period. Despite the fact that no rival brewer was driven from the market as a result of the price cuts, and despite the fact that rival brewers continued to exhibit profitability (albeit with lower market shares in the St. Louis area), the Supreme Court determined that Anheuser-Busch had injured competition and therefore enjoined it from similar pricing activities in the future. A later appeals-court decision softened this decision somewhat; nevertheless, Anheuser-Busch introduced its own nonpremium beer (Busch Bavarian) to be sold at lower prices, because it felt effectively restrained from price competition with Budweiser.[61]

Blair and others have strongly argued that predatory pricing does occur. They have not demonstrated, however, that it has substantially and adversely affected economic welfare. The consumer immediately benefits from price wars. These benefits must be weighed against the possible injury to competition that might result from competitors' being driven out of the

---

[60]*Federal Trade Commission* v. *Anheuser-Busch, Inc.*, 363 U.S. 536 (1960), 289 F. 2d 835 (1961).

[61] Busch Bavarian has therefore often been termed a "fighting brand," in the tradition of the "fighting brands" of cigarettes introduced at very low prices by the "Big Three" tobacco firms during the depression years.

market or being forced into pricing practices that are always harmonious with those of other competitors. Precise evidence of the ill effects of predatory pricing upon economic welfare is remarkably scant and usually is stated in terms of possible future harm. In any case, predatory pricing is usually an outgrowth of market structure. A ban on predatory pricing, even if it could be imposed, would treat a behavioral symptom rather than the basic cause of the alleged malaise.

RESALE-PRICE MAINTENANCE

Resale-price maintenance, also known as "fair trading," is an example of ill-advised governmental encouragement of price fixing. Fortunately, it has proved to be fairly ineffective in practice and is not a major subject of concern. A resale-price-maintenance agreement is a contract between a manufacturer and his distributors that specifies the prices that can be charged for the manufacturer's merchandise when it is resold by the distributors. Typically, the contract specifies a price below which the product cannot be legally sold.

Early court decisions often invalidated fair-trade agreements between manufacturers and sellers.[62] This judicial attitude eventually led to the passage of the first state fair-trade law, in 1931 in California. The California law made specific provision for the exception of fair-trade pricing contracts from antitrust prosecution. It was amended in 1933 to include an ingenious "nonsigner's clause," which made it unlawful for any retailer to knowingly undercut a fair-trade price, regardless of whether that retailer was himself party to any fair-trade agreement.

The passage of the Miller-Tydings Act in 1937 extended the legality of fair trading to interstate commerce. Considerable momentum was generated in support of fair-trade legislation at the state level, and by 1941, 45 states had some type of fair-trade pricing law. Fair traders received a blow in 1951 when the Supreme Court refused to read into the Miller-Tydings Act a nonsigner's provision.[63] This, however, led to the quick passage of the McGuire Act, which legalized the nonsigner's clause in interstate commerce, in 1952.

If resale-price maintenance were effective, it would closely approximate horizontal price fixing. Supporters of fair-trade legislation have argued that such agreements protect consumers in the long run, because they prevent large firms from engaging in predatory pricing and driving out smaller competitors. The empirical validity of this assertion is quite doubtful. What fair-trade pricing does is to eliminate price competition at the retail level.

---

[62]The first such decision was *Dr. Miles Medical Company* v. *John D. Park and Sons Company,* 220 U.S. 373 (1911).

[63]*Schwegmann Brothers et al.* v. *Calvert Distillers Corporation,* 341 U.S. 384 (1951).

As such, it is of primary benefit to the retailers rather than the manufacturers. This point has been made with great skill by Telser, who pointed out that a manufacturer who sells goods to a retailer should ordinarily desire that retailer to sell those goods at the lowest possible prices, since it is the rapid sale of those goods that will cause the retailer to purchase more units from the manufacturer.[64] The maintenance of an excessively high price by the retailer will discourage sales and therefore reduce the sales of the manufacturer to the retailer. A possible exception to this rule is the case in which a manufacturer wants his product sold at high prices in order to stimulate the retailers to sell it in a comfortable and stylish locale and manner. This "Cadillac" argument assumes that high-priced goods are usually sold in luxurious surroundings. Even if fair-trade agreements were not effective in imposing conditions of sale upon the retailer, they could nevertheless prevent him from altering a product image carefully cultivated by a manufacturer, by prohibiting him from pricing that product as a loss leader in order to draw patrons into his establishment.

A truly effective fair-trade agreement accompanied by a nonsigner's clause would duplicate a one-price monopoly situation. Despite the existence of a mass of law enabling and sustaining fair-trade pricing, the welfare effects of fair trading have been minimal, because the laws are often ignored. Large retailing chains such as Kresge's K-Mart consistently undercut fair-trade prices specified by manufacturers and do so with relative impunity, because manufacturers do not wish to antagonize such a large customer and because competitor retail firms do not have the resources or the energy either to police adherence to fair-trade agreements or to undertake the long legal fight necessary to sustain any price agreement that has been broken. Further, as Telser has shown, it is not ordinarily in the best interest of the manufacturer to insist upon fair-trade legislation. Consequently, while fair trade pricing is obnoxious and potentially destructive to competition, it has never attained the status of a substantial empirical evil.[65]

TYING CONTRACTS, REQUIREMENTS CONTRACTS, AND EXCLUSIVE DEALING

Tying contracts, requirements contracts, and exclusive-dealing arrangements are types of market conduct that are often closely related to the pricing structure of a market. A tying contract is an agreement between buyer and seller that binds the buyer to purchase one or more products in

---

[64]Lester G. Telser, "Why Should Manufacturers Want Fair Trade?" *Journal of Law and Economics,* 3 (October 1960), 86–105.

[65]Extensive analysis of resale-price maintenance may be found in two volumes by Basil S. Yamey *Economics of Resale Price Maintenance* (London: Pitman and Company, 1966); and *Resale Price Maintenance* (Chicago: Aldine-Atherton, Inc., 1966).

addition to the product in which he is primarily interested. Tying arrangements typically amount to the statement, "I won't sell you good X unless you also buy good Y from me." In certain cases, the tying device results in a practice known as "full-line forcing," in which the purchaser must purchase an entire line of goods in order to be able to purchase one particular good in that line.[66]

There is a multiplicity of reasons that a firm might wish to impose a tying arrangement on its customers. Perhaps the foremost of these is a simple desire to increase profits. If the sale of two items is tied together (for example, as IBM computers and IBM computer cards were for many years), then it is possible for the firm, by means of tying devices, to increase the joint profits it realizes on the two items.[67] A second and similar stimulus for tying contracts is the leverage that such agreements provides.[68] A firm with market power in one market might use a tying agreement to increase its profits in another market, where it has little market power.[69]

Tying contracts have also been touted as a quality-control device. In the *Jerrold Electronics Case,* Jerrold was allowed to tie the sale of a five-year service contract to the sale of its community-antenna television systems.[70] The same decision, however, made it clear that such permission would not generally be granted, and that such tying arrangements would be frowned upon as the market matured and more suppliers became available. In a similar case, IBM was not allowed to tie the sale of its computer cards to the sale of its computers, and was even urged to introduce conditions into its leases that would require computer cards of a certain minimum quality to be used.[71]

Both Bowman and Burstein have suggested that tying devices may be a means for a firm to evade government price controls or the tacit controls of an oligopolistic market.[72] Assume that the price of good X is controlled either by government fiat, or practically, by oligopolistic coordination. A

---

[66]Meyer L. Burstein, "A Theory of Full-Line Forcing," *Northwestern University Law Review,* 55 (March–April 1960), 62–95; see also Burstein, "The Economics of Tie-In Sales," *Review of Economics and Statistics,* 42 (February 1960), 68–73.

[67]Martin J. Bailey has demonstrated this in "Price and Output Determination by a Firm Selling Related Products," *American Economic Review,* 44 (March 1954), 82–93. A possible example of this practice, according to George Stigler, is the block booking of movies. See Stigler, *The Organization of Industry* (Homewood, Ill.: Richard D. Irwin, Inc., 1968), pp. 165–70.

[68]The Supreme Court explicitly noted this motive in *Times-Picayune Publishing Company* v. *United States,* 345 U.S. 594, 611 (1953).

[69]Burstein, in "A Theory of Full-Line Forcing" and "The Economics of Tie-In Sales," and Ward S. Bowman, Jr., in "Tying Arrangements and the Leverage Problem," *Yale Law Journal,* 67 (November 1957), 19–36, have doubted the ability of a firm to extend its monopoly power into a tied market by means of a tying contract.

[70]*United States* v. *Jerrold Electronics Company,* 187 F. Supp. 545 (E.D. Pa., 1960), affirmed in 365 U.S. 567 (1961).

[71]*International Business Machines* v. *United States,* 298 U.S. 131 (1936). It should be noted, however, that this decision did not prevent IBM from maintaining well over 80 percent of the computer-card market until the late 1950's.

[72]Bowman, "Tying Arrangements"; Burstein, "A Theory of Full-Line Forcing"; and Burstein, "The Economics of Tie-In Sales."

firm may decide to tie the sale of good Y to the sale of good X if the price of good Y is not controlled as is the price of good X. Such an arrangement would allow the firm to price freely in market Y, thus avoiding the displeasure of government and competitors alike.

A tying contract may also provide the firm with a convenient means to engage in price discrimination.[73] The firm may tie the sale of one item (where there is no price discrimination) to the sale of another item (where price discrimination is readily evident). The profits of the firm may even be derived largely from the sale of the tied item (the item one is forced to buy in addition to the item desired).[74]

It is also possible that a tying contract can enable a firm to realize some economies of scale. An example is the *Times-Picayune Case*, involving the two major daily newspapers in the city of New Orleans.[75] The Times-Picayune Publishing Company owned and published both the *Times-Picayune*, a morning paper, and the *States*, an evening paper. Anyone who wished to advertise in one newspaper was forced to purchase advertising in both, probably because such an arrangement permitted the publishing company to avoid certain costs associated with typesetting for each edition. Although the arrangement clearly involved a tied sale, the Supreme Court nevertheless refused to halt the practice.

From an economic standpoint, tying devices are typically undesirable because they are usually an attempt (sometimes unsuccessful) to foreclose a portion of a market from competition and/or to earn economic rents. The status of the law seems to be clear on the issue. Section Three of the Clayton Act expressly forbids conditions, agreements, or understandings that would tie the sale of one good to the sale of another where the effect might be to substantially lessen competition or to tend to create a monopoly. As we have seen, however, the courts have not chosen to interpret Section Three of the Clayton Act as a prohibition per se against tying contracts. Extenuating circumstances have been given great weight in several decisions, with the end result that the decision decries tying contracts but nevertheless allows one or more of them to pass by unrestricted.

Requirements contracts are also limited under Section Three of the Clayton Act. A requirements contract is an arrangement whereby a retailer agrees to sell only the products of a single manufacturer. Failure to follow that practice results in the manufacturer's refusal to sell any units of the product to the retailer. The aim of the manufacturer in such an agreement is to guarantee himself a share of the market, and perhaps to increase his

---

[73]Burstein, "A Theory of Full-Line Forcing."

[74]Cases involving this include *Heaton Peninsular Button-Fastener Company* v. *Eureka Specialty Company*, 77 F. 288 (6th Cir. 1896) and *Henry* v. *A.B. Dick and Company*, 224 U.S. 1 (1912). Both these cases, however, were decided prior to the passage of the Clayton Act in 1914. Section Three of the Clayton Act contains language specifically limiting the legality of tying contracts.

[75]*Times-Picayune Publishing Company* v. *United States*, 345 U.S. 594, 611 (1953).

share at the expense of other producers when cooperating retailers stop handling their merchandise.

The legal status of requirements contracts is somewhat hazy. The courts have typically invalidated requirements contracts that involved a large share of a given market,[76] while at the same time permitting other requirements contracts of substantial import.[77] The courts appear to be following some version of a rule of reason, in which the key factors are market share and the fact that requirements contracts permit manufacturers to plan more efficiently.

The benefit of a requirements contract to a manufacturer is in the fact that the manufacturer thereby has foreclosed a portion of the market from competition and has reduced uncertainty as well. If only manufacturers benefited from requirements contracts, however, few such agreements would probably be reached, because requirements contracts clearly bar the retailer from selling products produced by other manufacturers. The carrot used to attract retailers into such a contractual agreement is often a franchise. The manufacturer may grant the retailer a franchise that effectively guarantees the retailer that only he will be allowed to vend the manufacturer's products in a given area. Few phenomena have proved to be as prolific as franchising. One need only venture onto any main thoroughfare to see a profusion of franchised establishments such as Colonel Sanders, Ford, Shakey's, Rexall, and so on. The franchisee is often willing to pay a high price for the privilege of owning a franchise, because simultaneously, he inherits a known product with an established name; he is given instruction and counsel in operating and selling techniques when necessary; and he has a guarantee of some force against the granting of a similar franchise by the manufacturer in the nearby geographic area.

Antitrust cases have frequently arisen as a result of situations where a franchisee begins to sell the products of more than one manufacturer and thereby violates the exclusive-dealing agreement or understanding between manufacturer and retailer. In the *Hudson Case,* the now-defunct Hudson Motor Company was allowed to refuse to renew a franchisee's contract on the ground that the dealer in question was simultaneously selling automobiles produced by manufacturers other than Hudson.[78] The fact that

---

[76]For example, *Standard Fashion Company* v. *Magrane-Houston Company,* 258 U.S. 346 (1922), involved a requirements contract that covered more than 40 percent of all the retail dress-pattern outlets in the United States. *Standard Oil of California and Standard Stations, Inc.* v. *United States,* 337 U.S. 293 (1949), involved a requirements contract that covered 16 percent of the gasoline stations in the western area of the United States. In both cases, the Supreme Court declared the requirements contract to be destructive of competition because of the large market share involved.

[77]In *United States* v. *J.I. Case Company,* 101 F. Supp 856 (1951), the district court allowed what clearly functioned as a requirements contract to stand, because J.I. Case controlled only 7 percent of the relevant market and because the court felt that competition was not damaged by the arrangement, which was never overt and written. The *Tampa Electric Case* revolved around a requirements contract that related to a large dollar amount of sales (almost $130 million), but that nevertheless amounted to only about 1 percent of the total market. The Supreme Court allowed this arrangement to stand. *Tampa Electric Company* v. *Nashville Coal Company,* 365 U.S. 320 (1961).

[78]*Hudson Sales Corporation* v. *Waldrip,* 211 F. 2d 268 (1954).

Hudson controlled an insignificant portion of the automobile market was apparently the controlling factor in this decision, since in other cases involving larger market shares, such refusals to deal were judged illegal.[79] Once again, the courts have seemed to apply a form of the rule of reason in reaching their conclusions. A close reading of the *Standard Stations Case* encourages both the viewpoint that undue coercion upon a franchisee by a manufacturer to sell only the manufacturer's products will not be tolerated, and the view that the courts will typically apply some form of the rule of reason to franchising and exclusive-dealing cases.[80]

Requirements contracts and franchises that force exclusive dealing upon a retail firm can both raise and lower barriers to entry. Entry barriers are raised for a specific differentiated product such as Colonel Sanders' Fried Chicken, since it is not to the benefit of the Colonel Sanders franchisers to grant an unlimited number of franchises in a given market area. A particular franchising agreement will often contain provisions that limit or bar absolutely the granting of further franchises in a given geographic area. Taking a broader view, however, franchising may reduce barriers to entry. Consider the market for fried chicken. The existence of a franchiser such as Chicken Delight, which is willing and even eager to compete with Colonel Sanders in a given area, may make entry into that market easy. Location, training, and even a considerable amount of capital may be supplied by the franchiser in order to attract a franchisee.

Many requirements contracts and exclusive-dealing arrangements that depend upon franchising are harmless from an economic standpoint. Such cases should properly fall under the aegis of a *de minimis* provision that effectively ignores insignificant violations of the law. Other such arrangements exist primarily to erect barriers to entry, to foreclose markets, and to limit competition. Both the intent of the arrangement and its effects must be taken into consideration in order to arrive at an economic judgment.

CARTELIZATION

A cartel is an organization of firms that makes agreements concerning the production process. The subject and coverage of these agreements are almost infinitely diverse, but most often center upon prices, outputs, market areas, use and construction of productive capacity, and advertising expenditures. Cartelization concerning prices is illegal per se in the United States, and most other forms of outright collusion over important market variables have been almost continuously invalidated by the courts.[81] Hence,

---

[79]*Englander Motors, Incorporated* v. *Ford Motor Corporation*, 267 F. 2d 11 (1959).

[80]*Standard Oil of California and Standard Stations, Inc.* v. *United States*, 337 U.S. 293 (1949).

[81]Exceptions may include the momentary approval of price fixing based upon "reasonableness" granted by the Supreme Court in *Appalachian Coals, Inc.* v. *United States*, 288 U.S. 344 (1933), and the partial approval given certain of the practices of the National Recovery Administration during the 1930's.

American cartels are secretive, loosely knit, and based upon supposed common interest, and any agreements that result are unrecognized and unenforceable by law. Cartelization in Europe, however, is often given the sanction of law and has therefore become a very common phenomenon there.

Cartelization arises out of a desire of firms to stabilize market shares or prices, reduce competition, make use of excess market productive capacity, and outline spheres of interest. The diverse interests of oligopolists are seldom common for long periods of time, however, and the duration of a cartel has been described as being "short and turbulent."[82] As we shall see, the very existence of a cartel provides the incentive for profitable cheating by the participants. It is nearly always profitable for one or more producers to violate secretly the cartel agreement. Any successful cartel must therefore have the ability to detect quickly any cheating, as well as to impose some kind of meaningful sanction upon the cheater. Cheating is easiest to detect when (1) the existence of a sale and its terms and conditions cannot be hidden and are immediately and widely known; (2) products are homogeneous;[83] (3) the cost structures of the firms involved are the same;[84] and (4) market areas or even specific customers have been designated. The application of sanctions is easiest when the force of government can be utilized in the sanction. For example, legal action can be taken to prevent a cheating firm from using a patent license. Although patent pools have a doubtful status legally, the implied threat of losing the right to utilize many patents possessed by other firms can be a powerful influence in promoting adherence to a cartel agreement.

It is sometimes difficult for students of industrial organization to visualize precisely how a well-organized and public cartel would behave, because most forms of cartelization are illegal inside the United States.[85] The economics of a centralized cartel and the reasons for its eventual demise are not difficult to understand, however. In a centralized cartel, there exist complete collusion and cooperation. We will simplify the analysis, but not distort the lessons to be learned, by assuming that the cartelized market has

[82]Charles E. Ferguson, *Microeconomic Theory*, 3rd ed. (Homewood, Ill.: Richard D. Irwin, Inc. 1972), p. 359.

[83]When products are highly differentiated, it is easier to justify and/or explain the appearance of a price aberration that might otherwise not be excused.

[84]Similar cost structures and similar pricing methods make it less difficult to ascertain if cheating is actually occurring. Similar cost structures will tend to result in similar price structures; when two firms ordinarily charge the same price for a given product, a sudden price cut by one of those firms will often become obvious as sales shift.

[85]The reader is referred to James V. Koch, "The Economics of 'Big-Time' Intercollegiate Athletics," *Social Science Quarterly*, 52 (September 1971), 248–60, for a discussion of cartelization in intercollegiate athletics. The National Collegiate Athletic Association, the organization of universities that regulates collegiate athletic competition, behaves in the same fashion as any cartel whose actions are not substantially circumscribed by law. The reader who is uninitiated in the area of cartelization will find this particular view of cartelization instructive. Readers who desire more extensive coverage should see George W. Stocking and M.W. Watkins, *Cartels in Action* (New York: Twentieth Century Fund, 1946); and John P. Miller, ed., *Competition, Cartels, and Their Regulation* (Amsterdam, Netherlands: North-Holland Publishing Company, 1962).

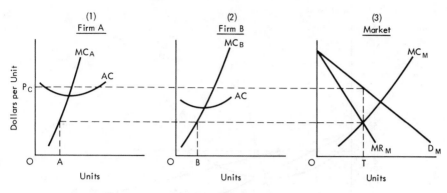

Figure 13.9

only two firms, which we label A and B. Firms A and B wish to collude in such a fashion that they maximize total profits earned in the market. The market-demand curve they face is labeled D_M in panel (3) of Figure 13.9. The firms possess different cost structures, as panels (1) and (2) indicate. The problem of profit maximization here is quite similar to the one facing a multiplant monopolist. Profits will be maximized when $MR_M = MC_M = MC_A = MC_B$. Each firm's production quota will be determined so that the marginal cost of producing a unit at either firm is the same. Such a strategy will minimize production costs as well. Figure 13.9 reveals that Firm A will produce A units, and Firm B will produce B units. Total market production will be T units.

The result presented in Figure 13.9 is not likely to be achieved in practice; the price, output, and profit decisions of most cartels are determined by the tug and pull of negotiation.[86] The more firms that exist in a market, the more heterogeneous their products, the greater the difference in cost conditions among firms, the more irregular and unpredictable demand is, the more depressed economic conditions are—the less likelihood there is that any mutually satisfactory agreement can be reached concerning important market variables such as prices, output, and profits.

We have already discussed the conditions under which cartel agreements will most likely endure, and we have also commented that there is a continual incentive for a member of the cartel to cheat. Figure 13.10 duplicates the cost apparatus of Firm A as found in panel (1) of Figure 13.9. Assume that Firm A faces demand curve AB in Figure 13.10 if it adopts a separate and independent pricing policy while Firm B continues to maintain the cartel price (P_C). Firm A will maximize its profits by equating its marginal cost with its marginal revenue. This will result in output Q_I and price P_I. Only a small price reduction is needed for Firm A to garner a considerable increase in sales (the increase being Q_I minus Q_C), because

[86]Bjarke Fog, "How Are Cartel Prices Determined?" *Journal of Industrial Economics,* 5 (November 1956), 16–23.

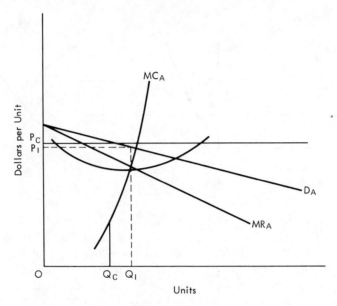

Figure 13.10

the demand curve facing any individual is considerably more price-elastic than the demand curve facing the entire market. Any price initiative below the cartel price, P_C, will be greeted with enthusiasm by customers, since it is the only alternative price available. Each individual firm is probably aware of this fact, and the increased sales and profits that a secretive independent price policy would bring are a constant incentive for individual firms to attempt to cheat.

Firm A, described in Figures 13.9 and 13.10, is not the low-cost firm in the cartel. The incentive for low-cost Firm B to cut prices may be considerably greater than that for Firm A. Firm B is the more efficient producer, and the cartel denies him the right to charge lower prices that would increase his sales and profits. Firm B can well afford to cut prices substantially, whereas Firm A can do so only to a limited extent. Cost differences such as those between Firms A and B are a major reason that many cartels are short-lived.

Since cartelization is not permissible in the United States, the frequency and duration of cartelization is considerably less than if legal approval had been given. The cartels about which we know most are therefore the ones from which the element of secrecy has been stripped. Certain international cartelization schemes may be openly participated in by American firms, under the terms of the Webb-Pomerene Act. One such cartel is the International Air Transport Association (IATA), a voluntary organization of airlines. The IATA claims in its membership nearly all the airlines that fly transatlantic routes. The IATA advises and solves problems for its members in the areas of finance, traffic, routes, schedules, and (almost inevitably) fares. It sponsors conferences at which transatlantic fares are discussed. If all participants agree on a given fare schedule, that schedule becomes binding upon all IATA members. When no agreement can be reached upon fares, members may price as they see fit. Substantial fines and penalties can be levied by the IATA against member airlines that violate fare agreements.

Certain airlines, notably Icelandic Airlines, are not members of the IATA. Icelandic has therefore pursued a predictable policy of pricing the seats on its flights well below the cartel price. Icelandic faces a price-elastic demand (similar to Firm A in Figure 13.10) and as a result has consistently been able to achieve higher load factors than the IATA airlines (load being the percent of seats occupied by paying customers). This has led to considerable grumbling inside the IATA and lobbying by some airlines for fare reductions. The cartel has responded by introducing more attractively priced charter and flight packages, and special youth and excursion fares. The progress has been slow, however, since unanimous approval of member airlines is necessary for each fare change or alteration. There is some indication recently that the price-fixing activities of the IATA may be severely limited or even terminated, because the self-interest of individual cartel members so dictates.

Trade associations such as the IATA are a convenient means (and sometimes a guise) for cartelization. Most trade associations in the United States disseminate legal, technical, financial, accounting, and market information to their members. For example, a trade association may dispense accounting advice in the form of recommended means of costing or pricing. When all firms follow such advice, parallel behavior can result that is similar to that of a cartel. Trade associations also provide the opportunity for their members to meet in order to discuss mutual problems. Such open and aboveboard meetings are a perfect setting for the formation of understandings and agreements that characterize collusion.

The role of trade associations has not escaped the attention of the Supreme Court. The first significant trade-association case to reach that body was the *Lumber Case* in 1921.[87] The American Hardwood Manufacturers Association operated what they termed an "open competition" plan. Those members who participated in the plan supplied to the association daily reports concerning their sales, prices, production, and stocks, submitting actual sales invoices to reduce the possibility of false reporting. These reports were then digested by the association and sent to each participating member. The effect of this information system was to discourage competitive pricing and market penetration, and also to make retaliation strong and organized. This particular arrangement was held to be illegal by the Supreme Court, although several subsequent trade-association cases

[87]*American Column and Lumber Company et al. v. United States,* 257 U.S. 377 (1921).

have resulted in approval for essentially similar informational schemes.[88] On the other hand, the more recent *Container Case* may have imposed stricter standards upon trade-association activities.[89]

The famous electrical-equipment price conspiracy is both an instructive and a fascinating example of cartel behavior.[90] Almost thirty manufacturers of electrical equipment were involved in the conspiracy, including such giants as General Electric and Westinghouse. Prices were fixed on items ranging from two-dollar insulators to huge turbine generators costing several million dollars.

The electrical-equipment price cartel operated in many different ways. Where standardized items were concerned, representatives of the firms would often meet and decide upon a common price structure. On other items, however, a common price would have aroused the suspicion of customers, since each prospective seller was required to submit bids (for example, when government was the purchaser). Hence, a system had to be devised that would rotate low bidders and do so in such a fashion as to maintain previously agreed-upon market shares for each firm. This required the development of complicated bidding systems in order to achieve the appearance of rigorous competition while at the same time predetermining the end result. One such scheme was the celebrated "phases of the moon" system used to develop bids for switchgears. Moon phases change each two weeks; when the moon phase designated one particular firm to be the low bidder, that firm would simply subtract a fixed percentage from a previously agreed-upon book price and thereby become the low bidder.

The electrical-equipment conspiracy was active for almost a decade during the 1950s, although the membership of the cartel sometimes varied. General Electric, for example, dropped out of the cartel and rejoined it as its interests seemed to dictate. A firm was sometimes a member of the cartel where one product was concerned, but not a member when the subject of discussion turned to other products. There is considerable evidence that cheating by cartel members was not uncommon; the departure of a member from the cartel was often caused by the reaction of the others to the discovery of its duplicity, or by that particular firm's anger over the cheating of others. Market shares were a constant source of bargaining and were often renegotiated as time passed.

The Antitrust Division of the Justice Department cracked the electrical-equipment pricing cartel in 1959. Fines were ultimately imposed upon the participant firms, and a series of consent decrees were signed by

[88]*Maple Flooring Manufacturers' Association* v. *United States*, 268 U.S. 563 (1925); *Sugar Institute* v. *United States*, 297 U.S. 553 (1936); *Tag Manufacturers Institute et al.* v. *Federal Trade Commission*, 194 F. 2d 452 (1st Cir., 1949).

[89]*United States* v. *Container Corporation of America et al.*, 273 F. Supp. 18 (1967), 393 U.S. 333 (1969).

[90]Extremely readable descriptions of the electrical-equipment price conspiracy may be found in Richard A. Smith, "The Incredible Electrical Equipment Price Conspiracy," Parts I and II, *Fortune*, 63 (April 1961), 132ff., and (May 1961), 161ff.

the ex-members, prohibiting them from similar activity in the future. Fines were also levied upon certain of the executives of the firms in the cartel. Judge Ganey of the Philadelphia District Court additionally took the almost unprecedented step of sending many of the guilty company executives to jail, thereby invoking a little-used legal penalty in cases involving collusion. Many of the individuals and firms that were victimized by the price fixing sued the guilty firms for "triple damages," as allowed under Section Seven of the Sherman Act. General Electric was reputed to have paid out over $225 million in such damages by late 1965.[91]

Cartelization seldom if ever benefits the consumer, even though cartel members sometimes attempt to rationalize the existence of restrictive arrangements by claiming welfare benefits owing to reduced uncertainty, increased price stability, and the removal of the excesses of cutthroat competition. Such benefits are unfortunately more imaginary than real, and the usual effect of a cartel is to increase prices, reduce output, and increase the profits of the participating firms. Hence, it is desirable that public policy be directed at discovering and eliminating cartels except in very special cases. It may plausibly be argued, however, that the worries of economists about cartelization are largely unnecessary, since few cartelized arrangements in the United States have ever exhibited much endurance. The conflict of interest among cartel members, the bickering over market shares and prices, and the ever-present incentive for a cartel member to cheat have made most cartels short-lived and substantially ineffective unless the arrangement has been given succor and assistance by government via grants of monopoly power.

SUMMARY

In this chapter we have centered our attention on applied aspects of oligopoly behavior. The diversity of the subjects covered reflects the nature of the oligopolistic phenomenon. A common thread in most issues surrounding oligopoly is a concern for the pricing process. Pricing was a recurring theme in the theoretical models surveyed in Chapter 12, and was once again of key importance when the applied aspects of oligopolistic conduct and performance were examined in this chapter.

Oligopolistic markets have often been criticized as being characterized by price inflexibility and price leadership. With respect to the price-inflexibility charge, the evidence is mixed, although the weight of the evidence indicates lessened price flexibility in oligopolistic markets. The quality of the evidence here has been clouded by methodological problems. Price leadership of various types is readily evident in many oligopolistic markets.

[91]"The High Cost of Price Fixing," *Time*, 86 (September 10, 1965), 82.

The price leader is sometimes the dominant firm (perhaps by virtue of size and/or efficiency), and sometimes a barometric firm that accurately reflects the needs of the firms in the market. In other cases, collusive price leadership is evident.

Basing-point pricing of the "Pittsburgh-plus-freight" variety has largely disappeared. In its place has arisen a host of multiple-basing-point pricing arrangements. Although these schemes reduce phantom freight and cross-hauling, such price structures still eliminate price competition among firms and are systematically discriminatory in nature. Discriminatory prices are prices that do not reflect the marginal costs of production and sale. Price discrimination is an extremely widespread practice, which cannot profitably exist unless (1) the discriminator possesses sufficient monopoly power to segment the market he faces, and (2) the market segments have differing price elasticities of demand. Even though price discrimination presupposes the existence of monopoly power, given the existence of irremovable imperfections in the economy, it may be the second-best solution in many circumstances.

Resale-price maintenance, also known as fair-trade pricing, involves an agreement between manufacturer and retailer concerning the prices the retailer may charge for the manufacturer's goods. When effective, it can approximate monopoly pricing at the retail level. Resale-price maintenance has not been effectively enforced, however, and therefore has had little chance to reduce consumer welfare.

Tying contracts, requirements contracts, and exclusive dealing are all arrangements between firms and their customers, designed to reduce competition in a particular market. Tying contracts attempt to force a purchaser to buy one product if he wishes to purchase another product; requirements contracts attempt to force a retailer to purchase given quantities of his goods (or even all his goods) from one manufacturer. The incentive for the retailer to engage in exclusive dealing is often a franchise that may carry with it an already-differentiated product, production know-how, and protection against entry by new competitors.

A cartel is an organization of firms that collusively decides upon prices, outputs, market shares, profits, and any other market variables of interest. Cartels are neither common nor extremely effective in the United States, possibly because of antitrust prosecution. It may be, however, that the real reason for the short life of American cartels and their seeming impotence is the fact that cartel members seldom if ever have common interests for long periods of time. Cartel agreements are not likely to endure if the agreement is injurious to one or more firms in the cartel. In any case, self-interests change over time, and cartels seldom possess stability. The incentive for one cartel member to cheat upon the others for the sake of increased profitability is always present.

PROBLEMS

1.   A November 1972 issue of the *Wall Street Journal* revealed that Kodak, the producer of film and cameras, is once again being accused of cutting prices on its cameras, with the expectation that it will easily make up the difference on the sales of its film. Under what circumstances can this be true?

2.   The Bureau of Labor Statistics has reported that the publicly published chemical-price quotations are altered only infrequently. Can we conclude from such data that prices are in fact rigid in the area of chemicals?

3.   For many years, distributors of motion pictures practiced "block booking." That is, they forced motion-picture theaters to book groups of films, some of which were desirable, and others of which were not. In order to be able to book the desirable films, one had to accept and pay for the less-desirable films. Under what circumstances will such a policy be profit maximizing for the distributors?

4.   The Potrzebie Manufacturing Company (PMC) is cutting prices in one market and raising them in other markets. The market in which the prices are being cut is characterized by a rising share of the total market sales for PMC. Is such pricing predatory?

5.   "Competition is at its perfection when all the sellers in a market must charge the same price. Hence, basing-point pricing, rather than being anticompetitive, actually approaches perfect competition." Comment.

6.   Lincoln Continental automobiles are priced higher than Ford Mustangs. One possible reason for this is the fact that the value of the inputs used to produce Continentals is considerably greater than the value of the inputs used to produce Mustangs. However, the markup of price over costs of production is also higher for Continentals than for Mustangs. Can you explain this?

14

A Brief Look at Regulation

Markets in which economic activity is actively regulated by government commissions are not the primary focus of this book. Such markets are by themselves a subject for legitimate study and concern. Regulated markets are nevertheless of direct interest to the student of industrial organization, because one often hears the contention that certain industrial markets should be subjected to regulation on account of present or anticipated departures from what is deemed to be desirable conduct or performance. Hence, our concern over market power (and what to do about it) would be quite incomplete if we did not at least briefly survey the regulatory policy option that is available. Fortunately, regulatory economics is yet another applied branch of price theory. Most of the same tools and concepts we have been using thus far have direct relevance to regulatory economics and therefore need not be discarded.

The scope and impact of economic regulation is not insignificant. As Table 14.1 indicates, over 7 percent of the national income generated by

TABLE 14.1

Amount and Percent of National Income Originating in Regulated Sectors of the Economy, 1969

Sector	National Income, 1969 (billions)	Percent of National Income, 1969
Transportation	$29.182	3.80
Motor Carriers	11.252	1.46
Railroads	7.360	.95
Air Carriers	4.415	.57
Water Carriers	2.582	.33
Local Carriers	2.235	.29
Transport Services	1.086	.14
Pipelines	.520	.06
Communications	15.920	2.06
Utilities	14.170	1.84
Total, Regulated Sectors	59.272	7.70

Source: Survey of Current Business, 50 (July 1970), 21.

the economic system originates in regulated sectors. Moreover, it does not seem likely that present regulatory coverage will narrow in the future, because popular opinion (in contrast to the views of a large number of economists) seems to favor a considerable extension and escalation of economic regulation. It therefore seems prudent to acquire a very basic understanding of regulatory economics.

THE WHAT AND WHO OF REGULATION

Although any law or rule might easily qualify as government regulation of economic activity, economic regulation as used here refers to the comprehensive rules, instructions, procedures, and attention that a governmental regulatory commission imposes upon a certain market. The regulatory commission often has statutory power to regulate and control nearly every significant economic variable, including price, quantity, safety, quality, firm size, market areas, and even the right to go out of business.

Regulation in the United States is typically carried out within a functional framework. Commissions undertake detailed regulation of economic activity in a given market on the basis of broadly worded legislation. The earliest regulatory commission, the Interstate Commerce Commission (ICC), was founded in the year 1887. The ICC regulates interstate rail, truck, and water transportation. In a similar fashion, there exist the Federal Power Commission (FPC), the Federal Communications Commission (FCC), and the Civil Aeronautics Board (CAB). A broader definition of regulation than that implied by Table 14.1 would also consider the Federal Reserve Board, the Federal Home Loan Bank Board, the Securities and Exchange Commission, the Federal Insurance Deposit Corporation, the Federal Savings and Loan Insurance Corporation, and the Office of the Comptroller of the Currency to be regulatory agencies.

The constitutional basis for economic regulation is contained in Article I, Section 8, of the U.S. Constitution, which gives Congress the power "...to regulate Commerce...among the several States...." Congress in its lawmaking, and the Supreme Court in its interpretations of the law, have interpreted this constitutional proviso very broadly. In the *Wolff Packing Company Case,* Chief Justice Taft argued:

> Property does become clothed with a public interest when used in a manner to make it of public consequence, and affect the community at large. When, therefore, one devotes his property to a use in which the public has an interest, he, in effect, grants to the public an interest in that use, and must submit to be controlled by the public for the common good....[1]

[1] *Wolff Packing Company v. Court of Industrial Relations,* 262 U.S. 522, 538–9 (1923).

The domain of public regulation is therefore almost infinite as far as the courts are concerned.

WHY REGULATE?

Markets have been subjected to economic regulation for four major reasons: (1) when a "natural" monopoly exists; (2) when there is need to conserve a natural resource that is publicly owned; (3) when the structure of a market is conducive to market conduct that sparks public indignation (for example, discriminatory price structures); or (4) where there is a desire among some to dilute or control large power blocs in the economy.

The natural-monopoly argument can be translated into price-theory terms with some ease. Figure 14.1 illustrates a firm that faces continually falling long-run average and marginal costs. As a result, there is a powerful incentive for that firm to expand its output, because output expansion brings with it lower unit costs. One cause of lower average unit costs is the fact that many natural-monopoly markets are characterized by high capital intensity and a high ratio of fixed to variable costs. Output expansion spreads the fixed element of costs over more and more units. Hence, as long as the marginal cost per unit is not rising rapidly, average cost per unit will fall. If demand is present at reasonable prices, the firm in Figure 14.1 will expand its output. Economic efficiency will eventually dictate that only one

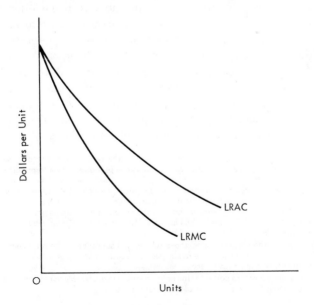

Figure 14.1

firm exist in that market, because the existence of two or more firms would cause each firm to realize higher unit costs than would be realized by a single firm. The rationale for regulating public utilities that provide electrical, water, gas, and telephone service is often couched in terms of the inevitability of a natural monopoly or the implied requirement of economic efficiency that only one firm exist.

A second major reason that markets are regulated is the desire of society to conserve and efficiently use scarce resources.[2] Certain natural resources, such as the radio spectrum, are found only in limited quantities. Further, in the absence of regulation, a zero private price would be attached to the use of the radio spectrum, since it would be a free, although limited, good. At a zero price, the radio spectrum might well be overused, or perhaps used in a less-than-optimal fashion. Hence, in order to increase social benefit, the use of the radio spectrum is regulated, and the right to use it is licensed. Presumably, licenses are granted to those applicants whose proposed use of the radio spectrum would maximize social welfare.[3] The conservation motive is present in much licensing in the field of communications, and also, to a lesser extent, in natural-resource regulation of commodities such as natural gas, oil, water, and electricity.

A regulatory agency such as the FCC grants only a limited number of licenses, and each gives the recipient the right to utilize only a particular portion of the radio spectrum. Once a license has been granted, FCC policy has usually been to renew that license unless obvious harm to economic welfare would result. The license has therefore assumed the stature of a semipermanent monopoly grant. In reaction to this, it has often been suggested that the FCC periodically allow the market to function in the licensing process by auctioning off portions of the available spectrum to the highest bidders. This suggestion is aimed at reducing the economic rents being earned by the monopolist licensees and instead transferring those economic rents to the public treasury.[4] Successful bidders might still be subject to other regulations with respect to their use of the radio spectrum —for example, the length and content of their programming.

A third reason for the introduction of regulation is the existence of

[2]It can be plausibly argued, however, that regulation of this type is not meant to conserve resources. Rather, it is championed by power blocs that wish to foreclose part of a market from competition and to limit entry into that market. In this view, the regulatory process is manipulatable by private interests for their own benefit. An increasing body of economists now subscribes at least partially to this view. For example, a well-known business textbook on government regulation describes the possibility that "a commission is systematically transformed from a vigorous protector of the public interest into an organization captured by the interests being regulated." Charles F. Phillips, Jr., *The Economics of Regulation* (Homewood, Ill.: Richard D. Irwin, Inc., 1969), p. 700.

[3]Although this is the ostensible aim, those who would subscribe to the sentiments voiced in the preceding footnote argue that the use of the radio spectrum (or the granting of television licenses) reflects political power rather than concern with economic welfare.

[4]The successful bidder for a portion of the radio spectrum might be able to pass on the cost of obtaining it to advertisers and others who seek to use the radio spectrum.

an obviously discriminatory pricing structure. Firms in certain markets (railroads, for example) have a very high ratio of fixed to variable costs. This type of cost structure frequently encouraged price-cutting orgies by the railroads in the nineteenth century, because they would lose only their small variable costs when they indulged in price cutting. The price cutting was often done selectively and did not include all customers or all products. Small customers did not benefit from the price wars as often as did large customers, because the promise of gain to the price cutter was less where the small customers were concerned.

The establishment of the ICC was a reaction to the seeming monopoly position of the railroads, as well as to their blatantly discriminatory price structures. The ICC pressured the railroads into a more uniform price structure, largely eliminated their ability to engage in price wars, and noticeably lessened the amount and degree of price discrimination against small customers. It has traditionally been assumed that this imposition of regulation was met with considerable disfavor by the railroads, but this interpretation has recently been challenged by those revisionists who have argued that the railroads secretly welcomed regulation as a means of eliminating "ruinous" price competition, and that the ICC protected the railroads from themselves by accomplishing a reduction in price competition that the railroads themselves could not achieve.[5]

In retrospect, it is highly doubtful that the price competition carried out by the railroads was economically ruinous to many of them, or even to many customers. The major impetus for regulation of the railroads seems to have been contained in a normative concept of a "just" price structure. Drawing upon economic thought that dates back at least to the Scholastics,[6] the just-price concept evidenced itself in the moral judgment that the discriminatory pricing structures of the railroads were morally indefensible.

A fourth thread found in proposals to impose regulation upon markets is a libertarian distrust of accumulated power, whether political or economic in character. Such an attitude may result in regulation even when the actual behavior of the firms in the market fails to be noteworthy. It is probable that the strategic position of firms that provide water, electric, gas, and telephone service, and the potential of these utilities to impose their economic will upon the public in the short run, would result in economic regulation even if the behavior of the firms supplying such services were beyond reproach. The potential for the exercise of market power has often been as important a stimulus to regulation and government ownership as has the actual exercise of that market power.

[5]An example of this train of thought is Gabriel Kolko, *Railroads and Regulation* (Princeton, N.J.: Princeton University Press, 1965).

[6]The Scholastics were medieval professors and men of science. See, for example, Joseph A. Schumpeter, *History of Economic Analysis* (New York: Oxford University Press, Inc., 1954), Chap. 2.

REGULATORY STRATEGIES

At least three identifiable regulatory strategies have been used or suggested with frequency. They are (1) the regulation of pricing such that price equals marginal cost $(P = MC)$, (2) the acceptance and promotion of discriminatory pricing structures as a means to the survival of the firm and economic efficiency, and (3) the concentration upon the rate base and the rate of return earned by the regulated firm. These strategies are not mutually exclusive. For example, the fact that a regulatory commission chooses to focus upon the rate base and the rate of return earned by the firms it regulates is consistent with either the presence or the absence of a discriminatory pricing structure.

Marginal-Cost Pricing

The price-equals-marginal-cost strategy occupies an old and honorable position in regulatory economics, even though it has seldom been implemented inside the United States.[7] Price equals marginal cost was commended to the reader as a welfare criterion in Chapter 2. Early work performed by Dupuit and work of a more recent vintage by Hotelling are the theoretical basis for the idea that $P = MC$ is a usable and economically efficient approach to pricing in public utilities.[8] Discussion of the $P = MC$ criterion has been lengthy and vigorous since Hotelling's contribution. From that discussion has emerged a better understanding of some of the difficulties that might arise if $P = MC$ pricing were imposed upon regulated firms, as well as an interesting new discussion of possible optimal departures from marginal-cost pricing.[9]

Marginal-cost price regulation might ideally operate in a fashion such as that indicated in Figure 14.2. The firm in Figure 14.2 possesses some monopoly power, and would in the absence of regulation maximize profits by producing price–output combination P_M, Q_M. If, however, the firm is forced to price such that $P = MC$, then it will maximize profits with price–output combination P_R, Q_R. Economic rents (pure profits) per unit are reduced from AB to CD; further, price is lowered and quantity produced is increased. Several caveats need to be introduced before the result of Figure 14.2 is accepted, however. It can be seen that the firm whose price

---

[7]$P = MC$ pricing may be used most often in the United States as a guide to minimum rates rather than as a guide to the appropriate rate. $P = MC$ has, however, gained more attention and use in Europe.

[8]Jules Dupuit, "On the Measurement of Public Works," translated, *International Economic Papers*, No. 2 (London: Macmillan & Company, Limited, 1952), pp. 83–110; and Harold Hotelling, "The General Welfare in Relation to Problems of Taxation and Railway and Utility Rates," *Econometrica*, 6 (July 1938), 242–69.

[9]An example is William J. Baumol and David J. Bradford, "Optimal Departures from Marginal Cost Pricing," *American Economic Review*, 60 (June 1970), 265–83.

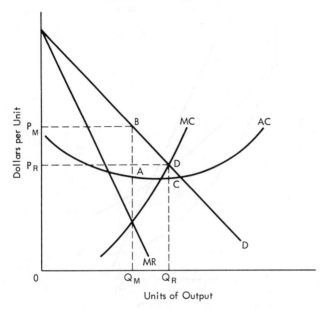

Figure 14.2

is thus regulated is forced by regulation to choose a greater-than-optimal scale from the standpoint of society. That is, the firm's scale is greater than the one that a perfect competitor would choose—namely, that scale where the lowest point on the average-cost curve is at the intersection of the marginal-cost and average-cost curves.[10] Additionally, there is the possibility that the firm described in Figure 14.2 might react to regulation by altering such things as product quality, or, as we shall shortly see, be tempted to change the size of its rate base in order to defend its previous level of profits. Finally, in many regulated markets, the cost curves of the firms do not assume the orthodox shapes presented in Figure 14.2. Instead, both marginal and average costs per unit may decline in the long run. This introduces a major complication into $P = MC$ pricing, and is deserving of further consideration.

One of the foremost objections to $P = MC$ rate making has been the contention that if such a pricing technique were imposed upon a firm that is realizing decreasing long-run unit costs, either that firm would be driven to the wall by recurring losses, or the public would be forced to subsidize it to avoid its disappearance. This argument is illustrated in Figure 14.3. The firm in Figure 14.3 enjoys declining long-run average and marginal costs per unit. If $P = MC$ were imposed, the regulated price–quantity combination would be P_1, Q_1, and a loss per unit of AB would be experi-

---

[10]The utilization of the scale is also slightly greater than optimal.

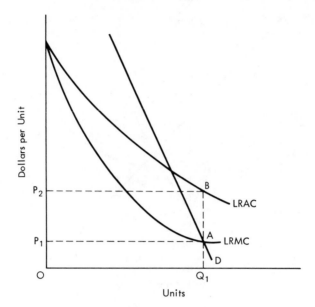

Figure 14.3

enced by the firm. A firm could not sustain such losses in the long run and therefore must be subsidized by amount *AB* per unit if marginal-cost pricing is desired.

The subsidization of firms, and even of whole markets, is not unheard of in American industry. The airlines and water carriers are examples in point. Yet the existence of a welfare transfer in the form of a subsidy is necessarily accompanied by the questions of where the funds for the subsidy came from, how they were raised, and the income-distributional consequences of the fund raising and subsidy. Subsidization, then, evokes substantial questions of equity and is a very dense political thicket.

Marginal-cost pricing has been attacked on still other grounds. One is that $P = MC$ pricing will not allow firms to cover their fixed costs, because all marginal costs are variable in nature. Although this may be true in the case where the unit-cost curves are declining in the long run, it is not true when the unit-cost curves are not declining and a long-run viewpoint is taken.[11] In the long run, all costs are variable, and $P = MC$ pricing need not doom the firm to losses.[12]

Any pricing rule, including marginal-cost pricing, suffers when applied widely, because of the nonconformity of real-world situations to a general

[11]Somewhat facetiously, one might ask if a firm ever operates in the long run. See William J. Baumol et al., "The Role of Cost in the Minimum Pricing of Railroad Services," *Journal of Business*, 35 (October 1962), 357–66.

[12]William G. Shepherd, "Marginal Cost Pricing in American Utilities," *Southern Economic Journal*, 23 (July 1966), 59–70.

rule. Joint costs, for example, are frequently a stumbling block to the implementation of pricing of any kind. The allocation of costs such as electricity and insurance to each product produced in a large multiproduct factory is often arbitrary. Multiplant firms may find it difficult to assign common costs to particular plants or products. Indivisibilities of both inputs and outputs also have the potential to confound the determination of any cost concept, including marginal cost. Still further complications to rational pricing are added when one admits to the possibility of a time dimension in production, which necessitates discounting. The need to make some sort of allowance for the appearance of risk and uncertainty is also a challenge to the perfect-certainty models we have developed. Finally, as our discussion of price discrimination in Chapter 13 indicated, certain departures from competitive optimality (and $P = MC$) may be advisable, in that they are "second-best" solutions and are welfare maximizing in an already imperfect world.

Troxel was clearly not too far wide of the mark when he argued that the imposition of marginal-cost pricing in utility regulation would result in "a general upheaval in utility rate-making."[13] In view of the sometimes incompetent and inefficient regulation churned out by many of the regulatory commissions, there is much to be said for some kind of upheaval. Major strides toward marginal-cost pricing would be desirable in a large number of cases. Nevertheless, marginal-cost pricing in regulated markets is not singularly appropriate. In any case, the current regulatory milieu is vulnerable to immediate and substantial improvement in a host of other areas by far less earthshaking means.[14]

Approval of Price Discrimination

Our work in Chapter 13 demonstrated that circumstances exist in which price discrimination can (1) permit the survival of the firm, when a nondiscriminatory pricing structure would result either in its disappearance or the need to subsidize it; (2) increase output and consumption; and (3) increase the utilization of the productive capacity of firms. It should be apparent that a completely rational regulatory strategy might condone and even encourage certain forms of price discrimination as approximating a "second-best" solution. (Utilities are often allowed second-degree price discrimination; railroads and motor carriers, third-degree.) Despite this fact, the existence of price discrimination does not guarantee that survival, output, and utilization of capacity goals will be realized. Price discrimination need not promote competition and technological progress. Further, a discriminatory price structure may stimulate regulated firms to toy with

---

[13]Emory Troxel, *Economics of Public Utilities* (New York: Holt, Rinehart & Winston, Inc., 1947), p. 463.

[14]A simple introduction and approval of competition between firms and modes would by itself have important salutary effects.

their rate bases in order to adjust their profits and earnings in the light of the price structure allowed them. We turn next to this possibility.

Control of Rate Base and Rate of Return

The rate base of a regulated company is the value assigned to the property of that company by the regulatory commission. The rate of return allowed by the regulatory commission is stated as some percent of the rate base. A rate base of $100 and an allowed rate of return of 6 percent will generate as much profit as a rate base of $120 and an allowed rate of return of 5 percent. It is understandable, therefore, that regulated firms and regulatory commissions do constant battle over the question of the proper rate base and of the proper rate of return.

Two concepts of what the rate base of a regulated firm should be have dominated the thoughts of regulators. The first view considers the rate base to be equal to the current reproduction cost of the firm's assets; the second, the historically incurred or original cost of the firm's assets, minus accumulated depreciation. The second view has predominated ever since the decision of the Supreme Court in the *Hope Case*.[15]

No court decision is capable of instructing regulators how to determine which assets the regulated firms should be allowed to count in their rate base, or how to specify the correct method of depreciation. Regulated firms will generally press for inclusion in their rate base of the widest possible range of items. The regulators must decide if items such as deposits and monies advanced by customers, property soon to be abandoned by the firm, the value of water rights, the value of patents, and property used for non-utility purposes may be included in the rate base. Further, the method of depreciating assets allowed in it can substantially alter the size of the rate base. Suffice it to say that both the determination of what items may be included in the rate base and the method of depreciating those assets may be chosen by the regulated firm for devious reasons and/or arbitrarily imposed by the regulatory commission for essentially noneconomic reasons.

There is no "correct" way to determine either the rate base or the method of depreciation. The Supreme Court has cryptically advised regulators to allow a "fair return upon...the fair value of the property being used."[16] In the same decision, the Court also cautioned regulatory commissions to take into account (1) risk and uncertainty, (2) current economic conditions, (3) the cost of obtaining capital, (4) the alternative uses of capital, (5) the financial structure and history of the firm, and (6) the competence and efficiency of management. Predictably, however, the Court was not so daring as to suggest the precise role or even the approximate importance or relationship of the factors mentioned.

[15]*Federal Power Commission* v. *Hope Natural Gas Company*, 320 U.S. 591 (1944).
[16]*Smith* v. *Ames et al.*, 169 U.S. 466, 546–7 (1898).

Even when a regulatory commission boldly decides upon a given method of determining the rate base and forms the opinion that a certain rate of return should be allowed, its wishes may not be carried out. Complicated accounting procedures and the bureaucracy of regulatory commissions can frustrate forthright and intelligent decisions, as well as those of a timorous and ignorant nature. The allowable rate of return must always be considered in relation to the allowed rate base; the actual rate of return earned by the utility may therefore vary significantly from the allowed rate of return. The tangled interplay of these factors was fully demonstrated in the long and involved investigation of the American Telephone and Telegraph Company (AT&T) in the middle of the 1960's.[17]

HOW WELL HAS REGULATION WORKED?

It would be incorrect to classify economic regulation as a disaster. It would, however, be doubly incorrect to label the American regulatory experience a success. Regulation has all too often had the end result of protecting monopoly power and discouraging competition. Regulatory commissions such as the ICC have consistently frowned upon price competition within modes of transportation as well as between modes of transportation. Walter Adams has caustically charged:

> ...regulation breeds regulation. Competition, even at the margin, is a source of disturbance, annoyance, and embarrassment to the bureaucracy. By providing a yardstick for performance, an outlet for innovation, and a laboratory for experiment, competition subverts the orthodox conformity prescribed by the regulatory establishment. It undermines the static, conservative, and unimaginative scheme of bureaucratic controls, and erodes the artificial values created by protective restrictionism. From the regulator's point of view, therefore, competition must be suppressed wherever it arises.[18]

The need for regulation has largely been eliminated in some markets, owing to technological change and the emergence of new competitors. The ICC was formed to protect the public from abuses perpetrated by the railroads. It has been clear for some time, however, that the monopoly position of the railroads has been substantially eroded, to the point where some railroads are fighting for their survival. Railroads now face intermodal competition from motor carriers, water carriers, and airlines. The ICC's response, unfortunately, has been to structure the competitive interface

---

[17]*Re American Telephone and Telegraph Company et al.,* 70, *Public Utilities Reports* (3rd Series), 129, 158, 160, 196 (Federal Communications Commission, 1967).

[18]Walter Adams, "Business Exemptions from the Antitrust Laws: Their Extent and Rationale," in Almarin Phillips, ed., *Perspectives on Antitrust Policy* (Princeton, N.J.: Princeton University Press, 1965), p. 283.

among the modes of transportation and the rate structure in such a way as to either eliminate competition or force the most inefficient carrier to handle a certain type of job. For example, one study of intermodal transport competition found that motor carriers were forced to handle goods on long hauls, when their most efficient usage would have dictated local or metropolitan hauls.[19] Wilcox, a noted authority on regulated markets, has commented that "regulation is a pallid substitute for competition."[20] This lesson seems to have eluded commissions that regulate markets such as transportation and communications, and even semiregulated markets such as banking.

The preceding indictment of economic regulation does not imply that competition would eliminate the need for all regulation. The existence of bona fide natural monopolies such as are often found in public utilities does require either regulation or public ownership. Rather, the criticism is a call for the introduction and extension of competition wherever possible. Regulatory commissions that were formed to protect the public from certain firms have with disturbing frequency subsequently assumed the role of protecting and assisting the regulated firms. The preempting of a regulatory commission by the firm or market it purports to regulate is an unfortunate theme that emerges from a study of the regulatory process.[21]

The regulatory commissions have become notorious for the profusion and complexity of their regulatory dictums. Supreme Court Justice Black once likened a decision of the ICC to something written in Sanskrit.[22] Moreover, the time lag in decision making has grown until years and even decades may separate a request for a decision and the final regulatory response on that matter. The FPC announced in 1960 that it would take until 2043 A.D. for the FPC to catch up with its current and projected case load, even if its staff were tripled.[23] Regulatory delay hampers resource allocation by preventing deserving consumers and firms from realizing their needs. New technologies are not introduced, rates are not lowered or raised when needed, and the expense of litigation is increased.

A crucial question in regulatory economics is whether regulation really makes a difference. That is, would an unregulated market or firm behave in essentially the same fashion as a regulated firm, or are observable differences in behavior apparent? This is a very difficult question to answer

[19]John R. Meyer, Merton J. Peck, John Stenason, and Charles Zwick, *The Economics of Competition in the Transportation Industries* (Cambridge, Mass.: Harvard University Press, 1959).

[20]Clair Wilcox, *Public Policies Toward Business*, 3rd ed. (Homewood, Ill.: Richard D. Irwin, Inc., 1966), p. 476.

[21]Blair has commented that "the attitude of a regulatory agency toward the industry under its jurisdiction undergoes a metamorphosis, changing gradually from initial hostility to a spirit of accommodation, and finally to protective concern with the industry's well-being." John M. Blair, *Economic Concentration: Structure, Behavior and Public Policy* (New York: Harcourt Brace Jovanovich, 1972), p. 401.

[22]*Chicago and Eastern Railroad v. United States*, 375 U.S. 150, 154 (1963).

[23]James Landis, *Report on the Regulatory Agencies to the President-Elect* (Washington, D.C.: U.S. Government Printing Office, 1960), pp. 5–6.

for two reasons. First, to what does one properly compare the performance of a utility such as a water company? Nearly all water companies of even moderate size are either owned or regulated by the public. Hence, a comparison between regulated and nonregulated water companies is impossible. Second, a methodologically correct study should attempt to hold outside influences constant, so that only the effects of regulation are being evaluated. This need presents considerable, although not insurmountable, statistical problems.

Three major thrusts have been made in the area of determining the efficiency of regulated firms and markets. The first study was performed by Stigler and Friedland, who attempted to ascertain if regulated electric-power companies behaved in a materially different fashion from their unregulated counterparts.[24] Presumably, economic regulation might be expected to result in lower prices and in larger quantities being consumed. Stigler and Friedland found no evidence of this during the time period 1912–37.[25] They concluded that the individual electric-power company did not possess a significant amount of market power in the long run and that regulatory commissions were seemingly unable to prevent the power companies from adjusting price, output, cost, or quality by a particular regulative order. One reason for this, of course, could be the fact that many regulatory actions are invalid or irrelevant by the time they become effective because of the previously noted time lag.

A related type of study has attempted to compare the relative efficiency of operation of regulated firms. Since, as Stigler and Friedland discovered, there are very few unregulated firms in most regulated markets, it is often impossible to compare in a meaningful fashion the efficiency of regulated and unregulated firms. Hence, it is frequently necessary to evaluate the performance of regulated firms in terms of themselves. An example in point is work performed by Iulo concerning the unit costs of production of a large number of electric-utility firms.[26] Iulo attempted to control a host of outside influences that differentiate the electric-power market of New York City from that of Morton, Illinois. He was able to rank the firms in his sample in terms of their relative efficiency. Even though such information will not tell us whether regulation itself is proceding efficiently, it does serve as a strong basis for evaluating the claims of regulated firms to efficient operation when they request rate changes and the like. The rewarding of efficient utilities and the penalizing of inefficient utilities would be a

[24]George J. Stigler and Clair Friedland, "What Can Regulators Regulate? The Case of Electricity," *Journal of Law and Economics*, 5 (October 1962), 1–16.

[25]By 1937, fully 39 states had established regulatory commissions. Hence, beyond that year, the legitimacy of comparison dwindled.

[26]William Iulo, *Electric Utilities—Costs and Performance* (Pullman, Wash.: Washington University Press, 1961); and Iulo, "The Relative Performance of Individual Electric Utilities," *Land Economics*, 38 (November 1962), 315–26.

noticeable improvement in regulation. Studies of the type noted here provide the means necessary for the implementation of such a policy.

The efficacy and ultimate effects of economic regulation have also been challenged in recent years by what has become popularly known as the Averch–Johnson hypothesis.[27] Averch and Johnson stimulated a plethora of studies and articles[28] when they contended that economic regulation often causes regulated firms to overinvest and use excessive amounts of capital. They contended:

> If the rate of return allowed by the regulatory agency is greater than the cost of capital but less than the rate of return that would be enjoyed by the firm were it free to maximize profit without regulatory constraint, then the firm will substitute capital for the other factor of production and operate at an output where cost is not minimized.[29]

The empirical predictions of the Averch–Johnson model are (1) an excessive widening of the rate base by inefficient purchases of capital, and (2) higher rates. The regulatory authorities, Averch and Johnson argued, could reduce or eliminate these undesirable effects by equating the allowable rate of return to the cost of capital.

It may be very difficult for any regulatory body to set the allowable rate of return equal to the cost of capital. The cost of capital varies over time, as well as among firms and particular projects. In point of fact, there is no single cost of capital. Additionally, if the regulatory body mistakenly placed the allowable rate of return below the current cost of capital, then in order for the regulated firm to raise capital, it might be forced to sell its stock at lower prices. A fall in the price of the regulated firm's stock, representing a capital loss to investors holding that stock, would be unpopular and would result in pressure upon the regulatory commission to mend its ways. All things considered, the cost of capital may frequently be below the allowable rate of return, which in turn will typically be less than the rate of return that the regulated firm would have realized in the absence of regulation. Unable to maximize profits, the firm will use available funds to expand its rate base. The resulting factor-input ratio is inefficient and not cost minimizing.

The Averch–Johnson hypothesis clearly requires the condition that the cost of capital be less than the allowable rate of return, which in turn

[27]Harvey Averch and Leland L. Johnson, "Behavior of the Firm Under Regulatory Constraint," *American Economic Review*, 52 (December 1962), 1052–69.

[28]The earliest and most prominent contributions were made by Stanislaw H. Wellicz, "Regulation of Natural Pipeline Companies: An Economic Analysis," *Journal of Political Economy*, 71 (February 1963), 30–43; Fred M. Westfield, "Regulation and Conspiracy," *American Economic Review*, 55 (June 1965), 424–43; Alvin K. Klevorick, "The Graduated Fair Return: A Regulatory Proposal," *American Economic Review*, 56 (June 1966), 477–84; and Shepherd, "Marginal Cost Pricing," *op. cit.*

[29]Averch and Johnson, "Behavior of the Firm," pp. 1052–53.

must be less than the profit-maximizing rate of return in the absence of regulation. This may frequently be the case, but it is not always so. Further, it is possible that the regulatory lag discussed earlier may largely cancel the effects of the Averch–Johnson phenomenon. The regulated firm will not be able to have the allowable rate of return adjusted in sufficient time to exercise the type of rate-base expansion predicted. This latter argument has two edges, however. The same regulatory lag that may prevent the Averch–Johnson hypothesis from becoming empirically valid can also lock a regulated firm into rate-base expansion that it would not otherwise undertake.

The Averch–Johnson thesis appears to have only selective empirical validity. It does not seem to be a valid explanation of the behavior of railroads and some utilities. It does, however, seem to explain the behavior of regulated firms such as AT&T. The evidence in support of the hypothesis is strongest when it relates to a circumstance in which a regulatory commission determines distinct rates of return allowable for individual regulated firms, rather than determining one rate of return for all firms in a market. When the identical allowable rate of return confronts all firms in a regulated market, one or more of the firms may choose not to indulge in the Averch–Johnson type of behavior. Such firms might choose instead to offer lower rates or increased service. The threat of one or more firms' behaving in such a fashion may deter some or all of the others from Averch–Johnson behavior.

The Averch–Johnson hypothesis has also been attacked on the ground that even if it is empirically valid, it does not follow that overexpansion of the rate base is necessarily a bad development. Kahn, for example, has pointed out that the static theory of the firm predicts that a firm with market power will engage in output restriction.[30] Expansion of the capital base, if it occurs, might help counteract this output-restricting tendency. It has also been argued that a preoccupation with expansion of the rate base may be a fertile background for technological change. Hence, one must balance the misallocation of resources that Averch–Johnson behavior implies against the increased efficiency and production resulting from more rapid technological change.[31]

The precise effects of regulation upon economic activity are not well known. The truth of the matter is that regulatory economics is a dark corner of economic science, in terms of the existence of sophisticated empirical evidence. Reliable studies are few in number because of methodological difficulties cited earlier, and because the field of regulatory economics has traditionally not attracted a large number of economists who possess the quantitative abilities necessary to perform the needed studies.

[30] Alfred E. Kahn, "The Graduated Fair Return : Comment," *American Economic Review*, 58 (March 1968), 170–74.

[31] Sidney Weintraub, "Rate Making and an Incentive Rate of Return," *Public Utilities Fortnightly*, 81 (April 25, 1968), 23–32.

SUMMARY

The economics of regulation is a subject of interest to the student of industrial organization, because regulation is a frequently mentioned palliative when market power is present. Regulated markets account for at least 7 percent of the national income generated by the American economy. There exists general agreement that some sort of economic regulation is desirable when a natural-monopoly situation exists in which a firm realizes falling unit costs of production in the long run. Regulation is also frequently imposed in circumstances where a scarce natural resource exists, where price-discriminatory behavior has attracted considerable public attention and disapproval, and where a firm possesses substantial political or market power. There is less agreement on the advisability and optimal extent of regulation in the last three cases mentioned.

Marginal-cost pricing long ago captured the imagination and support of many economists. Marginal-cost pricing is not generally practiced in economic regulation in the United States, because of possible economic and administrative problems. It is probable, however, that the selective introduction of marginal-cost pricing would improve the tenor of regulation in several markets. Regulatory commissions typically allow their wards to maintain a rate structure that is price discriminatory, on the grounds that price discrimination will increase welfare. The major attention of regulatory commissions, nevertheless, is upon the rate base and the rate of return realized by the regulated firms. The current regulatory vogue in measuring the rate base is that it is the value of the firm's assets in terms of their historic cost minus accumulated depreciation.

Economic regulation has been severely criticized on the ground that it has been inefficient, cumbersome, and ineffectual in some cases. It is undoubtedly true that economic regulation has been responsible for the development and prosperity of a large regulatory bureaucracy and apparatus, replete with rules, regulations, delays, and sometimes irrational decisions. Regulatory commissions sometimes appear to be the protectors of the firms that they regulate, rather than a representative and advocate of the public.[32] This attitude has evidenced itself in actions by regulatory commissions that appear to discourage or even eliminate the possibility of competition among firms or among transportation or communication modes. The encouragement of competition is a much-needed change in economic regulation.

For all its rules and regulations, there is disturbing evidence that economic regulation sometimes makes no difference, and/or that it stimulates

---

[32]The highly publicized work of several of the Nader Task Forces has done little to discourage this view. See, for example, Robert C. Fellmeth, *The Interstate Commerce Commission: The Public Interest and the ICC* (New York: Grossman Publishers, 1970); also, Edward F. Cox, Robert C. Fellmeth, and John E. Schultz, *The Nader Report on the Federal Trade Commission* (New York: Richard W. Baron Publishing Co., Inc., 1969).

firms to behave in a non-optimal fashion. The Averch–Johnson thesis, for example, predicts that regulated firms will often invest excessively in capital because of the rate decisions of regulatory commissions.

The empirical evidence available is altogether too sparse to merit the statement that regulation has been a failure. Nontheless, both theory and empirical evidence suggest that economic regulation is not what it could be and that fundamental reforms in the present regulatory framework should be accorded a high priority.

PROBLEMS

1.   Several regulatory bodies have argued that since they ordinarily regulate their markets by controlling rates of return on invested capital, the firms they regulate do not worry about the prices they pay for inputs because they can always get the regulatory agency to agree to an output price high enough to realize the permissible rate of return. That is, they will pay inflated input prices because they feel they will get it back on the price of the output they sell. Regulatory agencies have therefore argued that they must have the right to regulate the input markets connected to the output market they now regulate. Do you agree?

2.   What importance have the following concepts for regulation? (a) Original cost; (b) cost of reproduction; (c) cost of attracting capital.

3.   Can the Averch–Johnson thesis, as amended, ever explain undercapitalization of a regulated market?

4.   Compare and contrast a sheep and a telephone company, the object being to demonstrate the joint-cost problem that faces public-utility pricing.

15

Final Considerations

Our analysis of the field of industrial organization began some fourteen chapters back with the posing of a large number of important questions that we hoped to answer. Most of the questions dealt with the effects of market power or of firm size upon conduct and performance. For example, one question addressed itself to the effects of firm size upon innovation and invention. It is time now to evaluate our progress in dealing with the issues we raised earlier. Further, it is only appropriate that the last chapter of a book concerning the field of industrial organization should attempt to place in clear perspective the current status of the field and its problems. This chapter is largely a "where we stand now" statement.

THE EFFECTS OF MARKET POWER

Overgeneralization is a hobgoblin of the economist. Nevertheless, it is a necessity. The bushels of empirical evidence we have surveyed are generally supportive of the static theory of the firm. There is evidence that market power results in higher margins of price to costs of production, possibly lower output, and sometimes, slower technological change. This does not encourage the view that many, many firms in the American economy are larger in size than is necessary to realize available cost efficiencies. The contention that we live in an age where only large, diversified firms can be efficient cannot be supported by the evidence.

The empirical evidence is not so strong, however, that it often affords definite or even identifiable policy conclusions. The reasons for this are numerous. The methodology of many market-power studies is suspect (for example, of the studies that relate concentration and profit rates). Some studies suggest that welfare losses owing to the exercise of market power may be far less than 1 percent of national income. The widely quoted theory of the second best cautions us from making piecemeal adjustments in the economy in the direction of competitive norms. Hence, the empirical evidence in support of the static theory of the firm is neither very strong, nor necessarily a basis for important shifts in public policy.

Dewey, a seasoned observer of public policy in the area of industrial organization, has rhetorically asked whether the orthodox condemnation of market power and the support of a vigorous antitrust policy represent the result of scientific investigation or religious fervor.[1] On the one hand, reputable scholars such as Kaysen, Turner, and Blair call for a prohibition of many mergers and a policy of dissolution of many large firms, on the ground that mergers and bigness are harmful to competition and economic welfare. On the other hand, economists such as Bork, Bowman, and Weston have all contributed evidence that is advertised as destructive to the market-power hypothesis outlined above. Indeed, within the space of only a few years, two separate task forces appointed by different presidential administrations reached almost diametrically opposing conclusions about appropriate antitrust policy. The Neal Report, which was submitted to President Johnson, took a strong structuralist viewpoint and argued with force against permitting mergers between large firms, took a position in support of the dissolution of many large firms, and in general contended that oligopolistic structures would lead to undesirable conduct and performance.[2] The Stigler Report, which was submitted to President Nixon, found little reason to worry about firm bigness per se, conglomerate mergers, and higher-than-normal levels of market concentration.[3] Compounding (and illustrating) the division in the profession over these issues is the fact that both Neal and Stigler ply their trade at the University of Chicago.

There is general agreement among economists on the beneficial effects of competition in most situations. Most economists nearly always prefer more competition to less. The disagreement arises over what forms competition can take and in what circumstances it most often appears. If one had a sheet of paper containing a list of competitive and noncompetitive actions, a list of "good" and "bad" market structures, and a list of appropriate policy solutions for each problem, one could simplify antitrust policy to a series of rules indicating the permissible and the nonpermissible. The world does not, of course, align itself so easily. Although some black-and-white situations may exist, many more grey areas rear their unattractive heads.[4] It is these grey areas that are the real challenge to the field of industrial organization.

The Supreme Court, in developing the rule of reason, has done little

---

[1] Donald Dewey, "The Economic Theory of Antitrust: Science or Religion?" *Virginia Law Review*, 59 (April 1964), 413–34.

[2] *Report of the White House Task Force on Antitrust Policy*, as reprinted in *Antitrust Law and Economics Review*, 2 (Winter 1968–69), 11–52.

[3] *Report of the Task Force on Productivity and Competition*, as reprinted in *Antitrust Law and Economics Review*, 2 (Spring 1969), 13–36.

[4] For example, Kaysen and Turner call for the prohibition of only four actions: (1) price fixing, (2) collective refusals to deal, (3) grant-back clauses or exclusive licenses under patents, and (4) market-sharing agreements. Carl Kaysen and Donald F. Turner, *Antitrust Policy: An Economic and Legal Analysis* (Cambridge, Mass.: Harvard University Press, 1965), Chap. 3.

to clarify the grey situations.[5] Only undue or unreasonable restraints of competition and trade are prohibited in most cases. The rule of reason is a reflection of the nonspecific and very general wording of our basic anti-trust statutes, such as the Sherman Act, the Clayton Act, and the Federal Trade Commission Act. The antitrust laws leave immense latitude for un-burdened judicial interpretation and for the introduction of relevant empirical evidence in antitrust cases. It is the task of the industrial-organi-zation economist to shed light on the grey areas of public policy. We will shortly comment upon where the greatest needs for study lie.

THE PROPER ROLE FOR GOVERNMENT

The appropriate role for government in the antitrust area is most often viewed as one of prosecution and enforcement. This role, however, has never occupied much of government's attention. Active federal-government participation in economic regulation via commissions dates back only to the 1880's, and the first substantial piece of antitrust legislation, the Sher-man Act, was passed only in the year 1890. Even today, the total amount of resources devoted by the U.S. government to antitrust enforcement is far less than .01 percent of the gross national product. A generous congres-sional appropriation might allot a total of $20 to $30 million annually to antitrust enforcement in the Antitrust Division of the Department of Justice and the various arms of the Federal Trade Commission. This is eye-open-ing, since some of the current estimates of the welfare loss due to monopoly have been estimated (as we have seen) as being as high as $80 billion annually.[6]

It is not surprising, therefore, that the antitrust efforts of government have been ridiculed as being inconsequential and irrelevant. In some cases, the alleged ineffectiveness of antitrust policy is attributed to lack of re-sources devoted to the task. In other cases, however, antitrust policy is seen as foolish baying at the moon, on the ground that technological imperatives, economies of scale, and economic planning have long since abolished the free market in all but a few areas of the economy. The reader will recog-nize the thoughts of Galbraith and others here.[7]

The assertion that antitrust policy has had no impact is empirically not sustainable. The advent of amended Section Seven of the Clayton Act concerning mergers vastly changed the complexion of the merger phenome-non. The predominance of horizontal mergers gave way to vertical and

---

[5]The rule of reason was originally enunciated in *Standard Oil Company of New Jersey* v. *United States,* 221 U.S. 1 (1911), and has been utilized repeatedly since that time.

[6]Eighty billion dollars is 8 percent of a gross national product of one trillion dollars.

[7]The most recent contribution of this stripe is John Kenneth Galbraith, *The New Industrial State* (Boston: Houghton Mifflin Company, 1967).

particularly conglomerate mergers as a result of amended Section Seven and important test cases in the courts. This was the desired outcome, from the standpoint of most legislators and most economists. On the other side of the ledger, however, the Robinson-Patman Act, which is actually an amendment to the Clayton Act, has also influenced economic behavior, although in an adverse fashion. The Robinson-Patman Act, as we have previously argued, has encouraged soft competition and price rigidity, and has discouraged price competition and reduced price flexibility. The preceding examples reveal that antitrust policy can have an impact if the limited resources devoted to it are used to establish guideposts and landmark legal interpretations.

That government should encourage and attempt to maintain vigorous competition seems desirable and noncontroversial. Less attention has been given to the many other actions of government that reduce competition and establish or strengthen monopoly power. Machlup has noted that "our government has done much more to create monopoly than to destroy monopoly."[8] The imposition of tariffs, the granting of long-term patents accompanied by licensing, pools, and grant-back clauses, the selective application of taxes, the method of awarding government contracts, the exemptions given from antitrust prosecution, licensing, zoning, the actions of regulatory commissions that discourage or eliminate competition, the ill effects of laws such as the Robinson-Patman Act and those that pertain to resale-price maintenance, the granting of import and production quotas—the list of governmental monopoly grants is long and extensive. The democratic political process appears to be extremely susceptible to special pleadings on the part of power groups who argue that they must be given some measure of monopoly power in order to serve the purposes of equity. The tragic fact is that grants of monopoly power are often given to those who request or demand them even though the precise effects of such grants are unknown or unpredictable *a priori*. McKie has noted that "public policy seems to have undertaken a great many individual alterations of market structure for the sake of equity without even a partial equilibrium prediction of the economic effects."[9] Although there is no ready measure of the cost of governmental monopoly grants, the cost is apparently immense if the length and importance of the list above are to be taken seriously.

On balance, it is difficult to state that the net contribution of government to the competitive process has been positive. And yet the lesson of the theoretical models presented in this book, and the mass of the empirical evidence reviewed, is that a vigorous competition in which rivals knock

---

[8]Testimony of Fritz Machlup, in *Hearings on Administered Prices*, Part Ten, Subcommittee on Antitrust and Monopoly, Committee on the Judiciary, U.S. Senate (Washington, D.C.: U.S. Government Printing Office, 1959), pp. 4955–56.

[9]James W. McKie, "Industrial Organization: Boxing the Compass," in Victor R. Fuchs, ed., *Policy Issues and Research Opportunities in Industrial Organization* (New York: Columbia University Press, 1972), p. 5.

heads (and in which the possibility exists that some firms will be injured) will in the long run maximize welfare. Wherever possible, this lesson should guide government action.

A LOOK AT THE FUTURE

Theoretical advancement in the area of industrial organization has not been overwhelming in the last decade. Shubik has argued that the major theoretical advances in microeconomics (and hence in industrial organization) will be the result of insights provided by the application of game-theoretical and computer simulation approaches to firm and market behavior.[10] Theoretical breakthroughs are particularly needed in the area of oligopoly theory, where game theory and simulations would appear to hold great promise.

Even in the absence of further theoretical development, however, empirical advances are a necessity. The links between market structure and conduct and performance must be further illuminated in a multivariate and dynamic context. Topics such as the relationship between market power and profits, advertising and competition, and the motivations for merger have been the subject of numerous empirical studies in the last decade. It is a daring economist, nevertheless, who would claim to be in possession of the truth in these disputed and elusive areas. More work needs to be done.

Still other topics have yet to be attacked with any degree of vigor. The benefits and costs associated with the tradeoff between allocational efficiency and economic growth, the relationship between micro and macro aspects of conduct and performance, the understanding of vertical and conglomerate power, and the largely ignored internal behavior and decision-making process of the firm are deserving topics for further study. In this vein, Williamson (among others) has suggested that industrial organization might be appropriately considered a part of a general study of productive organizations and organizational behavior.[11] The construction of a general theory of organization, while not a new suggestion, may imply the blending and distillation of the work of many disciplines.[12] A good economist is always alert to the possibility of borrowing concepts and knowledge from other disciplines. Leontief and others have cautioned economists, however, that the millenium is not yet here in terms of the unity of science.[13] Hence, industrial organization may well achieve greater success by mastering the substance

---

[10]Martin Shubik, "A Curmudgeon's Guide to Microeconomics," *Journal of Economic Literature*, 8 (June 1970), 405–34.

[11]Oliver E. Williamson, "Antitrust Enforcement and the Modern Corporation," in Fuchs, ed., *Policy Issues and Research Opportunities in Industrial Organization*, pp. 16–33.

[12]Ronald H. Coase, "The Nature of the Firm," *Economica*, n.s., 4 (November 1937), 386–405.

[13]Wassily Leontief, "Note on the Pluralistic Interpretation of History and the Problem of Inter-Disciplinary Cooperation," *Journal of Philosophy*, 45 (November 1948), 617–24.

of essentially economic problems first, because the logics underpinning the various academic disciplines are not always commensurate.

In order for the student of industrial organization to wrestle more successfully with the problems suggested above, the current sources of data upon which empirical studies are based must be expanded. This might be accomplished by a closer alliance with particular business firms or groups of firms—an unlikely achievement unless the work of the industrial-organization economist becomes more useful to the businessman. There is another potential gold mine of data, however, which is hidden from economists' eyes by virtue of the strict rules concerning disclosure that burden the Bureau of the Census, the Federal Trade Commission, the Internal Revenue Service, and others whose secret caches of data might conceivably solve many problems currently vexing the field, as well as open new doors. Current rules prohibit government agencies that compile data of interest to economists from identifying individual firms. For example, four-firm concentration ratios do not identify the four firms covered in the ratio or the precise contribution and position of each of these firms within the ratio. A modification of disclosure rules would be a major victory for the field of industrial organization.

The number of unresolved empirical issues in the field of industrial organization is large and will probably grow in size, despite the surge of empirical studies that have appeared in recent years. The application of quantitative tools to the problems of industrial organization contains within it seeds of danger, however. Grabowski and Mueller have warned that "we stand in danger of seeing the period of infancy in the application of econometrics to industrial organization coincide with its zenith, unless we are able to develop better theories and/or come up with better data than are presently available."[14] The testing of faulty or misstated hypotheses on the basis of inadequate or poor data, and the drawing of inferences from exceedingly slender reeds of evidence, are not always better than doing nothing at all. Rather than lighting candles, faulty empirical work heightens the darkness by promoting possible falsehoods or misconceptions.

Quantitative methods, especially econometric methods, have much to contribute to the study of industrial organization. Such tools have nudged the field away from the danger of being too descriptive and too normative in nature. The use of sophisticated statistical techniques does not imply sophistication of application of those techniques, the logical correctness of the underlying model, the accuracy and representativeness of the empirical data being utilized, or application of the art of interpretation and information transfer. Quantitative tools, properly used, have revolutionized the field of industrial organization, and will continue to do so. The task confronting the field is to see that this revolution does not degenerate into a

---

[14]Henry Grabowski and Dennis Mueller, "Industrial Organization: The Role and Contribution of Econometrics," *American Economic Review*, 60 (May 1970), pp. 100–4.

sterile brandishing of high-powered techniques, devoid of an appreciation and perspective of appropriate usage.

An immediate challenge to the entire field of economics, and especially to the field of industrial organization, is the need to develop economic theory that is both operationally meaningful (in the sense that a test of the predictions of the theory is conceptually imaginable) and operationally feasible (in the sense that such a test can actually be performed). Moreover, such a theory would ideally be reducible to terminology, paradigms, or analogies that are understandable to the major practitioners of everyday economics. It is an unfortunate fact that economists have had strikingly little impact upon legislators, regulatory bodies, the judiciary, and businessmen, because the body of economic theory is sometimes neither readily understandable nor easily testable. The very individuals and institutions that are often derided for their lack of economic sophistication are themselves the victims of our own failure to communicate effectively. Needless to say, these individuals and groups exercise monumental influence upon resource allocation and competition. They cannot prudently be ignored.

The phenomena that the field of industrial organization conventionally treats are of vital interest to many individuals and groups other than trained economists. Our theoretical formulations must be capable of dealing with the major problems and issues of the day. Certain of the current tools of the field—for example, the static theory of the firm—may not ultimately prove to be the most ideal or effective vehicles to accomplish the task of increasing economic sophistication at all levels. A high priority must be accorded the search for new theoretical formulations that address important problems and whose implications can be understood, tested, and even implemented by decision makers of reasonable intelligence.

Any crystal-ball-gazing session concerning the future of the field of industrial organization would be derelict if it did not take notice of the increasing impact on all aspects of theorizing, research, and policy making that the "New Left" organizations (typified by the Union for Radical Political Economy—URPE) have had. URPE adherents profess a burning dissatisfaction with the type of economics that has traditionally been taught in American universities. URPE devotees, who are not always unified in their thoughts or desires, feel that modern economics (much of which is explicit throughout this book) incorrectly takes as given wholly debatable things, such as capitalism as *the* form of economic organization, and the prevailing income distribution. The dichotomy between positive and normative economics that was commended to the readers in Chapter 1 of this book is generally rejected by URPE members on the grounds that "what is" and "what ought to be" cannot be separated. The functioning of a market economy is said to lead to exploitation, as well as to inevitable monopoly. The economy is viewed as being heavily cartelized and supported by government subsidies, protections, and monopoly grants. In URPE eyes, the detrimental effects of monopoly power upon consumer welfare are grossly underestimated.

It cannot be predicted at this time whether the influence of URPE members and URPE thought will wax or wane in the near future. The introduction of interpersonal utility comparisons into economic analysis and the utilization of normative estimates of equity have not proved to be of lasting popularity in the field of economics in the past. The future, however, is (as always) uncertain. It is abundantly clear, however, that the ways in which economists study phenomena such as oligopoly, market power, and competition would be drastically altered by the ascendency of URPE followers in the field of industrial organization.

CONCLUSION

Industrial organization, like all of economics, has been buffeted by the winds of change. Increased use of quantitative tools and methods has vastly expanded the amount of empirical evidence available concerning the major issues confronting the field of industrial organization. Nevertheless, there exist few empirical laws in that field, and extended debate continues over substantive issues such as the effects of market power upon conduct and performance.

Significant theoretical developments have been sparse in the field of industrial organization in recent years. The received theory has been subjected to concerted attacks upon its relevancy by old and new guard alike. The impact of industrial organization upon public policy will undoubtedly rise *pari passu* with new theoretical developments that both address themselves to important problems and are understandable and teachable.

A host of important problems remain to be researched. The need for theoretical and empirical advance is particularly urgent in view of the important decisions relating to resource allocation that are often made on the basis of inadequate or even false information. The means necessary for important theoretical and empirical advances appear to be present. What is needed is inquisitiveness, mental ingenuity, and intellectual commitment. The readers of this book will, it is hoped, be suppliers of these commodities.

PROBLEMS

1. "Except for the meddling and bungling of government, monopoly cannot exist in the long run except in the natural-monopoly case." Comment.

2. "Some empirical evidence is better than no empirical evidence." Comment.

3. Does a market system have an inevitable tendency toward monopoly?

4. Is the refusal of many economists to mix positive and normative judgments a normative or a positive judgment?

Index

DATE DUE